THE NATURE AND FUNCTION OF PRIESTHOOD

By the same Author

THE NATURE
AND FUNCTION OF
PRIESTHOOD

A Comparative and Anthropological Study

by

E. O. JAMES

*D.Litt., Ph.D., F.S.A.. Hon. D.D. St. Andrews
Professor of the History and Philosophy of Religion
in the University of London. Fellow of
University College and Fellow of
King's College*

238.7
J

THAMES AND HUDSON
London

CONTENTS

PREFACE

SOME twenty years ago when I was engaged in the investigation of the origins and significance of sacrifice it came as a surprise to discover that while a voluminous literature existed on the theological, devotional and apologetic aspects of priesthood, together with a few scholarly regional adjacent studies, such as the late Buchanan Gray's admirable volume on *Sacrifice in the Old Testament,* no attempt had been made to pursue an objective anthropological and comparative inquiry into the nature and function of the institution as an integral element in social structure. Here, then, seemed to be a field for further research, and one which fell within my own particular domain. It soon became apparent, however, that priesthood is such a fundamental aspect of socio-religious phenomena, with so many ramifications, that to deal with the subject at all adequately would involve a protracted and extensive examination of the available data at a number of different cultural levels and in a variety of religious disciplines, both ancient and modern. These range from primitive society and the ancient civilizations of the Near East to Hinduism, Judaism and Christianity. Furthermore, the institution cannot be treated in isolation from either the kingship, and all that this signified in the religious and social organization of the civilizations of the Fertile Crescent, or from the specialized functions and techniques of diviners, exorcists, astrologers, seers and prophets in their several capacities.

Since Frazer, at the beginning of the century, concentrated attention on the sacred kingship in the formulation of his theory of the "dying god", his hypothesis has been critically examined and considerably modified in the light of fuller information and investigation, notably by the late Henri Frankfort and A. M. Hocart, and among those who happily are still with us, Professors Evans-Pritchard, S. H. Hooke Widengren and Engnell, together with the group of scholars collected round the International Association for the Study of the History of

9

Religions centred at Amsterdam and Paris. With these workers in this field I have been in intimate contact during the preparation of this volume.

An invitation to lecture in the University of Amsterdam in 1949 afforded an opportunity to put together some of the material I had collected on this aspect of the subject. Subsequently I developed the theme further in a course of lectures delivered on the Forwood Foundation in the University of Liverpool, and in papers contributed to the International Congress for the History of Religions during its meetings at Amsterdam and in Rome. The discussions arising out of these several interpretations of the data have been of considerable value in clarifying the situation, and in the presentation of the evidence in its present form in this book. I am also indebted to the group of English and Scandinavian scholars, such as Pedersen, Mowinckel, H. G. May, A. R. Johnson and A. Haldar, who in recent years have given a new emphasis to the cultic aspects of prophetism in ancient Semitic religions, thereby opening a fresh approach to the priestly tradition from this angle.

In Christendom the priesthood and its ministrations and jurisdiction have so long been a crucial issue, and unfortunately a storm-centre, that even an anthropological and comparative inquiry that aims at being objective and sympathetic is liable to come into conflict with the underlying highly controversial theological and ecclesiastical questions. It has been no part of my intention or purpose, however, to pass judgment upon the validity of the beliefs and practices in any of the sacerdotal regimes and traditions brought under review in these pages. Their function is independent of their truth or falsity. However erroneous some of them may appear to be, either in their present content or as they have obtained in former times, their effectiveness in the social and religious structure of a culture is not thereby necessarily impaired. It is for the apologist to defend or oppose the institution in its several manifestations in relation to religious truth. My business has been to endeavour to ascertain in the light of the available data, and with the aid of modern scholarship, the way in which it has in fact taken shape, and what has been, and is, its nature and function in the consolidation and stability of the group, nation, civilization or church of which it was, or still is, an integral element and potent force.

To-day one of the most pressing problems in our modern world, alike in the sacred and secular spheres, in Church, State and the Commonwealth of nations, is to find a unifying dynamic, such as the priestly tradition has supplied throughout the ages. Therefore, a re-consideration of how this has been accomplished by this discipline may be of some value as a guide, and perhaps as a warning, at a time when civilization is in search of social cohesion essential for survival, and the individual is seeking personal adjustment in his relations with his precarious and perplexing environment, which, it would seem, can be stabilized in the last resort only on a spiritual and transcendental basis.

Oxford   E. O. JAMES

CHAPTER I

Magico-Religious Practitioners in Primitive Society

IN opening an enquiry into the nature, status and function of priesthood in the social order and in the life of the individual we are confronted at once with the problem of the relation of the sacred to the secular in human society. At all times and in all states of culture religion has been and is the means whereby human beings adjust themselves to their physical, social and spiritual environment and categories of thought. Under the influence of its sanctions, beliefs and institutions they are enabled to live together in an orderly and co-operative manner, and to satisfy the needs of their impulses, desires and emotions as well as of their domestic, economic, political and social organization.

THE PRIESTHOOD AND THE MAGIC ART

Nowhere is this more apparent than in the function of priesthood. Notwithstanding the liability of abuse, where it has been established invariably it has been the official organ for maintaining a state of equilibrium between the sacred and the secular. Through the exercise of its prescribed techniques and disciplines it has been a stabilizing force in the social structure and in the religious life of the community by establishing efficacious relations with the transcendental power believed to control the universe and human affairs and destinies. Thus, in its several capacities it has become the dynamic centre of the sacred order with far reaching effects in the body politic.

Closely allied to, and often almost inseparable from, the priesthood is the parallel discipline in the magic art. In fact so difficult is it to distinguish the one from the other in the exercise of supernatural control in primitive society that some anthropologists feel that the time has come to drop the use of the term "magic" altogether.[1] But although both direct and mediated techniques may be employed in the same rite and exist side by side in identical operations, two fundamentally distinct kinds of thought, action and intention, each having its own essential distinguishing features, are of frequent occurrence, especially in primitive states of culture. On the one hand, there is the religious recourse to supernatural efficacy which resides in some transcendental source and is dispensed through human agency by the aid and intervention of a priesthood and its cultus. On the other hand, there is the manipulation of sacred power directly by the ritual employed, usually regarded as an impersonal, or only vaguely personal force *per se*, enshrined in the operator as a result of an elaborate process of initiation, training, instruction and filiation. This so-called magical efficacy is based on the utilization of sacred power by the aid of analogy, the association of ideas, autosuggestion, occult knowledge and practice, folk medicine, leechcraft, and similar devices calculated to bring about the desired results for the promotion of fertility, making rain, curing sickness, or conversely, for illicit, malevolent and destructive ends. The technique usually consists in uttering with precise accuracy mystic formulae in which the magical virtue is believed to reside, and in the performance of appropriate imitative gestures.

THE TECHNIQUE OF MAGIC

Most of these spells have been handed down from one generation to the next within the craft from immemorial antiquity, and so intimately are they bound up with the inherent power that not infrequently the slightest variation in the form of words, or in the prescribed actions, is thought to break the spell and render the rite null and void. Being impersonal in its operation, the efficacy of magic is uniform in its action, effectual of itself, and so *ex opere operato* it gives stability to a house or a canoe, makes the sun to shine or the rain to fall, wounds an enemy or attracts the sweetheart to her lover. Nevertheless, although the rite conveys the spell to the object through its own inherent power, it depends very largely on the skill and efficacy of the operator, since he is the actor rather than the agent of occult power. Therefore, the medicine-man or magician is the central figure in the magic art, and in consequence, while he enjoys very considerable social distinction and prestige and authority, so sacred and precarious is his office that he is surrounded with tabus to protect him against harmful contacts with influences which might render him ineffective.

Unlike the sacred man who acts as the agent of personal divine or spiritual beings, the magician is a variable quantity, dependent upon his own abilities for his very insecure status in the community because he is always liable to fall from his high estate. To acquire his position he has to undergo a strenuous course of training which may involve, in addition to a drastic process of initiation, some knowledge of meteorology, herbs, poisons, leechcraft, therapeutics, trephining, ligatures, massage, bleeding and childbirth. Sleight of hand, ventriloquism and similar subterfuges may also form part of his training, together with the development of the necessary psychical and occult qualities. But while charlatanry cannot be excluded, the office involves a personality, condition of mind and state of emotion calculated to bring about the results that are sought.

Sometimes certain physical and psychical peculiarities are regarded as an indispensable qualification for the exercise of magic, ranging from deformities of body to epilepsy. Hunchbacks or hermaphrodites, for example, frequently are thought to be potential medicine-men among people in a primitive state of culture,[2] and twins in Africa often become rain-makers, and are believed to be endowed with supernatural powers in various directions.[3] But the professional magician, whether or not he exhibits physical qualifications or a psychopathetic personality, or acquires his powers by inheritance, natural aptitude, purchase, gift or a personal "call", must be an expert in his craft. Therefore, a specialized training is a *sine qua non*.

Since magic is confined to its tradition and its efficacy is dependent on the human operator in whom its virtue resides, the magician must learn the technique before he can bring its power to bear upon situations through rite and spell. Material objects may be employed in a mimic fashion—a stick, bone or dart thrown or pointed at a victim, odours and inebriating stimulants used to repel or attract a person or spirit, or "medicines" dispensed to heal disease. But these can become effective only when the magician makes them the vehicles of magical potency by "singing" over them and employing them as part of the dramatic action in the rite. Thus, unlike the mystic power which is associated with awe-inspiring and mysterious phenomena in nature and human affairs, called by the Melanesians *mana,* magic is confined to its own technique. It cannot be conveyed in anything however "numinous" or sacred it may be unless it is brought within its sphere of operation through the appointed channels, known only to the practitioner of the magic art. Therefore, the discipline functions in a realm of its own, and only those who have been duly initiated into its mysteries can traffic with its potencies.

The methods adopted may vary according to whether the power resides in the medicines or instruments used; in the rite or in the spell. When it is operative in the magical object itself, such as a quartz crystal or a parasitic plant, the emphasis is on the things employed. In the case of the rite and the spell, the actions performed and the words spoken are the crucial elements. If they fail to produce the intended results, the failure is explained by counter-magic or some fault in the technique, or by the conditions under which they are performed, so that faith in the magic art and the prestige of its practitioners are not impaired. Nevertheless, magicians have to make and sustain their reputations. This can only be done by demonstrating their skill in the control of the unpredictable forces in nature thereby giving confidence to those who depend on their powers for their peace of mind and prosperity, their love-making, gardening, health, economy and protection,[4] or, conversely, as among the Azande in the Nile-Congo divide, enabling every detail of daily life to be determined by destructive magic in the form of a poison oracle.[5]

A belief so deeply rooted in the social structure and in personal affairs cannot be lightly esteemed, or its practitioners ignored, so long as they continue to fulfil their avocations successfully as wielders of supernatural power for good or ill. Being the instruments of one of the most dynamic forces in society their influence and significance are incalculable in inspiring hope, confidence and fear in the individual and in controlling the fortunes of the tribe as a whole. But where in this organization the line is to be drawn between magic and religion, the magician and the priest is not easy to determine since while the medicine-man may exercise his functions by virtue of his inherent magical powers and the rite and spell he manipulates, he may not infrequently have recourse to spirit "helpers" both during the period of his training and subsequently in the fulfilment of his vocation.

THE INITIATION OF THE MEDICINE-MAN

Thus, among the Central tribes of Australia, magic is regarded as an original endowment passed on throughout the ages from the *Alcheringa* or "dream time", when the ancestors were formed and the ceremonies and the religious and social organization were instituted. It was then that the ancestors wandered about and endowed certain rocks and pools with their supernatural powers in the form of spirit-individuals (*mai-aurli*) which ever since have been continually undergoing reincarnation. In addition to these sacred places magic also resides in various other spirits and their haunts, and in objects endowed with occult power, such as crystals which play an important part in the making and functioning of medicine-men.[6]

When a youth desires to enter the profession, among the Arunta and Ilpirra tribes three courses are open to him. The simplest and least-esteemed method is to seek initiation from members of the craft. The candidate is taken to a secluded spot where he is sworn to secrecy. The *nung-gara* (medicine-men) then withdraw from their bodies a number of small crystals which they press firmly against his head, along the front of his

B

leg and up his body to the sternum. After the scoring has been repeated three times on the first day and again on the following two days, and a hole has been made under the nail of the first finger of the right hand into which a crystal is supposed to be passed, his tongue is pierced with a crystal. At intervals he drinks water containing crystals, and he is given tobacco to chew and meat to eat fortified with the magic *ultunda* (crystals). His body is smeared with grease and painted with sacred designs of a special class of spirits called *oruncha*. Fur strings are placed on his head with leaves of a gum tree hanging down over his forehead. Until the wound in his tongue is healed a ban of silence is imposed upon him. He must also abstain from eating fat of any kind, and the flesh of wild dogs, fish or echnida for a long time. When he is fully recovered he returns to the camp, but lest his newly acquired power should depart from him he has to be careful to talk but little and to be temperate in all things. At night he must sleep with a fire between him and his wife, so that he shall be visible to the spirits and not be hindered in his intercourse with them.[7] Almost identical methods are followed among the other tribes in this area.[8]

An alternative to this form of initiation is to visit a cave which is believed to be occupied by the spiritual doubles of the Alcheringa ancestors, known as *iruntarinia,* who are supposed to be endowed with the power of making medicine-men. When a man feels he is called to the office he goes to the mouth of the cave and lies down and goes to sleep. Were he to go inside he would be spirited away for ever. At daybreak one of the *iruntarinia* comes to the mouth of the cave and throws an invisible lance at him. It pierces his neck from behind, passes through his tongue, making a large hole, and then comes out through his mouth. It is this hole in the tongue that is the outward and visible sign of the validity of his claims to be a duly initiated medicine-man. How in fact the novice makes it it is impossible to say, but that it is there on his return to the camp is beyond dispute; and, as Spencer and Gillen suggest, in course of time the man may really come to believe that it was not done by himself. The ancestral spirits then are supposed to throw a second lance which pierces him from ear to ear. This, it is alleged, kills him. Thereupon the *iruntarinia* carry him into the depths of the cave where they live in perpetual sunshine among streams of running water. Here he receives a new set of internal organs, together with a supply of magical stones (*atnongara*). He comes to life again in a state of temporary insanity, and is led back to the camp by one of the spirits who is invisible except to a few magicians and to dogs. For a few days he behaves in a strange manner, and then having regained his sanity he paints with charcoal a broad band across his nose as a sign that he has become a duly graduated medicine-man. He does not practice for a year, and if during this period the hole in his tongue closes up, as it does sometimes, he abandons the profession because he knows that his powers have departed from him. Meanwhile he learns from other medicine-men the secrets of the craft. These, it is said, consist chiefly in sleight-of-hand to enable him to produce at will quartz pebbles and little sticks, and "the power of looking prenaturally solemn, as if he were the possessor of knowledge quite hidden from ordinary men".[9]

The third method of initiation in Central Australia follows this procedure except that instead of the man going to the cave in which the *iruntarinia* are supposed to dwell, he resorts to a sacred spot where an ancestral spirit known as *oruncha* has his abode. During his sojourn there he is alleged to be taken down into the earth in order to become endowed with magic virtue. On the rare occasions when women are initiated into the profession in this region, this method usually is adopted.[10]

Sometimes, however, the "call" may come unsought. Thus, an old medicine-man of the Binbinga tribe explained to Spencer and Gillen that one day he walked into a cave in a hill and before he knew what was happening a spirit named Mundadji caught him by the neck and killed him, cut him open, took out his intestines and exchanged them for those of his own. He was then restored to life by a younger spirit, Munkaninja, and shown how to remove poison bones from sick men. Next he was taken to the sky, and finally brought back to earth near his camp where his people were mourning for him thinking he was dead. When he recovered from his dazed condition it was recognized that he had been made a medicine-man, and had gained a reputation which extended beyond his own tribe.[11] Similarly, in the Wotjobaluk tribe of Victoria a supernatural being, Ngatya, said to live in hollows in the ground, met a man in the bush, opened his side and inserted in it such magical objects as quartz crystals. Henceforth the man practised the occult art.[12]

Sometimes the Supreme Being or an ancestral spirit is regarded as responsible for making magicians. Thus, Dr Howitt was told by a medicine-man of the Wiradjuri tribe in South-eastern Australia that when he was a small boy he was taken by his father into the bush and two large crystals were pressed against his breast which vanished inside him. He was then given water to drink in which were crystals. After that he could see things which his mother could not see. At the age of ten he was initiated and shown a crystal in the bush. When he looked at it his father appeared to go down into the earth and to return covered with red dust. Next he was shown a dead man and his secret totem (a tiger snake) by whose aid he and his father visited Daramulun, the High God, and by means of a mystic cord they ascended to the camp of Baiama in the sky. Thus, they came into the presence of the All-Father who was the source of all magic power and of the social and religious organization of the tribe.[13]

Initiations of this kind, in which magical operations are combined with journeys to the spirit world whence the power is thought to be derived in its plenitude, show how very difficult it is at this level of culture to separate the practice of magic from that of religion. The techniques employed by the medicine-man may depend upon his inherent knowledge and skill in the manipulation of rites and spells, but, nevertheless, he exercises his functions by virtue of the supernatural power conferred upon him at his installation. Moreover, he may be thought periodically to converse with spirits during séances and seek from them guidance in the course of action to be taken in specific cases, and to gain from them information about current or future events.[14] In the control of the weather, behind rain-making ceremonies, for instance, may lie the activities of spirits or gods who actually produce the clouds under the influence of the rites performed on earth by those set apart for the purpose. Similarly, in everyday affairs the two disciplines co-exist. Thus, in Tikopia when a man is fishing it is not enough for him to cajole the fish to come to the nets by reciting a formula commanding them to bite on the hook. He also calls upon spiritual beings, his ancestors and guardian divinities to assist in bringing the fish to him. Again, in the seasonal canoe rites each sacred canoe has its own tutelary spirit (*atua*), and at the re-consecration ceremonies appeals are made to the guardians to stand by and procure fish for the owner, together with offerings of the first-fruits of the harvest from the sea.[15]

THE SUPERNATURAL CONTROL OF THE FOOD SUPPLY

This combination of magic and religion is apparent in the well-known *Intichiuma* ceremonies performed by the Arunta in Central Australia to produce rain and the increase of the totemic species upon which the food supply and the well-being of the community as a whole depend. Those who engage in these rites are themselves reincarnations of the mythological ancestors who first performed the rites and in the Alcheringa determined where they should be held, and ordained the prescribed technique and the economic organization on which the ritual is based. Their descendants exercise their sacred functions by virtue of their ancestry for the benefit of the rest of the tribe, though they themselves may only eat very sparingly of the species whose fertility they have procured.[16] Each clan, in fact, has the duty of performing *Intichiuma* on behalf of the other totems through the duly appointed and initiated agents of the source of providential bounty (i.e. the totems) by means of rites which are at once magical and religious in their form, content and purpose. Looked at from one standpoint they might appear imitative and coercive; from another angle they would seem to be not very different in intention from those performed by a priest at the altar.

It is true that the ritual is believed to be charged with super-natural power and is not addressed to a divine being, but it is the means by which man participates in the bounty of the totemic ancestors handed down from the Alcheringa and stimulated here and now by the enactment of the traditional ceremonial. The headman and his confederates are as it were intermediaries between the tribe and its totem, charged with the sacred duty of securing the two most urgent human needs, viz., propagation and nutrition. It is as a pre-figuration of the pur-pose of the rites that at some very sacred spots he strikes his companions on the stomach with one of the stones representing the totem (the witchetty grub) saying "you have eaten much food", when in fact they have not broken their fast.[17] By this pantomimic anticipation of the bounty the ceremonies are designed to produce, the performers partake of the plenty in a sacramental manner though it is not until the rites have been completed that they actually eat a little of the sacred food when the grub has become plentiful and fully grown, and dis-tribute what remains among men of the other moiety of the tribe.[18]

It is the duty of each group to make its contribution towards the food supply of the entire community by the due performance of the rites which are believed to cause the totems to increase and multiply, and from which those responsible for their enact-ment derive little or no material benefit. Thus, magic and altruism go hand in hand in the maintenance of the food supply based on the supernatural control of the economic organization and its underlying mythological tradition. More-over, there is a latent religious and sacramental element in the ritual inasmuch as the things done by the ancestors in the Alcheringa are the source of the supernatural power liberated by the rites. The performers identify themselves with the sacred ancestral species who ordained the ceremonies in the beginning and gave them their efficacy, and having fulfilled their functions at a critical juncture in the year when nature is in the balance, and thereby given a sense of assurance that all is well with the food supply, the natural function of eating is consecrated to a spiritual recreative meaning as well as to an economic purpose. A vital bond is ratified and sealed in a collective cooperative ritual by means of which a sacramental union is established with the beneficent source of Providence symbolized by the totem, and the tribe as a whole gains good hunting and collecting, and receives a plentiful food supply because it is in a right relationship with its ultimate controlling source in the sacred order.

The organized collective effort is so arranged that each group is made responsible for its own contribution to the common stock of food in a system of magico-religious cooperation.[19] The tabus on killing the species before it is abundant and fully grown, and on those engaged in the performance of the rites, requiring them to eat very sparingly, are directed towards the conservation of the supply. Moreover, this consumption of the first-fruits of their ritual activities appears to have a sacramental significance in which the first inklings of the conception of Providence may be detected, since by sharing in the food they have produced they enter into communion with the beneficent abundance and remove the tabu by their ceremonial "tasting", so that the rest of the tribe may freely enjoy the benefits that have been secured.[20] A common vital essence, or soul-substance, is believed to animate man and the animals and plants on which he feeds. This leads to restraints in the form of tabus in the matter of killing and in a desire to contribute ritually to the abundance of the species, to its increase and vitality. When, however, the sacred species is the principal source of the food supply for everybody, as in the case of the bear in Japan and Siberia, an individual animal is killed with great apology, thanked, venerated and eaten ceremonially, in order that the common life of the community may be reinforced and the daily slaughter for practical needs compounded for by a gesture of good-feeling and universal regret for an anomalous situation for which man is not ultimately responsible.[21] By sharing in the food sacramentally with the totems or divinities which represent the source of its supply, man shares with them the beneficent powers of his Providence. By so doing life is retained and renewed in a ritual which is most accurately described as "magico-religious".

It may be that originally the power to control the food supply by increase rites was vested in the chief magician. This is still the case in Malekula in the New Hebrides where the secret knowledge is handed on from father to son, or to his sister's son, unless the magician deems otherwise, for the choice of a successor lies within his personal competence. But while knowledge of the rites controlling the weather and the food supply is retained within the family circle, that of the lesser rites may be transmitted to anyone who is willing to pay the price.[22] Nevertheless, each clan, through its magician, carries out its ceremonies annually for the benefit of the whole district, as in Australia.[23] In the Trobriand Islands every village, and sometimes every subdivision of a village, has its own garden magician (*towosi*), who keeps a vigilant eye on the gardens under his care. In addition to performing the rites and observing the fasts which constitute the main content and purpose of his office, he has to make sure that each owner keeps his fences secure and his plot properly cultivated for the common good. His status is hereditary, and as the forces of fertility depend upon his activities, he occupies a position equal to that of the chief.[24]

THE MAGICIAN AND THE CHIEF

The equation of the magician with the headman of a clan or village is an indication of the way in which an office that may have begun as a family prerogative in course of time has acquired a wider significance as the group has become a specialized unity with its own obligations and departmentalized functions in relation to the tribe as a whole, organized on the basis of a magical co-operative system. As magicians form the intelligentsia of primitive society, able and successful practitioners naturally tend to attain positions of supreme importance and influence, and may gain a reputation outside their own domain. Therefore, they nearly always rank next to the chiefs, and sometimes may be equal or even superior to the headman. Their persons often are sacred by virtue of their inherent powers, though, as we have seen, they are always liable to suffer degradation should they lose their magic and consequently their prestige.

Magicians, however, are sacred men or ritual experts, not only on account of their status, knowledge, acuteness and personal gifts, but also because they often display supernatural insight attributed to their direct access to the transcendental sacred order as the agents of spiritual beings. Nevertheless, although for this reason they may become chiefs,[25] it is not by any means a universal rule. The two positions may be quite distinct,[26] since it does not follow that a gifted worker of magic is also a good administrator and in possession of the qualities necessary in a chief. In Australia, where chieftainship has never been developed, political authority is in the hands of the tribal elders independent of their magical powers.[27] In North America, although the Indian doctors invariably held influential positions in the tribe, they did not rise to power solely by virtue of their office.[28]

It cannot be maintained, therefore, that the chief has been the lineal successor of the magician, or, as Frazer contended,[29] that the priesthood developed out of the office of medicine-man by renunciation of the attempt to control directly the processes of nature, seeking instead to attain the same ends indirectly by appealing to the gods to do what the magician no longer fancied he could do for himself. This theory rests on the assumption that an age of magic preceded an age of religion so that "man essayed to bend nature to his wishes by the sheer force of spells and enchantments before he strove to coax and mollify a coy, capricious or irascible deity by the soft insinuation of prayer and sacrifice".[30]

Against this simple interpretation of a complex situation is the fact that among peoples in primitive states of culture the disciplines of magic and religion are so inextricably intermingled that it is impossible to reduce them to an orderly chronological sequence. Everywhere, and apparently at all times, cult leaders, priests, soothsayers, rain-makers and diviners have exercised their respective functions in relation to the sacred either by their own inherent powers or through the aid of superhuman and divine agencies. It is true that magic is a specific art for specific ends handed down from generation to generation as a highly specialized tradition in a craft which occupies a recognized position in the community. Religion, on the other hand, is a universal relationship with a transcendental sacredness which controls natural events and human affairs, made efficacious and accessible through a variety of channels. In practice, however, the respective techniques are so fused in bewildering confusion that neither of them can be reduced to a single category labelled magic or religion.

That a similar situation existed in Palaeolithic times is suggested by the use of magical life-giving agents, such as red ochre (as a surrogate for blood) and shells employed as revivifying amulets[31] to revitalize the dead in the hereafter. Again, in addition to the magical control of the chase exemplified in the Palaeolithic cave-paintings, attempts were made to establish beneficial relations with sacred species regarded as superior to man and as the ultimate source of the food supply by means of masked dances, as indicated for instance in the prehistoric cavern sanctuaries at Tuc d'Audoubert and Les Trois Frères in the Pyrenees.[32] It would appear, therefore, that magic and religion existed side by side as alternate techniques in relation to human needs and destinies in the earliest attempts of man to determine his fortunes by ritual devices. The agent may have executed his functions by spell and rite operative as a human possession enshrined in the magician and his tradition, and in certain objects employed for this purpose. Conversely, he appears to have appealed to transcendental powers outside himself located in a supramundane order of reality. There is nothing, however, to suggest in the evidence that one discipline and its personnel had priority over or developed out of the other in time and status and function.

THE PRESTIGE OF SUPERNATURAL POWER

Whichever methods may have been employed, the manipulation of supernatural power in primitive society has given prestige to those who have exercised it even though they may not necessarily have become chiefs or kings. To them recourse had been made when perplexing emotional situations have occurred outside the direct control of man by his own unaided efforts because it has been they who have had the knowledge, skill and techniques capable of dealing with the unpredictable elements in human experience and of overcoming the disabilities, frustrations and impasses of daily occurrence. Particularly at critical junctures, such as birth, adolescence, marriage and death, at the turn of the year or in times of drought, flood or famine, their services have been in demand in the capacity of priest or magician because upon the supernatural power they wield the well-being of the individual and of the community has been felt to depend. Therefore, as long as these conditions and beliefs prevail, the unique position and prestige of the successful practitioner are secure.

THE SHAMAN AND VISIONARY EXPERIENCE

Closely allied to the cult leader, but in a somewhat different category, is the occult functionary commonly described as a shaman. Like other sacred men in primitive society he is a complex figure, at once medicine-man, prophet and priest, but he relies almost exclusively on psychic influences and experiences gained through dreams and visions, trance and ecstasy. Indeed, without first-hand acquaintance with the occult it would not be possible for anyone to shamanize among the aboriginal tribes of Siberia, where the word "shaman" is derived from the Tungus term *saman* meaning "exalted", "excited", and is used exclusively in connexion with ecstatic individuals who exercise occult power through direct intercourse with, and as a gift from, the spirits with whom they claim to be *en rapport*.[33] Thus, only an individual who is able to show that he has the right disposition can hope to find a vocation to the office, and where the hereditary principle is maintained, signs of abnormal qualities are sought in childhood in prospective candidates.

Among the Ostyaks, for instance, a shaman chooses one of his sons as a likely subject and does all in his power to foster a neurotic condition in the youth, who is expected to be correspondingly co-operative. Fainting, excitability, moroseness and love of solitude are symptoms which indicate a call. These have to be carefully cultivated under the guidance of a practitioner, who also gives instruction in the lore of the spirits, and acquaints his pupil with the mode of invoking them. No one in this area becomes a shaman of his own free choice; the vocation comes to him *nolens volens,* as Miss Czaplicka says, like a hereditary disease.[34] Sometimes it is alleged that a deceased shaman has visited a particular man in a dream and commanded him to be his successor. He then shows himself "weakly as if dazed and nervous", and suddenly utters incoherent words, falls unconscious, runs through the forest and lives on the bark of trees, throws himself into fire and water, lays hold on weapons, wounds himself, and generally behaves in a crazy manner. He is then put under instruction and shown how to invoke the spirits. During the period of training some of them appear to him in various forms, sometimes as men and sometimes as birds, to endow him with power and reveal to him the mysteries of his art. But it is very important that he comes into contact with the right spirits, and, therefore, he has to learn to test them.[35]

Among the Yakuts, when a pupil is ready for consecration he is led up a high mountain or into the open fields by an old shaman who has been responsible for his training. There he is clothed with vestments appropriate to the office, given a tambourine and drumstick, and having clad him in his own robe the consecrator causes him to vow life-long allegiance to the tutelary spirit who has adopted him, and who will fulfil his requests. He is shown where the various demons live, which sickness they cause and how they may be propitiated. Finally the new shaman slays a sacrificial victim with the blood of which his clothing is sprinkled. A feast is then held on its flesh in which the spectators partake.[36]

In the Altai, on the other hand, it is alleged that shamans receive their commission purely by inspiration without having any kind of preliminary instruction. Suddenly the power falls upon a man (and occasionally on a woman), and makes him languid, seized with violent trembling and yawning. He feels a heavy weight upon his chest and is moved to utter inarticulate cries. He is shaken by "feverish shiverings, his eyes roll rapidly, he dashes forward and whirls round like one possessed until he collapses covered in sweat, and rolls on the ground a prey to epileptic convulsions". When these symptoms reach their climax he seizes the drum and begins to shamanize. The power of the ancestors has passed into him and in its strength he exercises his functions.[37] If this account is accurate, it would seem that the men who undergo these experiences must have been instructed in their youth and brought up in the occult tradition. Otherwise it would be impossible for them to display these frenzies and subsequently to perform the feats expected of them as shamans.

Whatever may constitute the call and training of these inspired men, that they are neuropathic persons, usually pathological from infancy, is fairly established. Thus, the dead ancestors of the Buriats are said to choose a boy among their living descendants who is pensive, a lover of solitude, subject to fits and prone to visions. While he is in this condition his soul is supposed to have gone to the abode of the spirits to learn under the guidance of dead shamans the secrets of the shamanistic art and the names and modes of worship of the gods. As the lad grows to maturity the dreams, swoons and ecstatic experiences increase. He leads a restless life, goes from village to village and tries to shamanize while at the same time continuing his occult exercises. This period of preparation extends over a number of years and few graduate under twenty years of age.[38]

Once they are duly professed they begin to shamanize. This consists in falling into an abnormal state to enable them to make periodic visits to the various regions of the heavens in order to converse with the spirits and ascertain from them whether or not a sacrifice is favourably received, predictions concerning the weather and the prospects for the crops and the harvest. The spirits, however, do not actually speak through the shaman, as in the case of a spiritistic medium, though he is able to produce most impressive effects by a kind of ventriloquism and the use of incomprehensible sounds resembling an approaching hurricane which passes and vanishes into the bowels of the earth. The whole performance, in fact, is very carefully arranged to make a strong dramatic and emotional appeal to his audience, though the visionary experience often amounts to a genuine state of ecstatic intoxication bordering on so-called "possession".[39]

It is nevertheless true that among the North Asiatic peoples the institution has lost its primitive spontaneity and in many cases has become little more than theatrical performances. While shamans take part in public festivals they occupy a relatively subordinate place in society. Their presence at sacrifices is not essential and the exercise of their occult power is not their exclusive privilege. Although to-day it is almost entirely a male occupation, there is some reason to think that in Siberia in earlier times shamanism was largely a female cult,[40] very much as in Africa, Indonesia and America female magicians sometimes outnumber their male competitors. But usually women confine their occult efforts to soothsaying and the interpretation of dreams and omens.

The shaman is the prevailing type of magician not only among the North Asiatic peoples but also in the Pacific islands, Malaysia, Dravidian southern India and Africa, and in some of the American Indian tribes, including, besides those of Alaska and Queen Charlotte Islands, the Yuma of Arizona, the Bororo of Brazil, the Jivaro of Ecuador and the Arecuna of Venezuela. As the intermediary between man and the spirit world, he is the mouthpiece of the beings by whom he is "possessed" during his ecstatic visionary experiences, and, therefore, he is in constant demand. It is true that occult power is seldom the exclusive privilege of the professional shamans, as in primitive society everybody usually engages in some forms of magic (e.g. spells and enchantments) and the exercise of supernatural gifts; but only those who exhibit a genuine psychopathic personality, involving a high degree of auto-suggestibility, inner discipline and specialized training, can produce the abnormal physiological state required to perform the feats their office demands.

Thus, the Seligmans were convinced that notwithstanding an element of humbug and display about some of the performances, especially in the presence of visitors, the less sophisticated Veddas did in fact nearly lose consciousness during the singing and movements of the dance in which they engaged to invoke the spirits, particularly the souls of the dead (*yaku*). Most sincere practitioners whom they interrogated in different localities were dominated by the belief in the reality of the *yaku,* and of their own coming possession, and explained their sensations while they were in a state of semi-consciousness. Occasionally women may become possessed among the Veddas, and in the only instance of female ecstasy which these observers witnessed, there was a large element of conscious deception. Normally, however, as they admit, the shaman surrenders himself completely to the dance, and this, combined with subconscious expectancy, produces a genuine psychic experience.[41]

In Sumatra the Bataks cross-examine the spirit of a dead person (*begu*) invoked during a shamanistic performance to assure themselves that they are not dealing with an impostor, and when the authenticity of the deceased called up by the medium has been established, he is questioned by his descendants after they have made the offerings demanded by the *begu.* Here, again, apart from an element of trickery, the possessed man finds himself in a state of insensibility and eclipse of personal consciousness. The spontaneity of the experience is shown by the fact that Batak Christians who were formerly mediums are liable against their will to find themselves invaded by forces they cannot control which "suspend both will and thought and replace them by an extraneous power". Moreover, this phenomenon occurs among persons who are not neurotic, epileptic or known to suffer from mental abnormalities.[42] But accidental possession is distinguished from the deliberate attempts to summon spirits through a professional medium (*basandaran*) by drumming, dancing and the shamanistic techniques. To execute these specialized functions of the shaman, who is highly esteemed, a psychic temperament is essential, and so exhausting are the experiences that the life of a medium is said usually to be short.[43] But as weak and sickly people are often selected for the office,[44] this may partly account for their early death. In some districts it is mainly women who practise as mediums.[45] In the Malay Peninsula Skeat records an invocation of the spirit of a tiger by the wife of a shaman in the exorcism of a sick man and the subsequent convulsions of the husband which involved his collapse with loss of consciousness.[46]

In Polynesia, on the other hand, inspiration often is produced by the drinking of the sacred kava, and utterance is given to divine declarations without music, dancing or ecstatic agitation, though sometimes symptoms of convulsion accompany the revelation.[47] In Melanesia when a man is possessed by a *tindalo* (spirit) he sneezes, trembles, foams at the mouth and is left in a state of exhaustion when the visitation is over.[48] But there is no order of shamans, and occult experiences of this kind may befall any unsuspecting person who is overpowered by the *mana* of a ghost. Sometimes a man may use magic to bring the possession upon himself but this is distinct from the spontaneous manifestation of such power by a spirit or ghost, and from deliberate attempts to become subjected to ghostly influence by visiting sacred places where this *mana* resides.[49] In New Guinea when a man or woman desires to become a shaman he or she joins a party of mourners sitting round a corpse in the hope that the spirit of the deceased will enter him. If he falls into an ecstasy he then undergoes his training for the profession.[50]

THE SHAMAN, THE MAGICIAN AND THE PRIEST

Thus, it is clear that the shaman derives his occult power and insight from the ghosts or spirits with whom he is *en rapport*, and it is upon them that he depends for his special endowments. Sometimes he may be also a professional magician, but when he shamanizes he is under the influence of supernatural forces external to himself. Notwithstanding the fact that the functions of the worker of magic may be combined in one and the same person, the distinction between the medicine-man and the shaman, the magician and the priest, is fundamental because the one relies solely upon the exercise of his own psychic power; the other seeks the aid of the spiritual beings with whom he is in constant intercourse. But while the shaman is in this way differentiated from the magician or medicine man, he is also distinguished from the priest by the very considerable measure of control that he is able to bring to bear upon the transcendental agencies he subordinates to his will. While on occasions he may engage in sacerdotal functions his real work is in connexion with healing and divination, and inasmuch as he has direct access to the spirit world and derives his powers from particular tutelary spirits who are more or less at his command, his marvellous feats are performed by virtue of supernatural gifts and exploits deriving from his power over or influence with spirits.

Therefore, he occupies an intermediate position between the magician who acts exclusively on his own authority and initiative, and the priest who supplicates and conciliates forces superior to himself, guards the sacred tradition in his care, and acts as the master of its sacrificial technique strictly within the limits of his office. The one officiates in his own name and by his occult methods; the other serves at the altar and in the temple or shrine as the representative of the community in its relations with the gods and the unseen world. Both have to undergo a specialized training and receive formal initiation, but the shaman virtually must have the right disposition and temperament, whether hereditary or chosen, whereas neither the magician nor the priest has to exhibit psychopathic ten-

C

dencies because they are masters of a technique, or holders of an office, conferred upon them by consecration. The medicine-man must be efficient in his craft, while the priest must have an expert knowledge of sacred learning and of all that pertains to the sacerdotal office, its ritual, mythology, law, doctrine and organization. The shaman and the magician may both be individualists, but since the priest is responsible for maintaining a right relationship between the community and its gods, he 'exercises his functions in a corporate capacity. As sacrifice is the vital bond of union in this relationship, the altar is his cult centre as against the shamanistic séance, visionary experience and ecstatic utterance, or the rite and spell of the magician put into operation either publicly or in secret for licit or illicit ends. In the shaman all three disciplines—inspiration, magic and religion—are loosely combined, but prophecy and divination, and the exercise of occult power, are the determining charac- teristics of the office.

Individuals richly endowed with these psychic gifts acquire considerable prestige, but shamans seldom, if ever, have an assured position in society comparable to that of an organized hierarchy, or of an outstanding magician, like for instance a renowned rain-maker. They are held in varying degrees of re- spect and fear according to their powers, but they do not con- stitute a distinct order, and unless they are also medicine-men or cult leaders, they do not exercise administrative functions, even though they may be honoured after death and become the centre of a cultus.[51] They may, however, combine the functions of a healer and an expert in the occult technique. Being in possession of a considerable psychological knowledge ac- quired by long training and experience in the exercise of their gifts, they occupy a key position in society. Their failures do not seriously diminish their prestige because it is recognized that like our own medical practitioners they have their limitations. The system is too firmly established to break down when their efforts do not succeed, the inability to effect a cure, as in the case of the medicine-men previously considered, being ex- plained by the intervention of a more powerful shaman.

In their structural relations they exercise a dual influence. Within their own group they tend to be a consolidating force inasmuch as they may use their good offices to settle disputes, guide opinion, persuade or coerce the spirits to promote the well-being of individuals and the body politic, and to establish and maintain harmony between the human and the divine orders. On the other hand, they may be malevolent in their intentions towards hostile neighbours, and therefore be regarded by them as a potent source of the evils that befall them. Consequently, there is a disruptive element in shamanism fostering ill-will and not infrequently causing prolonged enmity between opposed groups. But in either capacity, whether consolidating or disintegrating in his influence, the shaman is a central figure in structural relations and in social affairs, both reflecting and producing the existing organization and determining the attitudes of the spirits under his control for good or ill towards friends and foes alike.

CHAPTER II

The Seer and the Diviner

OUT of the fluid state which characterized the primitive conception of the magico-religious practitioner—neither exclusively priest, prophet nor magician—professional specializations in due course have emerged. While here again there has been an intermingling of functions, offices have tended to become more clearly defined. These have assumed the form of exorcists, seers, diviners and prophets on the one hand, and, on the other hand, of divine kings and priests devoted to the service of the altar and the techniques of worship on which the natural order and the well-being of man and society have been thought to depend. As the seers and the prophets have been the medium of revelations, so the priesthood has been the guardian of the sacred tradition, while in the higher religions their respective offices have acquired a spiritual, ethical and mystical significance.

THE SEER AND THE MANTIC TRADITION

Concentrating attention at this point in our inquiry on the seer and the diviner, as might be expected since the shamanistic tradition lies in the background, the methods employed to obtain oracular messages often are indistinguishable from those adopted by ecstatics in more primitive states of culture. In communicating their will and power to man, the gods have been believed to employ inspired men as their agents to whom they have given superhuman knowledge, foresight, and understanding to enable them to proclaim oracles and interpret signs and omens, dreams and the movements of the heavenly bodies. Thus, the mantic tradition developed into a pseudo-science under the direction of professional seers and diviners who by their psychic powers and technical training disclosed hidden wisdom and determined the course of events by ecstatic visionary experiences, or by portents, auspices, augury, hepato-scopy and astrological prognostications.

ORACLE-SEERS IN BABYLONIA

In Mesopotamia a special class of seers, the *bārû*, were set apart to communicate knowledge of the will of the gods concerning courses of action and future events in the form of oracles, omens, dreams and visions.[1] Etymologically the name is derived from the verb *barû* "to see", and while in practice the designation may include divinatory "inspection" of the entrails and liver of a sacrificial victim as the seat of its soul-substance, and, therefore, be employed to ascertain the will of the gods to whom it was offered, the natural meaning of the word is that of "beholding" in the mantic sense.[2] Therefore, in addition to hydromancy, hepatoscopy, the observation of celestial phenomena, physiognomical omens, the flight of birds and similar divinatory devices, the *bārû* occupied themselves with the interpretation of dreams, and with visionary experiences, as the official mediators between man and the gods.[3] In this capacity they questioned (*ša'ālu*) the deity, and so were sometimes called *šā'ilu*, "askers" or "inquirers".[4]

Their office, however, seems to have included that of the oracle-seer through whom the god spoke,[5] and in all probability it was intimately connected with the obscure officials called *šabrû* who appear to have been recipients of dream-visions in nocturnal occult experiences, though they may have been also simply interpreters of dreams in the usual manner.[6] If, however, their functions included spending the night at a shrine for the purpose of receiving a divine revelation (i.e. incubation), they must be regarded as dispensers of the incubation oracle;[7] a practice, as will be considered later, which has been commonly associated with the healing art.

WORDS OF POWER AND "PHATIC COMMUNION"

Besides these seers, there are indications of an ecstatic type (*maḫḫû*) who derived their powers direct from the god with whom they were *en rapport* and to whose words they gave utterance.[8] Doubtless their principal work was the interpretation of dreams and omens through the mantic oracle, but it may have included some of the wilder forms of ecstatic experience as well as incubation and priestly duties in connexion with the sacrificial rites.[9] Indeed, sacred utterance always has been an integral part of the office of the seer. From time immemorial the spoken word has been the instrument of *mana* so that the Word of Power has been regarded as the deity in action establishing a "phatic communion" between the speaker and the hearer by a sacramental exchange of words.[10] In this sacred action ecstatic experience has been the means whereby utterance has been given to the things revealed. The divine voice speaks through its human instrument in words which are intended to convey neither symbolic meaning, intellectual reflection, nor the transmission of thought. Their purpose is to give expression to the most intense and deep-seated states of emotion so that the agent feels himself to be so filled with the divine afflatus that he is compelled to give vent to prophetic oracles.

It may suffice merely to utter a sacred formula or exclamation indicating the intention for which a rite or gesture is performed whereby supernatural potency is made operative. When, for example, the Vedic priests in India, filled with divine power (*brahman*), sang the hymns of the Rig-veda they were believed to exercise a constraining influence alike over the gods and men, at once coercive, persuasive and propitiative.[11] The good will of the gods was cultivated and they were induced to bestow their benefits on their votaries in response to the service rendered in the cultus. Nevertheless, although they were constrained by the power of the sacred utterance to do what they were bidden by the priests, the brahmins did not claim to influence the course of events without their intervention. The words of power uttered and the ritual actions performed (e.g. the building of the Fire Altar representing the structure of the universe)[12] established a communal *rapport* in relation to the objective environment and its mysterious characteristics and hidden potencies. The utterances may be devoid of any precise

or intelligible meaning, like the puzzling syllable OM re-
iterated by the *hotṛ* priest in the consecration of a king as the
response to each verse of the Rig-veda.[13] Moreover, as a communal exercise ejaculations and utterances of this nature have a
consolidating effect on those repeating them in a common devotion, as in the recitation of verses of the Qur'an in Arabic in
the salat in Islam. The primary purpose, however, is to
establish union with the sacred order, to convey supernatural
power, and to gain access to superhuman knowledge.

Nevertheless, to utter Words of Power, or "speak with
tongues" (glossolaly) in a manner unintelligible to the hearers,[14]
though efficacious ecstatically and "phatically", does not fulfil
the practical purposes of the mantic art. Thus, in the Christian
Church while glossolaly continued in apostolic times and
ranked with other charismata, or spiritual gifts, in close association with prophecy,[15] it soon died out,[16] though the phenomenon has recurred in revivalist movements from the time of the
Franciscans to that of the Quakers, Ranters, Methodists,
Irvingites and other modern Adventist sects.[17] Since one of the
main functions of the seer has been to supply information
about current and future events thought to be known to the
gods with whom he is *en rapport,* unintelligible ecstatic utterances have not sufficed. In Greece, for example, Agis in-
quired of Zeus Naos and Dione whether his coverlets and
pillows had been lost or stolen, just as in Israel Saul repaired to
Samuel to discover the whereabouts of his father's asses. Before
engaging in battle with the Syrians for Ramoth Gilead, Ahab
consulted his prophets, and at Delphi the framing of laws, the
founding of colonies, the launching of wars, the fortunes of
dynasties, the healing of disease and the legal suits of individuals,
were referred to the judgment of the Pythian god from at least
the end of the eighth century B.C., or the beginning of the
seventh century. For a thousand years of recorded history the
Greeks and Romans consulted the prophetess (Pythia) seated
on her tripod, and probably long before Apollo occupied the
Delphic shrine it had an oracular tradition, going back perhaps to Minoan times.

THE DELPHIC ORACLE

Its foundation, however, is wrapped in obscurity. Before it was associated with Apollo, the Minoan Mother goddess whom the Greeks called Ge-Themis, and perhaps Poseidon, gave oracles at Delphi.[18] In the Homeric period its prestige was established as an Apolline centre,[19] but whether or not it was the home of the worship of Dionysos before it was occupied by Apollo has yet to be determined. In any case it exercised a moderating influence on the wilder Thracian orgies that had been held by night on the tops of mountains, when aided by tumultous dancing and music, and the free use of wine, the maenads became god-possessed "bacchoi", or "Sabazoi". In this state of *enthusiasmos* they saw visions and discerned the presence of Zagreus-Dionysos whose life they temporarily shared.[20]

Like the worship of the Phrygian Magna Mater, Kybele, the Dionysiac was orgiastic in the extreme, and, therefore, stood in the mantic tradition. Nevertheless, at Delphi inspiration took a different form from that manifested in the Thraco-Phrygian frenzies. At the shrine of Apollo, it would appear, the inspired prophetess when an oracle was demanded arrayed herself in long robes, a golden headdress and a wreath of laurel-leaves, and drank of the sacred spring Kassotis. She then, it is said, seated herself on a tripod over a vaporous cleft in a chasm or cave below, unless she actually entered the cave to encounter the vapour, in order to attain a state of enthusiasm. In this condition she gave counsel as the mouthpiece of Apollo.[21] As the accounts of this procedure are derived mainly from relatively late sources,[22] and no allusions to the cave or chasm occur earlier than the fourth century B.C., it is by no means certain that the vapour was the original cause of the inspiration. Clefts of this nature have been found in the limestone mountains in the neighbourhood of Delphi,[23] but excavations at the site of the shrine have not produced any conclusive results.[24] Therefore, while the ancient tradition is by no means improbable, it remains a conjecture. But whatever may have been the cause of the phenomenon, the words uttered by the Pythia, though probably not intelligible, were interpreted by the προφῆται, and often written down in hexameters as the oracles of Zeus given through Apollo, with whom the prophetess was thought to be *en rapport*. Like the Cumaean Sibyl, she was an inspired figure,[25] and in giving utterance to the divine voice she made known the will of Zeus through his son Apollo.

The Pythia, in fact, was but the Greek form of a prophetic tradition which belonged to the cult of Apollo, having its original home in all probability in Anatolia[26] before it became established at Delphi. While opinion is divided concerning the priority of Apollo and Dionysos at this shrine on "rocky Pytho",[27] that the one occupant reacted on the other can hardly be doubted. But although Apollo may have been a constraining influence on the voluptuous Dionysiac, he and his prophetess would seem to have had an ecstatic background.[28] In this connexion it is significant, as Mr Guthrie has emphasized, that the Hyperboreans with whom Apollo is traditionally associated, geographically and etymologically have Northern Asiatic affinities.[29] It is conceivable, therefore, that he stands in the shamanistic tradition by virtue of his antecedents long before the cultus was mellowed and modified in Anatolia, and combined with that of the Pythia. On taking up his abode with his prophetess at Delphi he was brought into relation with Dionysos who was established there, either before or after his arrival at the shrine. Having become the divine lawgiver,[30] the oracle would naturally be consulted to learn the will of Apollo on matters sacred and secular, and to secure his approval for what already had been done.[31] Whatever may have been the cause of the inspiration, the methods of the Pythia were ecstatic, and as the two cults coalesced the prophetess and her oracular utterances gave expression to a common tradition.

A third figure who found a place in this complex oracle was Orpheus, who, though never worshipped as a god, was a prophet and hero in the religion of Dionysos, and was venerated as "a priest, or in some other way satellite" of Apollo.[32] Here, again, it was Delphic influence which brought

the two gods and their respective cults together, and although
the Orphics could never have established the synthesis, they
introduced many Apolline modifications into the Thracian
orgiastic tradition. Under their influence apparently the
Delphians cultivated hero-worship,[33] and the ritual tendance
of the dead.[34] Moreover, the Dionysian-Orphic "enthusiasm"
bridged the gulf between mortals and immortals, first by crude
ecstatic frenzy and later by metempsychosis and *teletae* as a
means of getting into touch with the chthonian powers,
purging the soul of its titanic defilements, until at length release
from a hampering body might be secured.[35] Therefore, the
Pythian Apollo was responsible in no small measure for
directing the wilder forms of ecstatic revelation into new and
more refined channels, at once oracular and animistic, which
ultimately acquired a philosophic content in the Platonic
soma-sema doctrine of the soul and of its pre-existence and
reincarnation.[36]

So great became the fame and influence of Apollo that to the
Pythia at Delphi all Greece resorted for information on cult-
procedure, politics and law, questions of purification in cases of
homicide, and in all matters relating to the everyday life of the
state and of the individual. Therefore, at one time when empire
building made increasingly heavy demands on the seat of
divine omniscience, local *exegetai* had to be appointed to give
advice to the administration and to deal with the direction of
the citizens of Athens, Sparta and other cities. These officials
had to be equipped with some powers of divination to enable
them to act in the capacity of legal advisors to private individuals,[37] and in local affairs, within reasonable limits. But
Delphi remained the centre of spiritual authority and the
Pythian prophetess the final voice of the god, to whom bar-
barian kings turned in times of stress and crisis. Before a new
colony was founded the oracle had to be consulted,[38] and on
more than one occasion Socrates turned for guidance to
Delphi, the Pythia having declared him to be the wisest of
men.[39] Henceforth he regarded himself as in the service of
Apollo and under his protection, so long as he lived per-

petually in accordance with his divine direction. Thus, Apollo retained the allegiance of the entire nation from statesmen and sages to citizens and the athletes who assembled periodically at Delphi to take part in the sacred games held in his honour.

As a civilizing and consolidating force the influence of the oracle, therefore, was considerable. The Athenian *exegetoi* were chosen either by the oracle or elected by the citizens from among noble families with a hereditary qualification,[40] though Plato recommended appointment by popular vote.[41] He allowed, however, that the Pythian Apollo was the external authority to whom all must turn for advice on matters of worship but not to the exclusion of the local gods. If no attempt was made to unify the cults of the Greek States in a single deity, Delphi and its ministers occupied a unique position as the centre of oracular inquiry, both public and private. As such it exercised a powerful influence in respect of matters of legal and statutory procedure, the elucidation of ancestral custom, international affairs, colonization, vendetta, homicide, and in times of crisis. Thus, its sanctions bestowed on colonists a title of possession in the territory they occupied, and it was largely responsible for the abandonment of the blood-feud, and the substitution of ritual purification for homicide. In short, by 600 B.C. Apollo at Delphi became the chief standardizing agency in the welter of the city-states, with incalculable significance in the social structure and religious organization of the Greek world.

Nevertheless, the Delphic priesthood lacked any ultimate authority other than the pronouncements of the Pythia as the voice of Apollo announcing the purpose of Zeus. In the absence of a stable hierarchy independent of the oracular tradition, if these failed to be justified in practice its prestige was diminished and recourse might be made to other seats. Therefore, in the sixth century after the Persian wars when it proved to be unequal to the exacting demands made upon it, by its partial judgments it gradually lost the confidence of the nation. Delphi was despoiled of its treasures by the Phocian generals in the Second Sacred War (357–46 B.C.), and when they were

defeated by Philip of Macedon Delphi ceased to occupy its
focal position as the Panhellenic sanctuary, though the oracle
supported the conqueror and his successor, Alexander the
Great.[42] In the Hellenistic period, after the death of Alexander
in 323, it was little more than a local court of appeal on doubtful
questions touching the gods and moral conduct, giving advice
on matters of conscience. In the ethical sphere its standard was
generally high, but faith in its oracular pronouncements had so
declined in the prevailing conditions of decadence and scepticism that no attempt had been made to rebuild the temple after
its destruction (probably by an earthquake) in 371. In spite of
the legends to the contrary, the Hellenistic kings ignored the
Pythia, and on one occasion one of them is said to have
actually seduced her without incurring any penalties for his
sacrilege.[43] In short, they paid lip-service to Apollo without
honouring or consulting his oracle. It was not until 279 B.C.,
when Celtic hordes invaded Macedonia and sacked the temples,
that consolidated effort was made to save Delphi from their
hands on an assurance from the god that he would protect his
shrine—"I and the white maidens shall take care of these
matters."[44] National sentiment rallied to the cause and, convinced that Apollo had intervened by earthquake and thunder-
bolts, and, indeed, had himself appeared as a youth of superhuman size and surpassing beauty, the priests and prophetesses
rushed into the fray, clad in their sacred vestments, to complete
the discomfiture of the enemy who withdrew to the north and
was then driven back into Macedonia.[45] Nevertheless, the
shrine appears to have been plundered by the Celts,[46] though
the attack was beaten off with sufficient success to justify the
growth of the legend within six months of the invasion. The
festival of Σωτήρια was instituted to commemorate the event in
honour of Zeus Σωτήρια and the Pythian Apollo, and celebrated with sacred games.

The Celtic repulse marked a revival of the shrine, and during
the second century B.C. Delphi enjoyed renewed vitality. At
the end of the Hannibalic war Roman envoys consulted the
oracle before approaching Attalus of Pergamos (who had

founded his dynasty on the word of Apollo)[47] with a request that the meteoric stone, the symbol of the Phrygian Magna Mater, should be transported from Pessinus to Rome and the cult of Cybele established there.[48] Seleucus II (246–226 B.C.) sought the sanction of the Pythia before founding a temple of Aphrodite Stratonicis in Smyrna in honour of his wife,[49] and Ptolemy VI (173–146 B.C.) is alleged to have obtained the blessing of the Pythian Apollo on the transference of the image of Serapis from Sinope to Alexandria.[50] But while there may be no foundation in fact for this story, it suggests, nevertheless, that Delphi was occasionally consulted in the second century B.C.

In the early years of the Roman Empire, however, it seems to have been completely ignored in matters of state, and it was not until the beginning of the new era that it was revived, after the temple had been repaired by Domitian in A.D. 84,[51] and Pythian games reinstated. Then it came into prominence in the reigns of Trajan and Hadrian[52] when Delphi became again the sacred city (ἁ ἱερὰ πόλις). But its days were numbered for after a few sporadic utterances in the time of the Antonines and Severus,[53] the oracle became silent. The attempt on the part of Julian to resuscitate it failed completely,[54] and the last words of the Pythia were "tell the king, to earth has fallen the fair-wrought dwelling, no longer hath Phoebus shelter, nor a prophetic-laurel, nor a speaking spring. The water of speech is quenched".[55] In 390 the temple was closed by Theodosius and demolished by his successor, Arcadius.

THE SIBYLLINE ORACLES

Christianity, however, did not deny that behind the oracle were spiritual powers, but it regarded them as demoniacal, and, therefore, in line with all other manifestations of possession by evil spirits.[56] Moreover, the early Fathers and other Christian writers frequently quoted the collections of supposed prophecies bearing witness to Christ emanating from the mysterious sibyls. Like the Pythia, these seeresses originally were thought to have derived their inspiration from Apollo, and to

have become possessed (ἔν θέος) when uttering their prophecies "with frenzied lips".[57] The earliest of them was "the
sibyl of Erythrae in Asia Minor,[58] whose head appears on
ancient Erythraean coins, and, if she existed at all, she lived
probably in about the seventh century B.C. From Asia Minor
the movement spread to Greece where in the sixth and fifth
centuries floating oracular *dicta,* emanating from a weird
ecstatic female, flourished in connexion with the Orphic
movement. Thence it spread to Italy in the wake of the cult of
Apollo, and became established, probably by Greek settlers, at
Cumae near Naples.

Thus, a temple was said to have been dedicated there in 493
in obedience to directions found in the Sibylline Books, which
a strange old woman had succeeded in selling at an exhorbitant
price to the last of the Tarquin kings (Tarquinius Superbus),
after she had burned the earlier collections of prophecies which
he had refused to purchase. If this legend preserves the memory
of the foundation of the Cumaean temple in the fifth century
under Sibylline influence, it has the important implication that
the movement in Italy, which played a prominent part in the
introduction of Greek gods and their cultus at Rome, goes
back to this period, and gained a footing in the capital at the
beginning of the Republic.[59] In the disturbances that occurred
in the fifth century during the Etruscan struggle for the restoration of its dynasty, the Sibylline books were consulted and
called for the foundation of the cult of the Greek corn-deities,
Demeter, Dionysos and Kore, Latinized as Ceres, Liber and
Libera. Consequently, a temple was erected and dedicated in
their honour on the side of the Aventine towards the Circus
Maximus (496–493 B.C.). Nearly three hundred years later,
when, after a violent storm of pebble-rain in the strenuous days
of the Hannibalic war in 205 B.C. recourse was made to the
oracular books, the Phrygian Magna Mater was ordered to be
transported from Pessinus and installed in the temple of
Victoria until an edifice was erected in her honour on the
Palatine in 191 B.C.[60]

That at first it was at Cumae that the oracles were consulted is highly probable since they were established there in charge of *duouiri* before collections of the prophecies were kept in Rome at the Capitol early in the Republic,[61] under the care of *decemuiri sacris faciundis,* as the guardians then became. It was to them that the Senate made application for consultation when occasion demanded oracular direction, and they were responsible for carrying out what the Sibylline utterances declared. These included the introduction of new gods and new rites, some of which were not lacking in barbarity, including as they did burying alive or beating to death victims to whom were attributed widespread disasters.[62] Thus, for good in revitalizing Roman religion and bringing it into closer relation with current events, and for ill in the introduction of unedifying ecstatic and sometimes cruel innovations, the Sibylline movement changed the whole character of the state cult.

When the "books" perished in the fire that destroyed the Capitol in 82 B.C., men were sent to Erythrae seven years later in search of Sibylline verses. The thousands they brought back were submitted to the *duouiri* for inspection, but their selection was considerably reduced by Augustus. It was this residuum that was carefully protected and preserved for consultation when oracular guidance was needed at times of grave crisis, so that at the beginning of the Christian era it had an official position in the Empire and in due course gained a measure of recognition by the Church. Therefore, in the second and third centuries A.D. a new class of oracles came into being from Christian sources, closely related not only to the pagan prophecies but to those that had grown up at Alexandria in Hellenistic Jewish circles during the second century B.C. These adaptations of the Sibylline books consisted of hexameter verses written in the the same manner as those of the Graeco-Roman originals, and attributed to sibyls who were inspired, it was said, to propagate the faith and teaching of Israel among the heathen. Old Testament incidents were combined with legends borrowed from the Sibylline writings so that the destruction of the tower of Babel, for instance, was represented as the work of mighty winds before the reign of

Cronos, Titan and Iapetus and the birth of Zeus, and foretold by the prophetic seer.[63]

The success of this method of propaganda as a proselytising force led Christian writers in the second and third centuries to carry on the tradition. Some of the oracles were revised and worked over by Christian sibyllists,[64] while others were composed entirely afresh.[65] Most of them, however, are composite documents, and the last four books (XI–XIV) deal mainly with historical persons and events, with varying degrees of accuracy, written in Sibylline language by Jews and Christians from the third century onwards.[66] Notwithstanding the widespread acceptance by the Early Fathers of the inspiration of the sibyls as spontaneous witness to Christ,[67] the real nature of the fabrications was recognized by such discerning minds as those of Lucian and Celsus, who used all their skill and wit to discredit this method of Christian propaganda.[68] Nothing daunted, the Latins continued the tradition[69] and at Nicaea Constantine appealed to the oracles in addressing the Council,[70] while St Augustine placed the sibyl in the City of God.[71]

Thus, ecstatic inspiration survived in the Christian era and in an uncritical age it took a variety of forms, ranging from Sibylline prophesy and an oracular interpretation of Holy Writ and other ancient writings to the visions and occult experiences of saints and mystics and the widespread practice of exorcism. Indeed, as paganism declined it left behind a residuum of discredited beliefs and customs, gods and spirits, cults and esoteric mysteries, which were absorbed into and transformed by the new spiritual dynamic. Much of this inheritance came from the lower strata of society and by incorporation in the dominant faith and controlling influence of Christendom it acquired a new importance and significance.[72] The demon, for example, was raised from a position of relative unimportance to that of a member of a dreaded hierarchy of evil spirits ruled over by a supreme Author of Evil who became a serious rival to the Creator, and, as Mr C. S. Lewis has remarked, hardly less powerful and much more interesting than God. Therefore, ecstatic inspiration through divine charismatic forces had as its counterpart an equally potent possession by demoniacal influences which found expression in exorcism.

EXORCISM AND THE HEALING ART

In the primitive Church, as in Eastern Christendom to-day, the exorcising of demons was not confined to clerics,[73] but in the West in the middle of the third century an office of exorcist was instituted as a minor order,[74] a book of exorcisms was produced containing the formulae to be used in the expulsion of evil from "energumens" (i.e. persons suffering from mental and nervous disorders), catechumens, holy places and objects (churches, altars, and sacred vessels), and the elements employed as sacramentals (water, salt and oil). In course of time, however, as less stress was laid on demoniacal possession and contagion, the power of exorcism was transferred to the priesthood, and included in the gifts conferred by ordination. Moreover, under modern conditions care is taken in the exercise of this ministry to confine it to very special cases and certain forms of disease.

BABYLONIA AND ASSYRIA

All down the ages good and evil have been in opposition as two contending forces in perpetual conflict, so that the ritual of expulsion has been an essential element in sanctification and the impulsion of spiritual power and insight. Consequently, in this dual task of getting rid of evil in order to secure good the exorcist has exercised a function complementary to that of the seer. Not infrequently, as we have seen, the medicine-man or shaman has been responsible both for riddance and induction, and at a higher cultural level in Babylonia and Assyria the soothsayer and exorcist originally were hardly distinguishable. In process of time, however, the driving out of demons from human beings and buildings by incantations and ritual expulsions were separated from the interpretation of omens and astrological portents. This was necessitated by the development of an elaborate system of demonology entailing jinns, ghouls,

D

vampires, malignant disembodied ghosts (*edimmu*), and vast
hordes of hostile spirits (*utukku, gallû, labartu, labasu* and *ahhazu,
lilû, šêdu* and *lamassu*) which lurked in graves and solitary
places, on mountains and in dens of the earth, and in marshes.
They roamed about the streets, sliding through the doors and
walls of houses, and were borne on the wings of the mighty
winds that swept the land. Wherever they occurred they
brought misfortune, sickness and death in their train.[75] Small
wonder, then, that the exorcist was in constant demand. Thus,
the cuneiform texts from the middle of the third millennium
B.C. onwards bear witness to the numerous incantations employed to expel evil spirits and the ghosts of the dead. In the
case of the latter the exorcist threatened that no rites would be
performed on their behalf until they had departed:

> (Whatever spirit thou may be), until thou art removed:
> Until thou departest from the man, the son of his god,
> Thou shalt have no food to eat,
> Thou shalt have no drink to drink.[76]

In the healing of disease a Word of Power was uttered in the
name of Ea, the third god of the highest triad, the Lord of
Wisdom and ruler of the healing waters, and his son Marduk,
who as the god of Babylon became the head of the pantheon.
Standing nearest to mankind these deities were invoked by the
aid of the life-giving waters under the control of Ea and his
mediator (Marduk). "Marduk hath seen him (the sick person)
and hath entered the house of his father Ea, and hath said,
'Father, headache, from the underworld hath gone forth.'"
Then follows the prescription for the patient ending usually
with the incantation, "By Heaven be ye exorcized! By earth be
ye exorcized!", the appropriate god concerned with a particular
disease being addressed with this formula. But in addition to
pronouncing the name of the divine being in which the magic
virtue resides, the exorcist had to mention that of the demon to
be driven forth. This involved the recitation of long lists of
devils or ghosts in order to include the one that was the cause
of the malady.[77] The patient was then sprinkled with water,
censed, surrounded with flour, or some other magically pro-

tective substance, such as black and white yam fastened to his couch, the exorcist holding in his hand a branch of the sacred tamarisk, "the powerful weapon of Anu", the father of the great gods, during the incantation.[78]

From the potency ascribed to water the "curse of Eridu" (*sĭptu,* i.e. the curse of expiation) derived its efficacy as the incantation *par excellence* in overcoming the bans of demons, and in the consecration of sacred objects. The words of the formula have not been recorded but doubtless they contained the name of Ea since its mystic power was ascribed to the water-god, though originally it was the life-giving water itself that drove forth the malevolent influences and freed those beset by them from their evil contagions by absorbing them into itself. The act of expulsion (*kuppuru*) sometimes involved the offering of a kid or sucking-pig for the purpose of driving the demon into the body of the victim which was then destroyed.[79] In a Sumerian ritual-text, Ea is said to command Marduk to take a scapegoat in the form of a horned wild goat to the king bound by a curse, and place its head against his (the king's) head so that "his poisonous tabu into his mouth may be cast".

> May the king be pure, may he be clean,
> He who knows not the curse by which he is cured,
> From his body may he chase it away.
> May the demon of his device stand aside.[80]

Similarly, seven loaves of pure dough were carried into the desert after the exorcist had transferred to them the evil incurred by the breaking of a tabu in order to remove the pollution.[81] The Assyrians modelled the dough into an effigy of the sick man, censed and sprinkled it with water, but whether or not it was then treated as a "sin-carrier", or scapegoat, is not recorded.[82] But a specially woven white and black woollen cord bound upon the hand, head and foot of a man under a curse was sent forth to the desert as an expulsion rite.[83]

Surrounded on every side with such an array of ill-disposed forces personified in a variety of forms and guises, the exorcist occupied a position of supreme importance. Not only was he in constant demand in his capacity of "physician", but he

was called upon to assist at the consecration of temples, at
funerals, and the seasonal ceremonies—in short, on all occasions when hostile spiritual powers might be expected to be
lying in wait or already in possession of places, objects, or
persons. He was indeed one of the principal functionaries in
Babylonia and Assyria and without his aid and intervention at
every critical juncture evil was almost certain to befall the nation
and its people. In consequence he was held in high esteem, as
was Eridu, the seat of worship of Ea and the original centre of
the rites of exorcism. But the office had its responsibilities since
failure to effect a cure, or more particularly the infliction of any
injury on the patient, was calculated to render the practitioner
liable to a fine on the principle of the *jus talionis*. This, however,
applied more to the "surgeon" than to the exorcist proper who
was only concerned with internal diseases attributed to demons.
In this domain he reigned supreme.

ANCIENT EGYPT

Similarly, in ancient Egypt the exorcist was a doctor-priest
who engaged in a struggle with an indwelling adversary by the
aid of incantations and spells. First the name of the demon had
to be discovered and that of the god who could be adjured to
expel it by his divine power. When this secret knowledge had
been gained the exorcist either summoned the god or dis-
guised himself as the god and imitated his actions, unless he
was content simply to rely on the divine magical devices which
had proved efficacious on previous encounters. The hostile
force, however, was not always personified though usually it
was addressed in personal terms and bidden to depart. "Flow
out thou poison, come forth upon the ground. Horus conjures
thee, he cuts thee off, he *splits thee out,* and thou risest not up but
fallest down. Thou art weak and not strong, a coward and
dost not fight, blind and dost not see. Thou liftest not thy face.
Thou art turned back and findest not thy way. Thou mournest
and dost not rejoice. Thou creepest away and dost not appear.
So speaketh Horus, efficacious of magic!" When these words
were recited over a hawk made of isy-wood with two feathers

on its head, and bread, beer and incense offered to it, the poison was slain by the magic of Horus as soon as the object was placed on the face of a sufferer from snake-bite.[84]

Sometimes the exorcizing magician spoke in his own name, but when he gave vent to threatening utterances to the malignant power, demon, spirit, ghoul or vampire, he usually attributed the spell to a god: "It is Isis who says it", or "I am Re in this his mysterious name".[85] In addition to the knowledge of secret names and mystical numbers as a potent means of expelling and gaining control over evil influences, statues animated by the spirit of the god whose help was sought were employed, together with images and amulets charged with magical power derived from the statue in which the divine essence dwelt in its plenitude.[86] Then, again, the time and season had to be considered since exorcisms depended for their efficacy upon the hour or day on which they were performed. The temple calendars divided the year into lucky and unlucky days determined in relation to the struggle between good and evil that was continually going on in the cosmic order. Consequently, it was necessary that an incantation should correspond to the precise calendrical conditions so that the role of the god or spirit invoked should be reproduced by the sorcerer at the most advantageous moment—at the right time (e.g. the setting or rising of the sun) and on the right day.[87]

There was, however, no specific office of exorcist in Egypt. The priest-physician (*sunu*) exercised his functions as the controlling agent of supernatural powers, particularly the gods of healing on the one hand and the demons of disease on the other. He was believed to have secret sources of information and to have been the repository of magico-religious knowledge and potency which empowered him to work cures.[88] But although he might be specially trained[89] he was not necessarily a member of a priestly order, and mothers invariably invoked divine aid every night to keep their infants free from malign influences ever alert to slink through the open door, or hide away in dark corners of the house, to perform their nefarious deeds.[90] Nevertheless, the professions of magician, priest and physician frequently were combined, and exorcism constituted a common practice in the warding off and driving out of evil.

THE CULT OF ASKLEPIOS AND INCUBATION

Similarly, the Greeks did not possess a separate class or caste of exorcists, but when in the fifth century B.C. the cult of Asklepios was established in Argolis and elsewhere in Greece, and was brought into conjunction with that of Apollo, Epidaurus became the centre *par excellence* of miraculous healing. Thither the sick resorted to sleep in the temple, and having seen a vision in the night watches awoke cured of their ailments. Since in their hypnotic sleep sometimes they appear to have dreamed that they underwent experiences not unlike those of medicine-men in process of initiation, such as having their abdomens cut open by the attendants of the gods and then stitched up again, it is not improbable that the priests of Asklepios on occasions practised some form of augury which they attributed to the divinity. Be this as it may, the therapeutic methods were based on the mystic dreams, and while the priests of Asklepios were not exorcists in the proper sense of the term, they exercised their functions as divine agents in the healing art, depending on the therapeutic power of faith in their own technique and in the mind of the patient.

Whether it was a demon to be expelled or life and health to be impelled, the fundamental approach was the same—the driving out of evil in order to secure the good, for it was never enough just to get rid of the harmful influences. Something more positive was required; a specific act of healing, as in the New Testament story of the cure of the Gerasene maniac. In this episode the delusional insanity of the possessed man had first to be dealt with along the traditional lines. He believed himself to be invaded by a legion of devils, and until these were exorcized in some objective manner a cure could not be wrought. Once the dark secret concerning their name was revealed—"my name is legion for we are many"—power over them could be secured. Thus, the delusion was brought to an end by transference to a neighbouring herd of swine, the destruction of which brought relief to the hag-ridden fuddled mind of the maniac.[91]

At Epidaurus the cures were obtained by the aid of visions and dreams which carried the same sort of conviction to those who flocked thither from far and near to seek from Asklepios either immediate relief or advice about the remedy that would prove to be efficacious. The long list of cures recorded in the inscriptions at the sanctuary leaves no room for doubt that Epidaurus occupied a position in Greece from the end of the fifth century comparable to that of Lourdes in Western Christendom to-day. From Argolis the cult spread to Athens and thence to Memphis in Egypt, where the god reappeared under the guise of the sage Imhotep, until in 293 B.C., in response to a Sibylline oracle during a pestilence when the aid of Asklepios was sought, it found a home on an island (Insula Tiberina) in the Tiber. Here a shrine was erected in honour of the son of Apollo, Latinized as Aesculapius, and his partner Salus, the Roman counterpart of Hygieia (Health) in the Hellenic cult, and served by priests who probably were Greeks skilled in the healing art.[92] The island eventually was shaped like a ship in commemoration of the legendary arrival of the god under the form of a sacred serpent which escaped from the boat carrying it from Epidaurus, and there went ashore.[93] The tradition of healing was carried on by the Church which erected on the site of the ancient temple a church and hospital dedicated to San Bartolomeo. Elsewhere the functions of Asklepios were taken over by SS. Cosmas and Damian, the patrons of physicians and surgeons.

Although it would appear from the inscriptions that the remedies prescribed in the Roman Aesculapium were not wholly magical, the practice of incubation (i.e. sleeping in temples as a means of healing), so prevalent in Babylonia and Greece, and introduced into Egypt under the influence of Serapis worship in the Ptolemaic period, apparently was retained. The dream-oracles of Fannius in Virgil[94] may be merely poetic fancies,[95] but within the Epidaurian cult in Hellenized Rome incubation survived as an integral part of the healing art of Asklepios.[96] It was, however, foreign to the Roman tradition in which neither mantic possession nor exorcism was practised. Thus, in Italy there was nothing comparable to the ecstasis that reached its climax at Delphi, or the dream-oracles of Epidaurus, until inspired seers and seeresses and healers were introduced from Greece and made their influence felt in and after the fifth century B.C. largely as a result of Etruscan contacts with Hellenic civilization.

PURIFICATIONS IN ANCIENT ROME

An organized mythology and demonology alike were importations among the Latins and Romans whose conception of the supernatural centred in the belief in *numina* and their cultus. Some of these animistic forces and spirits were hostile and malign, so that in later times Petronius could affirm that it was "fear which first made gods in the world".[97] If this judgment requires a good deal of qualification, it calls attention to a prominent aspect of the religion of Ancient Rome which found expression in the purificatory procession, or *lustratio,* held for the purpose of expelling evil from the fields, the homestead, and subsequently from the city and its inhabitants, the army before engaging in a campaign, or on any occasion demanding the elimination of harmful contagions. A typical example is the Lupercalia of February 15th when two bands of youth, called Luperci, clad only in a loin-cloth, ran round the boundaries of the Palatine hill striking bystanders with their thongs of goat's hide to create as it were a magic circle to protect the settlement from evil influences.[98] Moreover, since women who were struck by the Luperci were alleged to be cured of barrenness, the rite appears to have been in the nature of an exorcism originating no doubt in a lustration-festival for the protection of the herds and the promotion of fertility, adapted to urban conditions. The dance of the Salii, or leaping dancers, in March and October, who as priests of Mars passed through the city from their respective settlements on the Palatine and Quirinal Hill arrayed in the bronze armour and cloaks of warriors and carrying shields and spears, may have been intended originally to drive away the demons of blight and barrenness.[99] Hence the selection of the spring and autumn for the rite. Demonology, however, never became an organized cultus with an order of exorcists, as in Babylonia, any more than mantic inspiration was practised to secure divine enlightenment or incubational dream-oracles except under foreign influences.

DIVINATION: AUSPICE AND AUGURY

Divination in Italy took a different line. Starting from the belief that the transcendental powers who controlled everything of importance expressed their approval or disapproval, willingness or otherwise to lend their aid, by signs such as the flight or cries of birds, lightning, dreams or the utterances of a human being, a State-authorized system of augury was established as the official means of determining the will of the gods in all matters of moment. To be efficacious augury depended ultimately on a right relationship existing between man and the sacred order—the *pax deorum*—since in Roman animism, in which the practice must have arisen, the numina were only hostile when tabus were broken or the prescribed ritual was neglected. As the spirits of the farm and of the field shared the life of the family in the home, they acquired a more intimate character, and might be expected to interest themselves in the fortunes of the homestead, which was largely dependent on the seasons and the weather for its well-being. Consequently, its inhabitants would be constantly on the lookout for signs as spontaneous expressions of the guiding hand. Hence, doubtless, arose the belief in omens and portents which eventually was systematized in auspice and augury and adapted to urban conditions as an appendage to the *ius divinum* of the State-cult. *Religio* was maintained by the *sacrificium* at the appointed times and seasons: the *lustratio,* or purifications of persons and places; the *piaculum,* or reparation for any infringement of the ritual order; and the *votum,* or bargain with the gods on the principle of *do ut des.* But in addition to this cultus and its duties the auspices were taken in order to ascertain whether the gods were willing that this or that should be done.[100]

Divine guidance could be obtained either by making formal request (*impetrativa*) to a deity to reveal his attitude to a proposed course of action, or by interpreting any unusual or arresting occurrence or phenomenon (*ostenta*) as an omen or a portent, good or ill as the case might be, in relation to what was about to be done.[101] This latter custom (*ostenta*), common to mankind all over the world and at all times, was so liable to become an obsession that it was condemned as a superstition by later writers.[102] Nevertheless, sufficient importance was attached to certain portents as indications of divine wrath that they had to be reported to the *pontifices* responsible for the administration of the State-cult, or to the *haruspices,* as the trained interpreters of auspices, whose duty it was to decide whether or not a *procuratio portente* should be offered as a kind of piacular sacrifice.

It was the *impetrativa,* however, that was developed into an official system of augury under the direction of the chief magistrate, or *Rex sacerorum* of the patrician body of citizens, the priest of Iannus, who having inherited the prestige of the divine kingship assumed the primacy of the priesthoods. Beside him stood three *augures* whose function was to ascertain the will of the gods and to advise the procedure to be adopted as a result of their interpretation of the auspices.[103] From three their number was increased to six, then to nine, and eventually to fifteen, to which a sixteenth is said to have been added by Caesar.[104] The oldest acted as president of the college of *augures,* an office held in high esteem. It was he who "inaugurated" the *Rex Sacrorum,*[105] and the three greater *flamines*— the priests of Jupiter (*flamen Dialis*), of Mars and of Quirinus— blessed the crops,[106] confirmed the election of magistrates and gave his benediction at the beginning of a military campaign.[107]

In the royal period in all probability sacerdotal functions were exercised by the *Rex,* and the *augures* subsequently took over his religious duties. In course of time they became chiefly concerned with the *auspicia*. That was the business of the magistrates who "watched the sky" (*servare caelum*), while the *augur,* seated blindfolded, pronounced upon the signs in virtue of his expert knowledge. To the behaviour of sacred chicken and celestial phenomena, originally connected with the flight and cries of birds, later were added omens from lightning, very likely as a result of contact with Etruscan methods of divination.[108] After the *templum,* or place of observation, had been marked, the magistrate stationed himself at a prescribed point and addressed the god whose counsel he sought asking for a specified sign to indicate divine approval of the proposed action. When this was given it was reported to the Senate, together with any manifestations of disapproval. When the *augures* were introduced as expert advisers the possibilities of a conflict of opinion respecting *signa impetrativa* were considerably reduced, and the danger of the annulment of the business transacted in response to a doubtful pronouncement by the Senate was lessened. Sacred edifices and territories—the *loca liberata et effata*—were inaugurated by the *augures* independently of the magistrates to make possible the transaction of business and the taking of auspices within them.[109] To prevent red mildew on the crops, for example, they performed the *augurium canarium,* probably in conjunction with the Robigalia on April 25.

THE HARUSPICES

Sometimes recourse was had to the specially trained Etruscan diviners known as *haruspices,* who besides interpreting lightning, also inspected entrails (*extispicium*), particularly the liver, and explained and expiated portents and *prodigia*.[110] This primitive form of divination acquired considerable importance and elaboration in Etruria before it was introduced into Rome at the time of the Second Punic War, and eventually in the closing century of the Republic, became a permanent military organization. It then was the duty of the *haruspices,* after an inspection of the entrails of an animal sacrificed for the purpose, to report on the attitude of the gods to a campaign, and if favourable to bring their influence to bear on the people.[111] In this crude procedure the liver was the most important organ because it was a seat of the soul-substance of the victim, containing as it does an abnormal amount of the blood of the body. Moreover, inasmuch as the victim stood in a mediatorial relationship with the god to whom it was offered, the divine mind readily came to be regarded as revealing itself in those parts of the anatomy of a sacrificial animal in which the soul-substance was believed to be located. Therefore, the liver, the entrails and sometimes the gall-bladder, were inspected with great care by professional diviners who usually combined the office of *haruspex* and priest, to discover the issue of a proposed action and to acquire information about the course of future events.

A survival of this aspect of Etruscan haruspicy in Rome occurred in the model of a sheep's liver found at Piacenza in 1877, divided into regions corresponding to the Etruscan divisions of the sky and inscribed all over with the names of the gods associated with the several parts.[112] Similar models in terra cotta have been discovered in Babylon[113] and there are constant references to hepatoscopy in the cuneiform texts. The Babylonian practice was to portion out the liver in the Etruscan manner into oracular squares on a cosmological plan, and to study the natural markings due to the subsidiary veins and ducts. The right and left lower lobes and the upper lobe were carefully examined by the *barû,* or diviner, together with the gall-bladder, the cystic duct, the hepatic duct and the hepatic vein, and the *porta hepatis.* A swollen gall-bladder indicated increase of power while, conversely, a depression in the *porta hepatis* portended a decrease in power. The right side represented the propitious, and the left the sinister omens.[114]

That it was from Babylonia and Assyria that hepatoscopy, and haruspicy in general, made their way among the Etruscans and thence into the Graeco-Roman world, is very probable. It is possible that clay models of livers with Hittite cuneiform inscriptions found at Boghaz-köy may constitute a connecting link between the Babylonian and Etruscan cults, while very occasional references in the Hebrew sacred literature to the liver as an organ of vitality[115] possessed of the power of divination by its convulsive movements when taken from a sacrificial victim, suggest that Judaism also came under the same influence. In the book of Tobit[116] the liver of a fish is referred to in connexion with exorcisms, and in Ezekiel xxi. 21 Nebuchadnezzar is said to have "looked in the liver" to divine the road he should take when he stood "at the parting of the ways" leading to Jerusalem and "Rabbah of the children of Ammon". This procedure, doubtless natural to a Chaldaean, does not appear to have caused any surprise to the Hebrew writer and so was not regarded as the occasion for comment. That the Hittites were a medium of cultural diffusion in the Middle East is not at all unlikely, and therefore it may have been through them that these forms of divination passed from Mesopotamia to Palestine and the Aegean.

ASTROLOGY

Be this as it may, the valley of the Tigris and Euphrates was one of the most potent centres of the practice of divination in the Ancient East, and in the hands of a highly organized body of *augurs,* seers and astrologers it became eventually a complicated science with an extensive omen literature comprising long series of tablets dealing with every aspect of augural phenomena.[117] If many of these belong to a relatively late period (i.e. Ashurbanipal, 668–626 B.C.) they refer to a long and firmly established tradition and represent the product of much earlier editing and redaction. Thus, recent excavation has brought to light omen texts and astrological inscriptions of a much earlier time, the earliest of which, the *Enuma Anu-enlil* series ("When Anu- and Enlil etc."), is believed to go back to the Sumerian period, since it contains references to the fourfold division of the world into the lands of Akkad, Elam, Subartu and Amurru, and to such early kings as Rimush and Ibin-sin, who belong to the middle of the third millennium B.C.

The two chief means of ascertaining the will of the gods (hepatoscopy and astrology) can in fact be traced back to about 3000 B.C., though it was not until much later that an elaborate system was devised based on the movements of the heavenly bodies and the identification of the planets and fixed stars with certain gods, and employed by professional astrologers in casting horoscopes and predicting future fortunes of individuals and the community at large. With the development of calendars of favourable and unfavourable days the royal astrologers were continually on the look-out for any events that might portend public and political disasters. But events like eclipses were too occasional to serve their general purposes. Therefore, while great importance was attached to them, it was the more ordinary and recurrent phenomena that were usually studied by astrologers, particularly the changes in the clouds and in the position of the planets and the stars.

Every celestial phenomenon, in fact, was held to have its counterpart in human events, and every individual was at length brought under the influence of a planet or a fixed star which determined his fate from the cradle to the grave. For example, if an eclipse of the moon took place in Nisan in the first watch there would be destruction, and brother would slay brother. If it happened in Iyyar the king would die and the king's son would not succeed to his father's throne. If it occurred in Tammuz agriculture would prosper and prices would rise. If it happened in Ab Adad would send a flood upon the land. But when Adad caused his voice to be heard in the thunder in Nisan, the rule of the enemy would cease; when it took place in Tammuz agriculture would prosper. Solar eclipses invariably were regarded as evil omens but Jupiter and Saturn in their various phases were usually propitious. The vagaries of the weather were under the control of Adad, the storm-god, and varied according to the month in which his voice was heard in the thunder, and the particular timbre of its sound.

The stars acquired a more personal significance, and together with the sun, moon, and the planets they determined human destinies, and gave rise to an elaborate astrological lore which passed from Mesopotamia to Greece and the Eastern Mediterranean in the wake of the conquests of Alexander the Great in the fourth century B.C. In the prevailing world-weariness and lack of stability which produced a sense of uncertainty and frustration, attention became concentrated on fate as an uncontrollable element in human experience. Therefore, if man was incapable of controlling his destinies, he might at least come to know his fate and so the better prepare himself to meet it. In such an atmosphere the wisdom of the Chaldaeans was eagerly sought and absorbed into the philosophical thought of Stoicism and the popular practice of the unsophisticated. The "Babylonian doctrine of the Chaldaeans", as Lucretius described the newly acquired Mesopotamian astrology,[118] was, however, a highly specialized art, the details of which were known only to the Chaldaean experts. In the Hellenistic world Alexandria became the centre of astrological learning and the birthplace of an occult mystical literature and of the hermetic sciences.[119] It was there that the casting of horoscopes and the whole paraphernalia of the astrological system were developed with minute elaboration by the *mathemmatici.*

At first these practices were confined mainly to the upper classes, doubtless largely because of the expense involved in obtaining the predictions by really competent observers. The growing popularity of the cult, nevertheless, gave rise to astrological charlatans who for a consideration gave a ruling on any matter upon which they were approached. Nothing was too trivial to come within their scope, as Juvenal has shown in his satire. The hour of a drive to the first milestone was settled "by the book; if a ribbed corner of an eye itches, the lady looks at her horoscope and asks for ointment; though she lies sick, no time seems right for taking a meal unless it has been appointed by Petosiris (a great name among the Egyptian astrologers)".[120] Therefore, despite the fact that the Stoics espoused the cause of astrology as evidence of the doctrine of Fate,[121] a warning against recourse to *Chaldaei, harioli* (soothsayers), *haruspices,* and the like, was given by the elder Cato to his bailiff, and in 139 B.C.[122] Chaldaeans were included with the Jews when ten days' notice was given to them to leave Rome.[123] But the practice was too firmly established to be eradicated. Thus, after the death of Marcus Aurelius in A.D. 189, the Chaldaeans occupied an important position in the imperial court, and as late as the time of Constantine, Firmicus Maternus, before he became a Christian, had written a vast treatise on "Mathematics, or the power and influence of the stars", which remained the *locus classicus* of astrology until the Renaissance.

CHRISTIANITY AND ASTROLOGY

Although the Church ranged itself on the side of the opponents of divination and the occult arts, the controversy concerning the date of Easter, arising from the discrepancies in the combination of the Babylonian lunar calendar with the Egyptian solar calendar, and the attempt to determine the year in which Christ was born, gave a new prominence to astrological calculations and their presuppositions. Moreover, since it was by the guidance of a star that the magi were held to have been led to Bethlehem, and in a dream Joseph was said to have been warned to seek safety in flight into Egypt,[124] it was difficult to repudiate altogether these types of divination. The successor of Judas, St Matthias, was chosen by divine lot:[125] a practice deeply laid in Judaism where, as we have seen, the counsel of Yahweh had been sought by the priest casting the lot to give *urim* or *thummim*,[126] and by dreams.[127] But if in the Jewish background of Christianity the rudiments of astrological lore were firmly established, and the "gnosis" had a peculiar fascination for the Jews of the Diaspora when they surrendered to syncretistic tendencies,[128] it was not encouraged officially, or by the religiously-minded section of the community. Thus, it was against these deceits that an orthodox Jew in Alexandria about 100 B.C. inveighed in no uncertain terms:

Verily all men by nature were but vain who had no perception of God,
And from the good things that are seen they gained no power to know him that is.
Neither by giving heed to the works did they recognise the artificer;
But either fire, or wind, or swift air,
Or circling stars, or raging water, or luminous heaven,
They thought to be gods that rule the world.[129]

The same opposition to Greek philosophy and Babylonian astrology recurs in the pseudepigraphic, the apocalyptic and the Rabbinic literatures, and in the attitude adopted by the Alexandrian Jewish thinker Philo at the turn of the era. Nevertheless, neither in Judaism nor in Christianity was the practice of divination completely eliminated. The more pagan aspects were discouraged and condemned by the rabbis and by most of the early Christian writers. In the Acts of the · Apostles the Christian Faith is represented as triumphing over sorcery in its various forms,[130] but the constant reference to the magic arts by the Patristic writers show that they survived in the sub-apostolic age largely through the influence of the followers of Simon Magus.[131] In the succeeding centuries divination became sufficiently a menace to require official prohibitions and disciplinary action at the Synod of Laodicea (*c.* 343–381), and subsequently at the Council of Toledo in 633. St Augustine recognized its dangers,[132] as did the *Decretals of Gratian* in the Carolingian Empire.[133]

In Talmudic Judaism much the same situation prevailed. Despite the efforts of the rabbis to prevent dabbling in divinatory and astrological practices the tradition and its techniques continued, though it was not until the ninth century A.D., under Muslim influence, that a Hebrew-Arabic occult science became definitely established, coincident with the Jewish scientific and Kabbalistic movements.[134] In Islam divination was so easily interpreted in terms of the accepted doctrine of predestination that the two hung together quite naturally. Under Greek, Christian and Jewish influences the polytheistic traits to a considerable extent had been shed, and it only remained for augury and astrology to be included in the "foreign" or "philosophic" sciences (*'ulum 'aqliyyah*) with mathematics, music, medicine and alchemy, to enable them to be pursued with impunity. Therefore, in the Middle Ages, when Arabic astral science flourished, Muslim astronomers prepared tables for the mathematical problems raised by astrology, and supplied the necessary astronomical data for the sacred art.

E

THE FUNCTION OF DIVINATION

The persistence and widespread distribution of astrology has been due to the environment in which it has functioned. Like auspice and augury, it has been a means of personal and communal adjustment to precarious and unpredictable situations, occasions and events under hazardous conditions when rational and empirical behaviour is in abeyance. It is then that ways and means are sought to bring under some measure of control the exigencies of fate, of determining human destinies and meeting all the uncertainties of everyday life with a technique based on causal interrelation, the association of ideas, the belief that happenings on earth can be influenced by the heavenly bodies, and a doctrine of fatalism combined with an innate desire to see into the future. Since divination in its various forms derives its strength from the certitude, security and hope it affords in the face of indecision, frustration and apprehension, the seer, professional diviner, healer and astrologer exercise a stabilizing influence in times of crisis, adversity and stress when rational knowledge and empirical observation are inadequate to render judgment possible on all the unknown and perhaps unknowable matters that it is desired to prejudge or ascertain. By virtue of their visionary experience and occult powers in relation to the forces of good and evil, oracular utterances and exorcisms, acute observations, therapeutic skill and technical knowledge of animal anatomy, the constellations, the flight of birds and other divinatory and astrological media, they stand in a class by themselves on the supra-rational plane. But, as we have seen, they are in a more precarious position than a sacerdotal hierarchy since, notwithstanding the care taken to protect themselves against the failure of their predictions and discoveries, they are always liable to a loss of prestige, as in the case of the Delphic oracle and the decline of astrology with the rise of scientific astronomy, physics, anatomy and biology. Therefore, while as an instrument of personal and social integration, stability and assurance, divination and the mantic art have played a significant role in the social structure, in personal adjustment to supranormal phenomena, and in inspirational insight (with the seer standing midway between the mystic and the medium), they have not been integrated in a hierarchic ritual order or political system to the same extent as a stable instititutional priesthood which forms an integral part of the structure of the community. As the instrument and mouthpiece of the divine will the seer or the diviner is primarily the interpreter of esoteric mysteries and knowledge by supernatural means. Therefore, his functions are closely allied to those of the prophetic office—which we have now to consider.

CHAPTER III

The Prophet and the Priest

FOR an examination of the prophetic tradition in its various manifestations in relation to priesthood Israel and Arabia afford a fruitful field of inquiry since in these two Semitic regions the classical type of prophetic religion occurs as a characteristic element in the social and sacred orders. Thus, in the Hebrew oracles of Balaam,[1] for example, a Syrian soothsayer (*kosēm*) is represented as having been bribed by Balak, the king of Moab, to pronounce a curse on the Israelites. After a series of magical operations, which included walking in a particular way and building an altar, he fell into a trance in order to become possessed by divine power with the intention of predicting the downfall of his patron's enemies. Instead, according to the present form of the composite oracles, the spirit of Yahweh reversed the inspired utterance thereby bringing a blessing on those whom he was directed to curse. Against his will he was transformed into a prophet of the god of Israel and in that capacity he foretold the destruction of Moab and Edom and the might and prosperity of Israel in the days of David and Solomon, to which the magnificently phrased poems appear to refer.

THE ORACLES OF BALAAM

In this lengthy and most characteristic monument of the earliest Hebrew prophecy the oracular utterances of a Syrian mantis were made subservient to the god who was believed to have chosen Israel to be the instrument of his purpose, and, therefore, the nation was represented as destined to be victorious over its neighbour and to be established by divine decree:

It is a people that dwells alone
And among the nations it is not reckoned—

Yet who can count the dust of Jacob,
Or number the fourth part of Israel?
If I die let me die the death of the righteous
And my end be the end of the just.[2]

The foreign soothsayer could but speak the words put in his mouth as an inspired utterance of his supernatural control, no matter what rewards might be offered to him by the King of Moab to curse them who were blessed by their god:

Rise up Balak, and hear;
Hearken unto me, thou son of Zippor;
God is not a man, that he should lie;
Neither the son of man, that he should repent;
Hath he said, and shall he not do it?
Or hath he spoken, and shall he not make good?
Behold I have received the word to bless:
And he hath blessed, and I cannot reverse it.
He hath not beheld iniquity in Jacob,
Neither hath he seen perverseness in Israel.
Yahweh their god is with them,
And the shout of a king is among them.
A god who bringeth them forth out of Egypt;
Horned like the horns of a buffalo.
For there is no spell against Jacob,
Neither is there any enchantment against Israel.
Now shall it be told to Jacob and to Israel
How God hath wrought.[3]

Thus, a foreign soothsayer of repute hired by a Moabite king to lay a curse on Israel was assigned the role of an inspired prophet of Yahweh, who used him to declare his revelation concerning the prosperity of his own chosen people and the doom of Moab.

The man whose eye was closed saith:
He saith, which heareth the words of God,
Who seeth the vision of the Almighty,
Falling down and having his eyes open.[4]

THEOPHANIES IN ANCIENT ISRAEL

For our present purpose the oracles of Balaam are significant inasmuch as they show how readily the professional ecstatic diviner may become the inspired prophet when he is transformed into the vehicle of divine revelation in a higher religion. If Hebrew prophecy in its later developments was a unique phenomenon, its antecedents were deeply laid in the ecstatic and divinatory tradition of the Ancient East so that the one easily passed into the other and both had much in common. In the pre-Mosaic period the cultus was to all intents and purposes identical with that of the Semitic peoples generally, and notwithstanding the drastic re-editing of the narratives by later compilers in an attempt to make them conform to the beliefs and customs of the ninth, or perhaps the tenth century B.C. and onwards, it is clear that the ancestors of Israel sought divine direction at local sanctuaries.

Thus, Abraham, who is represented as having been called out of Mesopotamia through a theophany, according to the narrative was the recipient of further disclosures at the oracle-giving terebinth at Shechem (Moreh), where he learnt that Canaan was the land of promise.[5] He is then said to have moved on twenty miles to the south and near Bethel to have built an altar, though no theophany is alleged to have occurred in connexion with it. This may be explained perhaps as an attempt to bring the story into line with the tradition of the foundation of Bethel by Jacob as a result of his accidental incubation there and the disclosure of the divine "owner" of the sacred place in a dream.[6] Under the influence of the later monotheistic religion the indwelling spirit of the megalithic sanctuary was interpreted in terms of a manifestation of Yahweh and the incubation described as accidental, though doubtless behind the legend lies the ancient custom of sleeping at shrines in order to obtain dream-oracles from the *'el* localized in the stones.

Similarly, the other important sanctuaries of early Hebrew tradition—e.g., Beersheba, Hebron, Mamre, Shechem, and later Sinai (Horeb), Gilgal and Jerusalem—are represented as places at which the god of Israel disclosed himself to the ancestors of the nation in special theophanies, either in person or by his angel. Not infrequently these manifestations were thought to have been spontaneous, as in the case of Jacob—"surely Yahweh is in this place, and I knew it not"[7] or in that of Moses in Midian. In the dual narrative of the burning bush,[8] the god of Israel was encountered under the form of fire in the midst of a bush which was not consumed when Moses came to "the mountain of God, unto Horeb", and "turned aside to see the great sight why the bush was not burnt". Then "he that dwelt in the bush" is said to have given his servant his instructions.[9]

In all these theophanic legends the divine disclosures are represented as direct manifestations at some specific sacred place, very often for the purpose of establishing the legitimacy of the sanctuary in the Yahweh religion. To Abraham, however, as the progenitor of the race and to Jacob as the eponymous ancestor of the twelve tribes, special revelations of national significance were vouchsafed, while to Moses, the cult founder, Yahweh was alleged to have spoken "mouth to mouth", "clearly not in riddles."[10] Instead of making known the divine will in visions or dreams, in the wilderness he is said to have descended to the "tent of meeting"[11] in the outward and visible sign of a pillar of cloud,[12] and stood at its door.[13] To Aaron and Miriam he gave his commands, but with Moses alone did he engage in intimate conversation as man to man, as previously in the seclusion of the holy mountain.[14]

These naïve anthropomorphisms are in striking contrast to the enigmatic utterances of the Pythia at Delphi, and the obscure oracular "observations" or "words" proclaimed by the cultic prophets in Israel. In Hebrew tradition Moses occupied a unique position and combined the offices and functions of prophet, priest and ruler[15] endowed with supernatural powers like a divine king.[16] In these several capacities he was enabled to have direct intercourse with Yahweh in a more intimate manner than was possible in the case of the ordinary prophetic instrument of the divine will. Nevertheless, notwithstanding his

privileged status, it was only at special times and places that a
theophany occurred, so that even Moses was virtually a cult
prophet in the sense that he exercised his functions in relation
to a prescribed ritual order. Exactly to what extent the practices in vogue in Palestine in the days of the monarchy, and the
temple cultus at Jerusalem, were transferred to the wilderness
and the tent of meeting by the later writers and compilers of the
Old Testament to give a divine and Mosaic sanction to the
established order, is not easy to determine. But there can be
little doubt that the general pattern of the prophetic tradition in
the Mosaic and pre-Mosaic periods was essentially the same in
form and content as that which prevailed in Canaan and
Mesopotamia, whatever particular interpretations may have been
given to the cultus as the Yahwistic faith took shape in Israel.

THE LOCAL SANCTUARIES

Thus, at any rate until the time of the Josiah reformation
about 621 B.C., the numerous Canaanite sanctuaries (*bāmôth*)
continued to flourish equipped with a sacred tree, a spring,
adytum, alignment, *maṣṣebah* or *gilgal,* as among all other
Semitic peoples, Aramaeans, Canaanites, Akkadians or
Phoenicians. It is true that in the Deuteronomic narrative an
injunction was inserted, purporting to have been laid upon
Israel at the time of the conquest of Palestine, ordering the
utter destruction of "all the places wherein the nations which
ye dispossessed served their gods, upon the high mountains, and
upon the hills, and under every green tree; and ye shall over-
throw their altars and break their pillars, and burn their
groves with fire; and ye shall hew down the graven images of
their gods, and destroy the names of them out of that place".[17]
This, of course, provided an excellent reason for the campaign
against the local shrines (*bāmôth*), if "the Book of the Law"
discovered during the restoration of the Temple in 621 was
in fact a portion of Deuteronomy.[18] But whatever attempts
may have been made either at the initial settlement in the
"Promised Land" or on subsequent occasions to eliminate the
Cananite cultus and disband its priesthood, the efforts proved

to be abortive until the centralization of all worship at the Temple in Jerusalem was of necessity imposed on the Jews who remained behind in Palestine at the time of the Exile. The Josiah reform was only a temporary expedient since although the Deuteronomic laws were established officially, in practice they lapsed during the reigns of the four last kings of Judah when all the old abuses returned,[19] together with those introduced from Babylonia,[20] and formed a composite non-Yahwistic cultus.

Among the less unedifying survivals that persisted in Israel throughout the period of the monarchy were the oracular divinations associated with the local sanctuaries. Thus, for example, the oak of Meonenim, "the soothsayer's terebinth[21] at Shechem in the days of Abimelech, doubtless was the same "oak which giveth oracles" (Moreh), well-known both in the pre-Yahwistic period[22] and in later times,[23] from which probably the diviners drew their omens by the rustling of the leaves.[24] It was to guard the shrine and carry on its traditions that a priesthood was established at these sacred places, the principal function of which was to consult the god rather than to engage in sacrificial worship. To this end it had to be in possession of the technical knowledge required to give oracular direction, which included augury, incubation, the drawing of lots and inspection. But although the service of the altar was subsidiary, sacrificial divination was an important element in the oracular tradition. Therefore, the cultic officials were at once prophets, priests and seers, endowed with divine insight and knowledge and oracular power as the instrument and representative of a particular god at the specific sanctuary to which they were attached.

THE LEVITICAL PRIESTHOOD

That this institution of cultic prophecy, common to all Semitic peoples, was practised in Israel little changed after the settlement in Palestine is clear from the available evidence. Thus, the Hebrew designations for those who exercised these functions were *kôhen, lēwi, nabi* and *roeh,* corresponding more or less to the renderings of priest, Levite, prophet and seer. The word *kôhen,* however, is the equivalent of the parallel Arabic root *kahin,* or diviner, and while in Hebrew (בֹּהֵן) it has the meaning of "priest" in a more specialized sense, nevertheless, it denoted essentially the office concerned mainly with obtaining oracles by the aid of the ephod for *urim* and *thummim,* and by inspiration.[25]

Under the influence of the cultus centralized in the Temple at Jerusalem, which cannot be earlier than the seventh century B.C., it became increasingly specialized and concentrated upon sacrificial worship, and after the Exile it was restricted by the Priestly School to the Levitical house of Aaron, probably of North-Israelite origin.[26] But these Levitical monopolies are later developments, and before the seventh century priests were drawn from many other lines of descent—those of David,[27] Nathan,[28] Micah[29] and Abinadab[30]—while neither Joshua nor Samuel was of the tribe of Levi,[31] although they exercised priestly functions. Whether in fact the Levites were ever members of a sacerdotal tribe[32] is open to question,[33] but in any case they represented a special fraternity set apart to give direction by the aid of the sacred lot.[34] Like Moses, Aaron and Samuel they were seers or prophets as well as priests, and they owed their prestige to their claim to have been the fellow-tribesmen of Moses, vindicated in their office by the intervention of Yahweh.[35] Moreover, if they were in possession of the sacred places of Kadesh, by maintaining a continuous supply of priests, they would secure a monopoly of the service of the sanctuary which in due course would be likely to harden into an established tradition.[36]

That their claims, however, were not unchallenged is suggested by the stories of the alleged rivalries in the desert between Moses and his allies and the non-Aaronic Levites, together with the prophets to whom Yahweh spoke only by dreams and visions. Thus, Dathan and Abiram, and even Miriam and Aaron, are depicted as questioning the authority and privileges of their leader to their undoing. In these narratives there would seem to be an indication of deeply laid jealousies and contentions among members of rival priestly confraternities and their respective sanctuaries in Palestine, reminiscences of which survived in the ninth century and onwards when the primacy of the Levites was becoming established.[37]

It was not, however, until after the Exile, when the Priestly Code was drawn up, that the distinction between priests and Levites became absolute,[38] and the priesthood was made exclusively Aaronic, despite the tradition that "a covenant of an everlasting priesthood" had been established with Phinehas, the son of Eleazar, from whom the Zadokites claimed descent.[39] This confusion probably arose from the existence of independent confraternities before the Exile associated with particular sanctuaries, some of whom enjoyed considerable prestige. Thus, those of Dan, and perhaps also of Shiloh, traced their descent from Moses,[40] while after the capture of Jerusalem by David, when it became the centre of the Yahweh cult, two outstanding figures, Zadok and Nathan, occupied a unique position in the hierarchy. It may be, as Mowinckel has suggested, that they were members of the ancient Jebusite royal priesthood.[41] In any case, the centralization of worship at Jerusalem and the degradation of those who had ministered at the local shrines as a result of the Josiah reformation, gave the sons of Zadok precedence in the temple ritual until they were carried away captives when the city fell to the Chaldaeans. If, as Kennett suggests, the Aaronites were already in possession at Bethel, and occupied Jerusalem after the removal of the Zadokites, granted that they remained there during the Exile, they would be in a strong position when the post-exilic Jewish community was re-established in Judah under Zerubbabel. By a genealogical fiction, it is urged, Joshua, the Bethelite (Aaronite) colleague of Zerubbabel, was made the son or grandson of Seraiah, the last of the Zadokites before the Exile.[42]

This ingenious interpretation of the situation, however, though plausible, involves placing Deuteronomy towards the end of the Exile instead of in its customary place a generation earlier. Nevertheless, the date of Deuteronomy is by no means finally established, and there seems to be some ground for thinking that the Aaronites were associated with Bethel and its bull cult.[43] Moreover, the story of the golden calf, which is doubtless later than the reform of Jeroboam, very probably reflects the cultus practised in the Northern Kingdom of Israel. Thus, the institution of the bull cult and of a non-Levitical priesthood at Bethel and Dan in fact were not the innovations in Yahwism that they were represented to have been by the later writers in Judah who viewed the situation in the light of the reform of Josiah in 621. The worship of Yahweh in association with image-symbolism was no more novel prior to the seventh century than the admission to the priesthood of men who were not Levites.[44] It is possible that at the accession of David the ark had been established at Bethel and Dan in place of the bull image,[45] and, therefore, that Jeroboam subsequently did restore there the earlier cultus and its hierarchy.

In any case, whatever may have been the relations between the northern and the southern cult centres in the early days of the monarchy, the rigid distinction between the descendants of Aaron, who alone were authorized to offer sacrifice, and the rest of the Levites, who were relegated to menial service of the sanctuary, was unknown before the Priestly Code was promulgated towards the end of the fifth century B.C. In the previous century the differentiation was between Levites who had "gone astray after their idols" at the local shrines, and the sons of Zadok who "had kept the charge" of the centralized sanctuary at Jerusalem. In the Temple that was to be established the localized "defaulters" were assigned oversight of the gates of the house of Yahweh and other lowly ministrations, such as slaying the sacrificial victims, while only the faithful Zadokites were permitted to make the actual sacrificial oblation of the life-giving blood at the altar, duly arrayed in their sacerdotal vestments.[46]

This constituted a compromise between the pre-exilic Deuteronomic code which conferred upon the tribe of Levi without qualification the custody of the sacrificial ritual, and the post-exilic Priestly legislation which limited it to the

Aaronic succession—a position which was adopted subsequently by the Chronicler. Thus, he described as Levites the foreign mercenaries collected by Jehoiada for the upkeep of the Temple of the earlier narrative[47] on the grounds that only such could have been admitted to these sacred duties.[48] Similarly, he interpreted the death of Uzzah by a breach of a tabu as the result of the absence of Levites to take charge of the ark.[49] In the pre-Deuteronomic literature, on the other hand, Levitical restrictions of this nature are entirely absent, just as the multiplicity of sanctuaries is taken for granted.[50]

Originally the Levites, without having a monopoly of the service of the altar, appear to have been engaged in sacerdotal and oracular functions,[51] the two being reciprocal aspects of one and the same office since divination was invariably accompanied by sacrificial rites. In this dual capacity, however, the principal duty was the giving of oracular direction, though divination by Urim and Thummim and the communication of the Torah and "the Sentence of Judgment", was not restricted to them. The Kôhen and the Levite were also equated with the prophet or seer (*roeh*), as in the case of Samuel,[52] who was endowed with special occult powers of foreseeing the future and of exercising ecstatic gifts. It is true that Samuel is never described as a priest (*kôhen*) but he is represented as having been consecrated by the service of the sanctuary at Shiloh, where the ark was kept, by a solemn sacrificial act of dedication, and to have been girded with a sacerdotal ephod, which was a symbol of priesthood.[53] Moreover, in the present narrative, he is represented as having been intimately associated throughout his career with the sacrificial aspects of the cultus,[54] though some of the incidents attributed to Samuel may in fact have been told of Saul originally and subsequently transferred to Samuel by an anti-monarchical school. Apart from the word-play in the story of the birth of Samuel[55] being more relevant to the name of Saul, since "because I have asked him of the Lord" is nearer to *shā'ül* (Saul) than to *shmü'el* (Samuel), the divine wrath which the king is alleged to have incurred for making the customary burnt offering at Gilgal to

consecrate the battle against the Philistines,[56] is inconsistent
with his having built an altar to Yahweh at the beginning of his
reign, at which apparently he offered the blood of the victims
brought to him by the people, without any indication of
sacrilege.[57]

THE PRIEST AND THE PROPHET

That it was the accepted practice for the king to exercise
priestly functions as soon as the monarchy was established in
Israel is shown, for example, by David taking over the cult
organization at Jerusalem as its leader and not hesitating himself to wear an ephod when he danced ecstatically before the
ark on its introduction into the sanctuary on Zion.[58] Similarly,
Solomon three times a year is said to have offered burnt
offerings and peace offerings on the altar which he had built
to Yahweh, and to have burnt incense upon it.[59] At a later
period as Jeroboam sacrificed at the altar that he had erected at
Bethel,[60] so Ahaz offered burnt offerings, meat offerings and
drink offerings upon an altar designed on an Assyrian pattern
he had seen at Damascus, and sprinkled the blood of the peace
offering upon it.[61]

Therefore, for reasons which will be considered later,[62] in
Israel as elsewhere in the Ancient East, the relation between the
kingship and the priesthood was so close that it carried with it
reciprocal functions. Nevertheless, the Hebrew monarchy was
never identical in its form and significance with that of Egypt
and Mesopotamia. The king was a sacred person, and in the
case of David the cult leader had among his retinue the traditional founder of the Zadokite hierarchy, and, in the person of
Nathan, an outstanding ecstatic prophet. But as the prophetic
movement developed, the two aspects of the theocracy became antagonistic until at length, in the period immediately preceding the Exile, (i.e. the eighth century B.C.) the monarchy
was regarded with the gravest suspicion by some of the Hebrew
prophets.[63] Thus, in one strand of the complex pattern in which
the rise of the monarchy is set in the book of Samuel, the new
departure from the earlier theocracy is represented as an affront

to Yahweh, who revealed to his servant Samuel the seer the consequences of the national apostasy.[64]

This Elohistic prophetic school regarded the kingship as one of the chief sources of the syncretistic perversions of mono-Yahwism, so that Hosea proclaimed in the eighth century that Israel had sinned since the days when Saul was anointed at Gibeah,[65] and became a rival to rather than the instrument of Yahweh. This is in striking contrast to the description of Othniel in the period of the Judges who was said to have been a mighty deliverer on whom the spirit of the Lord had descended in power.[66] Yet notwithstanding the re-editing of the narratives and their interpolations, traces remain of the original nature of the kings of Israel as the anointed viceroys of the divine ruler of the theocracy. Thus Saul is not only said to have been duly consecrated by Yahweh to be a prince over his people,[67] but at a sacred oracular oak he was met by three prophets going up to the sanctuary at Bethel who made a token-offering (*backsheesh*) of two loaves to him. On his arrival at Gibeah he was met by a company of ecstatics (*Nebi'im*) in a state of frenzy coming down from a local sanctuary to the accompaniment of an array of mystic instruments. Immediately the spirit (*ruach*) of Yahweh came mightily upon Saul and he was "turned into another man",[68] just as after the anointing of David the divine afflatus left him and descended upon his successor.[69]

THE PROPHETIC MOVEMENT

It was this aspect of shamanistic behaviour, characteristic of Semitic prophecy in general, that constituted the principal role of the professional ecstatics described in Israel as *Nebi'im*, or "sons of the prophets". Like the Kohnim and Levites they were associated with particular sacred places and exercised their functions as cult officials. Therefore, they were found as confraternities at centres such as Bethel, Gibeah, Gilgal, Rama, Jericho and Carmel,[70] in the service of the god who disclosed his will and purposes to them in a state of possession. That they were pre-Israelite in origin can hardly be questioned in view of the widespread range of this type of psychic phenomena. Thus, it was identical in its essential characteristics with that exhibited by the Mesopotamian *makku,* or visionary, believed to have been animated by a divine oracular "breath".[71] Indeed, as we have seen, shamanistic possession artificially stimulated to produce abnormal occult experiences has been a common feature in the civilizations of the Ancient East and the Graeco-oriental oracular cultus, as well as among peoples in a primitive state of culture, notably in the Siberian-Altaic region. What is less easy to determine is the extent to which, if at all, Hebrew practice differed from that of other nations where the phenomena occurred.

Professor Meek suggests that while priests and prophets (*Nebi'im*) had a common origin, as the priesthood became more professional and hereditary ecstatic experience was dependent upon a special predisposition and temperament it was confined to a restricted circle of individuals capable of this direct approach to deity.[72] Thus, he thinks the prophetic movement in Israel arose out of critical situations like the Philistine menace which caused recourse to be had to mechanical devices to induce ecstasy and so caused prophecy to become more and more professionalized and aggressive.[73]

Against this hypothesis is the fact that *Neb'ism* was widely practised in Asia Minor and Palestine before the Hebrew settlement in Canaan and it continued in a somewhat modified form throughout the period of the monarchy. Even the great prophets of the eighth century, as will be seen, did not entirely discard abnormal behaviour in their oracular utterances, and Jepsen thinks that it was in the *Nebi'istic* section of the community that the rationalistic theodicy and philosophy of history developed.[74] But he too draws a sharp distinction between the professional prophets (*Nebi'im*), whom he regards as pre-Israelite in origin, and the outstanding prophetic figures in the Old Testament record. When *Nebi'ism* was incorporated in Israel, he contends, it lost its ecstatic-mystical character and was transformed into the god-possessed man who disclosed the word of Yahweh and became a court official like Nathan and

Gad, and in the cases of Samuel and Elijah assumed the role of king-maker. Therefore, he agrees with Meek in giving prominence to the *Nebi'im* at times of crisis when the nation was ready for a divine pronouncement and intervention. But in order to exclude the canonical prophets from this development, apart from the textual emendations he is compelled to introduce, to justify this theory he has to resort to the unwarranted assumption that they were not inspired men in the god-possessed sense. The word of Yahweh came to them and they merely passed it on to their hearers, as against the *Nebi'im* who were animated by a lying spirit. This is a cleavage, as will appear later, that certainly cannot be maintained in the history of Hebrew prophecy. Nevertheless, within the movement two traditions did emerge and eventually achieved different results, notwithstanding the fact that throughout the common element was so substantial that it is often impossible to distinguish the one from the other.

So far as the *Nebi'im* are concerned, in Israel as elsewhere they functioned essentially in connexion with the cultus as the oracular mouthpiece of Yahweh. It is difficult to conclude from the available evidence that in the exercise of their office they differed to any appreciable extent in their methods from those adopted among the surrounding peoples. In the stories of Samuel and Saul at Gibeah, and of David and Saul at Rama, the ecstatic phenomena appear to be identical with non-Israelite manifestations of this kind elsewhere, and in the account of Elijah's contest on Mount Carmel the Phoenician *Nebi'im* of Baal were arrayed against the champion of Yahweh in a struggle to demonstrate the supremacy of one of the two gods whose rival claims for allegiance were at issue.[75]

If this dramatic episode is popular tradition rather than sober history, nevertheless, it illustrates the perennial prophetic struggle between two opposed groups—the *Nebi'im* of Baal and those of Yahweh—even though the Phoenician queen is said to have reduced the Yahwists to a single heroic figure.[76] This statement, however, is clearly an exaggeration since soon after the contest about four hundred of them apparently were still

F

functioning, and were summoned by Ahab to consult the oracle before the fatal battle at Ramoth-Gilead.[77] Acting as the mouthpiece of Yahweh on behalf of the king as was their custom whenever a war broke out, they engaged in a typical collective ecstasy which included the wearing of a horn mask by the leader, Zedekiah. Probably this was a cult object employed to give effect to the pronouncement;[78] namely, that the Syrians would be pushed until they were consumed. Therefore, the victory was proclaimed with one voice: "Go up to Ramoth-Gilead and prosper, for Yahweh will deliver it into the hand of the king." To make it complete Micaiah, the son of Imlah, was exhorted to confirm the favourable verdict, very much as Ahab had received a similar oracular assurance in a former conflict with the Syrians.[79] For the same purpose Joash later visited Elisha, and was told to open the window eastward and shoot "an arrow of victory over Syria".[80] But because subsequently the king smote upon the ground with the arrows only thrice instead of five or six times, he incurred the wrath of the prophet and reduced the force of the spell from a complete to a threefold victory.

In all these incidents shamanistic and magical methods are represented as having been adopted by the Hebrew *Nebi'im* which can hardly be differentiated in their fundamental forms and intentions from those in vogue among peoples in a relatively primitive state of culture. Transcendental power is projected by sacred utterances and symbolic actions because a ritual that involves a more or less realistic reproduction of an urgently desired effect is believed to establish the *ex post facto* idea of "sympathetic" causation. Moreover, it becomes a vent of pent up emotion and activity so that when an ecstatic condition is produced by a sacred dance and frantic music the underlying emotions and longings are uttered and represented symbolically in order to express in actions the underlying realities which often cannot adequately be described in words. The primitive is a man of action and, therefore, he dances out his religion and manipulates his magic by the aid of a prescribed technique. Thus, he expresses his inmost wishes and desires—the desire to act discharging itself on the symbol and in the spoken word. It is in this setting that the cultus of the Hebrew *Nebi'im* has to be placed to be correctly understood and evaluated.

THE WORD OF YAHWEH

Filled with the divine afflatus (*ruach*) these cult prophets were moved to speak words which were interpreted as divine oracles, and to give expression to the intention in appropriate ritual actions. This not infrequently approached divine intoxication bordering on a frenzied madness.[81] Their eccentric and wild behaviour made them objects of ridicule and scorn,[82] though this did not prevent credence being given to their predictions as the "Word of Yahweh". On the assumption that the god "siezes" or "enters into" his instrument, the word that is spoken becomes a divine utterance, an ecstatic oracle. Thus, under the influence of an overmastering emotion the Hebrew prophets proclaimed as they were moved by the transcendent power which invaded them, who was for them none other than the God of Israel. Consequently they frequently prefaced their oracles with the refrain, "Thus saith Yahweh," or concluded them with the words, "Oracle of Yahweh," and spoke in the first person.[83] The divine Word therefore, had objective reality,[84] and like the rite was efficacious in bringing to pass that which was proclaimed or affirmed. Indeed, the true prophet was the "Messenger of Yahweh,"[85] conscious of having been sent by him, and, like the supernatural being called the "Angel of Yahweh", almost indistinguishable from Yahweh himself.[86]

The sacred man, as we have seen, has been regarded essentially as a divine man by virtue of his office and functions, and, therefore, as A. R. Johnson has shown, the Hebrew prophet was for the time being an extension of Yahweh's Personality; i.e., he was Yahweh in Person.[87] By sharing in the divine nature (*ruach*) he partook of the Spirit of God and so he was brought within the "corporate personality" of the god of Israel as a living part of his divine being. This was a natural conclusion from the Hebrew conception of man as an aggregate of elements of the conscious life, physical and psychical, animated by a breath-soul, or *nephesh,* and standing in a peculiar relationship to his god and to the theocratic nation as a result of his creation in the divine image and likeness,[88] and of his membership of the holy covenant.[89] The initial creation of Adam was thought to be repeated and renewed in each subsequent birth,[90] though it is by no means certain whether originally the inbreathing of the breath of life was actually equated with the divine energy called *ruach* with which it was identified after the Exile. In any case the *ruach* cannot be confined to the breath-soul of man (*nephesh*) given by God at birth and regarded as the centre of consciousness of life diffused through the entire psycho-physical organism, and returning whence it came at death.[91] It had a wider significance denoting the spirit of Yahweh in its various and manifold operations in the natural order,[92] and filling his prophets with ecstatic power and vision.[93]

As the god of Israel was always conceived as a Person, the personality of the Israelite was directly related to his fellowship with the ultimate Source of his life. In the case of the prophet, however, this relationship was so intimate that it became a very projection of the divine Personality, rendering him when engaged in the service of Yahweh virtually a divine being like the *malach,* or divine "messenger". In this capacity he perceived some aspects of the being and nature of God and had a transcendental insight into His will and purpose for men and the world; be it a message of hope or of judgment, whether the people would hear or whether they would forbear.

Thus, the prophetic career of Samuel is represented as beginning with an incubational revelation when as a child he was sleeping in the sanctuary at Shiloh and heard an oracular voice calling him.[94] The sequel was a message concerning the destruction of the house of Eli. The setting of this incident certainly is pre-exilic, and it would seem to refer to a transitional stage in the development of the conception of the *malach* as virtually Yahweh and that which regarded him as a "man of

God" endowed with the spirit of Yahweh. It is not a dream that is described in the narrative since the youthful Samuel is made to experience an audition, though the Word of Yahweh had not been revealed to him. Eli, however, perceived the nature of the oracular event, and so gave appropriate instructions to the potential prophet who thereupon responded to the call. It was a call, however, and not an ecstatic possession that is recorded in this passage.

THE CANONICAL PROPHETS AND THEIR MESSAGE

In the case of the canonical prophets the transition to the human figure seems to have been almost complete since, with only two exceptions,[95] the messenger has ceased to be a supernatural *malach* and become a man in a particular relation with God. Thus, the prophet Haggai is given this title,[96] and in the last of the prophetic books of the Old Testament (the work of a fifth century prophet) the priest (*kohen*) is described as "the messenger of the Lord of hosts" (Yahweh Sabaoth).[97] The herald of the Messianic reign is also "the messenger of the covenant",[98] and assigned a role comparable to that of his counterpart in the enthronization of the king-god at the Annual Festival in the royal ritual.[99] But although it was still believed that Yahweh spoke directly through these functionaries, whose task it was to deliver a special "message", precisely how they were to be distinguished form "false prophets" when all alike spoke in oracles attributed to Yahweh was no easy matter. Jeremiah, for instance, condemned his contemporaries in the prophetic art in no uncertain terms[100] because they relied on "the visions of their own heart" and on "the dreams they had dreamed", rather than on the revelation of Yahweh spoken directly to them without any traditional oracular medium.

In this contention, however, he differed from the prevailing prophetic practice since, as we have seen, dreams and ecstatic visions were a recognized feature in pre-exilic prophecy in Israel. Where the canonical prophets were all agreed was in the matter of syncretism, since they presented a united front, from Amos to Ezekiel, in their opposition to the Canaanite cultus that had survived little changed at the local sanctuaries. For them Yahweh as a genuinely monotheistic Deity, the Creator and Sustainer of all things, transcended the universe and its processes. Moreover, he disclosed his essential nature in righteousness rather than in non-moral sacredness or in cosmic rhythm, though the control of the seasons and of fertility and the weather fell within his domain.[101] They saw behind all the phenomena of nature one omnipotent will, that of the righteous ruler of creation and doer of justice, whose law is holy and whose power is infinite. That such a Deity should intervene in the natural order and work out his purposes in human history was not extraordinary for them since he sends the winds, the ice and the snow, speaks in the thunder, appears in the form of fire in the midst of the burning bush, manifests himself in the earthquake and smites his enemies.[102]

Unlike the gods of the surrounding nations, he was not sporadically beneficent when in a favourable mood, or dependent upon the vicissitudes of competing priesthoods. His tender mercies were over all his works[103] but because he was the God of righteousness, the Holy One of Israel, he demanded of every member of the "holy nation" conformity to his standards of ethical conduct. His redemptive activity had been demonstrated in such historical events as the Exodus and the conquest of Palestine, but in the prophetic consciousness it became increasingly apparent that each individual had a personal responsibility in the maintenance of the prescribed theocratic religious and social order.[104] Right and wrong were defined not by reason, reflection, ethics, custom or common consent, but by the revealed will of God made known through the cultus, the sacred oracle and the voice of prophesy. Having the character of divine disclosures and precepts, the Word of Yahweh and the Torah constituted an absolute standard of conduct, binding on the consciousness of Israel as a theocracy and on the individual in his personal capacity in the covenant.[105]

Since the great prophets themselves received their message through their own individual experience of a direct encounter with Yahweh, they threw the social problem back upon the character of the individual. They became conscious of individual worth to God, and so of individual personality. In laying greater stress on the inward orientation of life and the ethical and spiritual standards of conduct in justice and mercy required of every Israelite,[106] while they proclaimed a social ethic the corporate personality of the nation could fulfil its vocation only by every single member in his personal capacity realizing his responsibilities and the demands made upon him by the divine righteousness of Yahweh in obedience and love.[107] This becomes more apparent in Jeremiah's conception of the new covenant which was based on the immediate relation of the individual to God.[108]

The authenticity of this oracle has been questioned,[109] but the position adopted in it is a natural development of the prophet's earlier teaching in connexion with the Josiah reformation inspired by the Code of Deuteronomy. The relation between Yahweh and Israel was conceived in personal terms as resting on divine graciousness (*ḥesed*) and human fidelity under the image of the nuptial bond.[110] While the public and social corruption destroyed the intimate fellowship, Jeremiah never lost hope of the ultimate restoration of Israel, and as his own personal relations with the Deity grew closer he thought less of the nation and more of the individual as the object of the divine care and purpose. True religion consisted in a right inward disposition of the human heart and its instinctive response to the self-disclosure of Yahweh, and this was of the very essence of the covenant. When it failed to be realized in the nation as a corporate personality it became individualized and internalized—"I will put my law in their inward parts and in their heart will I write it".[111] So in this new personal relationship He will be a God to them and they will be to him a people.[112] Therefore, while it was still a covenant with the house of Israel it was accomplished through a new fellowship with Yahweh on the part of each individual Israelite.

In place of a forensic external bond as a legal obligation between two contracting parties expressed in the ark and the temple, the law and the cultus, a deeper and more personal union was needed in view of the apostasy of the people in their corporate capacity. "The virgin of Israel" had done a very horrible thing in forsaking its God and worshipping vanity,[113] and the only hope for the future lay in a readjustment of relations to restore the position. This required a change of heart on the part of the defaulters; not merely collectively as a nation but by the conversion and re-orientation of the individual will and conscience. The old Torah and cultus were not abrogated, as they were later in the Christian Dispensation, but a new covenant (*běrîth*) in the sense of a fellowship of purpose between God and man ratified by an outward sign (in this case a change of heart), was to be established within the existing framework of Israel, giving fresh emphasis to individual moral responsibility and personal conduct in accordance with the righteousness of Yahweh.

This was endorsed by Ezekiel among the exiles in Babylon who proclaimed the ethical freedom and responsibility of each man before God, declaring that every one should die for his own iniquity,[114] in contradistinction to the earlier corporate vengeance meted out to the family of Achan for the breach of a tabu.[115] National misfortunes were no longer to be attributed to and punished by the sins and errors of the past, or by those of the body politic. Each man was now regarded as personally responsible for his deeds and treated according to his conduct as a free human being. Thus, God was represented as dealing with men impartially as individuals with absolute justice, rewarding the righteous and punishing the wicked. A new value was accorded to the individual at this stage in the prophetic consciousness based on a personal relation with God. In place of the former social solidarity the concept of personal responsibility in conduct, social and religious, became paramount,[116] so that when the community was re-established in and around Jerusalem the prophetic tradition was given expression in a sacerdotal theocrasy in which the individual was assigned an independent status in society.

However, notwithstanding the fact that the great prophets gave a new significance and interpretation to the Word of

Yahweh, they exercised their functions along the same lines as their predecessors, and their oracular methods were indistinguishable from the earlier cultus. Amos, it is true, appears to have repudiated the insinuation of Amaziah that he was a professional prophet by birth, professing rather to have been a "shepherd" and dresser of sycamore trees. But he claimed to have been taken by Yahweh and sent to prophesy unto Israel,[117] and it is not improbable that the term *nkd* suggests that in fact he was a cultic functionary.[118] Similarly, Isaiah was connected with the sanctuary,[119] as were Jeremiah and Ezekiel.[120] Their abnormal behaviour was shown by such actions as Isaiah going about Jerusalem naked and barefooted,[121] or by Jeremiah wearing a yoke round his neck,[122] while Ezekiel was essentially a visionary. Moreover, for him the cultus was the centre of the national life of Israel.

THE CANONICAL PROPHETS AND THE CULTUS

The attitude of the canonical prophets to the sacrifical worship has long been a matter of discussion. That they unreservedly repudiated the priesthood and the cultus seems most unlikely. It is true Amos appears to have looked back with approval to the golden age of the nomadic culture, and asked in the name of Yahweh, "Have ye offered unto me sacrifices and offerings in the wilderness forty years, O house of Israel?"[123] Similarly, Hosea proclaimed, "I have found Israel like grapes in the wilderness: I saw your fathers as the firstripe in the fig tree at her season: but they came to Baal-peor, and consecrated themselves unto that shame: and became abominable like that which they loved.[124] But if to go to Bethel was to transgress and to visit Gilgal was to multiply transgression,[125] this was because the syncretistic associations of these traditional sanctuaries obscured the ethical demands of Yahweh.

It does not follow, however, that the only service which God required was thought to be ethical, even though Jeremiah may have been driven to an extreme position in which he seemed to condemn the sacrifical system *in toto* in the course of the political controversy in which he became involved.[126] Reformers are always inclined to be reactionary and iconoclastic in their endeavours to sweep away abuses, but the great prophets in their anti-cultic denunciations were primarily concerned with the political implications of national degeneracy, warning the people persistently of the inevitable consequences of their actions, first in the Northern Kingdom and later in the destruction of Jerusalem and the Temple. Notwithstanding their warnings, however, when the crash came it was the optimistic oracles of those who proclaimed "Peace! Peace! where there was no peace" that so discredited prophecy in the eyes of the exiles that the movement virtually came to an end in Babylon.

Thus, when the community was restored it was the Priestly school that became predominant with the temple and its cultus as its consolidating centre, without seemingly any suggestion that this was contrary to the pre-exilic tradition. As Dr Welch says, "unless some vital connection can be made between prophetism and post-exilic Judaism, the consequence must be to make the prophetic testimony a mere interlude in the religious history of the nation."[127] If, on the other hand, the two movements are expressions of one and the same fundamental faith and practice which from time immemorial had exercised their respective functions as integral elements in the religion of Israel, the tension between priest and prophet in the period immediately preceding the Exile would seem to be in the nature of a protest against the failure of the cultus to fulfil its proper purposes.[128] Therefore, the prophets felt compelled to launch a vigorous campaign against current abuses and to recover what they believed to be the lost heritage of the nation in its relation to its god and his righteous demands. They saw the truth in the same measure as they were convinced they had received it from Yahweh. They were not just filled with his spirit in an ecstatic state like the *Nebi'im*. They knew the will and mind of the god in whose service they were enlisted and that any prophecy that was not strictly in accord with his demands was not in fact derived from him.[129] The Day of Yahweh was brought into relation with the ancient cosmogonic theme,[130] but although they not infrequently interpreted their message in the light of current myth and ritual,[131] for them faithfulness to Yahweh was the centre and core of all true prophecy.

During and after the Exile prophetism lost its spontaneity notwithstanding the activities of the Deutero-Isaiah and Ezekiel. Moreover, it had fufilled its function and although its influence was still strongly felt, in the reorganization of the social and religious structure of the post-exilic community it was the cultus that became the unifying dynamic. The Aaronic priesthood was re-established and the cultic functionaries were merged with the other Levitical orders to form the personnel of the choirs under its direction, and they may have constituted a connecting link with the former oracular tradition transmitted from one generation to another as inspired speech, often in poetic form accompanied by music.[132] In Haggai and Zechariah morality and ritualism were combined in an effort to bring back the nation to its God and fan the flames of Messianic hopes in their efforts to re-establish the Temple, until at length prophecy passed into apocalyptic as the earliest visions were detached from their origin and given a new and cryptic significance projected into an eschatological future. The Law canonized as the verbally inspired word of God to Moses had made prophecy of secondary importance just as the keeping of the Sabbath and the observance of the rest of the prescribed ritual order centred in the worship of the Temple produced a reaction against visionary experience and oracular divinatory exercises. The cultic prophets, as we have seen, became temple singers and merged with the other Levitical orders, and so were brought under the dominion of the Aaronite priesthood with its sacerdotal privileges.

PROPHECY IN ARABIA AND ISLAM

In the neighbouring Semitic culture of the desert prophecy tended to develop in the direction of mysticism because the Bedouins of Arabia had neither priesthood nor sacrificial worship, myth nor ritual. They were not concerned with the problems underlying the seasonal rhythm and the order of nature. In the agricultural civilizations of Egypt, Mesopotamia and Palestine, the Aegean and the Indus valley, it was possible to calculate and in a measure to control the environment on which the human communities depended for their subsistence. Therefore, they devised and elaborated mystery techniques to bring the divine order into relation with the natural order through sacerdotal intervention. Among the pastoral nomads of the Arabian peninsula, on the other hand, the desert dwellers, as distinct from those who made their habitation in oases and the semi-cultivatable lands, were continually at war with their surroundings and at the mercy of forces completely beyond either calculation or control, Therefore, they were driven to pit themselves against chance and, in the gamble, to seek such guidance and warning as might be ascertainable through divination and prophetic foresight.

In the background was the shadowy figure of the remote High God, or Supreme Being, who was rescued from oblivion by the mono-Yahwists in Israel and by Muhammad in Arabia. Thus, in both Judaism and Islam the prophetic movements gravitated towards the revelation of the desert while the settled agriculturists concentrated on the myth and ritual of the vegetation cultus. In Palestine nomadic conditions were at most ancestral and "idealistic", as among the Rechabites. Therefore, the cultus was fundamental, and however much the later canonical prophets may have reacted against it, the reaction was only a temporary expedient leading to the restoration of the Temple and its worship in a more spiritualized and moralized form. In Arabia the reverse obtained. There the desert nomadic régime was basic, notwithstanding the widespread centres of settled agricultural life with their holy places to which purely nomadic worshippers resorted, since it was from the desert that the true prophetic inspiration came, and where it was nurtured.

THE KAHIN AND THE SADIN

Unfortunately very little is known of the early history and conditions of the Arabian peninsula, but in the pre-Islamic era it would appear that in the localized centres the *kahin* occupied very much the same position as that of the Canaanite *kohen* as the cult official,[133] while the guardians were the *sadana*. This term originally meant "one who holds the curtain"; in other words, he through whom admission to the shrine was gained. The office very likely may have been hereditary and confined to a particular tribe or family as in some of the inscriptions members of what seem to be families are mentioned by name as serving this or that god.[134] Nöldeke thinks that the word *kahin* was borrowed from the Aramaic and applied to those in Arabia who were priests in the full sense of ministrants at a sanctuary.[135] On the other hand, Buchanan Gray regards it as a Hebrew loan word in Aramaic.[136] If in fact it was a common sacerdotal Semitic term[137] in general use everywhere except in the Eastern section of the region, where it does not occur, doubtless it was the designation of those definitely attached to the cult as against the guardians (*sadana*) and the door-keepers (*hajib*), though the *kohin* might also be a *sadin*.[138]

Both offices included sacrificial functions as well as those connected with the care of the shrine, together with the pronouncement of oracles and omens. In the case of sacrifice the ritual was not confined to sacred persons, but normally the chief or priest performed the rites, and his presence was essential when an offering was made in order to obtain an oracular response to a request for divine guidance. Thus *kahin*, from meaning originally "priest", was used by the later Arabs in the sense of "soothsayer" through whom revelations were received. At Mecca, for instance, before an image in the Ka'ba known as Hubal were seven divining arrows on each of which was an inscription which enabled the priest (*sadin*), here called *sahib al-kidah* ("master of the shafts"), to give an answer to inquirers when he "cast the arrows".[139] There are many stories in Arabic literature about *kahins* and *sadins* as omen observers showing that divination was their principal function.[140] The priest acted as seer (*hazi*) very much as in Israel, and the variety of names introduced to describe particular aspects of the office— e.g., *hazi, munaggim, zagir, 'arraf*—indicates the high degree of specialization and organization that was attained in pre-Islamic Arabia, ranging from diviner and presager to astrologer and sage. But as an observer of omens the *kahin* cannot be distinguished from the *sadin*.

INSPIRATION AND ECSTASY

His primary activity, however, was ecstatic, and in his shamanistic capacity he was possessed by one of the many *jinn* which abounded in Arabia. Before these spirits became regarded as mainly malicious objects of fear they were regarded as non-ethical and some at least were beneficent and well-disposed. Being capable of taking possession of men when they assumed the form of a familiar spirit, or guardian genius (*tabi,* or *ra'i*), they were thought to reveal hidden knowledge to the soothsayer when he was in a state of divine intoxication. Thus, he became the mouthpiece of the spirit with whom he was *en rapport,* until at length, in order to discourage pre-Islamic practice, the Moslem theologians degraded the tutelary spirits to the status of demons and represented the inspiration as proceeding from them rather than as an ecstasy which enabled the seer to receive divine knowledge through a spiritual medium.[141] The association of the inspiration with the *jinn* appears to have begun in the pre-Islamic period since local gods were in process of transformation into guardian spirits responsible for the ecstatic utterances of *kahins* and poets (*sha'ir*).[142] Indeed, Muhammad believed when he first began to receive revelations in the form of dreams and ecstatic experiences that he was possessed by a *jinni,* and it was in this way that the Meccans regarded him. Later, in conformity with Judaeo—Christian angelology, he attributed the visitations to Gabriel as the medium of divine communications vouchsafed by Allah to His prophet.

REVELATIONS TO MUHAMMAD

It would appear that when he approached his fortieth year Muhammad became increasingly contemplative and appalled at the idolatry and moral debasement of Arabia. In a state of indecision about the true religion and the rival claims of Judaism and Christianity, as he had encountered these two faiths in degenerate forms during his travels along the local trade routes to Aleppo and Damascus, he retired to a cave in mount Hira where he believed he was visited by an angel in a dream. After spending some time in retirement, returning intermittently to his family at Mecca, one day the angel (*malak*) again came to him and commanded him to "recite in the name of the Lord who had created man out of a clot of blood" the message recorded in the sacred Qur'an, written in Arabic as the inspired Word of God dictated by Him (Allah) from the "preserved tablet" in heaven.[143]

As poets in Arabia were thought to be under the inspiration and the power of *jinn,* it is not surprising that the earliest Qur'anic communications were in rhymed verse brought by Gabriel the archangel (who was also called the Holy Spirit), to the Prophet who repeated the messages he received. The revelations continued to the passive mind of Muhammad so that in addition to the one hundred and fourteen chapters of the sacred book delivered at Mecca and Medina respectively, there is a considerable body of tradition (*Sunna* and *hadīth*) which claims to contain the teaching of the Founder of Islam revealed to him, like the inspiration of saints and mystics, through an unknown medium (*ilham*), as against the angelic mode (*wahi*) employed in the bestowal of the Qur'an. Although in fact the collections of oracles attributed to Muhammad were not put together until after his death, a proportion of them in all probability are authentic, the earliest being the rhythmic Suras al-'Alaq (xcvi), al-Asr (ciii), al-'Adiyat (c) and al-Fatihah (i), in which the vigorous imagination and moral and religious earnestness of a seeker after God, rather than the pronouncements of prophetic utterance, is the characteristic feature. The reference to current events in the Medina period dates the section compiled during the establishment of the original theocrasy there, but the groups delivered at Mecca are less clearly defined by style or content. In these later revelations the sentences are long and unwieldly, denunciations of Jews and opponents are prevalent, public and local events are commented on, and the same stories repeated again and again in different words.

Notwithstanding the different periods and occasions which characterize the revelation, the whole of the Qur'an is regarded as equally the inspired uncreated Word of Allah interpreted as a divine attribute (*sifah*). Whether or not the archangel Gabriel or the Holy Spirit was regarded as the agent of inspiration at different times is not clear. Sometimes it came, Muhammad declared, like the noise of a bell; sometimes the angel appeared in the form of a man and held converse with the Prophet.[144] On occasions, however, Muhammad claimed to have been translated to the angelic realms like a shaman when bad news was conveyed to him. When the tinkling of a bell was employed, he alone could hear it and interpret the words of Gabriel by means of its sounds. He then became greatly agitated and suffered intense emotion. If he heard the bell when riding on a camel, the animal would fall to the ground owing to the weight of his body. When he ascended into the heavens during his noctural visions (*mi'raj*) he conversed with God like Moses face to face, without any intermediary. Sometimes Allah appeared to him in a dream, and made known His will by placing His hands on the Prophet's shoulders.[145]

To make quite certain that no error could enter into these revelations, if by chance he made a wrong deduction from a previous disclosure another was always sent to rectify it. Similarly, divine revelation abrogated not only principles of the original disclosures but the regulations which the Prophet had proclaimed, as, for example, in the case of the expansion of the two obligatory times of prayer to the five-fold salat. By this principle of abrogation the inconsistencies in the Qur'an are explained. Only in Medina, it is alleged, was the full revelation of Islam made known, regardless of the claim that the Qur'an represents an exact copy of the heavenly original so that "the text, words and phrases were communicated to the Prophet by an audible voice".[146] The reconciliation of these two opposed claims has constituted a problem with which

Muslim theologians have grappled with varying degrees of success, but notwithstanding the difficulties inherent in the situation, the Qur'an has remained an oracular authority unique in the history of prophetic literature.

THE ORACULAR AUTHORITY OF THE QUR'AN

The Hebrew prophets prefaced their utterances with the words, "Thus saith Yahweh," but they did not completely eliminate the human consciousness in the process of revelation. Muhammad regarded the message he received as having come direct from God on the "night of power" in the sacred month of Ramadan and consisting of isolated sections of the "concealed book" in heaven.[147] Therefore, those who arranged the Qur'an in its present form after his death began each of the suras with the words, "In the name of Allah, the Merciful, the Compassionate," or simply, in the case of the ninth sura, "In the name of Allah." It was, however, in the beginning an audible not a written revelation since Muhammad heard the voice of God speaking to him mainly through Gabriel as the intermediary sent down from heaven with "the spirit of His word" as a divine oracle (*kalam Allah*) existing from all eternity.[148] Like the shamans in primitive society who underwent similar ecstatic experiences, the Prophet had to struggle against evil influences—the whisperings of Iblis (Satan)[149]— and only by the help of Allah was he able to hear clearly and distinctly the admonitions of the "perspicuous scripture".

Whether or not any of these auditions have been recorded in fact can be but a matter of conjecture. It is possible that the oldest rhythmic sections may be in substance the messages he believed he received, but even these must have undergone considerable recasting. The rest is the work of his followers who after his death in A.D. 632 began a systematic collection of his alleged revelations. The results of the search were revised during the reign of 'Uthman, and in due course all the texts that departed from the standard version were suppressed. The suras were arranged in their present order in accordance with the length, beginning with the longest, and for liturgical pur-

G

poses the Qur'an has been divided into thirty equal parts. The revelations of the earlier prophets in Israel and those in the Christian scriptures were not denied, but in so far as they disclosed revealed truth it was said to be based on the original heavenly book, the contents of which were made known most completely to Muhammed alone. Therefore, it is maintained that the Qur'an confirms what was revealed to Abraham, Moses, David and Jesus, despite the Prophet's very imperfect knowledge of orthodox Judaism and Christianity. He denied that he was a *kahin* and forbade divination, but he conformed to the type of prophecy current in Arabia in his day so closely as to be almost indistinguishable from it. Thus, Gabriel virtually occupied the same position as the *jinn* acting in the capacity of a mouthpiece of the god with whom they were *en rapport*. The hidden contents of the "preserved tablet" were revealed during Mohammad's ecstatic experiences when they were made accessible to him on the "Night of Decree", having been taken to the lowest heaven for this purpose.

When Greek influences penetrated Islam the conflict between the Mu'tazilites and the orthodox Sunni arose concerning the eternity of the Divine Word (*kalam*) disclosed in the Qur'anic revelation. Against the orthodox contention that as a divine attribute the Word or speech of God is uncreated, the Mu'tazilites maintained that since the Qur'an was written in Arabic and descended to earth, it belongs to the temporal order and is created. Consequently, it has a human element and is not beyond reverent criticism and verification. In short, the movement was an attempt to introduce in Islam the conception of prophecy which regards the prophet as one illumined by God to reveal His words and will and purposes but subject to human limitations and environmental conditions.[150] But after a brief period of Mu'tazilite ascendancy between 833 and 848, the orthodox doctrine prevailed.

The attitude of the Mu'tazilites arose out of a fear that the doctrine of eternal attributes (*kalam*) would endanger the absolute unity of Allah; a problem similar to that which confronted the Christian Church in its Christological controversy. For both Islam and Christianity the question at issue was whether the highest revelations of the Godhead—the communication of the Qur'an and the Incarnation respectively—were divine accidents or essences. Was the *Kalam* the equivalent of the *Logos,* the Word of God Who was God? If so, its manifestation in a written record must be embodied in a preexistent uncreated book, as the Sunni perceived. Conversely, if, as the Mu'tazilites maintained, Allah alone existed in eternity, His revelation in the spoken word to Moses and Muhammad could not be identified with His essential Being since His attributes do not have independent existence.

SUFI AND DERVISHES

Thus, in the last analysis revelation becomes a question of the nature of Deity and of His relation to man and the universe. But it also presupposes a response from the divinely illumined human spirit, a capacity for visionary experience, a passing over from the material to the spiritual world. Therefore, the ecstatic prophetic tradition, so conspicuous in Semitic culture, is closely related to mysticism, as becomes apparent in the rise of an ascetic movement in Islam in spite of Muhammad's discouragement of this type of religious practice as unfitting for crusaders called to propagate the faith with the sword. His followers, however, soon began to display excessive zeal in their religious devotions which culminated in ecstasy. Owing to the custom of wearing wool as a mark of their spiritual status they were known as *sufi*. At first they represented merely a puritanical reaction against the luxury and licence of the wealthier classes and the formalism of orthodoxy, but in the seventh century, under the influence of Neoplatonism and Christian mysticism, they sought spiritual perfection and union with God in an organized asceticism.[151] Eventually, in the twelfth century, this found expression in the establishment of Orders in which the ecstatic state sometimes was produced by muscular movements in the recitation of mystic formulae (*hadrah*), solitude (*khalwah*) and sacred dances (*dhikr*). The members lived in monasteries composed of fully professed and lay brethren under the rule of elders (*shaikh*), but they did not take a vow of celibacy.

Among the Sufi were wandering mendicants, or dervishes, accredited with occult powers and marvellous feats, such as extinguishing the fire when they entered burning furnaces, and eating live serpents. This reputation, coupled with the disreputable practices in which they engaged, brought discredit upon the entire movement. Indeed, it can hardly be denied that although there have been holy men among the dervishes, for the most part they have been worthless beggars and scandalous fakirs who have exhibited all the worst features of ecstaticism. Sufism, on the other hand, in its original form was law abiding, quietistic and mystical rather than tumultuous, fanatical and licentious, and under the influence of Al Ghazali in the eleventh century, it was reconciled with the traditional faith and practice of Islam. Nevertheless, notwithstanding its political influence, Sufism has never been regarded with much favour by official Islam, the gulf between a monistic mysticism and a prophetic transcendentalism being too great to be bridged in the absence of a priesthood. Thus, the ultimate aim of Sufi spiritual exercises is a complete mystical union of the soul with Allah through seven stages, or "valleys"—the valley of search, or renunciation of earthly possessions; the valley of love in which ardent devotion to God is kindled, leading to the valleys of illumination (knowledge) and detachment until unity is attained in contemplation of the divine essence. Then follows a period of "amazement" at the failure to achieve the final goal which is the "passing away" (*fana*) or annihilation of the self. So in what is virtually a Nirvana transcendence becomes pantheistic immanence in which God and man are merged in a higher unity to the exclusion of all intervening agents human or divine.

THE FUNCTION OF PROPHECY AND PRIESTHOOD

To establish a mystic relationship with the eternal world has been a widespread form of religious experience ranging from shamanism to ecstatic contemplation of the divine and the *via negativa* of oriental pantheism. Where, as in Islam and Judaism, God has been regarded as essentially transcendent and ineffable, prophetic, angelic or priestly mediation usually has been introduced as against the meditative techniques resorted to to secure immediate identity with the Absolute without the aid of any intervening agents. The prophet, however, as the spokesman and interpreter of the divine will exercises his functions as an individual who is in personal contact with the supernatural order and the recipient of a revelational self-disclosure. He may or may not be a member of a cult organization, but he must be capable of becoming *en rapport* with the spiritual world and of receiving divine inspiration. Only so long as this relationship is maintained does he prophesy, but when he is filled with the prophetic afflatus he is compelled to deliver his message whether the people will hear or whether they will forebear.

Since the word which the prophet is called to utter may be in complete contradiction to the policy adopted by the ruling régime, as in the case of Jeremiah in Judah in the days immediately preceding the Exile, it may have a disintegrating effect on the social organization. Indeed, the Hebrew prophets constantly proclaimed oracles in direct opposition to the existing social, religious and economic order, and condemned in no unmeasured terms the iniquities, perversions, injustices and apostasy current in their own day and generation. As freelance critics and reformers they took an independent line at what they believed to be the command of God, speaking like Balaam as they were bidden by him regardless of the consequence. Thus, Muhammad was content to be a voice crying in a wilderness until at length he gathered around him a group of devoted followers who became the nucleus of a movement destined to weld together a great variety of peoples in a closely-knit civilization integrated in a common submission to Allah and his Prophet. As a result of his revelations and prophetic utterances some 250 million adherents have become united into a consolidated culture with a simple creed fervently believed and an equally simple cult punctiliously practised, bound together by participation in a common way of life and faith, obedient to a common law and the adoption of a common traditional and sacred language. As a result Islam has spread from its Arabian cradleland through Persia and India to the Far East, and westwards through Africa to the Atlantic, and left its mark on European history. So linked up with every vital aspect of human life has it become that it has transcended all other allegiances, and over this vast area it has produced a homogeneous society. Scholars in Alexandria, caravan attendants in Morocco, tradesmen in Syria and farmers in Java, regulate their lives and behaviour in accordance with the religious, social and political norm provided by the Holy Qur'an and the traditions derived from these sacred scriptures, to say nothing of the ninety-five million Muslims in the subcontinent of India.

It is true that sectarianism has been a feature of Islam, as of most religions based on the prophetic tradition. Muhammad is alleged to have affirmed that "diversity of opinion among my people is a mercy from God", and to have predicted that his followers would split up into seventy-three sects as "the children of Israel were divided into seventy-two sects".[152] The causes, however, have been political rather than doctrinal disagreements, concerned mainly with the vexed question of a successor to the Prophet. But behind these disputes and their disruptive influences there has been a remarkable solidarity deeply rooted in the Muslim ancestry and its prophetic tradition in which the revelations of Muhammad and his sayings, and those of his companions, have acquired divine authority and given coherence and unity to the social structure and religious organization of this vast civilization transcending the barriers of race, language and locality. Moreover, although Islam has never had a priesthood or sacrifical cultus as a stabilizing force, the hagg, or pilgrimage to Mecca, obligatory on all Muslims, has brought them all into personal contact with their common sacred centre, while the "five pillars" (comprising a confession of faith in the sovereignty of Allah and the prophetic role of Muhammad, daily prayer, alms-giving, fasting and the pilgrimage), together with the rigidly enforced canonical pre-scriptions, have served the purposes of a unifying dynamic.

In Israel prophetic religion was always counterbalanced by that of the priesthood. Thus, as we have seen, in its earlier manifestations it functioned very largely within the cultic tradition of the local sanctuaries, and when it assumed a more independent role in individuals of remarkable spiritual insight, such as Amos, Hosea, Isaiah, Micah and Jeremiah, after a period of reaction against "those who prophesied falsely and the priests who bore rule by their means", it became a leavening influence in the ecclesiastical structure of the post-exilic community. The demands of Ezekiel for a purer Zadokite priesthood to safeguard the "holiness" of Yahweh, defiled by priests and people alike, did not pass unheeded. Much that the prophets had condemned was reinterpreted in the later literature in terms of their ethical monotheism. The temple worship with its elaborate priestly ceremonial and organization was based on the pre-prophetic archetype and given a divine origin and sanction in relation to the prophetic ethical and spiritual conception of righteousness and holiness. Thus, the reforms initiated by the prophets acquired institutional expression through the priesthood in the regulation of the post-exilic religious organization, with all that this involved in the religious and social life of the community.

The stability afforded by this combination of the two traditions is shown by the remarkable persistence of Jewry as an entity through all the vicissitudes of its history both before and after the fall of Jerusalem in A.D. 70. Notwithstanding the cessation of the daily sacrifice and the other priestly ministrations in the temple, the practice of the faith continued, centred now in the Torah, in the synagogue and the domestic ritual with the underlying prophetic presuppositions. As in Islam, ecstatic contemplation was sometimes practised by the Talmudic rabbis through the recitation of a sacred text respecting the majesty of God in His heavenly glory, together with esoteric exercises,[153] but it was not in such phenomena that its strength lay. It was rather in maintaining its heritage as a sacred community, grounded in its covenant relationship with Yah-weh and expressed in the unity and common character of its religious observances as an integral part of its social structure, that its continuity and consolidation consisted. This was summed up in the Law imposed upon all as the bond which united the "holy nation" as the "kingdom of priests" with its officers, theologians, lawyers and administrators assuming col-lectively the role of an organized hierarchy in a theocratic community, giving it its stability and eagerly looking forward to the time when the temple worship and its priesthood, abrogated after the catastophe in A.D. 70, would be restored.

CHAPTER IV

Kingship and Priesthood

As prophetism is a characteristic and recurrent factor in Semitic culture so kingship as the embodiment of divine power is a fundamental feature in the agricultural civilizations of the ancient Near East. Moreover, in primitive states of culture, although a lineal succession from the medicine man through the chief to the divine king cannot be maintained, as Frazer contended, nevertheless, an affinity in office and function between kingship and priesthood does exist. In tribes organized in descent-groups hereditary chieftainship may be vested in a paramount chief who owes his position to descent from a mythical ancestor or god. This gives him a unique position among the rest of the hierarchy and may carry with it a divine status with corresponding tabus, responsibilities and sacred duties towards the community. His virility is so intimately associated with the fertility of the crops and the well-being of society generally that to prevent loss of potency in nature he may be put to death, either actually, in the person of a substitute, or symbolically by means of some ritual device, as soon as any indications appear that his natural forces are abating.

KINGSHIP AMONG THE SHILLUK

Since this practice was first recorded among the Shilluk of the Nilotic Sudan by Professor and Mrs Seligman in 1909,[1] and quoted by Frazer in corroboration of his theory of "the dying god",[2] king-killing to promote the welfare of the community has been revealed as a widespread custom in Africa and elsewhere,[3] though the precise significance of ceremonial regicide is still in dispute. That it has arisen out of his sacred character, supernatural potency and priestly status, partly life-giving and partly expiatory, is indicated by the circumstances in which, and the purposes for which, the rite is performed

(e.g., rain-making, vegetation renewal and vicarious offerings).
Among the Shilluk, for example, the king (*reth*) by virtue of
his descent from and embodiment of the soul of the culture-
hero Nyikang, who symbolizes the politico-religious structure
of the nation, occupies the central position in the ritual order
as the royal high-priest.[4] In this capacity he assists at the sacrifices for rain at the shrines of Nyikang invoking his ancestor to
send refreshing showers to renew the earth, and acts as the
mediator in the settlement of feuds.[5] But, as Professor Evans-
Pritchard has pointed out, "we can only understand the place
of kingship in Shilluk society when we realize that it is not the
individual at any time reigning who is king, but Nyikang who
is the medium between man and god (*Juok*) and is believed in
some way to participate in God as he does in the king."[6]

It is this relationship which gives the *reth* his sacerdotal
status and mediatorial functions, and lies behind whatever may
have happened in former times about killing kings when they
became sick or senile.[7] Thus, during the accession ceremonies
held about a year after the election, the image of Nyikang and
that of his son Dak are brought by the priests from Akurwa
in the north to Fashoda, the cult-centre, supported by an army.
Outside the capital a mock battle ensues with an army from the
south supporting the king-elect. The men of Akurwa, having
proved victorious, take the king to Fashoda and place the
image of Nyikang on the sacred stool which they have brought
with them. After a bullock has been sacrificed and eaten by
descendants of the third of the Shilluk kings, called *ororo,* the
image is removed and the king-elect is seated on the stool that
the spirit of Nyikang may enter into him and so complete his
accession by virtually becoming the culture hero. The royal
bride is then seized by Nyikang and a second combat is fought
between the two opposing forces in which the girl is captured
for the king. Peace is restored, the newly enthroned monarch
receives the homage of his chiefs and undertakes to rule well, by
virtue of the spirit and power of Nyikang with which he has
been indued, and of the relationship in which he stands to
Juok the High God.[8]

As the embodiment and representative of the creator of the nation the kingship sums up all that is divine in the Shilluk ritual order and consolidates the community as a single entity in a sacerdotal capacity. Transcendentally the sacred office stands over and against the social structure because it is rooted and grounded in the eternal world. This enables it to exercise a powerful unifying influence over all the various segments as the pivot of the political organization, and to become the connecting link between the earthly community and its supernatural foundations, very much as the medieval monarch was regarded as a *mixta persona,* both priest and ruler, having acquired his sacrosanct character by hereditary right confirmed by his sacramental "sacring" to act as God's viceroy in the secular and political sphere.

In primitive states of culture the divine kingship being mainly a ritual institution concerned essentially with the maintenance of the food supply and the integration of society, it has been devoted largely to the performance of sacerdotal functions to promote the welfare of the whole community. This finds expression especially in the control of the weather upon which the harvests depend. As the intermediary between the human and the natural orders, the supernatural potency embodied in the kingship flows through this appointed channel into the body politic establishing a state of harmony, equilibrium and beneficence in the integration of society and nature. It is on this basis that the institution exercises a sacerdotal function, and for this reason that the throne must always have a virile, healthy and alert occupant; for the king, symbolizing the community in its transcendental and temporal aspects, is its unifying and dynamic centre.

PHARAOH IN EGYPT

It is against this background that the rise of monarchical civilization in the Ancient East should be set. Thus, in the Nile valley, where so many of the characteristic features of the divine kingship among the Shilluk seem to recur, the traditional founder of the first dynasty, Menes, in about 3400 B.C. is assigned the combined rule of Upper and Lower Egypt in a supernatural capacity. Before him King "Scorpion" was considered to be an incarnation of Horus who may have been either one of the falcon gods in pre-dynastic Egypt, or the chief god of Pe (Buto) in Lower Egypt. When the Lower Kingdom conquered Upper Egypt the cult of Horus was established at Edfu (Behdet), and with the union of the country as a single nation, Horus (the Behdetite) became the predominant figure in the kingship.

Another ruler who apparently assisted in the unification of the "two lands" (i.e. Upper and Lower Egypt) was Narmer, who extended his sovereignty over the Delta. On an elaborately carved and inscribed slate palette found at Hierakonpolis he is depicted wearing the crown of Upper Egypt slaying the leader of his opponents, and on the obverse side arrayed in the crown of Lower Egypt inspecting his defeated enemies who had been beheaded. As in all probability he is to be identified with the traditional Menes,[9] the scenes would appear to represent episodes in the conquest of the North by the South. In any case, the unification of Upper and Lower Egypt eventually was accomplished by a ruler whose falcon-god, Horus, was a sky-god who became incarnate in the person of the Upper Egyptian king, and bestowed upon him a Horus-name. The capital was moved to Thinis until an imperial city, Memphis, was built, whose chief god was Ptah. There all subsequent Pharoahs were crowned in their dual capacity, and in the so-called "Memphite Theology" the theory of kingship was expounded.[10]

As the creator of the universe, himself the product of self-created thought[11] and the central figure of an Ennead representing manifestations of his essential nature, Ptah was too abstract to make much impression on the concrete Egyptian mind, occupied with the practical problems of an agricultural community. The priests of Memphis, therefore, at the beginning of the Dynastic period, under the influence of the cult of Osiris which had spread from its centre in the Delta at Busiris (Per-Usire, or Djedu, the capital of the ninth nome of Egypt) adapted the solar theology of the neighbouring sacred city, Heliopolis, to their own system and produced a composite "Memphite Theology" with the kingship and society placed in a cosmological context. Already, as we have seen, the king had been identified with Horus, and it only remained for the powerful Heliopolitan priesthood to bring into conjunction in the person of Pharaoh the two great cults centring in the all-enveloping glory and power of the Egyptian sun and the life-giving waters of the inundation, to place them in a position of predominance.

In the Pyramid texts, the chief source of our knowledge of the theology of Heliopolis, the solar line of kings had been equated with Re, the Sun-god, and then associated with Osiris, who was originally, in all probability, a deified civilizing king who in the Delta had become the centre of a death and resurrection cultus. Subsequently he became a composite figure as Lord of the dead, the god of vegetation and the personification of the fruitifying waters of the Nile, as his sister-wife Isis was the personification of his royal throne. In the Heliopolitan Ennead Osiris was incorporated as the son of Geb, the Earth-god, and given a place in the sun by descent from Atum-Re, the head of the pantheon. From prehistoric times Heliopolis had been a solar centre but it was during the fifth dynasty (*c.* 2580 B.C.) that its worship and theology were developed in great detail by its priesthood. It then became recognized as the home of the Re-cult with its temple, the "House of the Obelisk", erected on the primordial hill—the "sandhill"—which was supposed to have emerged out of the waters of Nun at the creation, on the top of which Atum first appeared in the form of a Phoenix.[12]

THE KINGSHIP AND THE PRIESTHOODS

Since Memphis also claimed to stand upon land that had arisen from the primordial water, personified as the god Tatjenen, a conciliation between the Heliopolitan and Memphite theologies was imperative. Heliopolis retained its supremacy and its system was accepted by practically every priesthood and every temple in Egypt. The theologians of Memphis adopted its Great Ennead but they made their god Ptah the head of it in place of Atum. He (Ptah) was represented as "the heart and the tongue" of the Ennead Atum as having come into being *ex nihilo* "on the tongue" as the creator-god. Therefore, Ptah in the Memphite Theology was the ultimate creative principle transmitting his power "in the form of Atum" (or "in the heart" as the texts affirm), to all the other divinities and to their embodiment, the king. In this way it succeeded in assimilating the Heliopolitan system without diminishing its claims for Ptah as "the Great One who begot the gods" and called all things into being by the thought of his heart (i.e. his mind). In addition to fashioning the gods he made the cities, settled the nomes and installed the gods in their temples.

Under the influence of the Heliopolitan solar cult, however, the victorious kings of Upper Egypt, having established the capital at Memphis and visiting it to celebrate their conquest of Lower Egypt, identified the falcon-god Horus with Re in the composite deity Harakhte," Horus of the Horizon". This opened the way for them to be declared to be the sons of Re. In the Second Dynasty the second king Re-neb was given a Horus-name, but it was not until the Fourth Dynasty (*c.* 2740 B.C.) that the Heliopolitan kings Khafre and Menkaure, the builders of the second and third pyramids, actually assumed officially the title "son of Re". From the middle of the next century the practice became more general and each king built a temple for the worship of the Sun-god in connexion with his royal residence on the margin of the Western desert.[13]

By the Sixth Dynasty (*c.* 2440–2250) the title was of universal application and the divine status of the reigning Pharaoh was further enhanced by the Osirianization of the solar cultus at Heliopolis. Not only was he begotten by his heavenly father who, it was maintained, assumed the form of the living king for purposes of procreation, but with the incorporation of the Osiris myth every living king was equated with Horus, the posthumous son of the culture hero Osiris who had been conceived by Isis when she hovered over his corpse. Thus, as at death every Pharaoh was Osiris, so he reigned in the guise of the living Horus (distinct from the falcon-god of Edfu), who had been established in the throne by the decree of the gods when Osiris was vindicated by the heavenly tribunal. Therefore, notwithstanding the complications in the royal title introduced by their several conceptions of the kingship, its divine origin and status were assured by the reigning king being at once the son of Re begotten of the Sun-god, the embodiment of all the deities of the "two lands", and the successor and son of the dead king Osiris, born of Isis, who avenged the death of his father in his contest with Seth.[14]

In the synthesis of these varying traditions under Heliopolitan influence the nation was consolidated in the throne as its dynamic centre. Having surrounded the king with all the glamour and prestige of solar descent, and added to this an Osirian status carrying with it universal sovereignty, the priesthood not only secured pre-eminence but gave greater stability to the social structure. Nevertheless, however pre-eminent Heliopolis might be with its deeply laid solar cultus, it was not the sacred centre. Memphis, as we have seen, remained the capital with its own cosmology and theology, while Hermopolis had its primeval hill, primordial deities and high priesthood of Thoth. It was not, in fact, until the middle of the second millennium B.C. that a permanent capital was established in Egypt at Thebes and its god Amon-Re was raised to the supreme place in the pantheon with the restoration of the Theban royal line at the beginning of the great Eighteenth Dynasty (c. 1570 B.C.), thereby giving stability to the New Kingdom.

The political disintegration and anarchy that set in at the end of the Sixth Dynasty (c. 2250 B.C.), and the foreign invasion of the Delta by Asiatic nomads, led to the establishment of local monarchs as feudal lords. This necessitated the creation of a host of local officials and a bureaucratic organization which constituted a serious embarrassment for weak Pharoahs, despite the supernatural sanctions that surrounded the throne. The monarchy, however, by virtue of its transcendental foundations and significance, remained the unifying centre which even under the disturbed conditions of the Middle Kingdom was a consolidating force in Egyptian civilization, and eventually became the rallying point when royal power was again able to assert itself as world power, cosmic in its range in the right ordering (*maat*) of nature and the nation by divine ordinance, as it was claimed.

Although priesthoods and tribal houses rose and fell, and Asiatic "shepherd kings", with the aid of their chariots and horses, set up an alien rule until they were expelled by Ahmose I about 1570 B.C., the enlightened rule of many kings in the Feudal Age did much to prepare the way for the new and glorious epoch that opened with the restoration of the Theban line and gave Egypt for the time being the leadership in the ancient world. The reconquest of Nubia, the extension of the empire to the second cataract, and the restoration of the suzerainty as far as the Euphrates and the Aegean, gave rise to a new conception of "world power". This carried with it the idea of a "world god" in the person of the Pharaoh who reigned over the entire area. For the first time the kingship now acquired an international significance with the Sun-god as an all-embracing divinity no longer confined to the Nile valley. Consequently, it only remained for Amenhotep IV when he came to the throne about 1375 B.C., to carry the conception a stage further to introduce a genuine solar monotheism. This he did by deposing Amon-Re in favour of an ancient designation of Re-Harakhty, known as Aton and symbolized by the luminous disk in which he shone upon the whole world, and declaring him to be the sole deity. "As the solar disk was one alone, without counterpart or equal, so thou reigned alone."[15]

Although the cult of Aton, or Show (an ancient god of light and air) in association with that of Re-Harakhte had long existed, the Heliopolitan Re in his various manifestations was essentially a syncretistic figure served by rival priesthoods, as we have seen. Therefore, when Amenhotep IV, having changed his name to Ikhnaton, transferred his allegiance from Amon-Re solely to Aton, he had to set up a new hierarchy and temple organization. Furthermore, not content with closing Karnak and the other temples of Amon-Re and confiscating the revenues of their priesthoods, the ardent reformer erased the names of all the other gods from the monuments, and in due course moved the capital from Thebes to a site near the present village of Amarna in Middle Egypt. This he designated Akhetaton, "the Horizon of Aton", and made it the centre of the new faith. Here the sole God in heaven and on earth was worshipped by his royal son and embodiment as the Creator and Sustainer of all things in a greatly simplified cultus consisting chiefly of monotheistic hymns, censings, libations and offerings of perfumes and flowers. All anthropomorphic and theriomorphic images were rigidly excluded, the only symbol employed being that of the solar disk with emanating rays.

Ikhnaton, however, was born out of due time. As a ruler he was weak and uninterested in imperial affairs. Egypt was full of dissatisfied soldiers and he had antagonized the dispossessed Amonite priesthood. Consequently, although the universalism of the Aton movement corresponded to the cosmopolitanism of the new imperial power, it lacked the support of an influential priesthood and made little or no appeal to the popular imagination. Moreover, as the Amarna Letters reveal, local rulers in the Western Asiatic provinces were apprehensive as the Empire began to fall into ruin. In the confusion that followed his death in 1350, the Amonite priesthood regained its power, and the old régime was restored with a new line of kings. These included Seti I and Rameses II as outstanding figures, under whom the Empire was consolidated. But it became stereotyped after the death of Rameses II. The Theban priesthood had annexed the greater part of the wealth and territory of Upper Egypt, and about 1100 B.C. Herihar, high priest of Amon-Re, seized the throne. The Delta thereupon set up a rival ruler in the person of Nesubenebded (Smendes) and virtually destroyed the unification of the "two lands" in a single divine head which had been the cohesive force since the end of the fourth millennium.

From this disintegration the Empire never recovered though

H

relations between the two rulers were cordial and intermarriage between their families occurred. A mercenary line of Libyan kings seems to have reigned concurrently in Thebes and in Tanis in the Delta in the Twenty-second and Twenty-third Dynasties, and they described themselves as "beloved of Amon" although they were votaries of the divinities of the Delta (e.g. Bastet of Bubastis). In Thebes they secured influence by appointing their sons as high priests of Amon, but the real sovereignty in the Theban sacerdotal State was exercised by the daughter of the ruling priestly house who assumed the role of the "god's wife" (i.e. of Amon).

Since Isis was the "throne-woman" as the sister-spouse of Osiris, the "occupier of the throne"[16] (and, later, as priestesses were "servants" of the god), so female musicians impersonated the god's hareem and their leader was regarded as the wife of the god in the guise of Hathor, the cow-goddess and the wife of the Sun-god at Heliopolis. To beget an heir, as we have seen, the Pharaoh visited the queen in all the glory of his royal divine majesty. Therefore, very deeply laid in the sacred kingship in Egypt was the status and function of the queen as the votaress of the god, and it is possible that the union took place in the temple.[17] In the Eighteenth Dynasty she was the priestess of Amon-Re, assisted by concubines over whom she presided,[18] and when the Saitic line was established at Thebes these sacerdotal princesses became the real governors of the State, the high-priest being a figure-head.

Egyptian religion, however, had now lost its vitality and with it the social structure was in steady decline. The divine kingship ceased to exercise its consolidating power and neither the throne nor its priesthoods could stay the political decay and disintegration. Vainly did the Ethiopian kings endeavour to revive and reassert the ancient tradition as a unifying force, and it only remained for Asur-bani-pal to conquer Thebes in 663 B.C. to reduce Amon-Re to the rank of a local god. After a temporary recovery with the help of Greek mercenaries Egypt was incorporated in the Persian Empire in 525 B.C. but without any fundamental change in its institutions. When Alexander established his Macedonian Empire in the Nile valley two hundred years later (332 B.C.) he was deified as the son of Amon, and offered sacrifice to the Egyptian gods at Memphis. Thus began the syncretism of the Egyptian and Greek pantheon and their cultus, as a result of which the Osirianized sacred bull Apis at Memphis became the state-god of Egypt in the Ptolemaic period in the form of Serapis with his principal sanctuary the serapeum at Alexandria, the capital of the Empire, where his original image was installed. It was he who under Ptolemy I was made the unifying centre of the Greek and Egyptian elements in the nation, and gradually absorbed the worship of all the gods who had a common origin in Osiris and Dionysos, thereby replacing the Heliopolitan solar cultus of Re as the consolidating dynamic.[19] The deification of the Ptolemaic sovereigns in the Graeco-Roman period and the institution of priesthoods in connexion with their worship gave a new emphasis to emperor-worship, and maintained the ancient tradition in which the king was the point of contact between the sacred and the secular orders responsible for the well-being of the community over which he ruled in a divine capacity as the priest *par excellence*.

When, however, the worship of the emperor eventually was revived in the Roman Empire it never acquired the position that the divine kingship occupied in Egypt. Augustus, it is true, was regarded as the beneficent representative of the mysterious divine power that sustained Rome and was given honours like those offered to the gods, but only on very rare occasions was he worshipped as *divus* during his life-time. It was not until after their death that the Senate conferred upon emperors this title (distinct from *deus*), and then it did not carry with it a cultus comparable in any sense to that of the divine kingship in the Ancient East. Officially prayers and offerings were not made to Divus Augustus, or supernatural benefits sought from him or his *Genius*. In legend his prototype was Hercules not Serapis, and he was never a cult-figure of a priesthood, though the worship had a political value in holding together the Empire.

THE KING AS A COSMIC FIGURE

In the Nile valley, on the other hand, once the monarchy emerged as a theocratic government centred in the Pharaoh and his priesthood, every aspect of life was a function of the State just as all the attributes and prerogatives of the gods were comprehended in the throne as the pivot of society in a permanent, changeless cosmic order.[20] It was the duty of the king as the son of Re, who had put order (*maat*) in the place of chaos when he called all things into being, to maintain "justice" (*maat*) in relation to the needs of the nation, ruling it with "truth ".[21]

This conception of "justice", summed up in the term *maat*, was essentially cosmic in its significance, involving the right ordering of the universe as well as good living and just government. As the Sun-god was "the begetter of truth" and from him proceeded the laws of nature, of society and of ethics as several parts of the universal divine order of the right and the good, so *maat* was personified as the "goddess of truth", the daughter of Re, whom the king offered daily to the god under the symbol of the little hieroglyph of the goddess.[22] To the official name of the king the epithet "living in truth (*maat*)" was appended, and during the Ikhnaton movement in one of the hymns the new capital at Amarna was described as "the seat of truth". Similarly, when Tutankhamen restored the worship of Amon-Re he was said to have "driven out disorder from the Two Lands so that order (truth) was again established in its place".[23] Thus, whether orthodox or heretical, the Pharaoh was regarded as the embodiment of *maat* with which he was endowed by its author and begetter the Sun-god, and which gave validity to his actions and commands.

THE ROYAL PREROGATIVES OF OFFICIALS

Originally the royal prerogatives of the throne were the exclusive possession of Pharaoh as a cosmic figure of elemental vastness whose powers were unlimited, and in theory he remained the high priest of every god. In all important ceremonies he alone was depicted in temple scenes as the officiant, but for practical purposes he delegated his functions to the professional priesthood. Similarly, as the elaborate funerary cult which at first was his sole privilege in the capacity of the living Horus, the falcon-headed god, and at death the personification of Osiris, was extended in due course to the nobility, and subsequently to all mankind in a simplified form of mummification, so all men became capable of understanding the nature of the universe, and of entering into harmonious relations with it, as well as of attaining immortality. Nevertheless, it was primarily officials, courtiers and priests who acquired sacred knowledge and shared the divine glory and privileges of the throne around which they were grouped.

The principle of substitution by which the king was the god he embodied and the priests were for practical purposes the Pharaoh they represented, modified the absolute rule of a single individual. Even though the royal deputies only acted on behalf of their divine ruler, they shared in some measure in his personality. The potency of the king remained unique because Re was his Ka, and when this vital force or transcendental self, at once the *alter ego* and the guardian spirit, was extended to the priesthood and nobility, and eventually to the rest of his subjects, it still belonged to the sovereign from whom it was derived. His Ka alone was depicted on the monuments as against the ghost-like Ba, or "external manifestation", which without respect of rank or status was represented as a human-headed bird often with human arms, especially in the reliefs and paintings of the New Kingdom. Nevertheless, although the priests and nobles submerged their individuality in their derivative office, as early as the Pyramid age they erected tombs for themselves, confident of being able to join their own Kas in the hereafter by virtue of their inherent divine vitality which they shared with Pharaoh. When the royal cult of the dead was Osirianized this privilege was extended to the rest of mankind with reciprocal effects on the conception of human beings as independent immortal personalities. Originally, however, the Ka was the exclusive possession of kings as an essential part of their divine constitution.[24]

With the extension of the funerary cult in the Middle Kingdom the maintenance of the tomb required the setting apart of
priests as "servants of the Ka" whose duty it was to make
offerings at the appointed times for the sustenance of the Ka of
the occupant, as it had been that of their predecessors to restore
to life the dead body (*sekhen hem*). The king being at once the
protector and sustainer of the individual in the Old Kingdom,
it was virtually his god, just as the king was the Ka whose
"mouth is abundance" (i.e. the vital force of the "two lands").
The function of the "servants of the Ka" was that of offering
food and other gifts for the Ka of a god in whatever tomb or
temple it might be present, very much as the funerary ritual was
performed daily in the royal temple to enable the dead king to
live in the hereafter as a god. When a future life was open to all
men they too could become Osiris and enjoy eternal bliss, but
since the king was the priest *par excellence* in whom all sacerdotal power was vested, his Ka alone is depicted on the monuments, thereby indicating that it was he who continued to
occupy the mediating position. By the time of the Middle
Kingdom the king had given permission for statues of eminent
persons to be erected in the courtyards of the temples so that they
might participate in the prayers and offerings of the priests on
festivals, such as those held at the New Year and on the 18th
of the first month, known as the *Wag*-festival. To avoid
frictions and pluralities funerary priests were reduced to a single
"servant of the Ka" and a "lector priest" for the recitation of the
liturgy at feasts. In the Fifth Dynasty those appointed for the
cult of the kings in their funerary temples were either *weeb*-priests
("pure ones") assigned to special sanctuaries of Re, or servants
of the god (*sandj*) as "instructors", while between these classes
there was the *yot-neter*, the "father of the god".

Being attached to specific kings, temples and tombs, from
which sources they derived their income, by the end of the
Sixth Dynasty they became an influential and well-endowed
element in society. Their principal function was to serve the
god, bathing, dressing and feeding the image, and to act as the
representative and mediator in his service. They might also be

state officials, acting in a variety of secular capacities on behalf of the Pharaoh. As the king represented the gods he embraced in his complex personality and office, so the hierarchy impersonated the gods or goddesses in whose service they were employed in the temples, as for example, in the funerary ritual where they played the role of Horus and Osiris, or of Hathor and Isis. Their wealth and power were determined by the revenues and status of the temple to which they were attached. Thus, in the New Kingdom the high-priest of Amon-Re and his hierarchy in the Twenty-first Dynasty were able to create a "state within a state" at Thebes under their own rule. Nevertheless, in theory the king remained the priest *par excellence,* and the entire sacerdotal order acted merely as his deputies or vicars.

THE CORONATION RITUAL

In view of the crucial position which the kingship occupied in the social structure and sacred organization in Egypt, it was essential that the throne should never be vacant. Therefore, as soon as one Pharaoh was translated to the celestial realms and reunited with his heavenly father, his successor must be duly installed in his divine office. To avoid any possible complications with regard to the hereditary principle inherent in the sacred monarchy, the son destined to succeed might become co-regent (described as "Horus appearing in the arms of his father Osiris") during the lifetime of the reigning sovereign, and so automatically acceded at the death of the old king. It then only remained for the accession to be accomplished by official authorization and installation. To this end a series of rites were held beginning with the administration of the oath, a visitation of the shrines in various centres, and the performance of a mystery play, leading up to the solemn recognition of the new ruler by the chief of the gods after ablutions with the water of Nun (the primeval ocean) in order to unite him with the Sun-god.[25] Lustrations formed an essential part in the daily royal renewal ritual from infancy onwards. In early childhood the heir apparent was sprinkled with water by priests in the guise of Atum and Mouth, or Re-Herakhte and Amon, and he was then publicly acknowledged by the god as his son.[26] After his accession the ablutions were repeated in the Toilet Ceremonies performed every morning in the House of the Morning as a re-enactment of the coronation rite, just as the coronation purification was a renewal of that undergone in infancy. At the time of the actual coronation it was performed by a priest impersonating the god Yahes (*I'ho*) with the words, "I purify thee with the water of all life and good fortune, all stability, all health and happiness,"[27] in order to endow the new sovereign with vital force and the divine qualities of his sacred office. This regeneration was symbolized in the scenes depicting the coronation lustrations by the water issuing from vessels as streams of *crux ansata*.[28]

Since the daily Toilet Ceremonies seem to have been a reproduction of the coronation ritual, it would appear that after the asperges the Pharaoh was censed to unite him with Horus, and he may have been given balls of natron to chew to complete his rebirth. This, at any rate, was the routine in the ceremonial toilet in the House of the Morning, and its counterpart in the temple liturgy, where after lustration at dawn the Pharaoh, or the cult-image of the Sun-god, was vested, anointed and crowned with the royal diadem of Upper and Lower Egypt, and presented with the flail and the crook or sceptre.[29]

In the Old Kingdom the royal ornaments were very simple. A fairly adequate girdle of matting or fur seems to have sufficed at first to mark the dignity of chieftainship. By the Fifth Dynasty this had become a skirt, sometimes made of gold material, with the front portion of the girdle hanging below. The head-dress consisted of two pleated lappets adorned with the *uraeus,* as the symbol of royalty, in the form of a snake. In addition to investiture with the double crown, the crook, flail, whip and sickle-shaped sword, at some point in the coronation ceremony a cloak regarded as the "garb of the god" was placed upon the king, together with a "bird-like gear" as a diadem, which signified that the spirit of the god had come upon him.[30]

Having been crowned and consecrated he assumed the

throne of Horus, "the lord of all living beings, like Re him-self,"[31] and arrayed in the royal attire of the Sun-god, holding his divine insignia, he was shown forth to the people on the throne in his royal splendour, and greeted with delight.[32] The great elaboration of this ceremony is depicted on the temple sculptures.[33] Above the "great seat of Horus", in the New Kingdom, a canopy was raised on wooden pillars with a thick carpet on the floor. The seat is represented as carried by negroes, and a royal sphinx, the destroyer of all enemies, is shown on either arm at the side. Under the feet of the monarch are the names of the enemies conquered, and above, on the roof, are two rows of *uraeus* snakes, another royal symbol.[34]

THE NEW YEAR FESTIVAL

It was not until he had received all his consecrations at Heliopolis that the Pharaoh existed in the fulness of his divine capacity because it was by virtue of these installation rites that he was transformed into a living incarnation of Re.[35] Con-sequently, Piankhi, the conqueror of Egypt, was not con-sidered to be the legitimate king of Egypt until he had under-gone all the coronation ceremonies in the ancient capital. Moreover, the reigning monarch had to be ritually renewed annually at the Spring Festival held in honour of the death and resurrection of Osiris in the latter half of the month of Khoiakh. In the Ptolemaic inscription engraved on the walls of the temple at Denderah in Upper Egypt on the western bank of the Nile, about forty miles north of Thebes, it is recorded that the effigy of Osiris, cast in a mould of gold in the form of a mummy with the white crown of Egypt on his head, was filled with a mixture of barley and sand, wrapped in rushes and laid in a shallow basin. From the 12th to the 21st of Khoiakh the image was watered daily and then the barley and sand were replaced by dry myrrh. Just before sunset it was exposed to the sun, and on the 22nd day of the month, at the eighth hour, it was taken in a boat on a mysterious voyage attended by a fleet of thirty-four vessels made of papyrus illuminated by 365 candles; each boat containing the image of a deity. Two hours after sunset on the 24th day of Khoiakh, the effigy of Osiris swathed as a mummy was placed in a coffin of mulberry wood and laid in a grave (*styt*), where its predecessor had been deposited until it was buried in a cemetery to make room for its successor. Finally, on the 30th day of the month it was rested on a bed of sand in the chamber to complete the interment of Osiris.[36]

That this was the day of the resurrection of Osiris, as Gardiner maintains, when "the dead king was recalled in the tomb to a semblance of his former life",[37] is suggested by a reference in a text at Denderah to his awaking from sleep and taking his place in the sky as the moon. Furthermore, in the bas-reliefs which accompany the inscription he is represented as a mummy, ithyphallic and bearded, lying on a bier at which various gods are stationed: Anubis, Isis, Nephthys, Hathor (the cow-goddess and manifestation of the Great Mother) and her brother Heqet, together with the frog-goddess, who was probably a symbol of resurrection. In the twentieth scene two hawks hover over the body and feet of Osiris, and in the twenty-second scene he is shown wearing the white crown of Upper Egypt with plumes, and holding in his hands the sceptre and flail, in process of raising himself on his knees. Finally, in the last relief, he appears as rising up out of the chest with Isis behind him stretching out her wings, while a male bearded god holds before him the *crux ansata* (i.e. the symbol of life).[38]

The resuscitation of the dead god hardly could be more graphically depicted unless it is in the representation of the same event in the temple of Isis at Philae where stalks of wheat are shown growing from the mummy and watered by a priest from a pitcher. Before the bier the *crux ansata* is figured, and the accompanying inscription declares the body to be that of him "who may not be named, Osiris of the mysteries, who springs from the returning waters".[39] The use of water as a vitalizing agent is illustrated by the numerous "beds of Osiris" made of barley which were watered during the Spring Festival to secure plentiful crops, and placed in tombs to give life to the dead. It is also significant that the Festival of Ploughing occurred in the latter part of the observance, held in a field known as "the place of rejuvenation".[40]

That these Osirian ceremonies were closely associated with the kingship is suggested by a bas-relief in the inner chamber of the hall of Sokar (the funerary god of Memphis) in the temple of Seti I at Abydos. At the head of the mummy of Osiris stands Isis calling her husband back to life, while over the body she is represented as a falcon in the act of fecundation. At the feet is Horus, and a falcon protects the head of Osiris, very much as in the Denderah scenes Nephthys assists Isis in his resurrection. But at Abydos the festival takes the form of a sacred marriage celebrated apparently on behalf of the king, since the inscription bears the words, "may Osiris Unnefer (the Good Being) give to king Menmaat-re (Seti I) life and power."[41]

That the Memphite Festival of Sokar on the 30th of Khoiakh, while the Osirian figures were still entombed, was connected with the royal cultus is further indicated by the raising of the *Djed*-column by the king in the presence of members of his own family, and assisted by the Memphite high-priest, as an integral part of the rites. The *Djed*-column, which in its conventional form resembled a telegraph post with four or five cross-bars at the top, sometimes is depicted in human form with hands holding the sceptre and flail, and a human head crowned with a pair of horns and two Osirian feathers, or adorned with the *crux ansata* and two arms supporting the solar disk.[42] On the tomb of Kheryaf at Thebes the king in association with the queen and her sixteen daughters holding rattles and sistrums, assisted by a priest, is represented as raising the *Djed*-column with ropes, while a ritual combat was in progress, and herds of cattle were driven round the walls of Memphis.[43] In the hall of the Osirian mysteries at Abydos, the reputed home of the body of Osiris, Seti I and Isis are shown as setting it up between them.[44]

If Sethe is correct in thinking that the Memphite Festival of Sokaris commemorated the accession of Menes, the traditional deified founder of Memphis and of the centralized Egyptian

State,[45] the suggestion of Gardiner that the Feast of Khoiakh was considered the proper occasion for any Pharaoh to ascend the throne,[46] gives a reason for the association of the king and queen with the erection of the pillar, regarded as the embodiment of Osiris, at the beginning of the spring, on the first day of the year.[47] It was this ceremonial action that was thought to secure the rebirth of Osiris in the celestial realms, but as he was entombed as a mummy while the rite was being enacted, it would seem that its primary purpose was that of enabling the living Horus (i.e. the king) to exercise his beneficent function during the forthcoming year.[48]

The sequel of the sacred marriage was the birth of the new Horus who was annually reborn to renew and maintain the vigour and prosperity of the land by the reciprocal effects of the rites on the occupant of the throne. It was only at death that the Pharaoh became the embodiment of Osiris. In life he reigned as Horus, not as the revivified Osiris. Nevertheless, although Osiris was always a dead king he impelled the growth of the grain and the rise of the inundation on which vegetation depended. Therefore, since he personified the emergence of life from death, he too had to be reborn at the turn of the year when the fertilizing waters of the Nile were due to begin their fructifying functions, and the grain was about to sprout as it were from his body. In the capacity of his son and avenger, Horus, the relation of the king to Osiris was so intimate that the renewal of the one depended upon the resuscitation of the other, as is indicated in the scene in the temple of Seti I at Abydos, and in the raising of the *Djed*-column. Sethe has shown, however, that the *Djed* was not exclusively an Osirian symbol. Indeed, it may be regarded as the prototype of rites celebrated all over the world by the king and queen of the May in conjunction with the May-pole, originally for the purpose of renewing the forces of nature at their vital source in the spring. Therefore, behind the raising of the *Djed* lay the fundamental theme of the New Year Festival in which Osiris, Horus and the Pharaoh were the central figures in their several roles in the reinvigoration of the natural order at its dynamic centre. Thus, while the column symbolized Osiris, it was raised by the king in his Horus capacity so that in the ritual combat at Memphis the cry was raised, "I choose the Horus N." according to the name of the Pharaoh whose renewal was being celebrated.[49]

THE SED-FESTIVAL

It was usually on the first day of spring that the renewal of the royal potency was held at the *Sed*-festival, celebrated either thirty years after the accession or at shorter intervals.[50] This is probably the oldest feast of which any trace remains in the records of Ancient Egypt, celebrated probably before the time of Menes.[51] It has been suggested that it goes back to a time when kings were killed on becoming senile, or after a given number of years.[52] This is merely a conjecture, and although regicide not infrequently has been practised in primitive society, as we have seen, expert opinion is divided about the extent and precise significance of the custom.[53] So far as the *Sed*-festival is concerned, it seems to have been a periodic ritual rejuvenescence and re-investiture for the purpose of confirming the beneficent rule of the reigning Pharaoh in his kingdom in his capacity of the sacerdotal mediator between heaven and earth.

Accompanied by the leading official, princes and royal kinsmen, he visited the shrines of the gods erected in the festival court of the temple in which the solemnities were held after the purifications had been duly performed, and made offerings to them. Processions followed for several days in which the king, the statues of the gods and their priesthood, the standard of the royal placenta, fan-bearers and attendants took part, while the Pharaoh himself received pledges of loyalty seated upon his throne. His feet were then ceremonially washed before he entered the robing room, or "palace" as it was called. Proceeding to a double throne the king sat alternately on each of the thrones symbolizing his rule over Upper and Lower Egypt. To assert his legitimate power over the land, he ceremonially crossed the area in the temple court known as the "field".[54] Finally, he was carried on a litter preceded by the standard of the jackal-god Upuaut of Siut to the chapel of Horus of Libya to receive the sceptre, flail and crook of his office. Wrapped in a cloak he was proclaimed four times and received the homage of his subjects and the blessing of the gods through their respective priests. In return the king made appropriate offerings to the gods. Taking off the cloak and clad in a kilt with an animal's tail, he ran four ritual courses, wearing the crown of Upper Egypt and carrying a short sceptre and whisk, and offered his insignia to Upuaut. The proceedings concluded with his visit to the chapels of Horus of Edfu and Seth of Ombos where he shot arrows of victory to the four cardinal points of the compass.[55]

The significance of the symbolism of the festival is obscure. It has been generally thought that the Pharaoh was arrayed in the costume and insignia of Osiris and impersonated him in his death and resurrection.[56] This, however, has been recently denied by Griffiths on the grounds that the purpose of the festival was to renew the existing kingship of the actual occupant of the throne rather than to establish the succession, as in the coronation rite.[57] Whether or not this was done by impersonating the restored Osiris in a death and resurrection ritual, or in the normal Horus capacity renewing the beneficial relations between heaven and earth which they controlled, as Frankfort maintained, in either case the king was strengthened and re-established in his divine office to enable him to exercise his functions in the nation as the incarnation of the gods he embodied and the priest *par excellence* in the sacerdotal hierarchy. Hence the declaration, "thou beginnest thy renewal, beginneth to flourish again like the infant god of the Moon, thou art young again year by year, like Nun at the beginning of the ages, thou art reborn by renewing thy festival of *Sed*."[58]

THE KINGSHIP IN MESOPOTAMIA

In Mesopotamia the kingship occupied a different position from that which it held in the Nile valley. Geographically and climatically the country did not lend itself to a stable social structure unified in a single ruler claiming absolute sovereignty by divine decree as the dynamic centre of the community and of the cosmic order. The unpredictable behaviour of the Tigris and Euphrates in striking contrast to the uniformity of the inundation in Egypt, coupled with the drought in summer and the torrential rainfall in winter, concentrated attention on the local group living under shifting and perennially precarious conditions in an insecure environment.[59] Thus, Mesopotamia came to be divided up into a series of city-states loosely bound together to meet the practical needs of recurrent emergencies governed by a secular ruler or king who in Sumer bore the title of *lugal* (i.e. "great man"), or by the high-priest (*sangu mah*) and the governor (*ensi*) of the city god. The main functions of these officials were to integrate the temple communities of the city, administer the temple revenues and fix the boundaries of its lands.[60] The city-state, therefore, was under a threefold control with the governor, or *ensi,* occupying a permanent position in the body politic and the high-priest, or *sangu-mah,* a corresponding status in the sacred organization, while the king only held office for a limited period at times of crisis, though as these often were of such frequent occurrence the kingship in fact seems to have been permanent in some cities. In any case, by Early Dynastic times one or other of these functionaries, as Frankfort points out, had established himself as a ruler in each of the Mesopotamian cities. For example, in the Gilgamesh Epic the hero of the story, Gilgamesh, is represented as the permanent despotic king of Erech (Uruk) in southern Babylonia, though he is said to have consulted the assembly of the elders before engaging in a military campaign.[61]

If originally the social structure in ancient Mesopotamia was that of a primitive democracy, as Jacobsen maintains,[62] with ultimate power resting in a general assembly of all adult free-men guided by a council of elders, by the beginning of the second millennium Hammurabi did not hesitate to declare that he had been called to be the exalted prince of Babylon by the gods Anu and Bel to make righteousness prevail in the land. No Sumerian king, however, was a cohesive force in the entire realm like Pharaoh in Egypt. In the king-lists, compiled about

2000 B.C., eleven cities are enumerated as having held a dominant position in Sumer. Ur, Erech, Larsa, Nippur and the other cities of the south were centres of small states with local dynasties of rulers subject to the vicissitudes of hegemonies established by conquest. Even when Hammurabi unified the State into an Empire and made Babylon the capital with its chief god, Marduk, as the head of the pantheon, it was only a temporary stability that was attained. The earlier triad of great gods, Anu, Enlil and Ea (Enki), with their respective priesthoods, were but partially eclipsed, each continuing to rule over one of the three divisions of the universe, heaven, earth and the waters. Thus, Marduk was never regarded as the Creator and Source of all the other gods like Re or Ptah in Egypt, being a syncretistic figure with whom the functions of the other gods were identified.

Until the end of the Assyrian empire divine election remained the foundation of kingship but as the favour of the gods could be withdrawn at will the monarchy lacked the secure and unique position it held in Egypt, even though an ancient formula maintained that "kingship descended from heaven" presumably as a gift of the gods. After the Flood in the third millennium B.C. the legendary "divine shepherd" *Dumu-zi* (Tammuz), under the designation of "the Fisherman", alone continued the antediluvian régime in the second Dynasty of Erech, between the god Lugal-banda and Gilgamesh in the traditional king-list. The Shepherd *par excellence* of Babylonia, however, was the historical Sumerian ruler Lugal-zaggesi who at the end of the Early Dynastic period introduced a new title, "King of the Land," under the sanction of Enlil,[63] suggesting a new conception of lordship over the entire country as distinct from local authority in a city-state.

Although these early kings were largely legendary Tammuz-like figures and were thought to have reigned by divine prerogative and selection, as each actual ruler aspired to hegemony his relation with the divine order became less clearly defined. Lugal-zaggesi claimed the sanction of Enlil for his sovereignty over Mesopotamia, and when he was conquered by

Sargon of Akkad the victor called himself "he who rules the Four Quarters", while his son Naram-Sin assumed the title "king of the Four Quarters", which was also borne by the great gods, Enlil, Anu and Shamash.[64] The use of this divine determinative was continued in the Third Dynasty of Ur, and to eleven kings of Ur and Isin it is appended in a Tammuz liturgy.[65] It was not, however, until Marduk was exalted over all the gods of the earth by Anu and Enlil, and at the same time declared Babylon to be the head of all the cities with Hammurabi as its ruler, that the kingship was brought into relation with a composite deity at all comparable to Re and Osiris in Egypt. But his son Nabu did not reign in the person of the earthly sovereign like Horus, and so while Marduk remained the supreme god and creator of mankind, instead of being relegated to the realm of the dead as in the case of Osiris before he was celestialized, Mesopotamian kings never attained to the divine status assigned to Pharaoh as god incarnate and the pivot of the social structure. They were not themselves divine though they were endowed with divinity by virtue of their office and its insignia in which it was inherent.[66] As human agents on earth of the gods they were primarily priests, and their principal function was the exercise of their sacerdotal duties, leaving little or no time or opportunity for secular rule and administration beyond the interpretation of the will of the gods as the official representative of their people.

The government of the highly developed temple organization and the performance of the seasonal rituals, spells and incantations, and the interpretation of omens, required an elaborate hierarchy under a chief priest, or *urigallu,* appointed by the king after divine consultation. It was he who functioned at the New Year Festival and the other great seasonal rituals, assisted by the *kalu*-priests who sang the liturgies and were responsible for the temple music in general. Exorcisms were in the hands of the *ashipu*- and *mashmashu*-priests as the specialists in deliverance from and protection against all kinds of evil influences, while the *barû,* as we have seen, were seers who observed the omens and interpreted dreams. Priestesses also were employed in the

I

service of the gods, and several of the kings dedicated their
daughters to the temples, where they might act as sacred
prostitutes at the great festivals.

THE DEIFICATION OF KINGS

The deification of kings in Mesopotamia, in fact, was closely
associated with a sacred marriage of the occupant of the throne
with a goddess who in the person of a priestess had chosen a
king to act as her bridegroom at the Annual Festival. Indeed,
Professor Frankfort suggests that it may well be that "only those
kings were deified who had been commanded by the goddess
to share her couch. In a general way the kings who use the
divine determinative before their names belong to the same
period as the texts mentioning the marriage of kings and
goddesses; and we have seen that some kings adopted the determinative, not at the beginning but at a later stage of their
reigns. If we assume that they did so on the strength of a divine
command, we remain within the normal scope of Mesopotamian thought, while the view that a king should have pre-
sumed of his own accord to pass the barrier between the human
and the divine conflicts with everything we know of Mesopotamian beliefs."[67] In support of this contention he quotes a
text known as "the deification of Lipit-Ishtar" in which that
king (Lipit-Ishtar) was deified as a preliminary to his sacred
marriage with the mother-goddess Ishtar by being fused with a
fertility god Urash, as son of Enlil, in order to enable him to
exercise his beneficent functions in the promotion of the prosperity of the land and to prolong his life.[68]

Whether or not the divine kingship in Mesopotamia was
confined to those kings who had become the bridegroom of the
goddess, it was apparently as the servants of the gods that they
attained their divine status rather than, as in Egypt, by virtue of
their heavenly birth and sonship. It would also seem that the
sacred marriage was an integral element in the royal ritual from
very early times. Thus, the annual marriage of the shepherd-
god Dumu-zi (Tammuz) to Inanna (Ishtar), the Sumerian
mother goddess, was celebrated at Isin in southern Mesopotamia

at the end of the third millennium B.C. by the king of the city, in the capacity of the divine bridegroom (i.e. Dumu-zi), having nuptial relations with a priestess, identified with Inanna, "to guard the life-breath of all lands"; in other words, to ensure prosperity in the forthcoming year.[69] After the physical act of union on a couch decorated with grass and plants, and described as a throne, a banquet was held to symbolize and make efficacious providential bounty.

Therefore, as in Egypt the emphasis was on the Pharaohs as the living Horus and son of Re, so in Mesopotamia it was on the earthly instrument of the goddess and the priestess who occupied the central position in the Annual Festival as the life-bestowing agents. In these rites the bride (the goddess) was the active partner while her bridegroom (the king) was her obedient servant, whereas in the Nile valley the queen was visited by her royal husband in all his divine majesty and potency to beget a successor to the throne and the upholder of the natural order.

THE SUFFERING GOD AND THE SORROWING MOTHER

As the prototype of the Pharaoh Osiris was at once a dead king, lord of the nether world and the author and giver of the life of the grain personified in the fructifying water of the Nile, living and reigning in his son Horus, whereas in Mesopotamia Tammuz, "the faithful son of the waters which came from the earth" (Dumu-zi), was a suffering god dependent upon the goddess, Ishtar, his mother-spouse. It was her annual descent to the underworld in search of Tammuz that was enacted in relation to the decline of life in the drought of summer and its revival when the beneficent waters of the Tigris and Euphrates flooded the valleys in the later winter.[70]

The withering sun was too devastating to be the source of life and bounty, as in the fertile oasis of the Nile. But the cyclic succession of the seasons, nevertheless, was under the control of a vegetation year-god who died in the scorching heat of summer and was revived when the revitalizing waters brought renewed life and hope. But neither the Tigris nor the Euphrates inspired the dwellers in Mesopotamia with the same sense of assurance in a static cosmic order that the never-failing inundation of the Nile gave to the ancient Egyptians. The Babylonians depended too much on the vagaries of an uncertain rainfall and were menaced by the fear of the incalculable floods of the two great rivers.[71] Therefore, it was not so easy to harmonize in a royal ritual order the life of the community with that of the natural environment.

Under these unstable conditions the ecclesiastical organization was concentrated on the social and sacred structure of the City-states. But since the power and influence of a particular deity waxed and waned with the course of political events, the pantheon was in a constant state of flux. Thus, Marduk rose to pre-eminence by the transference of political jurisdiction from Nippur to Babylon. His triumph, however, was short-lived and like his predecessors, Anu and Enlil, he was at the mercy of the fortunes of his cult-centre, even though in the creation story the oversight of the universe had been assigned to him by the gods after his victory over the forces of chaos and evil, personified by Tiamat and re-enacted annually at the New Year Festival.

This cosmogony, known as the *Enuma elish*, appeared in Akkadia in the middle of the second millennium B.C. when Babylon was the political and cultural centre, but behind it lay an earlier version in which Marduk replaced Tammuz. In this capacity he became the dying and reviving year-god personifying the generative power and preserving the harmony between nature and society on which the prosperity of the community depended. In some respects he had points of contact with Osiris and his counterparts in the Ancient Near East.[72] Nevertheless, the suffering god of Mesopotamia was a complex figure with peculiarities of his own which differentiated him from other comparable divinities elsewhere in the Fertile Crescent and the Aegean. As Tammuz he was the son and lover of the goddess and, therefore, his relation to Ishtar was quite different from that of Osiris to Isis. He was never represented as a dead god who lived and reigned in a posthumous son like Horus. When he had passed through the waters of the deep and visited the nether regions he returned in his own person to renew the face of the earth in spring as its generative force. In the Osirian cult the grain sprouted from the mummy of the hero just as Isis conceived Horus by hovering over his corpse, whereas in Mesopotamia Tammuz was brought again from the grave by Ishtar in all the fulness of his virile personality. Thus, he became responsible for the revival of the new life which burst forth when the spring and autumn rains renewed the parched ground by virtue of his relations with the Mother-goddess rather than by that of his own inherent vitality. Therefore, the Babylonian suffering god was inseparable from the sorrowing goddess who was at once his mother and his spouse, the author and giver of life and the liberator from death.

Now, it was in the Tammuz liturgies and the Annual Festival that this theme was enacted and brought into relation with the royal ritual, the renewal of nature being represented as dependent upon the sacred marriage of the king and the queen in the guise of the liberated god and the mother goddess. In the liturgies the death of the shepherd-god (Tammuz or Dumuzi) was celebrated with bitter lamentation and wailing,[73] and the singing of dirges over the effigy of the dead god, when the scorched earth seemed to threaten a return of the primeval woe and desolation that fell upon temple, city, people and nature while Ishtar wandered in barren fields and empty sheepfolds during her sorrowful search for Tammuz in the underworld.[74] From these sinister regions the cry of the suffering shepherd-god was echoed in the laments of the priests and people until he was released by the goddess and restored to the upper world as her "resurrected child". Then sorrow was turned into joy and defeat into victory, celebrated by a royal banquet furnished with gifts from deified kings (e.g. Ur-Nammu, Pur-Sin) offered to Ishtar to rejoice her heart. The liturgies end with a doxology addressed to the reunited gods in the bridal chamber for having restored fecundity as the new life springs forth after the rains.

THE NEW YEAR FESTIVAL

In this recreative ritual Sumerian rulers as the servants of the gods played the rôle of Tammuz-Dumuzi incarnating the creative forces of spring through union with the goddess Inanna-Ishtar, the source of all life, with whom respectively the king and the priestess became identified for the purpose of engaging in a sacred marriage as the culmination of the rites. Thus, in Babylon where Marduk replaced Tammuz as the central figure in the spring festival known in Akkadian as *Akitu,* his defeat of Tiamat, the primeval water-goddess, and her demons was enacted in the cult-legend (the *Enuma elish,* or creation epic). On the fifth day the king was conducted to the shrine of Marduk escorted by the priests, and left there alone. The high-priest thereupon emerged from the inner sanctuary where the statue of the god stood, and divested the monarch of his regalia, slapped his face, pulled his ears, forced him to his knees before the image, and extracted from him a negative confession:

I have not sinned, O Lord of the lands,
I have not been negligent regarding thy divinity,
I have not destroyed Babylon.

After a kind of absolution the insignia were restored to him and he was duly re-established in his royal office.

The reinstated king then summoned each god in a carefully arranged order of precedence to leave the chapel, holding his sceptre in his hand. "Taking the hand of Marduk", he proceeded to the great hall to receive the special divine power conferred upon him. A procession to the Festival House (*Bit Akitu*) on the outskirts of the city was formed representing apparently the victorious army of the gods as depicted on the copper doors of the *Bit Akitu* of Assur.[75] It was here that the victory over Tiamat was celebrated at a great banquet[76] before a return was made to the city for the consummation of the sacred marriage in the *Esagila,* enacted by the king and a priestess of royal birth,[77] perhaps in a *gigunu* erected on one of the stages of the ziggurat and decorated with greenery.[78] The destinies of the coming year were then fixed as at the creation when "the table of destiny" was bestowed upon Marduk as the champion of the gods when he was elected to the kingship and given absolute power.

In Mesopotamia, however, the monarchy was a social institution rather than the dynamic centre of the cosmic order, even though kings reigned by divine prerogative and selection. In Assyria, in fact, they stood outside nature, the control of the processes of which belonged exclusively to the gods. In Babylonia the city-god and his ruler, even when raised to temporary supremacy, as in the case of Marduk at Babylon, were never conceived in terms of a single cosmic Power, operative in and through a permanent static universe, as unchangeable as it was all-embracing. Neither the king, the central government, nor the nation at large had an assured and completely secure position rooted and grounded in a transcendent unifying principle standing over and above the mutable order. Marduk rose to pre-eminence by the transference of political jurisdiction from Nippur to Babylon. His triumph, however, was short-lived, and like his predecessors, Anu and Enlil, he was at the mercy of the fortunes of his cult-centre. He was in truth a "dying god", and neither his supremacy nor the Empire in which he held predominance, so magnificently organized by Hammurabi, were destined to survive the death of the founder.

THE CANAANITE TEXTS FROM RAS SHAMRA

Nevertheless, the recurrence of the Tammuz-Marduk cult drama in the Canaanite ritual texts discovered between 1930 and 1933 at Ras Shamra (Ugarit) on the north coast of Syria, shows how fundamental was the divine kingship and its theme in the Ancient East. These tablets unfortunately are neither complete nor consecutive, and are inscribed in the characters of an hitherto unknown cuneiform script. But those that have come to light leave little room for doubt concerning their purpose and significance since they constitute a part of the archives of a local temple in the Amarna Age in the middle of the second millennium B.C. However fragmentary, they nevertheless record a traditional mythology concerning the exploits and adventures of a sky-god named Aleyan, son of Baal, and his enemy Mot, son of El, lord of the underworld.[79]

After a struggle with a dragon, Yam or Nahar, culminating in the victory of Aleyan and his installation in a royal palace, his combat with Mot is recorded.[80] In the heat of summer Aleyan is represented as having been killed by his adversary, his descent into the underworld being symbolized by the withering plants and parched ground during the season of drought. Then follows an account of the search for his body by Anath his consort, the Ishtar of the episode, and her encounter with Mot, who feigned ignorance of the whereabouts of Aleyan, and tried to persuade her to secure water from the nether regions to revive the earth. This she refused to do, and instead seized him, split his body with a ritual sickle (*harpé*), winnowed him, scorched him in the fire, ground him in a mill, scattered his flesh over the fields, like the dismembered body of Osiris, and gave him to the birds to eat. In short, she treated him as the reaped grain. Eventually after many conflicts with other gods in which Aleyan was always victorious in the end, he (Aleyan) was restored as king.[81] Mot, who in the meantime had been revived, was urged by the Sun-goddess to capitulate since further resistance was futile. El "overturned his (Mot's) throne" and "broke the sceptre of his dominion". Therefore, the adversary surrendered and acknowledged the kingship of Aleyan. The Sun-goddess was then commended for her assistance in the fray which thus ended in the defeat of drought and death and the re-establishment of fertility on the earth.

If the interpretation of these fragmentary and confused texts is largely a matter of conjecture, that they were New Year liturgical rituals rather than, as Virolleaud maintained, poetic legends,[82] seems to be highly probable.[83] The central theme is the battle between life and death in nature and the measures taken to secure the renewal of the beneficent forces of fertility at their ultimate source, along the lines of the kingship cultus in the Ancient East. Moreover, there are indications that the rites concluded with a sacred marriage to ensure the continuance of the fructifying forces, celebrated by the temple priests and priestesses in their official capacities, and it is not improbable that the king as the incarnation of El had nuptial relations with the high-priestess.[84] The Nikal-Kotarot text in the Ras Shamra series seems to refer to the marriage of the Moon-god and the moon goddess,[85] describing perhaps, as Gaster suggests,[86] the wooing of the goddess Nikal by the god Y-r-h in the form of a wedding song. Since it was recited at "the hour when at the sinking of the sun, the moon is to be seen", it may have led up to a nuptial ceremony based on the precedent of the sacred marriage of the divine prototypes, the new moon being propitious at childbirth. Similarly, in the parallel Danel text, the childless king (Danel) is represented as beseeching El to give him a son, and after fasting and lamentation he is said to repair to the nuptial couch to beget the offspring, as in a royal connubium.[87]

Therefore, notwithstanding the confusion of the theme in the present condition of the texts, there is reason to think that they contain a Canaanite version of the Tammuz-Marduk cult. The death of the hero Aleyan-Baal, lord of the rain and verdure, and his descent into the underworld would appear to symbolize the decline in the processes of vegetation and their subsequent revival enacted at the Annual Festival and personified by the king. This ritual, as we have seen, culminated in Babylonia in a sacred marriage as the union of heaven and earth to promote the fertility of the crops, the beasts and mankind, and secure the proper functioning of the natural universe and of human society. By driving away or destroying the malign forces of decay, death, hunger and barreness, and establishing right relations with divine beneficence, the streams of life were re-enforced through a ritual drama in which the king and queen, personifying the gods and goddesses responsible for providential bounty, played their respective roles in the promotion of the well-being of the community.

THE THEOCRATIC COVENANT AND THE MONARCHY IN ISRAEL

After the settlement of nomadic Hebrew tribes in Canaan, the establishment of a monarchy in Israel might be expected to follow this same pattern, as in other agricultural communities in the Fertile Crescent. There was, however, an important distinction which differentiated the invaders from the indigenous civilization. Some of the Hebrew tribes had been welded together in the desert under the powerful leadership of Moses in a peculiar covenant relation with one particular deity, Yahweh. The origins of this Western Semitic Supreme Being, whose name occurs as *Ya, Yami, Yahweh,* in Aramaean, Canaanite, Babylonian and Hebrew inscriptions and documents, are obscure.[88] It is possible that he was known in Canaan before the Israelite settlement since the name *Ahi-yahu* occurs on a cuneiform tablet found at Taanach dated between 2000 and 1500 B.C. But, even so, he could have been only a minor god among the Canaanites. Primarily he was a desert deity, prominent among the Kenites where he may have been worshipped by Jethro, the father-in-law of Moses, before he became known to the future leader of the Hebrews in the theophany at the burning bush. According to the J narrative in the Book of Genesis, his cult had been practised by the ancestors of Israel from the time of the mythical Enoch,[89] and unless he was in some sense the god of Abraham, Isaac and Jacob (i.e. the ancestral god of the Hebrew tribes) he could hardly have become the rallying point of the oppressed captives in Egypt,[90] despite the contrary view adopted by the E and P documents.[91] In any case, he stands in a different tradition from Re and Osiris in Egypt, Tammuz and Marduk in Babyonia and Aleyan-Baal in Canaan.

If the popular Hebrew etymology of the divine name be accepted, the form "Yahweh" may be interpreted as "He who is", or "He Who causes to be"—a conception not very far removed from that of the more abstract aspects of Egyptian solar theology, or, indeed, of the Thomist concept of Deity in scholastic philosophy. But the immediate associations of Yahweh were nationalistic rather than cosmic or ontological. He was essentially the god of the desert tribes, and if the Kenites were largely responsible for the introduction of Yahwism among the Hebrews, it was with Israel that his covenant was established, before the conquest of Palestine. Since in ancient society a change of territory normally involved a transference of allegiance to the gods of the land,[92] that he retained his unique position in Israel after it had established itself in an agricultural country in spite of the powerful influence of the indigenous cults, shows how deeply laid was the corporate conception of the Sinaitic covenant in the Yahwistic minority.

That the nature and attributes of the Palestinian baals were transferred to Yahweh in pre-exilic Israel is beyond dispute, and in the sanctuaries devoted solely or primarily to him the cultus was indistinguishable from that of the Canaanite occupants. In fact, the struggle between the two religions continued until the Exile in the sixth century B.C., as is shown by the prophetic denunciations of the syncretism that prevailed in the days of Amos and Hosea, Isaiah and Jeremiah, and, as we have seen, found a home in the central sanctuary at Jerusalem.[93] Nevertheless, Palestine officially was "the land of Yahweh", and his relation to the country of his adoption was not identical with that of the gods who ruled over the Nile valley in the person of the reigning Pharaoh, or of those who rose and fell in power and prestige with the changing fortunes of the city-states in Mesopotamia.

In the Hebrew theocracy the bond between the nation and its god was dependent upon the observance of the covenant (*běrîth,* i.e. the cultus) the first condition of which was absolute loyalty to Yahweh, and him alone, and obedience to his commands. If this ideal of the prophets and the post-exilic priestly school was never realized until after the dissolution of the monarchy, it was inherent in the mono-Yahwist tradition. While Saul and David and their successors exercised sacrificial functions like divine kings in the neighbouring countries[94] they were not intermediaries, still less were they earthly embodiments of Yahweh. Thus, although Saul was "turned into another man" at the time of his anointing, when the spirit of Yahweh came mightily upon him, it left him and descended upon his successor when the Benjamite leader fell from divine favour.[95]

To arrive at an accurate estimate of the actual situation in respect of the kingship in Israel before the Exile is very difficult because the records have been distorted under the influence of the prophetic movement. The representation of the monarchy as an affront to Yahweh[96] may have been occasioned by the prevailing conception of the kingship in the Fertile Crescent being contrary to the interpretation placed upon the Sinaitic covenant by the eighth century prophets. Nevertheless, although the Hebrew monarch was regarded as the anointed of Yahweh he was never the dynamic centre of the social structure and the religious organization, as was the Egyptian Pharaoh or the deified bridegroom of the Mother-goddess as in Mesopotamia. The emphasis in Israel was on the covenant, first with Abraham, then with Moses, and finally with the house of David. But the theocratic relationship was with God not the king. Thus, the northern kingdom did not hesitate to repudiate its inheritance in the house of the son of Jesse when his grandson refused to listen to their demands.[97] Indeed, notwithstanding Nathan's decree that the Davidic dynasty should endure for ever,[98] in fact the Hebrew monarchy was brought to an end summarily at the time of the Exile in the sixth century B.C., and it has never been restored.

THE DAVIDIC KING

To resolve this dilemma the royal office and the divine promises associated with it were re-interpreted in the post-exilic period in terms of a Messianic reign of a Davidic king and an eternal priesthood of the elusive Melchizedek, "king of Salem and priest of the most high God, without descent, having neither beginning nor end of life."[99] In Israel king, priest and prophet always had been inseparably bound together so that, despite the attempts of later writers to separate their respective functions and status in the nation, no rigid distinctions can be maintained. Kings from the time of Saul onwards offered sacrifice, wore the ephod and prophesied in their royal capacity as the head of the priesthood, the anointed of Yahweh and his accredited messenger (*melek*).[100] David took over the priesthood of the god Zedek at Jerusalem when he captured the city and placed himself at the head of the hierarchy. Zadok and Nathan served under him as *kohen* and *nabi* respectively, while prophets as well as priests were grouped round sanctuaries and had their part in the ritual procedures.[101]

The covenant with the house of David, however, had a wider significance than the monarchy and was independent of the earthly throne since behind it lay the covenant of Yahweh with the nation as a whole, thereby differentiating it from that of the surrounding civilizations in the Nile valley, Mesopotamia and Syria. The Hebrew king was a sacred person and exercised sacerdotal functions, but he rules only by divine permission and the will of the people, just as the priesthood was secure only so long as it was faithful in the discharge of its duties.[102] Thus, both kingship and priesthood lacked stability, the unifying and consolidating force being the covenant of which they were the instruments and agents. It was not until later that the Davidic king acquired a Messianic significance as the firstborn of many brethren,[103] walking in meekness and righteousness,[104] having a priesthood different from that of Aaron and Zadok and their descendants, called by a new name (viz., that of Melchizedek) which suggested righteousness (*sedek*) and prosperity.[105]

After the fall of the monarchy the title "Messiah" (*māshiakh*) was variously applied to kings, priests and rulers like Cyrus, Zerubbabel and Simon Maccabaeus who acted as prince, priest and governor, even though, as in the case of Simon, they were not in the direct line of the high-priestly family.[106] It was, in fact, assigned to any deliverer who was regarded as the agent of Yahweh and partook of His attributes, or even to the nation as a whole.[107] The Maccabaean princes were not of the lines of Zadok but they were certainly engaged in a mighty struggle against those who were regarded as the enemies of Yahweh. It was their purpose and function to bring "salvation" (i.e. victory) to the holy nation and so to exercise what was virtually a "messianic" role in the deeply laid conviction that God always intervened through his appointed agents. Moreover, in the apocalyptic movement that arose out of the prevailing conditions of widespread unrest when the sacrificial worship of the temple and the all-sufficiency of the Torah were beginning to prove inadequate to the needs of a much-tried people, the vindication of divine justice in the presence of innocent suffering and persecution was felt to require a supernatural intervention. Therefore, in the transitional period between B.C. and A.D. the time was ripe for a new interpretation of Messiahship such as found expression in Jewish apocalyptic and its Christian re-interpretation.

THE SUFFERING MESSIAH

It has generally been maintained that in post-exilic Judaism the concepts of the Davidic Messiah, the Son of Man and the Servant of the Lord were quite distinct and that it remained for Christianity to bring them together in a single complex Figure. This doubtless is true, but, nevertheless, they were not wholly unrelated eschatological hopes, and, as Professor Rowley has said, beneath all their varying forms and phases there is a deep underlying unity of conception.[108] It has long been a matter of debate among theologians to what extent, if at all, the anointed of Yahweh was expected to fulfil his office through suffering and death in terms of the Isaianic Servant Songs.[109] While the weight of expert opinion has been against the theory of a suffering Messiah in pre-Christian Judaism,[110] several scholars have taken the contrary view.[111] Indeed, Dr Engnell has not hesitated to affirm that the Servant of Yahweh in Deutero-Isaiah was the Davidic Messiah.[112] But, as the Septuagint shows (Is. xlii. 1), the hero of the poems is Israel as a nation, and his sufferings appear to be those endured by Jehoiachin and the exiles of 597 B.C. and their predecessors in 586.[113]

The idea of a suffering Messiah first appears in Rabbinic literature in the Messiah ben Ephraim, in the post-Christian Targum of pseudo-Jonathan and in the Babylonian Targum. Later it recurs in the Targum of the Song of Songs. If it had been familiar when the Gospel tradition was in process of formulation the disciples of Jesus could hardly have been represented as being confused and bewildered by his announcement that in his Messianic role he must suffer.[114] Neither the figure of the Davidic King nor that of the Son of Man could have been equated in their minds with the Suffering Servant. If in fact he did apply to himself the role of the Son of Man, as is doubted by some modern commentators,[115] it did not suggest to his contemporaries the idea of suffering, nor prevent his followers from regarding his death when it actually occurred as the tragic end of all their hopes and aspirations. But once the significance of the Servant prophecies was realized in relation to the Messiahship of Jesus it was the crucifixion and all that this involved and implied which made the most permanent impression upon the early Christian Church. Calvary was the one factor which above all others was destined to determine for Christianity the conception not only of the Messianic office and its purposes, but also of the whole redemptive process. The functions first attributed to the Davidic King and then invested with apocalyptic glory in the supernatural Son of Man became transfigured with suffering in the person of the defeated yet victorious Saviour of mankind who, it would seem, in some measure in his own Messianic consciousness applied the Servant prophecies to himself.

There can be no doubt, however, that in the days of his flesh his disciples, as well as the rest of their compatriots, were looking for a Davidic Messiah to the exclusion of any idea of suffering and death as part of this office and vocation. Nevertheless, in the Messianic tradition the three figures, the King, the Son of Man and the Servant, not only had a common pattern of thought[116] but also retained a common theme very deeply laid in the Kingship myth and ritual of the Ancient East, where, as we have seen, in Mesopotamia the cult of the suffering god and the mourning goddess gave expression to the anxiety inherent in an uncertain destiny and unstable environment. As a combination of weakness and strength the defeated hero was a virile figure triumphing over death and the powers of evil, who, unlike Osiris in Egypt, was restored to the land of the living, reflecting the annual ebb and flow in nature.

In Christian tradition this theme of the dying and reviving god was brought into relation with that of the conquering Christ under the apocalyptic symbolism of the lamb slain from the foundation of the world to ensure the final triumph of good over evil and of life over death. The malign forces were personified in the dragon and his host, and their destination was celebrated by the sacred marriage of the victor (the Lamb) as the prelude to the reign of universal peace, prosperity and righteousness.[117] Behind this imagery lay a complex mythology derived from Babylonian, Egyptian, Iranian and possibly Mandean sources, but however much Christian Messiology may have been influenced by current and more remote apocalyptic mythology; Jewish and pagan, it was unquestionably the historic Jesus who in the first instance produced the conviction of his Messiahship among his intimate followers. No doubt the cult of the kingship, the ritual combat, the sacred marriage and the Heavenly Man exercised a formative influence on the development of the doctrine of redemption. We have seen, however, that the Frazerian conception of the divine kingship did not in fact exist anywhere in the Fertile Crescent in precisely the manner set forth in *The Golden Bough,* as has been commonly supposed in recent years, and least of all in Palestine among the Hebrews, notwithstanding the fact that there are traces of the royal cultus and its humiliated king having survived in Israel during and after the monarchy. But it was around the figure of Christ the King that at the break-up of the Roman Empire, and in the Dark Ages that followed, the social structure and its moral values found a new unifying centre with a priesthood and cultus deeply laid in the civilization in which Christendom emerged.

CHAPTER V

Priesthood and Sacrifice

THE powerful influence exercised by the priesthood as a stabilizing force in the structure of society has been due above all to the primary function of the institution in the control of the supernatural forces upon which the well-being of mankind has been thought to depend. This has found its fullest expression in sacrifice. As the king was the son or instrument of the god he embodied or served as the divinely commissioned agent, so the priest, through a process of delegation, has been the wielder of transcendental potency as the master of the sacrificial oblation, and all that this has implied in the maintenance of a vital bond between man and the sacred order.

THE NATURE AND PURPOSE OF SACRIFICE

Although the origin and significance of sacrifice has long been a matter of debate, the essential element in the institution clearly is centred in the offering of a sacred victim for the purpose of establishing beneficial relations between a source of spiritual strength and those in need of such strength. This relationship may be one of communion, when strength is imparted to man or to a deity and a bond of union is effected with the beneficent powers who either participate in a communal meal, or become the actual sacrifice by a process of identification. Conversely, it may be one whereby a human weakness, error or transgression is held to be "covered", "wiped out", neutralized or carried away by a piacular offering.[1] From these primary considerations secondary motives have arisen, such as the notion of securing the favour of an offended god by offerings which are in the nature of fines rather than of efficacious oblations, made either in kind or money, as in the later Hebrew ritual. Honorific free-will or thank-offerings also have been made in grateful recognition of the mercies and blessings received. Thus, the first-fruits of the crops and the firstlings of man and beast, and many other gift sacrifices, have been conceived more in the nature of honoraria, sometimes not far removed from bribes, on the utilitarian *do-ut-des* principle— "I give that thou mayest give".

The fundamental conception of the institution of sacrifice seems to have been the giving of life to promote and preserve life, and to maintain a vital relationship between the worshipper and the object of worship in order to gain free communication between the natural and the transcendent orders.[2] When E. B. Tylor enunciated his "gift theory" of the origin of sacrifice in terms of offerings to secure the favour or minimize the hostility of supernatural beings[3] he forgot that the word *dare*, employed in Ovid's maxim, *do-ut-des,* contains the implication of placing oneself in relation to, and participating in, a second person by an instrumental agent which is part of oneself. As Van der Leeuw has pointed out, "to give is to convey something of oneself to the strange being, so that a firm bond may be forged."[4] Thus, a victim is first consecrated to the service of the altar and so identified with both the offerers and the recipient of the oblation. It is then killed in order that its life-giving blood may be poured out sacrificially to establish a "blood covenant" between them. The gift is the inherent vital principle and the ritual shedding of blood is the giving rather than the taking of life, death being merely incidental in the process of liberation. As Loisy says, "to die is but to live again; life issues from death, and death is the condition and means of life. To destroy in order to create, to liberate through death, the power that lies latent in a living being."[5]

SACRIFICE AND THE SACRAMENTAL MEAL

Approaching the rite from the side of the sacramental meal, Robertson Smith elaborated his theory of the "theanthropic animal", at once god and kinsman, as the source of sacrifice of the communal type.[6] Frazer, he thought, had proved the existence of animal totemic sacraments involving communion in the flesh and blood of the sacred animal; and since by eating the god sacramentally man absorbs its nature or life into his own, he shares its divine attributes and enters into a mystic union with the theanthropic species. Therefore, "the fundamental idea of sacrifice", he maintained "is not that of a sacred tribute, but of communion between the god and his worshippers by joint participation in the living flesh and blood of a sacred victim." But the kinship of man with divinity in a common meal is not necessarily a sacramental communion in which the deity and his worshippers enter into a vital relationship by the latter partaking of sacred food. Moreover, the totem in primitive society is not a sacrificial victim, as Robertson Smith supposed, and priesthood plays no part in totemic rites like the Intichiuma ceremonies in Central Australia on which Frazer and Durkheim largely relied. The totem is the potent agent in welding together the clan into a sacred brotherhood united in a common relationship with its supernatural ally. The communion is with the totem rather than with the sacred food itself, and through the totem with the group as a whole. The outward and visible become the channel of the inward and spiritual, independent of sacerdotal intervention, to enable the human group to enter into communion with the supernatural sources of its life (i.e. the totem), and to share in its animating essence. The relationship thus established is sacramental but not sacrificial.

EXPIATION AND ATONEMENT

In sacrifice the consecration and destruction of the victim as an intermediary are fundamental.[7] In it (i.e. the victim) the sacred and the profane are fused, and through it the supernatural potency is transmitted either positively to the sacrificer or negatively away from him by a process of desacralization. In the first case divine life and its qualities are transferred from their ultimate source and a bond of union is established between the sacred and the profane. In the second type of sacrifice —the piacular and expiatory—harmful influences and dangerous tabu conditions are rendered innocuous. Death or sickness is met with a fresh outpouring of life, and atonement for evil, or misfortune incurred, is made by way of expiation to re-establish a right relationship with the sacred order and the gods on whom well-being depends. The source of the evil may lie in an offended deity whose anger has been aroused and whose hostility has been encountered by reason of an offence committed wittingly or unwittingly, ranging from the breach of a tabu to an ethical fault. To restore right relations and to blot out the offence, expiation has to be made by appropriate offerings, usually at the hands of those set apart for the purpose in a sacerdotal capacity. If the evil is in the nature of a pollution contracted through contact with some defiling object, such as a corpse or a newly delivered mother, the contagion may be wiped out, covered, or in some way removed by cathartic agents (e.g., water or blood), propitiatory offerings, or carried away by transference to running water or a scapegoat, which may or may not be killed as a sacrificial victim.

SUBSTITUTION AND VICARIOUS SACRIFICE

Underlying these expiatory redemptive offerings is the idea of substitution, the life of the victim being offered and received in the place of the sacrificer (or the person for whom it is made) with whom it is identified by the act of consecration, so that virtually he is giving part of himself.[8] As Emerson recognized, a gift to be true must be the flowing of the giver to the receiver and of the recipient to the donor, a principle which finds its highest expression in altruistic self-giving wherein a life is laid down voluntarily to give life in greatest abundance and to eliminate harmful and evil forces and conditions. The animal victim can only assume this rôle by being set apart as a substitute for, and an efficacious symbol of, the offerer with whom it becomes identified. At a higher level the king in the capacity of the suffering or dying god combined the office of victim and chief worshipper, either actually, through a ritual act, or by means of a substitute, immolating himself on behalf of the community over which he reigned to renew its life at its vital centre.

By offering himself vicariously he became at once both priest and victim, sacrificing his life in a representative capacity. But the dynamic centre of the sacrificial act was the life-giving and death-defeating offering, the oblation of which caused the vitalizing stream continually to flow. The reigning monarch might rise and set like the sun from which so often he claimed descent, but the throne remained unshaken because as the source of potency its occupant was for ever young and virile, crowned with glory, honour and power. Since he was merely the representative in an instrumental sense of the ultimate source of all that he embodied and transmitted in this capacity he was required either to immolate himself as a patriotic duty when his natural forces abated, or to provide a substitute to play the fatal rôle in his stead, as among the Aztecs in Mexico.[9] It was the offering that mattered. Therefore, when the sacrificial action was transferred solely to the ritual sphere, as in Vedic India, the professional priesthood became supreme and the king receded more and more into the background. The Brahmins then were left in absolute control of the cosmic situation as the masters of the technique upon which the existence of the universe and of the gods depended.

THE BRAHMANIC CONCEPTION OF PRIESTHOOD AND SACRIFICE

Thus, the king in the Vedic literature is a member of the Kshatriya, or warrior caste, and, therefore, he was subordinate to the Brahmins who occupied the first place in the segmentation of Hindu society. In the Code of Manu, however, variously dated from 300 B.C. to A.D. 150, he is described as "a great deity in human form" whom for the protection of the world Brahman created from the eternal particles of Indra, of Yama, of the Sun, of the Moon, of Fire, of Varuna and of Kubera, thereby assigning to him divine status. "He showers benefits upon his realm as Indra sends rain upon the earth; he must be as omnipresent as the wind; he must control all his subjects as does Yama; he must draw revenues from his kingdom as the sun draws water from the earth; he must be brilliant and blazing anger against crime like the radiance of the fire; he must bind criminals as the fetters of Varuna enchain the wicked; he must be beautiful in the sight of his subjects as is the moon in the eyes of mankind; like the earth he must support all his subjects."[10]

Similarly, in the Rig-veda he is equated with the sun and the sky through his relationship with Mitra, Agni, Indra and Varuna.[11] This association with the gods who gave life and birth made him the bestower of universal beneficence. As the Sun-god he was the motive force and fertilizing agent; as Mitra he was Lord of Justice; as Indra, the controller of storms and the giver of victory; as Varuna he regulated the moral order and upheld the universe; as Agni he was equated with the sacred fire and the sacrificial flame by which all creation was sustained. But since he was not himself invested with authority to offer sacrifice, it was the priests as the official sacrificers who upheld all things in heaven and earth by their sacerdotal functions, and it was they who controlled the gods whose attributes and status they assumed.

"The universe is the Brahmin's", says Manu, "for the Brahmin is entitled to this universe by his superiority and his birth."[12] Thus, the priesthood in Vedic India usurped the position previously held by the divine kingship in the supreme control of the fortunes of heaven and earth, of the gods and men, and of the state; though not infrequently priests worked in the service of princes, sometimes apparently, as in the case of sacerdotal families like the Vashishtras and Visvamitras, assisting them in battle. But as the masters of the all-sustaining sacrifice they were able to bring within their sphere of absolute jurisdiction every aspect of creative supernatural power. This was facilitated by the conception of a single cosmic divine principle, *rta,* beyond the gods governing alike the mundane and the transcendental orders, and associated in particular with Varuna, the king of heaven, and with Agni the lord of sacrifice. Consequently, it only required this fundamental principle (*rta*) to be made subject to the control of the Brahmanic ritual technique as the "womb of *rta*",[13] to establish the complete supremacy of the priestly offering and all that this implied.

In bringing together all the gods involved in the sacrificial ritual, thought moved away from the individual and personal towards a pantheistic interpretation of the universe. The wielders of supreme power were manipulators of an impersonal dynamic process immanent in the cosmic order. Thus, in the Rig-Veda creation was represented in terms of the sacrifice of the Primal Man, Purusha, with his thousand heads, eyes and feet pervading the earth, while in the Brahmanas, Prajapati, as the Lord of Production and the personification of the creative principle, was at once Creator and creation. Being the ruler of macrocosm and microcosm he pervaded the universal cosmic and moral order (*rta*) pantheistically. By his primal sacrifice at the hands of the gods the phenomenal universe came into being as so many parts of his body. Having produced the waters, the sun, the stars and the earth, he created the animals and man, and finally the gods. By the repetition of this sacrifice by the king and the Brahmins the unity was reconstituted. As "the sacrificer is the god Prajapati at his own sacrifice", so the king and the priest, upon whom the duty of carrying on the ritual of creation devolved, exercised his functions on earth.[14] Furthermore, since the offering was the god, the king and the priest became Prajapati, renewing the creative processes and inaugurating the social organization.

THE FIRE-ALTAR SYMBOLISM

The altar (Agni) on which the sacred fire was kindled consisted of a quantity of bricks built up in seven layers in the form of a falcon, representing the body, wings and tail of the seven "persons" composing Agni, who became Prajapati as the Lord of generation. In the midst a fire-pan was carefully fashioned as a reproduction of the creation of the universe, for "the sacrificer who makes the fire-pan thereby makes the world." And as it is also the "self" of Agni, "he who makes the fire-pan thereby makes Agni."[15] Moreover, since Agni was "yonder sun", when he was born anew every morning the sacred flame kindled by the fire-sticks of the priests recreated the life that pervaded the universe and sustained it. Therefore, since Agni as the personification of fire (which in its turn was connected with the sun as the ultimate source of life and heat and regenerative power) became identified with the cosmic figure Prajapati, the building of the Fire-Altar was a repetition of creation, and the fire deposited upon it derived its vitalizing essence from him (Prajapati).[16]

This remarkable Vedic ritual was virtually the equivalent of the royal renewal rites of the Ancient East, since the priests as gods played the same rôle as the divine king in the seasonal drama of regeneration, and for the same purpose; viz., to ensure the continuance of the cosmic order and the prosperity of the community. But by assuming the offices and functions of composite divinities, who were rapidly losing almost every vestige of individuality and self-identity,[17] the Brahmins were the chief actors in an impersonal cosmic sacrificial drama. The same unifying element permeated nature and man just as creation and creator were comprehended in Prajapati as the One and the Many, with the neuter Brahman as the first-born of the All.[18] Through *Rta,* the cosmic principle and the moral law, he (Prajapati) fulfilled his operations in the universe he had called into being by his primal sacrifice at the hands of the gods, while the Brahmins kept all things in existence by the continual repetition of the offering. Every part of the altar was identified with some part of the universe and the god who was responsible for it. Similarly, the victim also represented the universe, and its parts were the parts of the universe. Thus, in the case of the cosmic sacrificial horse, the head was the dawn, the eye was the sun, the breath the wind, the back the sky, the belly the air and the earth, the limbs the seasons.[19] The sacrificer in becoming the sacrifice was united with the universe in all its parts resolved into a unity and sustained by a cosmic offering in which the body of the Creator (Prajapati) was broken anew and restored for the conservation of the world. The victim (the horse), however, was only the equivalent of the chief worshipper, and so it was slain.[20]

THE DOMINATION OF THE PRIESTHOOD

The principle of substitution, which played a prominent part in the later developments of the institution of sacrifice, was readily adopted in Vedic India since there it was pre-eminently the cultus that vitalized all things. The priests who alone had a correct knowledge of the texts (Brahmanas) and their prescribed actions, handed on by tradition from age to age, held the secret of the universe in their grasp. They not less than the king had the power, and they alone knew precisely how the cosmic order could be sustained, so that the sacerdotal rites and their officiants became the real source of potency. The efficacy lay in the things done by the priests. The gods were merely names or symbols for certain powers and principles liberated and made efficacious by the ritual duly performed. Even the king dropped into the background as a shadowy figure behind his deputies who actually controlled the situation. When Soma, the sacred plant equated with the royal god, was crushed to extract its life-giving juice, the king-god (Soma) was thought to be slain as a sacrificial victim to revivify those who partook sacramentally of this nectar of immortality.[21] But it was essentially a priestly action like the Fraction of the consecrated Host in the offering of the Mass, though differing from its Christian counterpart in that the power manipulated governed the world of the gods as well as the world of man. Apart from the rite, in fact, the gods had no independent existence or function as personal beings. Therefore, in the Brahmanic tradition all individuality was submerged in the priestly office and its offering until at length existence was reduced to one single event—the universal sacrifice of the Primal Man (Purusha) from which everything emanated. It then only remained to equate the divine principle in the universe (*Brahman*) with the self (*Atman*), to resolve all ultimate existence into an impersonal unity which rendered the ritual order itself an anachronism.[22]

This was the inevitable result of making the gods subservient to their own priestly agents. To function normally the institution of sacrifice requires a theistic framework. So long as the divine is identified with the inner life of the universe, or with absolute self-existent Being in and beyond the human spirit, and the highest aims and ideals can be secured without the external aid of any supramundane power, an intervening god is excluded. Consequently, in India when the Vedic gods were made subservient to, or absorbed in, an ultimate pantheistic principle, the priestly oblation became an all-sustaining magical rite until it lost its place and significance in a Way of Knowledge and a Way of Self-salvation. The sacerdotal tradition, however, was too deeply laid to remain permanently in abeyance. Therefore, in the Vedantic schools and the later Upanishads there was a tendency to revert to Vedic ceremonial and the chief sacrificial deities in an attempt to reconcile the claims of the Veda, the offering and asceticism with the search for true knowledge.[23] But the ritual had ceased to be a priestly device to uphold the universe; rather was it a means of purifying the heart (*durita-ksaya*) and of securing emancipation (*moksa*). Even in the most orthodox school of *Karma-marga* (the Way of Works), although the aim of revelation was said to be that of teaching the doctrine of sacrifice (*karman*), the offering was subordinated to the attainment of *moksa*. Similarly, in Buddhism, while a sacrificial mode of life was adopted by the monks, priestly intervention and sacrificial ritual had had no place in the search for salvation and release from the burden of *Dukka* grounded in Desire (*Tanha*). Only in Tibet has a ritual technique survived which in Tantrism is indistinguishable from magic.

PRIESTHOOD AND SACRIFICE IN ISRAEL

Notwithstanding the specialized development of priesthood and sacrifice in India, and the rôle of the Brahmins in the social structure, it has been in the Near Eastern religions, and in Judaism and Christianity which emerged very largely under their influence, that the sacerdotal tradition and its sacrificial cultus has occupied the central position. As we have seen, in the civilizations of Egypt and Mesopotamia the organized priesthoods were the consolidating force as the representatives of the gods who ruled the lands or the city and its temple, while in Israel the elaborate sacrificial system developed by the post-exilic priesthood became the unifying theocratic centre of Jewry. The centralization of the cultus at Jerusalem may have begun during the reforms said to have been carried out by Hezekiah,[24] if the account is not an anticipation of those undertaken by Josiah when the temple was repaired in 621 B.C. and a law-book was discovered, generally thought to be that of Deuteronomy (i.e. of Dt. xii–xxvi, xxviii).[25] Be this as it may, it seems to have been on the basis of this Deuteronomic Code that the centralization of worship and sacrifice was effected, the provincial shrines and their cult objects were destroyed, and the Passover was celebrated in Jerusalem as the climax of the reformation.[26]

THE BLOOD-COVENANT

Prior to these reforms the ancient conceptions of sacrifice appear to have been of universal occurrence. Thus, the Mosaic covenant was alleged to have been ratified in blood because it was the life (*nephesh*) in the blood that made atonement.[27] In the sprinkling of the blood of the victim on the altar and on the people, the ancient method of ratifying a covenant was adopted by the leader of the group, regardless of the post-exilic legislation restricting the manipulation of sacrificial blood to the priesthood. As the occasion was unique so, it might be argued, was the ritual, yet the procedure followed well-established precedents in connexion with blood-covenants. The sprinkling of the life-giving essence on the altar and on the people meant that Yahweh and his chosen nation were thereby brought together in a sacred bond of a common life, symbolized by the blood of the sacrifice.[28] It was the poured-out blood rather than the priestly agent that united the contracting parties in a vital relationship, like the bond created by the common meal,[29] or the eating of salt together.[30] Here, again, it was the blood that was the active principle "by reason of the *nephesh*," or soul-substance, contained in it.[31]

HUMAN SACRIFICE

Whether or not behind these blood rites there lay a grimmer practice suggested by the redemption of the firstborn before an animal replaced a human victim,[32] it is difficult to say. That human sacrifice was a recognized and widely adopted custom among the Semites and was condoned in Israel there can be no doubt. The numerous bodies of children excavated from the foundations of buildings in Palestine unquestionably are the relics of oblations to strengthen the walls of houses and cities;[33] while prior to the Josiah reformation in 621 B.C., children were passed through the fire to Moloch (i.e. the king) in the valley of Hinnom.[34] Or, again, when the king of Moab had been driven to his last fastness he did not hesitate to offer up his eldest son as a burnt-offering on the wall to propitiate Chemosh, with the result that the god turned his anger upon Israel.[35] That such human sacrifices were thought to be acceptable to Yahweh is apparent in the account of the vow of Jephthah which without scruple describes the sacrifice of the hero's daughter by her father.[36] If the story of the offering of Isaac[37] is in the form of an eighth-century prophetic Midrash, it is based upon a legend of a sanctuary where at one time human victims were offered, before the sacrifice of rams was substituted by way of amelioration of the original rite. As told with exquisite simplicity and fine literary skill in the present Elohistic narrative, its purpose no doubt was to suggest that human oblations are not acceptable to Yahweh, but despite the horror of the situation brought out by the later author with restrained emotion, the lingering tradition of the original episode can hardly fail to be apparent, going back to the time when the injunction in the Book of the Covenant, "the firstborn of the sons shall thou give unto me,"[38] was in some measure at least literally enforced. The place taken on the altar by the ram is represented, in fact, as a concession to Abraham whose "faith" was rewarded by the provision of a substitutionary victim.

THE PASCHAL RITUAL

Although the sacrifice of the firstborn is quite explicitly stated in the Hebrew legislation,[39] it is difficult to believe that it was ever of universal application as the drain on the population would have been too heavy. Nevertheless, that it was a recognized institution is indicated by the annual commemoration of the historic night on which the angel of Yahweh was alleged to have set forth on his bloody campaign against the Egyptians.[40] The origins of the Paschal ritual are wrapped in obscurity, but as Frazer says, "the one thing that looms clear through the haze of this weird tradition is the memory of a great massacre of firstborn."[41] As part of the New Year Festival in the spring (Nisan), it may have been originally a ritual offering on behalf of the divine king: the firstborn having been slain as a substitute for the royal victim. Since in Israel, however, there is no suggestion that this aspect of the cultus was practised, the rite doubtless had undergone very considerable modification before, or when, it was adopted as part of the complicated spring festival.

A male lamb, kid or goat ritually without blemish replaced the firstborn sons who may have been killed originally at the full moon at the vernal equinox. During the night of the 14th of Nisan, the animal, having been slain for the purpose in the fully developed rite, was eaten with bitter herbs and unleavened bread. The prohibition forbidding the eating of the flesh raw is evidence that originally the flesh was eaten raw,[42] the purpose of the sacred meal being that of imbibing sacramentally the inherent vitality of the victim, as in the Arabic camel sacrifice described by Nilus in the fifth century A.D. Like the Thraco-Phrygian worshippers of Zagreus who consumed the raw flesh of bulls and calves,[43] the Arabs appear to have drunk the warm blood of the slain camel before "hacking off pieces of the quivering flesh and devouring them raw with such haste, that in the short interval between the rise of the day star which marked the hour for the service to begin, and the disappearance of its rays before the rising sun, the entire camel, his body and bones, skin, blood and entrails, is wholly devoured".[44] In this way the life of the sacred victim, symbolized by the "living flesh" as raw flesh is called in Hebrew and Arabic, which originally was regarded as itself divine, was absorbed by all who shared in the ceremony. The living blood was conveyed to the god, and the divine life inherent in the living flesh and blood was absorbed by the worshippers. Throughout, the fundamental conception was that of liberating vitality—of giving life that it might be received in greater abundance.

The sprinkling of the blood on the lintel and door-posts of the houses in which fugitive Israelites are said to have concealed themselves, protected by a sacred barrier or "a re-enforced door",[45] seems to be a later addition to the Paschal ritual, derived from the practice of smearing houses with blood to repel demons.[46] This very ancient protective device, which may go back to Palaeolithic times in view of the hand designs in red ochre and black manganese in some of the decorated caves (e.g. Gargas in the Pyrenees, and Castillo in Cantabria) similar to those daubed on the lintels and door posts by Arabs, would be regarded as an efficacious barrier against "the destroyer" when the story was formulated. But the rite has nothing to do with the Paschal feast as such, and the explanations given for it are inconsistent, the "destroyer" and Yahweh being confused.[47] Furthermore, it is not clear whether it was to be a sign to the Israelites or to the "angel".[48] As Buchanan Gray has pointed out, "either the story is intended to correct a popular conception of Yahweh, or to counteract a popular recognition of other divine powers than Yahweh." In any case, the apotropaic function of the Paschal blood ritual is clear.[49]

A more important and significant addition to the *Pesach* was the *Maṣṣoth,* or Feast of Unleavened Bread,[50] which belongs essentially to the agricultural tradition as an offering of the first-fruits. The mention of a second Passover in Numbers ix. 6–12 reflects the unsettled relations which the pastoral *Pesach,* or firstborn rite, originally bore to the vegetation harvest festival. Although at first both were distinct they were celebrated at the vernal equinox at the time of barley harvest[51] when in Babylonia, on the seventh of Nisan, the Annual Festival in honour of Shamesh, the Sun-god, was held in Sippar. As a nocturnal festival[52] doubtless it had a lunar significance to ensure the increase of the flocks and herds, since the Moon-god was a fertility deity.[53] The haste with which the victim had to be eaten so that none of the flesh should remain until the morning, suggests that it had to be consumed before the god withdrew his presence on the night when it appeared at its height at the vernal equinox.

In the J document and in Deuteronomy, however, the predominant observance was the Feast of Unleavened Bread, or *Maṣṣoth,* when at the beginning of barley harvest a sheaf of the new crop (*'omer*) was waved before Yahweh on the second day to promote the fertility of the crops during the forthcoming season,[54] just as seven days later, at the end of barley harvest and the beginning of wheat harvest, the "wave-loaves made of fine flour and baked with leaven were offered at the Feast of Weeks (*Shabu'oth*)".[55] These rites doubtless represent survivals of the indigenous Canaanite vegetation ritual connected with the firstfruits, with perhaps solar influences in the background, since in the Jewish liturgy Psalm lxxx occurs with its references to Yahweh shining forth from between the cherubim.[56]

Be this as it may, the *Pesach,* celebrated under nomadic and pastoral conditions and centring in the offering of the firstlings of man and beast, was combined with an agricultural harvest festival after the settlement in Palestine as a composite spring feast. The purpose of the *Pesach* was the offering of the firstborn to promote the annual increase of the flocks and herds on which the pastoral people depended for their subsistence. Similarly, the *Maṣṣoth* had as its chief aim the fertility of the crops for the ensuing season. Since the two occurred at approximately the same time of year (i.e. the spring) they readily became a seasonal sacrificial and sacramental ritual for a common purpose in which a number of allied, though formerly distinct, primitive practices associated with the Annual Festival were united and reinterpreted as a commemoration of the great deliverance from Egypt.[57] The oblation and eating of the Paschal lamb, sheep, or goat remained the principal feature until its place was taken by a roast shank-bone when animal sacrifice was abrogated in Judaism, thereby perpetuating the primacy of the blood rite (*Pesach*). Moreover, it continued to be essentially a domestic observance, and even when in post-exilic times it was celebrated in Jerusalem and the victims were slain in the Temple (i.e. until A.D. 70) and the blood was offered at the altar by the priests, small groups of ten to twenty of the pilgrims assembled for the sacred communal meal with its prescribed ingredients and procedures. These included the sweeping of the house to remove any traces of leaven, and the eating of unleavened cake and bitter herbs, the recitation of deliverance from Egypt and the singing of the Hallel (Ps. cxiii.–cxviii.).

After the destruction of the Temple in A.D. 70, the more specifically sacrificial aspects of the Passover necessarily ceased, since it was no longer possible for the priestly oblation of the blood of the victims to be conveyed to the altar. It then reverted to its earlier non-sacerdotal character. The head of the family resumed his primitive function as the priest of the household surrounded by his children and guests, and gave the customary explanation to the question, "why is this night different from other nights?"[58] The grimmer side of the rite gave place to a joyous festal spirit in which the deeper religious significance of the event and its commemoration was and still is combined with an element of festivity and hopeful anticipation of the restoration of Israel. Originally, if the *Pesach* was connected with the slaying of a substitute for the firstborn, it must have been a priestly sacrificial offering, as no doubt was the vegetation spring rite with which it became combined. But in its Hebrew form the annual celebration had lost these characteristics. In some measure they were restored after the Exile when the Passover was centralized at Jerusalem, and the killing of the victims became a definitely priestly function which included the oblation of the blood at the altar. That these sacerdotal ministrations were not, however, regarded as integral parts of the rite is shown by the ease with which the earlier domestic sacramental meal fell into its natural place in the home as an aetiological observance of the Exodus.

After the Exile when the sacrificial system became the means by which the nation fulfilled its functions and responsibilities as a theocracy both individually and corporately, the high-priest and the ritual he controlled occupied much the same position as that of the kingship in the surrounding civilizations. The covenant idea being fundamental in Judaism, the sacred community was resolved into a unified whole consolidated by the official worship of the Temple, through which the spiritual bond of the nation and its god was maintained. The personal character of Yahweh and his transcendence as Lord of the universe and of history prevented the ritual order from gaining supreme control of cosmic events, as in India, making all things in heaven and on earth subject to the sacrificial offering. The priesthood was the instrument of the God who had adopted the nation for his own purposes, but although it was indispensable for the proper functioning of the covenant, its authority was delegated, not absolute. Moreover, under the influence of the prophetic movement, a personal relationship between Yahweh and the individual Israelite had emerged which found expression in a deepened sense of sin, fostered by the post-exilic conception of the Law.

THE DAY OF ATONEMENT

The ancient symbolism of the blood as the life was retained,[59] but it was re-evaluated in terms of the teaching of Ezekiel and the Deutero-Isaiah so that the need of atonement was felt to be an act of reconciliation, alike for the nation and the individual. This reached its climax in the rites performed on the tenth day of the seventh month when the annual expiation was made for the temple, the priesthood and the whole congregation of Israel. According to Ezekiel[60] the sanctuary was cleansed ritually twice a year—on the first day of the first month, and on the first day of the seventh month—but no mention of this twofold purification occurs elsewhere in the Old Testament. After the time of Ezra (i.e. *c.* 397 B.C.), when the high priesthood was definitely established and the priestly legislation was in full operation, the Day of Atonement

L

described in Leviticus xvi was instituted. In the present Levitical narrative three observances, or stages in the development of
the rite, can be detected. The first, belonging to the middle of
the fourth century and recorded in Lev. xvi. 3, 5–10, com-
prised the priest taking a bullock for a sin-offering to make
atonement for himself and the priesthood. A ram was then
offered and two he-goats were "set before Yahweh". Upon
them lots were cast to determine the goat to be assigned to Yahweh as a sin-offering and the one to be presented to Azazel as a
sin-receiver, to carry away the iniquity to the demon of the
waste in the wilderness. After Yahweh's victim had been
slain, the one selected for Azazel was "set before Yahweh
alive" and despatched to the desert.

In the next stage (11–28) this relatively simple cleansing of
the sanctuary was transformed into an elaborate atonement
ritual with minute details concerning censings, the manipulation of the blood of the bullock sprinkled on the mercy-seat
in the holy of holies and on the altar "to make atonement for
the holy place, and because of the uncleanness of the children
of Israel". The casting of lots over the victims, if it was practised, is not mentioned, but the transference of the iniquities of
the people was effected by the priest laying his hands on the
head of the live goat as he confessed all their sins over it to bear
them away to a solitary land. The carcasses of the bullock and
the goat offered as the sin-offering were taken without the
camp to be destroyed by fire, the man performing this task
being required to engage in a thorough ablution of himself and
of his clothes to remove the defilement before re-entering the
community. Finally, (29–34a) a note was added explaining
that the Day of Atonement was to be regarded as a "high
sabbath", and set apart as a fast to enable the people to "afflict
their souls", and to do "no manner of work".

In this very primitive ceremonial the original idea of evil as a
substantive pollution removable by the sprinkling of blood,
censings and lustrations, together with a sin-carrier in the form
of an animal, was prominent. The blood made atonement "by
reason of the *nephesh*", or soul-substance, contained in it,[61]

liberating it as a life-giving agent and wiping away, or covering up, sin. Moreover, it conferred "holiness" on everything it touched as sanctifying power by virtue of its atoning efficacy. Similarly, the smoke of the incense and the holy water were endowed with the same potency, while the "scapegoat", like the bird in the purification of the leper,[62] was a vehicle for the removal of the pollution transferred to it.

Yet in post-exilic Israel it was Yahweh who alone could release from sin, and his first demand was the offering of a clean heart and a broken spirit, in which sacrifice did not necessarily play an essential part.[63] Only an all-righteous and merciful God could forgive sin and pardon iniquity,[64] and He had no need of the blood of bulls and goats and the ashes of a heifer, inasmuch as He stood over and above the ritual order, however integral the priestly oblation may have been in the religious organization of the community. It was generally supposed that the daily sacrifice expiated unintentional breaches of the Law—the evening oblation removed those committed during the day, and the morning holocausts those of the night —while the Day of Atonement piacular *ex opera operato* removed sins committed with a "high hand", but always on the condition that the offering was accompanied by repentance.

Behind this conception of sin and expiation lay the covenant relationship of Yahweh and Israel. This required an appropriate act of repentance and ceremonial amendment to effect expiation when there had been any departure from the prescribed rule of life, conduct and worship, whether in the sphere of ethics, theology or ritual, made either intentionally or accidentally. The entire action moved on the spiritual plane since it was directed Godwards, and it was sacrificial inasmuch as it presupposed a relationship between a living God and His people established and maintained by the worship at the altar. Sin as the violation of the divine law was an affront to the holiness of God and resulted in an estrangement between the creature and his Creator; the cutting off of the soul from the source of its life. Therefore, any breach committed wittingly or unwittingly had this effect, without respect of its nature and

character, or the intentions of the sinner. Animals and inanimate objects like the sanctuary and its vessels, partook of this
"uncleanness" and so required the same purification as human
beings who ministered at the altar.

This sacredness, in short, was as synonymous as in non-
moral holiness and demanded a sin-offering by way of appeasement to restore the covenant relationship and secure release from harmful supernatural influences. But the fact that on
the Day of Atonement the goat was laden with *all* the sins of
the nation (i.e. ethical as well as ceremonial), and that the
Rabbinic doctrine maintained that the rite was efficacious only
when it was performed with sincerity of heart and true repentance,[65] suggests that it was more than an act of ritual
expiation. The book of Leviticus is a *rituale* rather than a
manual of devotion like the Psalms, and in such a work it is the
things to be done, set forth in terms of liturgical rubrics, rather
than their ethical significance, that are described. Nevertheless,
in the Mishna the Day itself was represented as expiating sin,[66]
the objective efficacy attributed to the rites being dependent on
the use made of them by God Himself. As His duly appointed
divine instruments and dramatic symbols of forgiveness, to
neglect them would be equivalent to spurning the atonement
offered by the penitent sinner through them. Therefore, the Day
was set apart as a Sabbath of great sanctity[67] on which work of
every description was absolutely forbidden and a strict fast
enjoined.[68] To enable those who could not take part in the
observances in the temple at Jerusalem to share in their
efficacy, the penitential aspects of the ritual performed by the
high-priest in the holy of holies were reproduced in the form of
confessions of sin, and in the prayer for forgiveness in the
synagogue liturgy. In this way greater emphasis was given to the
purification of the heart, and with the destruction of the temple
in A.D. 70, the ceremonial expiation necessarily ceased, leaving
the symbolic synagogue service as a devout spiritual exercise set
against the background of the earlier sacrificial priestly expiation and the piaculum.

The prophetic movement had prepared the way for an

ethical conception of repentance independent of ceremonial atonement, but the loss of the scapegoat ritual was keenly felt in Rabbinical circles because it was so intimately related to the need for the expiation of sin, regulated by the belief in the covenant relationship between Yahweh and Israel.[69] It was not that an angry God had to be propitiated by gifts and offerings. That notion had been dispelled by Jeremiah and the eighth-century prophets. Evil, however, remained as a taint that had to be "covered" or "wiped out" if the divine fellowship of the theocracy was to be maintained. With the cessation of the temple and its sacrificial system repentance was left the sole condition of remission of sins, as neither the manipulation of the blood of the victim nor the offices of a scapegoat was available.

EXPIATORY SUFFERING

The vicarious principle inherent in the institution of sacrifice had found expression in the idea of expiatory suffering in the Servant Saga embedded in the later portion of the book of Isaiah,[70] where the righteous servant, however he may have been interpreted, was represented as bearing the penalties which others should have borne because of their transgressions. Indeed, he had been commissioned by Yahweh not only to raise up the tribes of Jacob and restore the preserved of Israel, but also to be a light to the Gentiles that salvation might be unto the ends of the earth. This mission was accomplished by much suffering, and notwithstanding his innocence, it pleased Yahweh to bruise him and put him to grief in order that his soul might be "an offering for sin". He was led as a lamb to the slaughter that he might make an act of vicarious atonement— —"He shall see the travail of his soul and shall be satisfied: by his knowledge shall my righteous servant justify many: and he shall bear their iniquities."[71]

Why sinners should be forgiven because an innocent man had suffered is not explained, but it is recognized that sin must be atoned for, and the sufferings of the righteous Servant are compared to the guilt-offering (*āshām*),[72] as the death of Miriam elsewhere is related to the ritual of the red heifer,[73] suggesting that as the red heifer expiates so does the death of the righteous. The death of Aaron, again, appears in a similar context.[74] The underlying principle is that something has to be done to remove the consequences of sin, and while the function of the Servant was to restore the captivity of the exiles and to renew their prosperity, like a divine king,[75] the deeper problem of vicarious atonement lay behind the concept.

THE SACRIFICE AND PRIESTHOOD OF CHRIST

It remained for Christianity to interpret the crucifixion in terms of a vicarious self-offering of surpassing magnitude in which the sufferer assumed the role of the victim in a sacrificial oblation to effect reconciliation between an all-righteous God and sinful humanity.[76] Exalted as a prince and a saviour at the right hand of the divine majesty on high, in Christian theology Christ became at once the victorious ascended king and the high-priest, ever-living in the heavenly places to offer perpetually his eternal sacrifice as the lamb slain from the foundation of the world, and in his mediatorial capacity to make intercession for those who come unto God by him.[77]

The traditional conception of the atoning efficacy of sacrificial blood being axiomatic for the elusive author of the Epistle to the Hebrews, communion with God for him required the pouring out of the vital essence of a victim.[78] Yet he recognized that it was impossible that the blood of bulls and goats should take away sin,[79] and so he fell back upon the perfect self-offering of the dedicated life of Christ, immolated on the Cross, as the only true sacrifice of supreme validity, effecting what had only been accomplished partially and symbolically in the cultus of the covenant.[80] The Aaronic priesthood and its ritual were merely copies or shadows in a Platonic sense of the archetypal order of eternal reality, and, therefore, failed to make perfect those who drew near to them.[81] Only Christ "beyond the veil" was "able to save to the uttermost those who come unto God through him", because for those who were in a state of grace, he had removed the barrier of sin separating man and God.

Thus, in this Epistle the emphasis was placed on the analogy between the work of Christ in the heavenly tabernacle and that of the Jewish high-priest on earth, particularly on the Day of Atonement. Of the mystery conception of a participation in the divine nature, or of a union with Christ in his death and resurrection, so prominent in Pauline theology and in the royal myth and ritual, nothing appears to have been known. But, nevertheless, its theology has deeply influenced Eucharistic thought and liturgical language. This has found expression in the placing of the action of the Mass in heaven whither the worshippers are as it were caught up to the celestial realms where the sacrifice is pleaded. Ambrose, Chrysostom and Gregory the Great, all connected the Eucharist with the heavenly life of Christ,[82] and in the Western Church the offering of the gifts on the altar on earth symbolized their presentation by the eternal High-priest at the heavenly altar.[83]

THE EUCHARISTIC SACRIFICE

In an age saturated with sacrificial ideas and dramatic-mythical metaphors and conceptions, the interpretation of the death, resurrection and ascension of Christ as a priestly oblation inevitably involved the perpetuation of the offering in the heavenly sanctuary in a cultus on earth. For, if the sin-offering had been made once and for all the thank-offering remained to be offered "until he come".[84] The Old Dispensation, it is true, was regarded as having been abolished so far as its cultic demands were concerned, and the sacrifice once offered on the Cross was thought to have made divine grace operative in redeemed humanity in the capacity of a "royal priesthood".[85] The concept of "spiritual sacrifice" was also stressed,[86] as, indeed, it was in Judaism, but in neither case to the exclusion of a cultus. In Christianity the last gathering of the apostolic company on the night of the betrayal constituted the nucleus of a liturgical rite which, whatever may have been the original intention, could hardly fail to become the *anamnesis* of the drama of redemption analogous to the Jewish Paschal memorial, once the death of Christ had been given a sacrificial significance. This in fact is what occurred.

Although the textual evidence is involved and incapable of precise determination, it is generally agreed, in spite of such variants as Lk. xxii. 19 ff., that at the Last Supper Jesus as the Host took bread, gave thanks over it, broke it, and distributed it among his apostles with words which identified it with his own body about to be broken on the Cross. He also took a cup containing wine and water (or if the Lucan variant is correct, two cups) and performed the same actions as those employed in the blessing and distribution of the bread.[87] The Marcan narrative would seem to have been derived from a primitive Palestinian Christian liturgy of which the Matthaean account represents an expanded version. The variant texts of Lk. xxii and I. Cor. xi. 23–6 are probably independent versions, but all agree that the institution of the Eucharist occurred at a communal gathering (*koinonia*) which was given a special significance in relation to the Passover and the approaching events recorded in the Passion narratives.

Whether it actually coincided with the Passover meal is still a matter of debate.[88] The Synoptists appear to take the view that the Supper was the actual Passover while the Fourth Gospel implies that it took place before the Paschal celebration,[89] probably at a *chabrûah*, an informal quasi-religious gathering of the disciples with their master, such as had been held on many previous occasions.[90] Although *charubôth* were especially associated with legal observances,[91] communal meals of this kind were held on the eve of Sabbaths or Holy Days when a cup of wine was blessed and drunk at sunset at a *Kiddûsh*, or Sanctification, consisting of (*a*) the benediction over the wine, and (*b*) the sanctification of the day, followed by the passing round of the cup and the solemn washing of hands.[92] In the case of the Last Supper, if it was the *Kiddûsh* it must have been put forward a day by Jesus in view of the approaching crisis. Realizing that the blow might fall at any moment he assembled the little company, it may be conjectured, on the Thursday evening for the purpose of enacting under the very shadow of the

Passover and of his own Passion a Eucharistic symbolization of the events which he realized only too well were about to take place, and which apparently it was his intention should be commemorated in this manner.

This interpretation of what may have occurred avoids the serious difficulties and inconsistencies involved in accepting the Synoptic chronology and equating the Last Supper with the Passover meal, but it does not dispose of the confused nature of the documentary evidence. The most that can be said is that the gathering in the Upper Room was a hurried and haphazard anticipation of the Passover meal to which Jesus had been looking forward with eagerness.[93] This may explain certain departures from the normal order of a *chabûrah,* and the *kiddûsh* with which it so often closed. Either the meal did not begin with bread and wine and Jesus blessed these elements when they came; or, if the meal began with the blessing of the bread and wine, the duplication of the blessings points to an innovation implying that the previous blessings, *Kiddûsh* or otherwise, were invalid, and they were repeated because henceforth they were to have a new significance. If Christ had been in the habit of assembling the apostolic band from time to time to convey to them the inner meaning of his Messianic mission by sacramental signs, as symbolized in the feeding stories, the final banquet was the climax of these rites. Thus, Leitzmann maintains that "in offering himself like the Paschal lamb, at the last of the solemn banquets with his disciples, Christ in effect said, 'I am the sacrificial victim whose blood is poured out for you—that is, for the believing folk—to seal a new covenant with God, and whose blood is slain for you.' "[94]

Whether or not Jesus commanded the rite to be perpetuated depends on the interpretation of I. Cor. xi. 24 f., but that his followers did in fact continue the observance is not open to doubt. If it began as a *charûbah* and if *charubôth* were an institution at the beginning of the first century A.D. as many (though not all) scholars maintain, for the apostolic company to meet together in this way after their Master had passed from their midst would be a natural procedure. At such weekly gatherings when they assembled to "break bread",[95] they would hardly fail to recall with increasing vividness the unique occasion on which they foregathered with him for the last time on the same night in which he was betrayed. If, as seems probable, the crucifixion took place on the day on which the Passover lambs were sacrificed, his death at that precise moment inevitably would become associated in their minds with the historical and theological significance the festival had for them, first as Jews and then as Christians.

But although the Last Supper *Kiddûsh* readily could have become equated with the Paschal meal and so acquired a sacrificial interpretation, a potent reason is required to explain how these pious Jews brought themselves to partake even symbolically of a cup that was represented to be the *blood* of the new covenant, in view of the deeply laid tabu on such an act of sacrilege.[96] Indeed, unless the traditional narratives are substantially accurate, it is difficult to explain the subsequent course of liturgical development in the Church, notwithstanding the textual discrepancies. The persistent tradition requires the words and actions recorded in the New Testament to give it its historical setting, place and function in Christendom as the central act of worship and the permanent means whereby the faithful throughout the ages have commemorated before God and participated in the self-offering of Christ as priest and victim.

Important, however, as is the problem of the origin of the Eucharist with all its historical and theological obscurities, for our present purpose it is the part it has played in, and the contribution it has made to, the integration and continuity of the Church as a whole that constitutes its essential function, irrespective of precisely how it came to assume its final mode of celebration and interpretation. Around it developed a sacrificial mystery theology and a sacred ministry which became the consolidating force in the New Israel, occupying a position and having a purpose comparable in some respects to the seasonal drama in the Graeco-oriental cultus and the sacrificial worship in Judaism prior to A.D. 70, yet having its own distinctive features.

While the Christian liturgy took its shape in an environment in which the influence of the hellenistic mysteries was strongly felt,[97] the immediate background in the first instance was Jewish rather than pagan. Thus, St Paul in his Eucharistic discourses, apart from a passing reference to eating in an idolatrous temple, takes all his illustrations from the Old Testament;[98] and the structure of the Christian rite in the second century developed along the lines of the synagogue pattern, opening with lections and prayers leading up to the dismissal of the catechumens as the introductory portion of the liturgy, subsequently known as the *Missa catechumenorum,* or "service of the word", as distinct from the *Missa fidelium.*[99]

When the Agape, or common meal, was separated from the Eucharist with which originally it was associated, the synagogue type of worship was confined to this preliminary section with its prayers, lections and homily, as an introduction to the Eucharistic oblation which began with the offertory (i.e. the placing of the bread and wine on the altar and their presentation to the bishop, assisted by the presbyters). After "the prayer of the faithful" the bishop consecrated and broke the bread, gave the kiss of peace, and made his own communion while the concelebrating presbyters and the deacons broke the bread before them on glass dishes or linen cloths for the communion of the clergy and the people, administered by the deacons. After the ablutions the congregation was dismissed by the deacons with the words, *Ite missa est.* They then carried the consecrated Elements to the absent.

THE APOSTOLIC MINISTRY

In the pre-Nicene period the principal function of the episcopate seems to have been to "offer the gifts", while that of the deacons was to "bring up (or present) that which is offered",[100] though until the fourth century when the practice was forbidden at the Council of Arles in 314,[101] they (the deacons) appear to have celebrated the holy mysteries in some local churches. But the offering of the Eucharist was normally confined to the *sacerdos* (i.e. the bishops and presbyters), though at first it was always a delegated episcopal prerogative exercised in the absence of the bishop, except in the case of concelebration (i.e. joint consecration of the sacred Elements).[102] So firmly established was the practice of presbyteral celebration in the fourth century that at the Council of Nicaea the cessation of communicating presbyters by deacons was urged.[103]

With the development of parish churches in rural areas under the spiritual care of local presbyters the right to consecrate the Elements was of necessity bestowed upon them as the official deputies of the bishop under whom they served. The exercise of episcopal powers, however, remained vested in the episcopate, and at joint gatherings of the corporate presbytery of the local churches the bishop presided.[104] It is probably true that in theory he was the normal celebrant of the Eucharist, as in ancient Egypt the divine king was the officiant in all the temples in the solar cultus, but in practice the place of the bishop, like that of the Pharaoh, was taken by his sacerdotal deputies, assisted at first by the deacons who administered communion.[105] The sending of the *fermentum,* or particle of the consecrated Host from a preceding episcopal consecration, symbolized the formal "presidency" of the bishop in all Eucharistic worship.[106] Indeed, "the history of the episcopate is in one sense the history of the breaking down of its primitive liturgical monopoly."[107] The bishop, in fact, was the heir of the divine king, reserving to himself the fullness of priesthood but compelled by force of circumstances arising out of the development of ecclesiastical organization and the expansion of the Church to delegate his functions to his subordinates.[108] Moreover, in the West the absolute supremacy and universal jurisdiction claimed by the occupants of the Holy See as the successors of the Prince of the Apostles, under the title of *Pontifex Maximus* conferred on Augustus in 13 B.C.,[109] retained in Christendom the essential principle of the royal priesthood re-interpreted in terms of Judaeo-Christian faith and practice.

As the episcopal status and office centred in the Eucharist of which originally the bishop was the proper minister, so the conception of priesthood necessarily was bound up with the sacrificial interpretation of the rite. Therefore, those who were commissioned to offer the Eucharistic oblation were *sacerdos,* irrespective of their other administrative and pastoral offices and duties. The Mass took the place in the "Israel of God", as Christendom regarded itself, of the sacrificial worship of the temple in the Old Covenant, while the sacred ministry was regarded as the continuation of the Aaronic priestly succession. When in the later Patristic period, from the fifth to the eighth centuries, the Eucharistic sacrifice acquired a propitiatory character, a new emphasis was given to the unique status and function of the priesthood, which in the Middle Ages was further enhanced by the promulgation of the dogma of Transubstantiation at the Lateran Council in 1215. As a result of these doctrinal developments the Mass and the priesthood became the unifying centre of medieval civilization, with the altar as the focal point of the whole structure, together with the Papacy.

Having reached its zenith in the thirteenth century the decline that set in during the Later Middle Ages culminated in the disintegration of the ecclesiastical structure in Northern and Central Europe under the influence of the Reformation. It is true that the sacrificial death of Christ retained its central position in Christian theology, but the Mass and the priesthood lost their status and function as the essential element in faith and worship. Except in the British Isles, the apostolic succession of bishops, priests and deacons, together with the historic episcopate, were abandoned, while the Eucharist was interinterpreted as a commemorative sacramental meal in thankful remembrance of the sacrifice once offered on the Cross, but with such a variety of meanings and emphasis that a bitter controversy tore the ranks of the Continental Reformers asunder from the beginning. Instead of being the unifying dynamic as heretofore, the Lord's Supper became the primary cause of disunion with Lutherans, Zwinglians and Calvinists maintaining distinct and opposed doctrines ranging from consubstantiation to receptionism, united only in their rejection of the medieval faith and practice.

In England the Reformation followed a course which is of considerable interest and significance for our present inquiry. While the continental anti-sacerdotal influences were strongly felt, there was never as in Protestant Europe a complete break with medieval Catholicism after the Henrician breach with the Papacy. The Mass was specifically safeguarded in the Six Articles of 1539, and with the subsequent swing of the pendulum, first in one direction and then in another, it came to rest with a Zwinglian and Calvinistic set of "Articles of Religion", combined with an Ordinal based on the pre-Reformation pontificals with an unequivocal assertion of the apostolic origin and essential nature of the threefold ministry. The succession was to be "continued and reverently used and esteemed in the Church of England"; none being permitted to exercise episcopal, priestly or diaconal functions unless he had been duly ordained by prayer, the imposition of hands and the prescribed rite. The importance attached to this principle of continuity is shown by the care taken to secure the valid consecration of Matthew Parker to the Primatial See of Canterbury in 1559 by a proper quorum of bishops at a time when very few Anglican bishops were available.[110] This was achieved in the face of strenuous opposition from the reforming party which had adopted the Calvinistic, Zwinglian and Lutheran doctrine of the ministry and the Eucharist.

The celebration of the Eucharist was confined to the priesthood, as was the bestowal of absolution on the penitent, while Ordination and Confirmation were exclusively episcopal ministries. The word "priest" was deliberately retained in the Prayer Book and Ordinal despite Puritan opposition, and in the seventeenth century the altars were restored to their original position in the sanctuary after the Restoration in 1660. The Ornaments Rubric inserted before the Order of Morning and Evening Prayer made provision for the old arrangement of the chancel to be continued, and notwithstanding the determined efforts to sweep away the traditional sacerdotal vestments, the Act of Uniformity of 1559 ordered those that had been in use in the second year of the reign of Edward VI to be retained.[111]

Whatever may have been the defects, deficiencies and anomalies of the Elizabethan Settlement and its aftermath, at least it was directed towards the maintenance of the existing ecclesiastical structure in respect of the apostolic ministry and the sacraments, while allowing considerable latitude in the underlying doctrinal interpretations. If it failed to embrace in a single Establishment all the divergent religious elements in the country, it succeeded in retaining the allegiance of a considerable section of the community in a comprehensive Anglican Communion claiming to be both Catholic and Reformed. The unity may have been in the nature of a compromise stabilized by the official status it held in the English constitution within which it emerged. But the preservation of the traditional fundamental structure has kept in being the corporate body as an entity for four hundred years, and prevented its breaking up into a number of sects and schisms when sectarianism was rife, and long after the major portion has ceased to function as an Established Church.[112]

Moreover, notwithstanding the doctrinal divergences concerning the nature and purpose of the ministry and of the Eucharist, in recent years a new approach has been made by both Catholic and Protestant scholars to the underlying theological problems with a view to a clearer understanding of the fundamental issues and the removal of at any rate some of the causes of division on all sides. By common consent the Ordinal and the Liturgy, and all that lies behind them, constitute the crucial factors in the problem of the re-integration of a divided Christendom because priesthood and sacrifice always have been the unifying and stablizing force in the ecclesiastical structure, and not least in that of the Christian Church in West and East alike.

CHAPTER VI

Priesthood and Absolution

IF the primary function of the priest is to offer sacrifice, closely
related to it in significance and importance is the sacerdotal
ministry of absolution in which evil, sin and guilt hindering
communion and reconciliation between the human and divine
orders are removed. As we have seen, exorcism and expiation
have played a prominent part in the expulsion of harmful contagions and malevolent influences,[1] and the priest in absolution
stands in this tradition. When ceremonial uncleanness was the
condition most to be dreaded and avoided, cathartic devices
were employed to remove the miasma or ritual defilement.
Water, for example, has been used very widely to wash away
harmful contagions resulting from contact with sacredness, and
at a higher level of religious development ablution and absolution have been almost synonymous, as in the case of the
immersion-bath in Judaism, the lustrations in Mithraic initiations, and baptism for the remission of sins in Christianity.
Similarly, the application of the blood of a sacrificial victim,
as we have considered, has been regarded as efficacious in
making atonement, removing the taint of evil and re-
establishing harmonious relations with the transcendental source
of beneficence.[2]

THE HEBREW CONCEPTION OF SIN AND RECONCILIATION

In Israel, where the expiation ritual reached its climax in the
Day of Atonement observances, the conception of sin arose out
of the covenant relationship assumed between Yahweh and the
nation. Therefore, any departure from the rule of life, conduct
and worship prescribed by the Law, whether in the sphere of
ethics, theology or ritual, made either intentionally or accidentally, required an appropriate act of repentance and cere-

monial amendment to effect reconciliation. The entire action moved on the transcendental plane since it was directed Godwards, and it was sacramental inasmuch as it established a vital relationship between Yahweh and his people by means of efficacious signs.

It was not, however, necessarily ethical in the modern sense of the term. The sin-offering was not an offering for sin as a moral quality. It was essentially an expiation for the involuntary violation of the divine law as an affront to the holiness of God, conceived as sacredness rather than in terms of ethical righteousness.[3] Sin was uncleanness and apostasy resulting in the estrangement of the creature from his Creator; the cutting off of the soul from the source of its life. Therefore, since all customs and precepts were regarded as of divine origin and sanction, and as an integral part of the holy covenant of Israel, any breach committed wittingly or unwittingly had the same effect, without respect of its nature and character and the intentions of the sinner. Moreover, animals and inanimate objects could and frequently did partake of this "uncleanness", together with particular states and conditions of life, such as pregnancy and the priesthood. Consequently, the altar and the sanctuary and those who like the high-priest or the man who led away the "scapegoat", performed sacred functions, required ritual cleansing to remove the taint, Thus, sin was synonymous with sacredness and ceased to have any specific relation with even unintentional error. It was simply non-moral holiness creating a supernaturally dangerous and tabu condition for all persons and things that became affected by it. To "wipe off" (*le-kapper*) the contagion an "atonement" (*kippurim*) had to be made[4] in order that it might be no more seen by God or man. But this Semitic notion of forgiveness as a "covering", or "wiping out", readily becomes that of "propitiation" when it is applied to an offended deity who hides his face from those who infringe his laws. Hence the need of a sin-offering by way of appeasement to restore the covenant relationship as well as to secure release from harmful supernatural influences.

M

THE DUAL PURPOSE OF RITUAL PURIFICATION

Ritual purification, therefore, has a dual purpose. It is an attempt to begin afresh, especially at the turn of the year, by driving away the accumulation of evil that hinders divine benevolence and separates both the individual sinner and the entire community from the transcendent source of all well-being. It is also the means whereby a fresh outpouring of vitality and energy, spiritual and physical, may be secured by the maintenance of a correct relationship with the supernatural order, interpreted in Judaism in terms of the living God. In its negative and positive aspects atonement is thus at once purificatory, propitiatory and sacramental. It cleanses, appeases, and renews by averting evil and imparting new life through the duly appointed channels of divine activity.

The rites employed to this end may be very primitive in character, as in the Hebrew piacula, and devoid of any genuinely moral quality, but, nevertheless, they are regarded as the divinely ordained means by which "a state of grace" is maintained in an imperfect world. Sin in the form of ritual defilement, or the unwitting infringement of a prescribed custom, law or tabu, is removed by some material substance, such as water, blood or fire, or carried away by an animal or bird, or neutralized by a revitalizing sacrificial offering. But throughout this sacramental process the purpose is the restoration of the state of religious purity and holiness on which the continuance of divine beneficence depends. In other words, it is to raise mankind, either in an individual or corporate capacity, to a higher spiritual status in which the transcendent exercises control over the physical and human, and the eternal over the temporal, but always through human agents and material instruments employed as the vehicle of purifying efficacy.

THE RABBINIC CONCEPTION OF SIN AND FORGIVENESS

With the rise of more ethical conceptions of sin and the righteousness of God, atonement and purification have undergone a corresponding change in interpretation, but while the methods have altered the underlying concepts have remained the same. Thus, for example, in post-exilic Judaism it was never questioned that the blood of the sacrificial victim atoned for sin,[5] but the *modus operandi* of the atonement was not considered by the Old Testament writers or in the Rabbinic schools. The followers of Shammai maintained that sins were "trampled down" by the morning and evening sacrifice, while the school of Hillel contended that what is trampled down comes up again, and the sacrificial lambs "washed off" the iniquities of Israel—the play being on the etymological meaning of the noun *kebes,* a lamb, rather than on the verb *kipper,* to expiate.

It was repentance that atoned as the condition of forgiveness and this rested ultimately on the love of God which covers all transgression.[6] But there was no general agreement concerning the precise way in which this was effected by the piacula offerings. Those like the Rabbi Judah, who held that the Day of Atonement removed all evil from the entire congregation of Israel other than apostates, were inclined to an *ex opere operato* doctrine of expiation. On the other hand, those who maintained that repentance was the *sine quâ non* of forgiveness adopted the prophetic view that God had no delight in sacrifice and oblation unless the rites were the expression of a contrite heart.[7] Therefore, they placed the emphasis on sincere confession with prayer for an inward purification and ethical dispositions of mind and spirit.

The destruction of the temple in A.D. 70 had a profound effect on the relation of atonement and repentance inasmuch as the cessation of the sacrificial system drove the rabbis to adopt the prophetic idea of "justice" and "righteousness", and of "obeying the voice of God" as the condition of remission of sins. "Beneficence, devotion and repentance, and the words of the Torah" were said to be "more than all sacrifices". It was never suggested, of course, that objective worship and expiation were unnecessary, but unless the outward and visible channels of divine grace were related to conduct the cultus ceased to be efficacious. Thus, in the Wisdom literature, for instance, Ben-Sira made an eloquent appeal for the support of the priesthood, and eulogized the splendour of the ritual of the temple on the Day of Atonement as conducted by the High-Priest.[8] But he was equally insistent that all this magnificence was of no avail unless it was accompanied by the observance of the moral law and of right living.[9] Indeed, it was said that "he that keepeth the law bringeth offerings enough, and to forsake unrighteousness is a propitiation".[10] Therefore, from the time of the eighth century Prophets onwards, the rabbis had excellent precedents for making repentance and good deeds an efficacious substitute for the sacrificial offerings and the temple festivals.

The elimination of the cultus after A.D. 70, however, raised the question of the nature of genuine repentance and the way in which forgiveness was to be secured. The abrogation of the sacrificial system made it necessary to rely on interior powers of resolute turning from sin and on purpose of amendment after confession of the transgressions committed, and the making of such restitution as might be demanded in the case of material injury.[11] This might involve an expression of guilt in the presence of several witnesses and of a desire for reconciliation, together with the propitiation of the injured party.[12] But in either case, it was by man's own effort that forgiveness was to be secured by returning to God and thereby forming himself anew. In the words of Rabbi Chanina, "If you obey and fulfil the commandments of God, it is as if you fulfilled yourselves, as if you created yourselves." And as God accepts repentance thus expressed, so when the wrong-doer makes this amends, it is the duty of the injured party to forgive him.[13]

CONFESSION IN JUDAISM

The obligation to make confession of sins is explicit in the Old Testament.[14] In the ritual of the scapegoat, as we have seen, it occupied a central position. Thus, the high-priest laid his hands on the goat for Azazel, confessing over it all the iniquities of Israel, having first performed the same ceremony in connexion with the bullock which he offered as a sin-offering for himself and his house.[15] He is said, in fact, to have confessed three times on the Day of Atonement. Standing by his own victim between the porch and the altar and facing west with his hands on its head he declared: "I beseech thee, Yahweh, I have committed iniquity, I have transgressed, I have sinned before thee, I and my house. I beseech thee, Yahweh, forgive now the iniquities and the transgressions and the sins wherein I have committed iniquity and transgressed and sinned before thee, I and my house. As it is written in the law of thy servant Moses, "For on this day shall atonement be made for you, to cleanse you from all your sins." The priests and the people responded: "Blessed be the name of His glory for ever." This was repeated over the sin-offering of the priests and over the scapegoat.[16]

Thus, according to the Rabbinical interpretation of the post-exilic observance, and the current liturgical practice preserved in the Midrash Torat Kohanim (*Sifra*) on Leviticus XVI, and in the Midrash and Tosephta on the Day of Atonement, penitence expressed in confession took the place of the earlier cleansing from ritual pollution after the destruction of the temple. This was given a personal application following the scriptural precedents of such notable individual penitents as David, Solomon and Daniel.[17] At first it sufficed to say, "I have sinned, transgressed, rebelled," but very soon the formula was elaborated. Thus, the form of confession appended to the Tephillah for the Day of Atonement in Jewish Prayer Books is attributed to Hamnuna in the fourth century A.D.:

O my God, before I was formed, I was nothing worth, and now that I have been formed, I am but as though I had not been formed. Dust I am in my life; how much more so in my death. Behold I am before thee like a vessel filled with shame and confusion. O may it be thy will, O Lord my God and God of my fathers, that I may sin no more, and so to the sins I have committed, purge them away in thine abounding compassion though not by means of affliction and sore diseases.[18]

Since it was not considered necessary or desirable to enumerate in the presence of a priest or before the congregation the actual sins committed, auricular confession has not been practised in Judaism.[19] The synagogue services were penitential in character, based on the confessions of the high-priest in the temple worship, but the Talmud expressly states that "when one utters the simple expression, 'Verily we have sinned,' he need say no more".[20] The opening words of the confessions of certain teachers in the third century A.D., made after the public prayers, are given, and some of them have been perpetuated in the later prayer books. That recited in the name of Rab is still retained, and runs as follows:

> Thou knowest the secrets of eternity and the most hidden mysteries of all living. Thou searchest the innermost recesses, and triest the reins and the heart. Nought is concealed from thee, or hidden from thine eyes.
>
> May it then be thy will, O Lord our God and God of our fathers, to forgive us for all our sins, to pardon us for all our iniquities, and to grant us remission for all our transgressions.[21]

At the approach of death the dying man is exhorted to make a general confession in terms such as these, as are criminals on their way to execution. If a confession cannot be framed, it suffices to say, "let my death be an atonement for all my iniquities."[22]

Since in Judaism the forgiveness of sin is essentially a divine prerogative which is not deputed to men, while ritual expiation, as we have seen, had a sacramental character, priestly absolution was never practised. The only remedy for the violation of the law of God is His forgiving grace, having its ground in His mercy, love and benevolence towards His people, and indeed to the entire human race, righteous and wicked alike.[23] So great is His goodness and compassion, in fact, that even the animal creation partakes of His beneficence, and no genuine penitent is ever refused forgiveness, though, according to the Rabbinical authorities, certain individuals

(Jeroboam, Ahab, Balaam, Doeg etc.) and classes of sinners (heretics, unbelievers, apostates etc.) are denied a share in the world to come.[24] But the sinner must reveal the right dispositions of repentance and amendment—the *contritio cordis,* the *confessio oris* and *satisfactio operis*—as in Christian moral theology.

Moreover, since sin is social as well as individual in character, the responsibility of each member of the Jewish community not only for his own conduct but also for that of his fellow men has been maintained. "Thou shalt surely rebuke thy neighbour, and not bear sin because of him" is a Talmudic injunction because the effects of sin are not confined to the individual sinner, as is shown in Hebrew tradition in the case of Akan and Korah. Indeed, when one sins not only do all suffer, but the evil is liable to become a contagion since a sinner is prone to lead others into sin.[25] Therefore, if the whole structure of society is to be preserved from contamination the avertion of guilt must be avoided and every effort made to bring the sinner to repentance (*Teshubah*).

In Judaism the conception of a community attains its full meaning and significance. This found expression in a union of *Teshubah,* of repentance and atonement, in which the righteous and the wicked are "joined together in a single bundle that the one may atone for the other". Before the destruction of the Temple, sacrifice for sin, and expiation, removed guilt. After that catastrophe the study of the Torah together with works of mercy, good actions, prayer and confession were thought to be as efficacious as the sacrificial offerings, provided they were accompanied by right moral dispositions and a firm determination to avoid a repetition of specific sins and their occasions.[26] No intervening priestly agent or mediator, however, was required to effect divine forgiveness. God alone forgives and this He does fully and freely without any mediation, notwithstanding the fact that man never entirely ceases to be in need of atonement, as the earlier ritual testifies and the later prayers confirm.

THE CHRISTIAN DOCTRINE OF RECONCILIATION

It was here that Christianity parted company with the Judaism in which it emerged, by concentrating attention upon salvation as the reverse side of guilt requiring a recreative act of atonement for sin, at once a deliverance and new birth; a reconciliation and regeneration. The Day of Atonement, it is true, was regarded by the rabbis as constituting an annulment of the past under the figure of a new creation.[27] But it differed fundamentally from the Pauline doctrine of rebirth based on the idea of the need of man to be reconciled with God through a process of redemption.[28] So far from the study of the Torah being efficacious in repentance, for the Apostle the Mosaic Law was the focal point of his attack on the Old Dispensation because he regarded its "works" to be wholly inadequate to secure "justification".[29]

In formulating his doctrine of atonement in terms of justification by faith in contrast to the Jewish contention that salvation must be attained by individual effort, obedience to the demands of the Law, and corporate responsibility, St Paul by devious ways and side-tracks, involved arguments and mixed metaphors, arrived at the conclusion that in the process of reconciliation a change of status rather than of character is a first requirement.[30] Therefore, baptism into the Church as the "mystical body of Christ" was a *sine quâ non,* since until this had been accomplished justification, sanctification and communion with the risen Christ as mediator could not be realized.[31] But once the new status had been acquired it became possible for the reborn to reckon themselves "to be dead unto sin but alive unto God in Christ Jesus".[32]

The Pauline interpretation of the new relationship between God and man that it was claimed the death and resurrection of Christ had established, raised a number of theoretical and practical problems for the Early Church. If in fact "God was in Christ reconciling the world unto Himself", that which had been accomplished once and for all by the Saviour of mankind had to be made actual in the life of the individual and in that of the redeemed humanity as a whole, i.e. in the Church. This involved the establishment of an ecclesiastical structure adequate for the purpose. Therefore, when the apostolic ministry replaced the Jewish priesthood and its ordinances, its function included the exercise of a "ministry of reconciliation" as the means whereby man might be reconciled to God through His duly appointed ambassadors commissioned to act on behalf of Christ in the dispensation of the grace of forgiveness, and in the maintenance of the solidarity of Christ with his people.[33]

THE JOHANNINE COMMISSION

Although in the first instance the power to "bind and loose", assigned according to the Matthaean tradition to St Peter in a viceregental capacity and then to the disciples collectively as an *ecclesia*,[34] appears to have referred to administration and arbitration rather than to absolution,[35] in the Fourth Gospel the commission to remit and retain sins is represented as the counterpart of the Matthaean binding and loosing. In the form in which it is said to have been given, according to the Fourth Evangelist, Jesus is depicted as appearing on the evening of Easter Day to the apostolic company assembled behind closed doors, perhaps in the cenaculum. After saluting them in the customary Eastern manner and displaying to them his wounds, he breathed on them and said, "receive ye the Holy Ghost; whosoever sins ye forgive they are forgiven unto them; whosoever sins ye retain they are retained."[36]

The symbolism would seem to have been based on the Hebrew creation story, where, according to the J narrative in the book of Genesis, Yahweh Elohim moulded man out of the clay of the earth and to animate his body breathed into his nostrils the breath of life.[37] So in the Fourth Gospel it is affirmed that the new creation of the Church as the Mystical Body of Christ was quickened by the risen life of the Second Adam,[38] bestowed in the first instance upon those who were to form its vital centre. With this equipment and in virtue of the command which accompanied the inbreathing of the quickening spirit—"whosoever sins ye forgive they are forgiven"—they were commissioned to carry on his work of salvation in the world by his delegated authority as the channel of his liberating and reconciling power issuing from his death and resurrection.

If the Evangelist has recorded an historical event, it would seem likely that the commission was given to the ten apostles re-assembled in the room in which they had foregathered for their last *chabûrah* with their Master on the previous Thursday evening. The setting and circumstances suggest such a gathering, which would be an appropriate sequel to their original sending forth and to the promises recorded earlier in the narrative.[39] In any case, the Johannine commission was generally assumed by the early Church to have been a special endowment prior to the Pentecostal afflatus on the whole body of the faithful recorded in Acts ii. 1–4.[40]

THE SACRAMENTS OF BAPTISM AND PENANCE

From Apostolic times the spiritual life of the Christian was thought to begin with a baptism of repentance,[41] closely associated with a confession of sins.[42] As this initiatory rite took shape confession and absolution were brought into juxta-position, together with the laying on of hands conveying the charismatic gift, to form one complete whole in the process of rebirth.[43] By these means it was believed "justification" from actual sin was effected and the initiate mystically united with the crucified and risen Saviour in whose victory he participated sacramentally. Through a symbolic death and resurrection made efficacious by a cathartic and therapeutic rite, the "body of sin" was "annulled" so that henceforth those who had been cleansed, washed and sanctified lived in a state of grace.

This conclusion, however, raised a practical difficulty for the Early Church. If those who had embraced "the life of the age to come" by sacramental initiation were *renatas in aeternum,* in the sense that they were incapable of contracting actual sin after baptism, how was this theoretical affirmation to be equated with the practical experience of a Christian sinning and coming short of the glory of God when already he was in a regenerate condition? It was as a result of this enigma that the sacrament of penance in due course emerged to provide a sacramental method of dealing with the post-baptismal offender. At first it was exercised only on very rare occasions, restricted to the three capital sins, homicide, adultery and apostasy; or to times of persecution, when it was confined to one μετάνωα. In the Gospels the only unforgivable sin is said to be blasphemy against the Holy Spirit,[44] but the threefold prohibition in Acts xv. 6—pollutions of idols, fornication and blood—became in the early centuries the three mortal offences which were either beyond the scope of absolution altogether, or demanded special treatment by a system of penance before reconciliation could be admitted. The distinction between "mortal" and "venial" sin mentioned in the Johannine epistle[45] was developed by later Christian writers. The capital or deadly sins at first were left to the justice and mercy of God, not because they were regarded as unforgivable but because the Church felt itself unable to take the responsibility of exercising reconciliation on its own initiative. Homicide, idolatry and fornication incurred the penalty of excommunication, very much as St Paul delivered to Satan the incestuous Corinthian for "the destruction of the flesh that the spirit may be saved in the day of the Lord Jesus Christ".[46]

This rigorist attitude, however, was soon modified, though relapse into paganism, which was considered to be the gravest crime, remained an inexpiable sin till the time of St Cyprian (A.D. 252), when the havoc of the Decian persecution made some means of restoration imperative if the Church was to survive. At the beginning of the second century Hermas of Rome claimed to have received a revelation to the effect that as persecution, and possibly the Parousia, were imminent reconciliation could be made once after baptism.[47] This, however, was admittedly an exception, the normal rule being that to "apostates, blasphemers, betrayers of the brethren, repentance is not open".[48] The teaching of Hermas was endorsed by Clement of Alexandria who maintained that "it behoves him who has received the remission of sins that he sin no more. For a regards the first and only penitence (μετανοία) of sins, that is to say, the sins which formerly found place in the course of

the ethnic and earlier life, I mean the life of ignorance, penitence is forthwith incumbent upon those who are called,
cleansing the region of the soul from offences, in order that
faith may be established. And the Lord, who knoweth hearts
and foreknoweth things to come, the fickleness of man, and the
perversity and subtilty of the devil, foresaw of old time from on
high, that he being envious of man on account of the remission
of sins, would inflict certain occasions of sin upon the servants
of God, astutely plotting evil in order that these might share his
fall with him. (God) accordingly being exceedingly merciful,
gave another and a second penitence (μετάνοιαν) to those
among the faithful who fell into some transgression. If any be
tempted after his call, and be overborne by compulsion or per-
suasion he may yet receive this one penitence not to be repented
of."[49]

Thus, in Alexandria at the beginning of the third century, it
was admitted by the head of the great catechetical school that
one opportunity of repentance and reconciliation was given to
those who had committed grievous sin after their baptism, not
merely as an exceptional concession, as in Hermas in the
previous century, but as a general rule of the Church, covering
even the case of the unfaithful wife.[50] This latter lapse, however,
was rejected by Origin,[51] as in the West it had been condemned
by Hippolytus in his attack on Callistus, bishop of Rome between 218 and 222,[52] and by Tertullian at Carthage.[53] The
charge brought against Callistus included the reconciliation of
sinners in the matter of impurity, after they had done penance.
This was an innovation in the rigorist tradition of the Roman
Church highly distasteful to Tertullian. Thus, while in his
earlier treatise, *De Poenitentia,* the first of the great Latin Fathers
expressly declared that all sins, of flesh and spirit, of will and
deed, were pardoned by baptism, and admitted one post-
baptismal repentance,[54] in his later work, *De Pudicitia,* written
after he became a Montanist, he placed sins against purity in the
same category as idolatry and murder. Therefore, they were
unpardonable[55] unless the adulterer became a martyr.[56]

Nevertheless, although this was the position which predominated in the second and third centuries, a more lenient view had its advocates in Dionysius of Corinth, and in Cornelius, who became bishop of Rome in 251, as well as in Callistus, who prepared the way for the work of Cyprian at Carthage after the Decian persecution (250). In Spain the earlier rigorist practice survived throughout the century, and in 303 the Council of Elvira refused even the last sacraments to those who had lapsed into paganism under the strain of the Diocletian persecution in progress at the time. But the Church as a whole recognized that the apostate could not be debarred from all hope of reconciliation in this world, and it set to work, therefore, to institute a penitential system in order that the lapsed might be re-admitted to Communion after proper restitution. In due course homicides and other grave offenders were included, so that by the time the Nicene Council assembled in 325 a canon could be enacted to cover the reconciliation of all penitents irrespective of the nature of their sins and offences.

PUBLIC PENANCE AND PRIVATE CONFESSION

Since the capital sins for the most part were of a public character they demanded public penance. This involved confession followed by prescribed penitential exercises administered under episcopal authority; or, in the East, by a special penitentiary appointed by the bishop. The discipline, known as *exomologesis,* included fasting, prostration, the wearing of sackcloth, lying in ashes, mortification in food and drink and exclusion from the sacraments. The preliminary avowal of sin was not necessarily made in public, but, as St Augustine declared, "if the sin is not only grievous in itself, but involves scandal given to others, and if the bishop (*antistites*) judges that it will be useful to the Church, let not the sinner refuse to do penance in the sight of many or even of the people at large, let him not resist, nor through shame add to his mortal wound a greater evil."[57] It seems, then, that it rested with the confessor to determine whether or not the penance should be performed publicly, and the confession published.

That confession to a priest in private was the normal

practice is suggested by the counsel of Origen urging penitents to consider the character of the priest to whom they should show their sins and seek the remedy. "If it be one who will be weak with the weak, who will weep with the sorrowful, and who understands the discipline of condolence and fellow-feeling, so that when his skill shall be known and his pity felt, you may follow what he shall advise. Should he think your disease to be such that it should be declared in the assembly of the faithful—whereby others may be edified, and yourself easily reformed—this must be done with much deliberation, and the skilful advice of the physician."[58]

From this passage it is clear that the first duty of the sinner was to confess to the priest or bishop in private and leave it to him to decide what the subsequent procedure should be. So far from public penance being the general rule, St Basil expressly states that in the case of an adulteress "who had made confession through piety or whose sin was otherwise proved," to avoid the matter becoming public knowledge she should be admitted to the Eucharist though debarred from receiving Communion.[59] In the West, Leo the Great appealed to the "Apostolic rule" against "the recitation of the nature of particular sins in a written statement (*libellus*)," maintaining that "it sufficed that the accusation of conscience be indicated to the priests (*sacerdotibus*) alone in secret confession".[60]

This ordinance, issued in 461, marks the end of public confession in the Western Church, and in the East the office of *poenitentiarius* had already (390) been abolished by Nestorius owing to the scandal that was occasioned by the practice. The four "stations", or grades of penitents, known as "weepers", stationed outside the church, "hearers" in the narthex, "prostrators" between the door and the chancel or ambo, and "bystanders" permitted to be present at the Liturgy while awaiting their final restoration to the status of a communicant, soon fell into abeyance. In the West in place of this system of graded penance the tendency was to treat penitents as catechumens throughout, leaving it to the priest, after he had heard the confession in secret, to assign such private and public exercises and duration as he thought meet and right in particular cases.[61] Gradually, however, as in the East, the penitential system was mitigated, and although the Church has never ceased to exercise the power of excommunication, the primitive discipline has been allowed to lapse into desuetude.

The practice of expiating public sins by public penance tended in the Middle Ages to take the form of works of piety, such as the making of a pilgrimage to the Holy Land, or to the shrine of St James at Santiago de Compostela in Spain, of equipping a soldier to go on a crusade, or fasting, almsgiving, scourging, prayer and other devout exercises, in remission of punishment due to sin (i.e. indulgence). By commuting an enjoined penance in this way it became possible to devise a method of redemption, or substitution, to cover the entire penitential discipline by one act. This inevitably led to abuses, and the familiar scandals connected with the traffic in indulgences by "alms-gatherers", which persisted until they were finally abolished by the Tridentine decree in 1551.[62] But long before this the Fourth Council of the Lateran in 1215 had imposed on every Christian in Western Christendom who had reached maturity the obligation to confess to a priest at least once a year at Eastertide, and to fulfil the penance imposed by the confessor.

Thus, the ancient system of public penance, universal in the West from A.D. 450, gradually gave place to the practice of private confession for the purpose of receiving absolution by a priest duly authorized to exercise the ministry of reconciliation be delegated jurisdiction. Although recourse to the sacrament of penance had not become obligatory until the thirteenth century, it had long been widely adopted by the devout, largely under Celtic and Anglo-Saxon influences, after the abandonment of the rigorist attitude to post-baptismal sin and the system of graded penances. Once the practice was definitely established and officially enjoined, it was systematized by the medieval theologians and canonists,[63] and subsequently their conclusions were endorsed and defined by the Council of Trent in 1551.

THE PRIEST IN ABSOLUTION

As a result of these deliberations priestly absolution acquired a judicial significance since the confessor acted in the capacity of a judge.[64] Therefore, the general commission to absolve sins confessed, given at ordination to the priesthood, did not *ipso facto* carry with it the right to exercise the ministry of reconciliation in the tribunal of penance without further authorization. Ordination to the priesthood bestowed sacramental power (*potestas sacramentalis*) to declare divine forgiveness on behalf of the Church, but it remained for the bishop to authorize a priest to hear confessions within the limits of a given delegated internal jurisdiction (i.e. a parish or some other ecclesiastical area, such as a Religious Order or the services of the crown). In short, a priest to pronounce a valid and regular absolution must have jurisdiction conferred upon him by his superiors (i.e. the bishop, or in the case of a Religious the superior of his Order), except in the event of danger of death when any priest may absolve as an emergency measure.[65] In normal circumstances, parish priests exercise those aspects of their office in virtue of their institution to their benefice; other priests by licence. But even so, certain sins may be taken out of the jurisdiction of a priest and required to be submitted to a higher ecclesiastical tribunal. In these so-called "reserved cases" absolution may be given only by the bishop of the diocese, or some authority superior to him, unless a licence or faculty (*specialis facultas*) is issued for the purpose to a particular priest.[66]

To fulfil his office as Judge the confessor must have a competent knowledge of moral theology in order to ascertain whether the penitent has the right dispositions for receiving absolution, since the validity of the sacrament depends on the worthiness of its reception. In other words, the penitent must reveal genuine contrition (i.e., sorrow for the sins committed, a hatred of them, and a firm purpose and resolution not to repeat them in the future). Since what is technically known as "perfect contrition" is held to arise from the motive of perfect love of God, as a special divine gift which justifies the soul without recourse to absolution, contrary to the opinion of some of the early Scholastics it is not now regarded as an essential requirement of a good confession. Therefore, the Council of Trent affirmed that "attrition", or "imperfect contrition"—viz. sorrow for sin arising from motives lower than perfect love—is sufficient for the reception of a valid absolution.

Contrition is expressed by a detailed confession of all mortal sins committed since the last absolution which can sincerely be remembered, together with their circumstances in each case. It is only when such a disclosure has been made that the priest is in a position to pass judgment on the spiritual condition of the sinner and to impose an appropriate penance by way of satisfaction; for the penalties attached to sin, even when the guilt has been forgiven, are an integral part of the process of reconciliation. Therefore, self-accusation finds its completion in self-chastisement, and until the penance has been imposed and duly performed, though the absolution is valid the sacramental grace is not effective, unless the penitent is physically, or for some other sound reason, incapable of fulfilling this condition. Appeal against a penance to the confessor is permissible.[67]

THE SEAL OF CONFESSION

If the purpose of amendment and the making of satisfaction are obligatory on the part of the penitent, the seal of confession (*sigillum confessionis*) is not less stringently imposed upon the priest. Thus, no public penance may be required, or any demand which might disclose the nature of a sin committed. Neither "by word, sign, or in any manner whatever", as the Fourth Lateran Council declared in 1215, may a confessor disclose anything learnt in the tribunal of penance, with no possible exception, unless the penitent relaxes the obligation. Moreover, outside the confessional the priest may not discuss the contents of a confession with his penitent on his own initiative, or answer any questions put to him by a third party which might break the seal, even to save his own life.[68] He can merely state that he has no communicable knowledge on the subject and refuse to enter into a discussion about it. The obli-

N

gation extends to any ecclesiastical superior who confers with the confessor or with the penitent, and to any correspondence or consultations that might involve violation. In short, the seal has been made as absolutely binding as is humanly possible.

THE CONTINENTAL REFORMERS AND ABSOLUTION

Since the valid administration of the sacrament requires both "the power of the keys" conferred in absolution and internal jurisdiction, either "ordinary" or "delegated",[69] it presupposes the Catholic constitution of the Church as the ultimate authority in the process of "loosing" and "binding", resting on the Johannine commission as interpreted by the patristic writers and the medieval doctors. Therefore, when this conception of divine forgiveness and reconciliation was repudiated by the Protestant reformers in the sixteenth century, the sacrament of penance and its minister necessarily were abandoned, together with the penitential system with which it was so intimately connected. In violent revolt against the principle of vicarious satisfaction for the penalties attached to sin, which found expression in the doctrine and practice of extra-sacramental indulgences (subsequently endorsed by the Council of Trent and the Counter-Reformation), Luther took his stand on justification through faith alone in the saving merits of the sacrificial death of Christ. Having taken upon himself the guilt of man, the righteousness of the Saviour, it was maintained, in all its perfection is transferred to the sinner who in genuine repentance surrenders himself wholly and unconditionally to him, without any further requirement or sacramental intervention. Consequently, there can be no remission by sanctifying grace other than that bestowed through justifying faith, and the illuminating regenerative ministry of the Word making known by the Holy Spirit the promises of the Gospel concerning the forgiveness of sins. Although Luther recommended the voluntary use of private confession as a pious practice, absolution having ceased to be an integral part of a divinely ordained sacramental system, the custom gradually died out and was replaced by a service of public confession and "absolution" as a preparation for Communion, in which the intending communicants promised amendment and the pastor declared the forgiveness that had been secured by Christ.

Zwingli instituted a court of discipline for the exclusion of unworthy communicants from the Lord's Supper, though the right of excommunication was left to the State. The *First Helvetian Confession* provided for excommunication and for reinstatement after repentance, but it was careful to affirm that "God alone forgives sin, and that through Christ Jesus, our Lord, alone". Confession to a priest or neighbour, therefore, ought not to be for remission of sins but for consultation. Calvin, like Luther, at first advocated private confession but since he denied all idea of sacramental absolution, the only merit obtained thereby was a greater guarantee of forgiveness when pardon was expressed by a minister. Discipline was rigidly maintained by a Consistory Court composed of six pastors and twelve elders who lived in different parts of Geneva in order to exercise oversight of Genevan households and report on their moral integrity and religious fidelity from time to time. Those who failed to attend church on Sundays were reported by watchmen appointed for the purpose, and appropriate fines were levied. More serious offences such as blasphemy, heresy and idolatry, were punished by the State, which was regarded by Calvin as a Christian institution established to defend the cause of religion, though it was denied the power of excommunication.

PENITENTIAL DISCIPLINE IN ENGLAND AFTER THE
   REFORMATION

While this rigorous discipline was readily adopted by the Puritans in England and the Presbyterians in Scotland, it never was accepted by the English Church. The various Acts of Uniformity passed between 1549 and 1662, as we have seen, were an abortive attempt to enforce a common faith and worship throughout the country rather than to impose penalties on sinners and the lapsed. Nevertheless, the need of ecclesiastical discipline was recognized officially in the commendation of excommunication in the Articles of Religion (XXXIII), and of public penance in the Commination drawn up in 1549 for use on Ash Wednesday, presumably in place of the sentence of the Greater Excommunication read in the medieval Church at the beginning of Advent, Lent, on Trinity Sunday and the Sunday within the octave of the Assumption. Moreover, in the rubrics prefixed to the Liturgy, the curate is directed to "call and advertise" any member of the congregation who is known to be "an open and notorious evil liver, or to have done any wrong to his neighbours by word or deed so that the congregation be thereby offended", that "he may in no wise presume to come to the Lord's Table until he have openly declared himself to have truly repented and amended his former naughty life".[70]

To the need of such discipline Thorndike bore witness. "If a Christian after Baptism, fall into any grievous sin, voiding the effect of Baptism, can it fall within the sense of a Christian to imagine; that hee can bee restored by a *Lord have mercy upon mee?* No, it must cost him hot tears, and sighs and groans, and extraordinary prayers, with fasting and alms; to take Revenge upon himself, to appease God's wrath, and to mortifie his Concupiscence; If hee mean not to leave an entrance for the same sin again. If his sin bee notorious, so much the more; Because hee must then satisfie the Church, that hee doth what is requisite to satisfie God; that is, to appease his wrath, and to recover his grace. The Church may bee many ways hindred, to take account of notorious sin. But the Power of the Keyes, which God hath trusted it with, is exercised only in keeping such sinners from the Communion, till the Church bee so satisfied. And for this exercise, the time of Lent hath always been deputed by the Church."[71]

That public penance was enforced in England after the Restoration is shown by the numerous references to the practice in the literature of the period. Thus Pepys records a declaration of penitence of a man who had undergone "the Church's censure for his wicked life" which he witnessed on July 16th, 1665. Similarly, on June 16th, 1686 a verger of Durham Cathedral

did penance for drunkenness, and in the next century in
January 1799 for the same sin a parish clerk was cited by the
Dean of Middleham and ordered on the first Sunday in Lent
to read after the Nicene creed a public confession of his mis-
conduct.[72] In like manner women were proclaimed in church
for breaches of the seventh commandment, and Wordsworth
affirms that before 1778 he saw a woman doing penance in
church arrayed in a white sheet.[73] On August 5th, 1733
William Pells and Amy King were required to appear in
their respective parish churches of Otley and Helmingham in
Suffolk, clothed in a white sheet and holding a white wand in
their hands humbly to acknowledge the sin of fornication,
repeating "after the minister" a public confession "before the
Psalms and Sermon".[74]

PRIESTLY ABSOLUTION IN THE ENGLISH PRAYER BOOK

As regards the sacrament of penance, the position taken up
by the Church of England after the Reformation was to leave
the use of private confession to the conscience of the penitent.
The power of absolution vested in the priesthood was maintained in the Book of Common Prayer from 1549 onwards.
This is most apparent in the Ordinal where the Johannine
Commission, "whose sins thou dost forgive, they are forgiven:
whose sins thou dost retain, they are retained"—was deliberately
made an essential part of the Ordering of Priests in the First
Edwardian rite in 1550, although it is not found in the ancient
and medieval Pontificals prior to the twelfth or thirteenth
centuries. Therefore, since on an appeal to antiquity it could
have been omitted, presumably it was retained for the express
purpose of continuing the exercise of the ministry of reconciliation. In 1538 Cranmer in his Injunctions recognized private
confession as a regular part of the sacramental discipline of
the Church, and while he allowed that the practice is not enjoined in Scripture, he recommended those with troubled consciences to seek "consolation, counsel and absolution *singulatim
a sacerdote*". Furthermore, according to the pamphlet *Recantae-
yans*, published privately from a MS. in the Bibliothèque

Nationale in Paris and found among the papers of Harpsfield, he made his confession to a priest on the morning of his execution. Therefore, his action in 1550 in transferring the Johannine commission from the subordinate position it occupied in the Sarum Pontifical before the post-communion in the Mass as a final laying on of hands, to the central place in the Edwardian Ordinal is significant, viewed in the light of his own practice and of the course that events took under his guidance.

In the first year of the reign of Edward VI (1547) the clergy were exhorted in a royal injunction to examine each Lent "every person that cometh to confession, whether they can recite the articles of their faith, and the Ten Commandments in English, and hear them say the same particularly". In the First Prayer Book issued two years later, a general confession and absolution were included in the new Liturgy; and in the Order for the Visitation of the Sick a rubric was inserted requiring the priest to urge the sick person to make a special confession, "if he fele his conscience troubled with any weightie matter. After which confession the priest shall absolue hym after thys forme:

> Our Lord Jesus Christ, who hath lefte power to his Churche to absolue all sinners, which truely repent and beleue in hym; of his great mercy forgeue thee thyne offences: and by his autoritie committed to me I absolue thee frō all thy synnes, in the name of the Father, and of the sonne, and of the holy gost. Amen.

"And this same forme of absolucion shal be used in all pryuate confession."[75]

This absolution differs from the precatory form in the Liturgy, in that it was modelled on that used with the traditional *confiteor* in the Mass and at Prime and Compline, in being indicative and personal "I absolve thee from all thy sins." This formula was not adopted until the eleventh century,[76] and then it only gradually replaced the earlier deprecatory forms which still survive in the Roman formulary in combination with the later indicative language:

May the Almighty God have mercy on you, forgiving your sins, bring you to life everlasting. Amen.

May the Almighty and Merciful God grant you pardon, absolution and remission of your sins. May our Lord Jesus Christ absolve you, and I, by His authority, absolve you from every bond of excommunication and interdict so far as I can and you may need. I absolve you from your sins in the name of the Father and of the Son, and of the Holy Ghost. Amen.

May the Passion of our Lord Jesus Christ, the merits of the Blessed Virgin Mary and of all the Saints, what good you have done and what evil you have suffered, be to you for the remission of your sins, growth in grace, and the reward of everlasting life. Amen.

In the decree *Pro Armenis* (1439) Eugene IV declared that the "form" of the sacrament of penance is in the words *Ego absolvo te a peccatis tuis in nomine Patris* etc. Therefore, regarded in terms of the Scholastic doctrine of "matter" and "form" in the sacraments, the Anglican absolution in the Order of the Visitation of the Sick is valid, so far as the formula is concerned, whatever may be the position regarding the minister. And in the light of the evidence of the Ordinal there can be little doubt that the English Reformers intended to perpetuate the established practice of priestly absolution, while at the same time making the use of the sacrament of penance voluntary; throwing the responsibility on the individual to decide for himself whether he should or should not seek this method of reconciliation. Thus, in the absolution composed in 1552 and prefixed to the Daily Offices, it was clearly affirmed that "God has given power and commandment to His ministers to declare and pronounce to His people, being penitent, the absolution and remission of their sins". Furthermore, in 1661 the word "minister" in the earlier rubric—"the absolution to be pronounced by the minister alone"—was altered to "priest" to restrict its use to those who had been duly commissioned to exercise this sacerdotal ministry, in accordance with the terms

of the Ordinal. This declaration, therefore, was then brought
into line with those parts of the Order of Holy Communion
which might be performed by the priest alone.

Again, in the Exhortation introduced into the Liturgy in
1549, to be read after the Sermon or Homily, intending communicants, when "full trust in God's mercy and a quiet conscience" cannot be obtained by self-examination and repentance, were urged to resort to the parish priest, or "to some other
discreet and learned minister of God's Word and to open
their grief; that by the ministry of God's Holy Word they
may receive the benefit of absolution, together with ghostly
counsel and advice". In the original form in which it was
drawn up in 1549, the voluntary nature of private confession
was stressed by the addition of the words (omitted in the revisions of 1552 and 1662) requiring "such as shall be satisfied
with a general confession not to be offended with them that do
use to their further satisfying, the auricular and secret confession
to the priest: nor those also which think needful or convenient
for the quietness of their own consciences particularly to open
their sins to the priest to be offended with them that are satisfied with their humble confession to God and the general
confession to the Church. But in all things to follow and
keep the rule of charity, and every man to be satisfied with
his own conscience, not judging other men's minds and consciences; where as he hath no warrant of God's Word to the
same."

PRIVATE CONFESSION BEFORE AND AFTER THE RESTORATION

In the second Book of the Homilies published in 1563 and
appointed to be read in all parish churches by royal command,
the same position was maintained. While absolution was described as having "the promise of forgiveness of sins", and
confession represented as a laudable custom for those who found
themselves troubled and doubtful in conscience, it was not
obligatory as it was in what is described as "the time of blind-
ness and ignorance". Nevertheless, the sacrament of Penance

appears to have been widely used in the English Church both before and after the Restoration in 1660. Whitgift (1530–1604), for example, did not hesitate to affirm that pronouncing remission of sins in terms of the Ordinal was "the principal duty of a minister",[77] while Hooker (1554–1600) maintained that "confession to man, not to God only, is not in reformed churches denied by the learneder sort of divines, but, cleared from all errors, is both lawful and behoveful for God's people".[78] Indeed, "to use the benefit of this help, for the better satisfaction" in cases of mortal sin is "so natural that it can be forbidden no man". Though, in accordance with the Anglican post-reformation tradition, he added, "yet not so necessary, that all men should be in case to need it."[79] Nevertheless, he himself sought the comfort and consolation of this means of reconciliation, and on the day before his own death sent for his confessor, Dr Saravin, to receive absolution and the Viaticum.[80]

In the next century Jeremy Taylor (1613–1667), the son of a Protestant martyr, acted as confessor to John Evelyn, who in the days of the Commonwealth, when only one church in London was suffered to remain for the administration of the sacraments, went to town to make his confession to the saintly Caroline divine.[81] Charles I confessed to William Juxon, Bishop of London, who absolved him at Whitehall before his execution on January 30th, 1649, and after the Restoration of the monarchy in 1660, in the capacity of Archbishop of Canterbury he crowned the son of "the royal martyr". During the succeeding years the practice was resumed as part of the sacramental tradition, but with the same latitude in respect of conscience. Dr Sanderson, Bishop of Lincoln, was absolved by his chaplain before his death in 1663, and on his return from exile in France in 1879, Dennis Granville unburdened his conscience to the Bishop of Ely, whom he described as his "first spiritual father".[82] Thomas Ken (1637–1711) exercised considerable influence as a confessor, and was censured by Burnet for giving absolution to Charles II on his death-bed. John Sharp (1645–1714), who eventually became Archbishop of York, acted as spiritual adviser to Queen Anne but it is doubtful whether the office was that of confessor.[83]

Be this as it may, the literature of the period bears witness to the prevalence of resort to the sacrament of penance as a recognized preparation for death, as, for example, in *Tom Jones* where Fielding makes Parson Thwackum ask, "who but an atheist could think of leaving the world without having first made up his account? without confessing his sins, and receiving that absolution which he knew he had one in the house duly authorised to give him?"[84] In Cosin's *Collection of Private Devotions,* which ran through a series of editions from 1627 to the end of the century, "to disburden and quiet our consciences of those sins that may grieve us, or scruples that may trouble us," recourse is recommended "to a learned and discreet priest, and from him to receive advice and the benefit of absolution".[85] Similar instructions recur in other manuals of devotion drawn up by such divines as Ken, Wetenhall and Hammond, and are confirmed by the theologians, Thorndike, Pearson, Barrow, Wake and Beveridge, all of whom maintain that private confession and absolution are legitimate though not obligatory practices in the Church of England.[86] The position is summarized in a catechism drawn up in 1723 to differentiate the teaching of the Anglican and Roman Communions. The English Church, it is declared, is "not against Confessing to a Minister". On the contrary, "our Church presses it, both publick and private, to God chiefly, and to a pious and able Divine, if the Conscience be burthened, and particularly upon a sick or death bed, and before receiving the Sacrament."[87]

In the eighteenth century, however, a decline in sacramental religion set in, and while the practice of private confession never entirely ceased, in the period immediately before the rise of the Oxford Movement in 1833 it was doubtless much less frequently used than formerly. Nevertheless, Dr Seeker, who became Archbishop of Canterbury in 1758, affirmed that "in many Cases acknowledging the Errors of our Lives, and opening the State of our Souls to the Ministers of God's Word, for their Opinion, their Advice and their Prayers, may be extremely useful, sometimes necessary. And whenever Persons think so, we are ready both to hear them with the utmost Secresy, and to assist them with our best Care; to direct them how they may be forgiven, if we think they are not; to pronounce them forgiven, if we think they are."[88] Sir George Pretyman Tornline, Bishop of Lincoln (and subsequently translated to Winchester), regarded "confessing to priests as sometimes useful by leading to effectual repentance".[89]

It is by no means clear, however, that these divines attached a sacramental significance to absolution, as in the earlier period, and although in isolated cases[90] the practice of confession lingered on, notably at times of crisis and as a preparation for death (and then apparently often surreptitiously), it cannot be regarded as having been in fact an integral part of the Anglican tradition at the beginning of the nineteenth century.

It was no doubt partly on account of the prevailing unfamiliarity with the sacrament of Penance that its revival by the Tractarians after 1833 met with such strenuous opposition, frequently coupled with gross misrepresentation of the procedure, and a lingering memory of the medieval abuses of the penitential system. Nevertheless, it could not be denied that few doctrines were more firmly embedded in the Prayer Book and the other official formularies of the English Church, or could claim greater support from the teaching and practice of some of the most reputable Anglican divines in the preceding centuries.[91] Moreover, it met a human need, especially when its voluntary character was maintained, as has become increasingly clear in recent years. In the intervening period during the past century, a more balanced judgment has been brought to bear upon this ancient practice, and to-day, in addition to the theological significance of "the benefits of absolution", the recognition of the importance and value of wisely given direction under adequate safeguards is not confined to one tradition or school of thought. This has found expression in a demand for properly trained and duly qualified confessors performing their functions, as in times past, under delegated jurisdiction, in accordance with the provisions of Canon Law.

THE FUNCTION OF PRIESTLY ABSOLUTION

Thus, it has been widely recognized that the exercise of a "ministry of reconciliation" and the "direction of souls" is an integral part of the priestly office. As we have seen, the function of the priesthood essentially has been to maintain a right relationship between man and the sacred order of which it is the instrument and agent. In the case of expiation and absolution this has been accomplished by expelling evil and remitting sin in order to get rid of harmful contagions and malign influences, or, at a higher level, to prevent permanent alienation from God and to secure freedom from guilt, designated in theological language sin and applied to a breach of a moral law which expresses the divine will. So long as evil was or is interpreted in terms of ritual uncleanness and prohibitions (tabus), priestly intervention employing mechanical methods and agencies—e.g. blood, water, or a scapegoat—removes the taint and its consequences. This primitive conception of evil and its removal not infrequently recurs even when wrong-doing has become sin against an ethically righteous God, like many other survivals from a lower substratum of culture. But the doctrine and practice of priestly absolution in a religion like Christianity moves on an entirely different plane.

In the Christian scheme of salvation priestly absolution is the means, as we have seen, whereby those who have been admitted to the Church by baptism can be restored to and maintained in a state of grace (i.e. of divine favour) by the expression of genuine contrition, confession and purpose of amendment. Thus, the function of the priest in the sacrament of Penance is twofold; the one negative the other positive, corresponding to the expulsion and impulsion aspects of the expiation ritual. Firstly, he exercises his office as the duly authorized instrument of the Church to remit sins committed after baptism by virtue of the powers bestowed upon him at his ordination, and delegated to him by the bishop under whom he serves. But his functions do not cease with the authoritative declaration of absolution when the necessary conditions and dispositions of repentance and satisfaction (penance) have been fulfilled.

In practice his secondary function is of a more positive nature. The sins having been remitted the spiritual life of the penitent has to be built up and strengthened. Therefore, the priest is required to act as the director of the consciences of those who seek his ministrations in the tribunal of penance. The penitent must submit to his guidance in the cultivation of the Christian virtues, and in progress towards perfection as the ultimate end and ideal of the Christian vocation.[92] The office of the confessor, therefore, involves a variety of functions which include, in addition to the giving or withholding of absolution, those of judge, father, physician and teacher.

Before he can pass judgment upon a particular case he must be in possession of the facts and circumstances of the sins committed, if these are in doubt, and of the dispositions of the penitent. It is his duty, therefore, to be sure of the integrity and veracity of the confession. This may involve judicious questioning as a secondary function to assist the penitent to submit fully his own sins and give outward evidence of contrition in a willingness to make satisfaction as an expression of a genuine desire for forgiveness and for reconciliation to God. He may also be called upon to estimate the guilt of apparently unconscious habits or involuntary acts[93]. Accessory to the function of judge is that of a fatherly attitude to the penitent calculated to give confidence and encouragement by patience and kindness, and the skill of a physician responsible for the cure of sick and suffering souls and the prevention or relapse by prophylactic treatment, involving an adequate knowledge of moral theology.[94] Similarly, a proper understanding of the faith and practice on which the Christian life is based is required, and for the fulfilment of his office as teacher an ability to apply such knowledge to particular cases in the tribunal.

In the exercise of this ministry the priesthood has under its control the means whereby internal moral conflicts can be resolved by bringing them to the level of consciousness and opening them to another person who, if he is adequately trained, is reasonably competent to deal with most ordinary cases,[95] and so prevent their becoming the source of morbid obsessions and other neuroses. It is now a matter of common knowledge that nervous strain and inhibitions due to the consciousness of wrong-doing are overcome by discovering and facing up to their causes. When this is done in the presence of one who is believed to have the authority of Christ and the Church behind him in the granting of absolution, the relief to the mind from the conflicts and repressions characteristic of a sense of sin can hardly be over-estimated, even though the confession may not disclose and interpret deep-rooted suppressed unconscious factors. As Jung has pointed out, "a psycho-neurosis must be understood as the suffering of a human being who has not discovered what life means for him, and it is spiritual stagnation, psychic sterility, which causes this state."[96] As the function of analysis is to reinstall the individual life-stream harmoniously in the general stream of life and to restore its direction and goal, so that of absolution is to reintegrate the spiritual life of the penitent and restore him to a state of grace and a right relationship with God Who is the source and ground of his being.

The declaration of forgiveness is the primary need of those in moral distress, and it is this which is made operative and efficacious in the sacrament of Penance, over and above the psychological interpretation of sin in terms of faulty sentiments or complexes; i.e. symptoms of a pathological condition susceptible to scientific treatment. It is true that the consciousness of guilt can readily become a repression and form a complex when relegated to the unconscious, and so make for the disruption of personality. For this reason the cultivation of the regular habit of confession prevents the development of a state equally disastrous in the mental and spiritual spheres, inasmuch as it eliminates the sense of guilt before it can become a seriously disturbing influence. This doubtless largely explains the relative absence of neurotic disorders in communities in which resort to the sacrament of penance is an established practice, in contrast to their prevalence under conditions where no such relief obtains. Thus, long before psychologists concentrated attention upon the problem, a way had been found to enable the individual to meet his own personal re-adjustments by the ministry of absolution and spiritual direction. In the exercise of this function the priesthood has provided the means of satisfying basic human needs at a personal level in the perpetuation of sentiments on which, as we have seen, the maintenance of society, both sacred and profane, depends.

Guilt, however it is regarded, is not limited to the individual in isolation from the rest of mankind. No man lives or sins to himself alone. As he is affected by his physical and social environment, so he in his turn affects the world around him of which he is an integral part. Not only is sin a personal act of rebellion but it produces a sinful human environment, as well as a condition of alienation from God. It follows, therefore, that the absolution or remission of sin has a wider reference, extending to the society in which the sinner lives, and to his relations within and towards it. In providing an outlet for individual internal conflicts, priestly intervention, notwithstanding its liability to abuse and frustration, performs a role of fundamental importance as an integrating force in those personal adjustments which have such far-reaching consequences in the right ordering of human life and of the structure of society.

CHAPTER VII

Priesthood and Sacred Learning

ALTHOUGH the primary function of the priest is to offer sacrifice, absolve the penitent and exorcise and expiate the forces of evil, he has also been a man of learning and the guardian of sacred tradition. Thus, in primitive states of culture where the esoteric lore of the tribe and its ritual techniques are the most treasured and carefully preserved heritage, it has been the duty of the religious leaders of the community to protect and pass on from one generation to another the cultic wisdom of the ages. This comprises the knowledge and technical equipment of the magic art acquired by an elaborate course of training prior to initiation into the profession, and the skill involved in the practice of exorcism, augury, divination and the service of the sanctuary.

THE ZUÑI SACERDOTAL FRATERNITIES

In the Pueblo region in Western New Mexico, for example, the Zuñi hierarchy is organized into thirteen fraternities for the meticulous performance of the ritual on which the growth and fertilization of the maize is thought to depend. This requires the memorizing of a vast amount of word-perfect ritual which, as Miss Ruth Benedict says, "staggers our less trained minds, and the performance of neatly dovetailed ceremonies that are charted by the calendar and complexly interlock all the different cults and the governing body in endless formal procedure."[1] The prayers and rites are standardized and assigned to particular societies within the organization, all arranged on the same patterns, but, as among the neighbouring Hopi of Arizona, each administering special and distinct ritual meticulously recited and performed.

The primary need in this desert country is rain. Therefore, the purpose of the religious observances is the bestowal of the first requisite for the growth of the crops. But the whole daily round is accompanied by ritual procedures, and each group of priests has its own appointed tasks and its proper times in the process. These include the recitation of the fixed epithets to the gods, masked dances, calendrical ceremonials, astronomical observations, and everything connected with fertility, curing disease, hunting, warfare, and tribal prosperity, health and well-being. While the rituals are essentially magical and centre in the sacred "medicine-bundles" in which the mystic power resides, they involve a very considerable knowledge of maize planting and nurture, and most of their functions are exercised in secret in the fastnesses of their priestly "retreats" when they "make their days" (i.e. retire in seclusion to sit motionless before their "bundles" at the appropriate seasons of rain-making). It is then that they call upon the vast stores of eso-teric knowledge and techniques which they go on accumu-lating throughout their lives as they proceed from one initiation to another, until at length they attain the highest degree in their Orders. Consequently, Zuñi priests are called "those who know how", having "learned their power verbatim from traditional sources".[2]

THE MAYA AND AZTEC CALENDRICAL CULTUS

In the adjoining region in Central Mexico an elaborate priestly organization developed among the Maya and Aztecs in association with the calendrical system which provided the re-ligious programme for each day in the year. The complete cycle of never-ending services was a reflection of the cosmic order, and eventually became overshadowed by the practice of human sacrifice on a gigantic scale. There is no indication, however, that this custom was in vogue among the Mayas, for when the civilization reached its climax about A.D. 1000 it was a peace-ful confederation of cities extending from north-west Honduras to the plateau of Yucatan. Dependence upon the seasons for the regulation of the crops led to the study of celestial pheno-mena and the invention of an ingenious system of interlocking cycles based on the solar and planetary years. The heliacal

o

rising or setting of constellations were correlated with seasonal changes in nature; the solstices and equinoxes were determined with considerable accuracy, and the short measurement of time by the phases of the moon. The five brighter planets were distinguished, and their synodic periods correctly estimated.

Since the sun was thought to have been destroyed several times with disastrous consequences, eclipses were regarded with dread as foreshadowing a repetition of the catastrophe. It is possible that in the first millennium B.C., in their efforts to establish the interval between the eclipse seasons, the Maya priesthood may have arrived at the *tzolkin,* or direct permutation of twenty names and thirteen numbers making a cycle of 260 designations for the days of the ceremonial year. Three eclipse seasons being equal to nearly two *tzolkins,* any considerable series of eclipses, either of the sun or of the moon, clustered around three focal days in the double *tzolkin.*[3] By the seventh century the Maya count day was established, and a book of lucky and unlucky days (*Tonalamatl*) eventually was compiled to indicate propitious and unpropitious times for performing certain actions. But although, as in other ancient civilizations, these early astronomical observations rapidly degenerated into astrological portents, they seem to have equalled, and in some respects to have surpassed, those of any other people prior to the invention of the telescope. Thus, the Mayas reached a higher degree of accuracy in the true length of the year than is found in our present Gregorian calendar.

Before the collapse of the Old Empire, Maya civilization had spread to the Mexican Valley, where it was adopted by the Toltecs from the north. In the twelfth century A.D. the Toltecs were overthrown by the Chichimec, and by the fourteenth century the Aztecs, or Tenochca, the last of the Nahua-speaking invaders, became the dominant power in Mexico.[4] Absorbing the culture of their neighbours, they became conspicuous for their genius for political and religious organization, and from the Zapotecs, in all probability, they acquired the calendar and other features of the Maya civilization.

Having transformed the gods connected with the weather and the crops into a sanguinary pantheon demanding thousands of human victims annually to maintain the seasonal sequence, this aspect of the calendrical ritual became the chief preoccupation of the priesthood. Nevertheless, under sacerdotal influence and guidance a complex culture arose with highly developed arts and crafts, a communal system of land administration, and guilds of craftsmen, and a ceremonial year (*tonalpohualli*) for divination based on the Maya calendar.[5]

Thus, in addition to the service of the bewildering multiplicity of gods and their innumerable festivals, higher knowledge was cultivated by the well-organized priesthoods in whose hands was the education of youth.[5] Every temple had a vast retinue of priests, probationers, vestal virgins and scholars, and on the arrival of the Spaniards Torquemada claimed that no less than five hundred persons were employed in the cultus of the warrior-god Huitzilpochtli in Mexico city (Tenochtitlán). Immediately below the chief-priest of this god and the high-priest of Tlaloc, the rain-god, the dual heads of the Aztec priesthood, was the chief instructor of the Calmecac, or school for the sons of the nobility. This office carried with it great responsibility and importance, so highly esteemed was sacred learning and the education of the rising generation of religious and civic leaders. All priests had an intimate knowledge of the *Tonalamatl* since they had to consult this sacred calendar continually in the course of their ritual observances, and the control of events, ranging from the declaration of war to the saving of the smallest field of maize.

SACRED SCIENCE IN MESOPOTAMIA

Although in the last resort it might be the will of the gods that shaped the course of events, in the Mexican pyramids and the Babylonian ziggurats a considerable amount of astronomical knowledge was obtained by the skilled observers in the pursuit of their cult. Thus, the Babylonian omen texts are the result of many centuries of such observations, going back to a much earlier period than in Central America, since the most ancient manual of Mesopotamian astrology belongs to the Sumerian period.[6]

Of all the heavenly bodies the moon in this region probably was the first to become the subject of observation in the *ziqqurats* and *bittamarti,* or "houses of observation" in the temples. Being the nearest to the earth, and its changes regular and spectacular, its importance for divination was recognized very early. Since its phases could not be determined with mathematical precision, its appearance and disappearance had to be observed with great care, and the variations given ominous and astrological significance. The concurrence of the sun and the moon in the sky could also be seen between the 12th and 20th days of the month, and this phenomenon was noted and interpreted in relation to the fall of the dynasty, and other unpropitious events, until on and after the 14th day it betokened prosperity. The periodic repetition in the movements of the heavenly bodies was calculated and tabulated for future reference so that each astrologer had at his disposal collections of these observations which he could consult in arriving at his prognostications.

As a result of these careful and exact observations and calculations the year was divided into months in which the occult character of each day was noted, and observations were made in the clear air of Mesopotamia which were quite remarkable for their accuracy, taking into account the absence of instruments. Thus, the greater part of the twelve constellations in our modern zodiac are identical with those distinguished by the Chaldaean astrologers, and the zodiacal system as a whole is a product of their attempts to map out that part of the sky in in which the apparent movements of the sun, the moon and the planets occurred as a circle or "girdle of signs". The course of the moon and of the planets was determined with reference to the sun's ecliptic, and the five planets (which in modern terminology are called after the Roman deities, Venus, Mercury, Mars, Jupiter and Saturn) were identified with the corresponding Babylonian deities—Ishtar, Nabu, Nergal, Marduk and Ninib—whose movements were thought to be related to the fortunes of mankind. Groups of stars or asterisms, were formed with a well-defined system of star names, and the chief constellations known to the Greeks seem to have had their origin in Mesopotamia. In its passage to the Eastern Mediterranean, astrological lore, in fact, underwent very little change until the seventeenth century of the Christian era, when Kepler (1571–1630) discovered the three laws which govern the motion of the planets, thereby opening the way for Newton's epoch-making inquiries.

Nevertheless, towards the close of the Assyrian period after the death of Ashurbanipal in 626 B.C.—notwithstanding the application to omens and portents relating to the king and the state of the ancient learning of the hereditary guilds of priests preserved in the voluminous cuneiform texts and commentaries and elaborate rituals[7]—the decline of astrology set in before the rising tide of a genuine astronomical interpretation of celestial phenomena. Behind the practice of consulting the omens and determining the course of events by the position and behaviour of the heavenly bodies lay the recognition of laws governing their movements amenable to calculation. The gods might be thought to behave in an arbitrary manner but at least their ways and purposes were sufficiently intelligible to be ascertainable by natural occurrences, so that the time of the appearance of the new moon, and the periodical appearance of lunar and solar eclipses, could be calculated, This was made possible by the learning of the priests based on observation and the association of ideas, though it was not until after the fall of the Babylonian Empire in 539 B.C. that a definite break was made with the earlier astrological tradition, and genuine astronomical inquiries were conducted on a scientific basis.

IRANIAN INFLUENCES

With the advent of the Persian sovereignty in the Euphrates valley, Zoroastrian monotheism and Mazdaean dualism introduced a new approach to the problem of the universe by resolving its ultimate ground into a single supreme Deity, Ahura Mazdah, the all-wise Lord, whose power was only limited by the existence of a spirit of evil, Angra Mainyu, or the Druj, later transformed into Ahriman as a rival of Ahura.[8] As the sole Creator Ahura Mazdah was the one supreme controller of the universe, its laws and processes, even though the prince of the kingdom of darkness had dominion over the calamitous and vicious elements in creation, from evil spirits and constellations to loathsome pests and catastrophic events. The old struggle between Marduk and Tiamat survived in the Mazdaean dualistic conflict between the forces of good and evil, and the universe was divided into two diametrically opposed and balanced creations. But the conception of an all-wide and all-righteous Ultimate Reality (Ahura Mazdah) ordering all things to a final consummation as the *summum bonum* of creation, was a definite move away from the pluralism of ancient polytheism in which the activities of a departmental pantheon were manifest in the movements of the sun, the moon and the planets. Astrology, it is true, was widely practised by the Iranian Magi, who were highly skilled in the knowledge of star-lore, while the heavenly bodies were venerated and invoked in the Zoroastrian cultus, and the signs of the zodiac recurred, at least in the Sasanian period, though the nomenclature was different from that used in Mesopotamia. But if the astrological interpretation of the universe continued, behind all phenomena, normal or abnormal, a universal law under the control of a single Creator was gradually becoming recognized, and attempts were being made to explain in quasi-scientific terms the supposed influence of the heavenly bodies upon natural occurrences and human destinies.

This introduced a more serious feature into astrological learning and facilitated the pursuit of astronomical inquiry as a priestly occupation, especially in the Seleucid period when Greek influences were felt in Persia and the Euphrates valley. Elaborate calculations began to be made of the movements of the planets in their orbits, and it was then that the theory was evolved of the ecliptic as representing the course of the sun through the year, divided among twelve constellations with a measurement of 30° to each division. The zodiac was made to represent the world-cycle in the year and in the world-year, and the calendar was regulated with greater precision. Eclipses ceased to be regarded as evil portents, and unusual celestial phenomena were investigated in terms of natural law rather than of divine wrath and vengeance.

THE DIFFUSION OF ASTRAL SCIENCE

Thus, in the three centuries after the Persian occupation of Mesopotamia the Babylonian priests under Iranian influence made remarkable strides in astronomical learning which were destined ultimately to dethrone astrology from its exalted position in sacred tradition, and at last to reduce it to the level of a superstition. But established beliefs and practices die hard, and outside the Euphrates valley the imaginary science created by the Babylonians survived in Persia until, under Moslem rule, it was brought into relation with Arabic science and the Islamic doctrine of Fate. Consequently, it became the sister of astronomy and in Moslem nomenclature no distinction was drawn between the astrologer and the astronomer, both being comprehended in the term *munajjim* (or *najjim*). In the Graeco-Roman world, as in Ancient Egypt, prediction from the stars and planets, borrowed from Chaldaean sources, flourished at Alexandria in the Ptolemaic period under Greek and Egyptian influence in a powerful school devoted to this type of sacred learning, which embraced all the known sciences.

If this did not prevent the continuance of the scientific study of the heavens initiated by the Ionian philosophers in the sixth century B.C., and carried on by thinkers like Aristarchus of Samos in the third century, and by his successor Hipparchus (190–120 B.C.), it opened the way for an elaborate development of horoscopic lore and practice, which survived into the Middle Ages. Pythagoreans, Cynics and Epicureans might scoff, but, as the Stoics maintained, if the gods existed divination was a logical conclusion.[9] Therefore, there was nothing to prevent the wisdom of the East being grafted on to the fruitful tree of

Greek scientific learning in its several departments, biological, astronomical, anatomical and medical.

HEBREW AND ARABIC SCIENCE

The spread of the three great monotheistic religions in the West—Judaism, Christianity and Islam—altered, however, the character of the astrological tradition, inasmuch as it eliminated the polytheism on which the practice had been founded. Nevertheless, in all these faiths, although the divine government of the universe was vested in the omnipotent will of a single Creator, the conception of and approach to the natural order was not as scientific as had been that of the later Babylonian astronomers or of the Greek philosophers. That God should, and in fact did, intervene in the course of events was taken for granted. Moreover, the will of Yahweh came to be regarded as executed by a multitude of angelic beings who in the realm of nature fulfilled their functions as messengers and agents of divine Providence. The movements of the heavenly bodies were thought to be regulated by them, though sometimes the planets were venerated or feared as living and intelligent organisms.[10] The repeated condemnation of the worship of the sun, moon and stars, and the burning of incense to the "twelve signs" (i.e. the zodiac), and all the host of heaven,[11] indicate that the abuses were prevalent. Indeed after the Exile attempts were made to give astrology a divine sanction, since the stars were said to have been created to be "signs" for man.[12]

For nearly a century intimate contact with the Chaldaeans had aroused in the captive Jews a desire to know the future revealed by those in Babylonia who "divided the heavens" and engaged in "monthly prognostications".[13] Consequently, despite the efforts of the rigid monotheists of the prophetic tradition to eliminate astral theology and techniques, together with all other divinatory devices, they spread so rapidly that by the Hellenistic period an astral literature had come into existence. Though the rabbis made a determined effort to discourage the more pagan aspects of the cult,[14] its hold on Talmudic Judaism became considerable.[15] The mysterious connexion between mankind and the planets was affirmed,[16] and celestial phenomena such as eclipses came to be regarded as portents of good and evil, particularly in relation to the astral calendar of lucky and unlucky days and months.[17]

The rapid spread of Islam in and after the seventh century in the countries in which the Jews had settled had a very considerable effect on the development of astrology in both cultures. If some of the most notable books in Jewish astrological literature (e.g. those of Abraham ibn Ezra in the middle of the twelfth century A.D.) were based on Arabic sources, the Arabic scholars also borrowed from Jewish works. It was a Jewish astrologer, Jacob ben Tarik, who founded a school at Baghdad, and in Europe the Hebrew and Spanish translations of the Moslem writers popularized the system. The Kabbala was also a medium of astrological speculations. Therefore, notwithstanding the efforts of Maimonides to free prophecy from magic, soothsaying and astrology,[18] the Arabo-Judaic astral science of divination became an established feature in the Middle Ages.

In the form in which it was received and developed by Islam, astrology was an eclectic movement derived from a variety of sources—Greek, Iranian, Indian, Babylonian, Syrian and Egyptian. As all possible combinations concerning the relation of the constellations to human events had been worked out, instead of attempting new prognostications the Moslem astrologers and astronomers endeavoured to perfect the mathematical processes involved in the observations. These they embodied in mathematical tables applied to spherical astronomy and trigonometry based on exact calculations requiring very considerable scientific knowledge. If these remarkable achievements were not the work of organized priesthoods, as in Babylonia and Persia, nevertheless they were products of the ancient sacred learning in which they arose.

In Islam, as has been considered,[19] predictions fell into line with the Moslem doctrine of predestination. If all human actions were predetermined, that the course of events should be revealed in the positions and behaviour of the stars and planets was readily accepted in an age steeped in astral theology. In due course, however, despite the efforts of philosophers like Al-Kindi in the ninth century to rationalize the system, theologians and thinkers who came under the influence of the Aristotelian movement adopted a critical and hostile attitude towards it as repugnant to good sense and incompatible with the rigid monotheism of Islam.[20]

ASTRAL SCIENCE IN THE MIDDLE AGES AND THE RENAISSANCE

In the eleventh century philosophers and theologians joined forces against the astrologers who still held sway in heretical sects like the Iharān as-Safā (Sincere Companions). Thus, Avicenna (d. A.D. 1037), notwithstanding his leanings to various kinds of occultism and emanationist cosmology, was as forthright in his condemnation of their practices as were Ibn Hazm, Averroës and al-Ghazali,[21] though it remained for Íbn Qayyim al-Jauziyyah (1350) to complete the refutation.[22] But the discipline was too firmly established to be uprooted by theological anathemas, and astrologers continued to occupy important official positions in Islamic states. In Turkey and in many other Moslem countries, the office of chief astrologer survived until the last century, and in Morocco and Southern Arabia the cult has never been abandoned.

In Western Europe in addition to the spread of Islam and the Jewish Kabbala in the Middle Ages, the revival of classical learning in the fifteenth century gave a new impetus to astro-logical pursuits. The emperors and popes of the Renaissance openly and without apology had their official astrologers who virtually regulated the life and decisions of the imperial and papal courts, and often attained considerable eminence and prestige. At Bologna, Pavia and Sapianza academic chairs in the subject were established, distinct from those of astro-nomy as a scientific discipline. Indeed, it became the primary duty of the astronomers to supply the astrologers with the data for their prognostications, and themselves to cast horoscopes and make predictions. These practices continued long after the

Copernican system had become established, and in England it was not until after the Thirty Years' War that astrology and the astrologer lost their official status. As a popular superstition and pseudo-science they have survived to the present day very little changed. The "planetary books" still sold at fairs are essentially the same as those in vogue in the Middle Ages, the Renaissance and in the time of Cromwell and his contemporaries.

The immense prestige and duration which astral science and theology have secured throughout the ages doubtless have been due in no small part to the fact that the observations have made the sky and the heavenly bodies intelligible in the context of human destinies and mundane events. This has given the astrologer a recognized position as a highly-trained member of a learned sacred order, engaged in carrying out what were virtually astronomical observations and calculations and then interpreting the results of his inquiries in astrological terms as divine prognostications. That these interpretations often were fallacious and even ridiculous does not alter the fact that astrologers were largely responsible for laying the foundations on which a rational scientific cosmology was built long before they had abandoned their astral theories and presuppositions. Plato and Aristotle retained the current belief in celestial animism but this did not prevent their arriving at a profound conception of the universe and its processes and ends. Thus, astrology and the occult arts, like other forms of divination, have not been without their influence in the evolution of higher types of knowledge and a clearer understanding of things human and divine.

THE ORDER OF NATURE

Closely associated with this astral aspect of sacred science has been the rhythmic sequence in nature which has found expression and evaluation in the ritual cycle, especially in agricultural communities. With the observance of the solstices and the establishment of the solar calendar emerged not only the dependence of human destinies on the Power manifested in the celestial bodies, but also the divine control of all life and the orderly processes of the cosmos. Since the calendrical cultus in which the natural order was thought to depend for its continuance and well-being was in the hands of the temple priesthoods, it was they who developed a cosmological pseudo-science and mythology to give an adequate reason for and efficacy to the things done in the course of their ritual procedures.

It is true that myth is neither a primitive explanation of the world and its natural processes nor a scientific philosophy in embryo. Primarily it is the utterance of a rite possessing supernatural power in its repetition, certifying the sacred actions performed and embodying a situation of profound significance.[23] But, nevertheless, for the practical purposes of good living depending largely upon fruitful harvests, seasonal rains and sunshine, and the arts and crafts of agriculture, in addition to the correct and efficacious performance of the prescribed ceremonial, there must be a knowledge and understanding of nature itself together with the technical abilities requisite for a rational mastery of the situation. Therefore, the sacred and the profane, the spiritual and the physical, must be brought into conjunction since the one is largely dependent upon the other. Even in primitive states of culture, knowledge based on observation and experiment, and crops raised by dint of manual labour, occur side by side with recourse to magico-religious traditions and techniques.

Thus, for example in Melanesia, as Malinowski has pointed out, "if you were to suggest to a native that he should make his garden mainly by magic and scamp his work, he would simply smile on your simplicity. He knows as well as you do that there are natural conditions and causes, and by his observations he knows also that he is able to control these natural forces by mental and physical effort. His knowledge is limited, no doubt, but as far as it goes it is sound and proof against mysticism. If the fences are broken down, if the seed is destroyed or has been dried or washed away, he will have recourse not to magic but to work, guided by knowledge and reason. His experience has taught him also, on the other hand, that in spite of all his forethought and beyond all his efforts there are agencies and forces which one year bestow unwonted and unearned benefits of fertility, making everything run smooth and well, rain and sun appear at the right moment, noxious insects remain in abeyance, the harvest yield a superabundant crop; and another year again the same agencies bring ill-luck and bad chance, pursue him from beginning till end and thwart all his most strenuous efforts and his best-founded knowledge. To control these influences and these only he employs magic."[24]

There is no indication, as Lévy Bruhl and the French sociologists of the school of Durkheim would have us suppose,[25] that at any period in the history of the human race of which we have knowledge the ordinary processes of reasoning were not in operation, either in the collective consciousness of mankind or in individual members of society. The primitive and the civilized alike are at once rational and mystical in their re-actions to their natural environment, according to the particular circumstances of a given situation. The distinction between the sacred and the profane does not belong to the category of logic or rationality any more than the workings of the human mind are governed exclusively by the principle of "participation" in opposition to that of "contradiction". When man was dependent completely upon the vagaries of nature for his food as well as for other things, and was confronted at every turn with situations beyond his understanding or control, having postulated a transcendental order of reality as the ultimate controlling Power or Providence, it is neither surprising nor irrational that he sought its aid and intervention in supplying his primary needs, as does the primitive today.

THE PRIESTHOOD AS THE MASTER OF SACRED SCIENCE

The business of the priesthood was to devise and elaborate techniques to deal effectively with the inauspicious and unpredictable elements in human experience, whether individual or collective, in relation to natural processes. Having been set apart for this purpose, it was for those equipped with this sacred knowledge to strengthen and control the vital forces in nature—to make the rain to fall, or assist the spiritual beings responsible for the weather in carrying out their functions for the well-being of mankind, to drive away storms, tempests, plagues and noxious pests, and to augment the fertility of the earth and its products. But in so doing they did not exclude empirical knowledge based on careful observation and accurate deduction within the limits of their capacity. On the contrary, as we have seen in connexion with the early developments of astronomy, a very considerable corpus of valuable scientific data has emerged from the sacred learning of the ancient priesthoods in their attempts to adapt the life of man to his physical environment and to correlate it with transcendental reality.

Similarly, in the order of nature in its terrestrial aspects, ritual and empirical understanding of the weather and the seasons, of plants and pests, of soils and seedlings, were so intimately associated that it is exceedingly difficult for the sophisticated observer to differentiate the one from the other. This is because for the priests themselves the two domains of knowledge were complementary rather than contradictory, there being no clear-cut distinction between the "natural" and the "supernatural". The universe was regarded as a composite whole made up of laws and processes and techniques and controls, some of which fell within the sphere of rational empirical inquiry, others in the domain of the magical and transcendental. Up to a point it was recognized that nature works in regular and ascertainable ways, and upon this supposition the seasonal cultus was based, though not to the exclusion of supranatural or sacred forces and influences always liable to introduce an unpredictable element into the situation, and subject to ritual control. It was the function of the priesthood to bring together the two disciplines into a comprehensive system of organized knowledge and techniques, partly sacred and partly profane (i.e. empirical), esoteric and mysterious yet intelligible and knowable, given the right conditions. It was into the secrets of this higher gnosis that the priesthoods were initiated, of which they were the custodians, and to a considerable degree the originators and promoters as the masters of sacred science, set apart for the co-ordination of the cycle of nature with the cycles of heaven and earth and human life.[26]

Thus, in the learned temple priesthoods of antiquity, myth and ritual and science flourished, and found expression on the one hand in astral theology and observation, and on the other hand in the seasonal calendrical observances and their underlying traditions, Their intellectual activity was revealed in the ingenuity displayed in evolving theological systems corresponding to theoretical divisions of the universe, in the regulation of the calendar with increasing scientific precision, and the minute observation involved in hepatoscopy in Babylonia, which led to a genuine study of the anatomy of the liver. Since the first step towards the scientific interpretation of nature is the recognition of immutable laws of universal application, while the ancient priesthoods could not emancipate themselves from the primitive conception of the magico-religious control of the inexplicable and unpredictable events and causes in the natural order, nevertheless they laid the foundations of a systematic attempt to understand the universe in the operation of regular laws.

Behind their ritual techniques a law can be discerned which extended far beyond the operations over which they claimed to exercise control, and which they sought to imitate and represent in their dramatic and mimetic rites. If it was the practical problems of every day life rather than abstract questions concerning the origin and nature of the universe with which they were concerned, their object was to produce certain effects— viz., to ensure the prosperity and stability of the community by causing the celestial bodies and the physical processes on which the means of subsistence depended to perform their proper functions. These ends were attained by an imitative reproduction in dramatic form of the supposed operation of the natural forces themselves, in order to recreate and re-enforce them at critical junctures, such as the turn of the year in spring and autumn. This they accomplished by identifying themselves with the order of nature in their priestly capacity as the instruments and agents of the god or gods responsible for the bestowal of providential bounty and the right ordering of the cosmos, and by virtue of their relationship with the throne as the connecting link between the world of men and the world of the gods. Thus, as the masters of sacred science and the manipulators of the techniques whereby the divine order and the order of nature were maintained in juxtaposition, the highly organized priesthoods occupied the key position in society. In Egypt at last they usurped the kingship and in India they were the power beyond even the gods because, as we have seen, it was they who controlled the cosmic order (*Rta*) by their sacrificial ministrations.

TEMPLE ORGANIZATION

Thus, from an expert knowledge and supreme control of natural laws and processes the powerful priesthoods in the Ancient East exercised an immense influence in civic life and statecraft upon which they brought to bear their intellectual superiority, their understanding of affairs and all the prestige of their learning and status. In Mesopotamia, for example, the chief edifice in the principal towns was the temple of the patron deity, with smaller sanctuaries grouped round it within the sacred area, dedicated to the gods and goddesses associated with its cultus. Its activities were manifold and included, in addition to the religious functions, mercantile pursuits of various kinds, medicine, mathematics, administration, commercial undertakings, trading and monetary transactions. To meet all these demands the training in the temple schools became more and more diverse as the functions of the priests were increasingly differentiated. Instruction was given in the drawing up of legal documents, in the study of the laws, in business methods, the calculation of interest, and possibly in clay modelling, as well as in divination, exorcism, astral theology and astronomy, since all learning was a sacerdotal prerogative.

SACRED LITERATURE AND LEARNING IN VEDIC INDIA

In India, again, the Brahmanic priesthood represented a special class in the community with very extensive and unique powers, functions and knowledge. The office was hereditary and included apparently the practice of medicine as a quasi-magical art, but its chief concern was with sacred literature and the sacrificial liturgy. Thus, the main theme in the great collection of sacerdotal poetry known as the *Rig-veda* is the *Soma*-sacrifice in which a very large number of priests were employed in a great variety of offices. But it was in literary activities that they excelled.

As the official exponents of the Dharma of Hinduism the Brahmins divided the sacred literature into *sruti,* that which had been heard, and *smriti,* that which had been remembered (i.e. tradition). In the first division they included the sacred knowledge known as the Vedas, comprising the Rig-veda, a collection of hymns dating from about 1500 to 1000 B.C.; the ritual books (Brahmanas) and the philosophical mystical treatises (Upanishads); the manual of the chants arranged for the second order of priests (Samaveda); the formulas recited at sacrifices (Yajurveda); and finally the mantras and spells contained in the rather later Atharvaveda. The word "veda" coming from the root *vid,* "to know", means "knowledge" or "sacred science", revealed through the inspired seers (*rishi*) and charged with magical power residing in the words.

The Rig-veda contains 1028 hymns and is divided into ten books, six of which were grouped round a particular family or school of *rishi.* Two hundred hymns are addressed to Agni as the divine counterpart of the priesthood, officiating at the sacrifice and acting as the messenger between the gods and men.[27] So sacred were these potent utterances that they were not written down for several centuries lest some unauthorized profane person should get hold of them. Therefore, as a precious part of Brahmanic esoteric knowledge and learning they were kept secret by the priests, and after they had been committed to script they were jealously guarded. Their sacredness, however, lay not in their being regarded as a divine revelation or philo-

P

sophical interpretation of the cosmic process, but in the belief that magical power resided in them.

It was not until about 700 B.C. that this *veda* (Knowledge) was transformed into an intuitive disclosure on the part of the seers as a series of cosmic vibrations interpreted verbally by the *rishi* who received them. Thus, in the schools of priestly learning there grew up different recensions (*sakha*) of the sacred texts as oral transmission was replaced by written records of the canonical scriptures. These schools became numerous, especially in the Samaveda and Yajurveda, teachers and their followers dividing into schematic groups as "black" or "white", "older" or "younger", according to the recensions adopted. The rest of the Sanskrit literature, that known as *sruti,* and regarded as tradition in contradiction to the "heard" or perceived sacred knowledge, consists largely of sectarian literature together with epics, plays, *Puranas* (quasi-historical and mythological treatises) and *sutras* in the form of ritual manuals, and treatises on domestic ceremonial and conduct and law-books.

Originally the first three Vedas (*trayi vidya*) constituted the sacred canon to which later was added the Atharvaveda with its special brahmanic associations. As the brahmins were responsible for the entire sacrificial system no single book can be assigned to them in the sense that the Samaveda and the Yajurveda belonged essentially to the chanters (*udgatar*) and the offerers (*adhvaryu*). But the sacred literature as a whole grew up and took shape under priestly influence, and embodied the sacred learning of the respective schools in which it arose for specific purposes. From the time of the Rig-veda those who exercised sacerdotal functions were called loosely "brahmins", but the term very seldom indicates a particular class of priests having peculiar duties and prerogatives.[28] It was not until later, as sacred learning and literature accumulated, that their function became that of applying their superior knowledge to the ordering of the sacrificial system as a whole, and to atonement of the errors committed by the offerers, chanters and reciters (*hotṛ*). Then they were credited with literary learning, the Atharvaveda was devoted especially to them, and they were required to become conversant with all the Vedas.

THE EGYPTIAN HIEROGLYPHIC TEXTS

Throughout the ages literacy has been essentially a priestly accomplishment, and in this connexion it is significant that the name given by the Greeks to the most ancient of the three kinds of Egyptian script was "hieroglyphic" (ἱερός γλύφω, "sacred carvings"). If originally these pictures were of men, animals and concrete objects, their use was extended to express cognate concepts and abstract ideas, and adopted by the very considerable and leisured class of priests engaged upon the transcription and compilation of sacred texts and inscriptions. Thus, the Pyramid Texts represent a notable example of a vast collection of sacred writings drawn from every available source at a very early period (c. 2980–2475 B.C.), having as its purpose the bestowal of immortality on the Pharaoh, on the walls of whose tomb they were inscribed. This oldest surviving body of sacred literature, which now fills two quarto volumes with no less than 1051 texts,[29] consists of funeral ritual and mortuary offerings, magical charms, hymns, myths, sacred dramas, and prayers, some of which go back to predynastic times. The material is arranged in sections in a haphazard manner, each headed as "Utterances". Of these the first of the five pyramids (Unis) contains 228 sections, and the rest make up a total of 714.[30] Being a series of spells to enable the dead king to enter the celestial realms of Re, their order and disorder were of little consequence, so the priestly editor was content to copy anything and everything he could find that was considered to be magically efficacious as charms.

Similarly, the later collection of texts known originally as "The Book of the Coming Forth from the Day" (and now erroneously called "The Book of the Dead"), after the time of the Theban domination in the sixteenth century B.C., was buried with the mummy as a guide in the next life and a protection against its dangers, when immortality was no longer exclusively a royal prerogative. When the effectiveness of the

uttered word on behalf of the dead was extended to the priesthood, the nobility and the ruling classes, and ultimately to the
whole community, the mortuary literature became more
voluminous in the Feudal Age so that by the Middle Kingdom
texts were written on the inner surface of coffins setting forth the
claims of the deceased to righteousness and justification before
the gods. These "Coffin Texts" prepared the way for the New
Kingdom papyri, commonly known as The Book of the Dead,
and deposited in the tomb in the form of a roll of papyrus on
which mortuary texts were inscribed. Some of them were as
much as 60 to 80 feet in length and contained up to a hundred
and thirty chapters of spells and charms. Others were of more
modest proportions and might be meagre rolls only a few feet
long.

In the eighteenth dynasty ornamentation of the text with
vignettes in black outline began. In the next dynasty these
developed into elaborate illumination at the expense of the
text. It was not until the twenty-sixth dynasty, when the Saïte
Recension was produced, that attempts were made to systema-
tize the contents and to reduce the collection to some sort of
order. As theological documents concerning the Egyptian
conception of immortality these sacred texts are neither
edifying nor enlightening, but they justify the application to
them of the term "hieroglyphic", since in the first instance the
script was used by priestly scribes who for at least three thousand years continued to be preoccupied with the production of
a sacred literature written in these characters.

THE CUNEIFORM TABLETS IN MESOPOTAMIA

In Mesopotamia, again, the clay tablets inscribed with
cuneiform characters were the work of the Sumerian priests, but
while their purpose was largely magical and religious, the
contents of the literature were more varied than in Egypt. The
hieroglyphic texts, as we have seen, were mainly concerned with
the cult of the dead, apart from a miscellaneous collection of
hymns and legends. The Sumerian and Babylonian tablets, on
the other hand, are a mine of information on omens, astrology,

incantations, spells, the gods, ritual texts, myth and legends, together with lists of kings, royal inscriptions and the year-names of kings, contracts, administration, legal procedure, and excerpts from political history. From them we are able to gain a reasonably accurate and continuous picture of belief and practice in Mesopotamia from about 3000 B.C., when the Sumerians invented the art of writing in their wedge-shaped script on clay tablets in an ever-increasing stylization of the original pictographic signs.

When their agglutinative language ceased to be spoken at the end of the third dynasty of Ur (*c.* 1939 B.C.) it continued to be used as the sacred language by the priests, and the ancient Sumerian texts were copied for religious purposes until it fell into oblivion at the beginning of the Christian era. When it was taken over by the Accadians the Sumerian syllabary and word-signs were adopted and new values added based on their own script. From them the cuneiform writing and its literature passed to the Assyrians, the Hittites, the Mitannians and the Elamites. But behind this diffusion there appears to have been a Proto-Elamite Ugaritic and Persian type of cuneiform, the earliest example of which occurs in a Proto-Elamite tablet from Susa belonging probably to the fourth millennium B.C.

It was very largely in the temple schools that the priestly scribes engaged in the literary activities from which our knowledge of Babylonian myth and ritual is derived. If they were primarily concerned with the provision of text-books for candidates for the priesthood, they, nevertheless, stimulated a literary spirit in giving the myths and legends a literary form. Moreover, they created an interest in and appreciation of the traditions, learning and wisdom of the former generations. The earlier rituals, omen-texts, incantations, hymns, lamentations, astrological inscriptions, popular stories and medical treatises were not only copied but commented upon and edited, and sometimes transliterated in bilingual versions, Semitic and Sumerian.

Thus, in the famous collection of texts preserved in the great Royal Library at Nineveh, founded by Ashurbanipal during the last days of the Assyrian Empire (668–626 B.C.), almost every branch of Sumerian and Babylonian learning and knowledge in the possession of the priesthood is to be found. Commissioned by their royal patron to collect, revise and catalogue the extant texts, the priests made a thorough search of the oldest temple archives throughout the country and succeeded in bringing together a vast and comprehensive collection of literary material, some of which was of considerable antiquity. The bulk of it was of a religious character, the product of the temple schools harbouring large bodies of priests equipped with literary knowledge and skill, and an understanding and appreciation of the documentary material with which they dealt.

Among the most important tablets recovered from this great royal collection were the fragments of the Gilgamesh epic—one of the finest literary products of Babylonia, the earliest version of which goes back to about 2000 B.C. This story of the legendary founder of the city of Erech and the temple of Ea Anna is a composite narrative containing elements originating at different times unified in and around the hero, Gilgamesh, as a national epic. Within it may be found sections containing the Tammuz theme in a specialized form, the story of Enki-du, the deluge myth and the adventures of Ut-Napishtim (Zisudra), all intermingled with nature myths, necromancy and the cult of the dead.

Here is illustrated the skill of the Babylonian and Assyrian priests in weaving into a single narrative covering twelve tablets, and containing not less than 3000 lines of text, a mass of legendary and quasi-historical material to give a particular significance to the established cultus. The final form is the product of a long and complicated literary process determined throughout by the underlying theological motives, and leading to certain practical conclusions, such as proper burial being absolutely essential to secure peace for the dead in the cheerless nether world which was the ultimate destination of everyman. Similarly, as has been considered,[31] the epic of Creation lay behind the Annual Festival as a renewal ritual to "fix the destinies" and ensure a prosperous New Year.

THE UGARIT CULTIC TEXTS

The part played by sacred drama in ancient priestly literature
is demonstrated in the library of alphabetic cuneiform tablets
belonging to the fifteenth and fourteenth centuries B.C. discovered since 1929 at Ras Shamra (Ugarit). Inasmuch as this
series of very fragmentary and incomplete texts appears to be
part of the archives of the local temple, it belongs to a period
prior to the fourteenth century,[32] and, therefore, represents a
parallel literature to that of the Babylonian tablets. Variant
examples of the same alphabetic script have been found at Beth
Shemesh and Mount Tabor, but, as it was suitable only for use
on clay tablets, which were not the normal Palestinian medium
of writing, it was a Canaanite-Hurrian dialectal adaptation of
the cuneiform of short duration. Nevertheless, the very considerable number of cultic texts produced, treating of events
connected with the death and resurrection of Baal, the marriage
of Keret, and with Danel, shows that while it lasted it was an
active and prolific literary enterprise directly related to a ritual
which found its climax in the enthronement of the year-god,
apparently at the autumnal festival. In short, it was a priestly
movement centred in the temple of Ugarit, and the texts were
essentially religious documents for the purpose of giving
efficacy to the sacred drama enacted.

Indeed, as Dr Gilbert Murray has recently affirmed, "it is
hardly an exaggeration to say that when we look back to the
beginning of European literature we find everywhere drama,
and always drama derived from a religious ritual designed to
ensure the rebirth of the dead world."[33] And the priesthood
was responsible for the dramatic ritual on which the social
structure and the welfare of mankind depended. Being the
learned and literate section of the community its function was
the conservation of the sacred tradition, essential to the consolidation of society, embodied in the sacred literature, ritual,
myth and philosophy which holds together the culture as an
integrated whole. Thus, as the repositories of sacred learning
and specialized knowledge, the guardians of traditional lore
and its ritual, the keepers of the archives, the custodians and the

interpreters of religious literature, esoteric mysteries, mythologies and cult legends, and the systematizers of the liturgical drama, the organized priesthoods have been a powerful influence in cultural development and intellectual achievement. Their innate conservatism and intolerance of any rival institutions unquestionably have retarded progress beyond the range of their own jurisdictions and disciplines. But even so the dead hand has not been without its effects as a consolidating dynamic in the stabilization of society, the preservation of learning and the cultivation of scholarship within the limits of a prescribed tradition.

THE TORĂH IN ISRAEL

To impart sacred knowledge, or *torâh,* hidden from the rest of the community was an essential function in the priestly office in Israel, and to neglect this duty was a serious offence.[34] Since the term as it is used in the Old Testament suggests that the priests assumed the office of judge, it involved more than oracular decisions. Moses, for instance, is said to have given *torôth* in the desert like a sheikh,[35] making known the mind and will of Yahweh in accordance with the priestly method of revelation from the depositories of traditional knowledge divinely ascertained, rather than in the form of spontaneous prophetic utterances.[36] These "statutes and directions (*torôth*) of God" became the nucleus of an oral Mosaic tradition which eventually gave rise to the Pentateuch when it was committed to writing and assigned the status of "scripture", with all that this implied as a special revelation of divine truth and knowledge. In this way ancient priestly traditions readily acquire a fixity and supernatural authority which once established and adapted to the stabilization of faith, worship, moral conduct, and the social structure, attain a new character and sanction, social rather than individual in origin. Thus, the five books ascribed to Moses were grouped together in the Jewish Canon and given a degree of sanctity far above that of the rest of the literature of the Old Testament (i.e. the *Prophets* or *Nebi'im,* and the *Writings* or *Kethubim*).

REVELATION AND REASON

The raising of tradition to the level of revelation places this type of sacred knowledge in a unique category distinguishing it from every other form of literature or learning. As stereotyped in the Talmud, revelation began with the Patriarchs and under the inspiration of the Holy Spirit continued throughout the prophetical period from Moses to Ezra[37] thereby rendering all "the holy writings" from Genesis to Malachi sacred and tabu, described by the rabbis as "defiling the hands". This conception of the sacredness of the canonical scriptures, which has been a recurrent feature in the interpretation of revelation known as "fundamentalism", has had the effect of making the verbal form and traditions of authorship inviolable, and the contents of the documents of unquestionable divine authority and inerrancy, whether it be the Law and the Prophets of Judaism, the books of the New Testament, or the Qur'an, and places them in very much the same position as that occupied by traditional lore among peoples in a primitive state of culture.

Now it cannot be denied that for the purposes of giving stability to established belief, custom and social and religious organization and behaviour, this point of view exercises a powerful consolidating influence. It is, however, an attitude that can be maintained only as it were behind closed doors securely barred against the advance in knowledge from outside and so long as it is possible to prevent critical investigation and independent inquiry within its own domain. Therefore, it can be but a temporary expedient. To make a permanent contribution to knowledge, and to fulfil its proper function in society, sacred learning must keep abreast of the progress of thought in other fields and be capable of adjustment to their disciplines. Otherwise it becomes hidebound and static. Nevertheless, permanence presupposes continuity, and in the preservation, adaptation and re-integration of sacred traditions in relation to secular knowledge the priesthood as a stable institution has occupied the key position in the integration and dissemination of learning.

THE TRANSITION FROM SACRED TRADITION TO PHILOSOPHY

Thus, in the sixth century B.C., when an attempt was made at Miletus under the inspiration of Thales to discover how the universe arose as an intelligible rational cosmic order reducible to a single underlying principle as the cause of all things, the break with the earlier mythical tradition was by no means as pronounced as has been commonly supposed. It is true that the quest of "the One that remains" was in great measure lost in the confusion and complexity of the "Many", and the cosmos as subject to the operation of fixed laws admitting of no predictability ceased to be regarded as being under transcendental control. Nevertheless, the cosmological problems of which a rational solution was sought by natural causes were not very different from those inherited from the religious pattern of ideas concerning the cosmic order and the causes of phenomena, except that divine intervention was eliminated and with it the functions hitherto exercised by the priesthood.

Ionian speculation, however, was only one aspect of the new movements in thought and practice which swept over the Hellenic world in the middle of the first millenium B.C. A religious revival was no less in evidence, characterized by an emotional mysticism which found ecstatic expression in the Thracian orgiastic worship of Dionysos before it was sobered on being brought into relation with Orphism.[38] It was from this Orphic source that a new conception of revelation was introduced, together with sacramental purification, to secure the release of the soul from the hampering body in which it was incarcerated with all its Titanic defilements. Unfortunately we know little about the organization of Orphic communities and their sacred literature since the poems and hymns bearing the name of Orpheus belong to the end of the Roman imperial period and are of uncertain antiquity. In their present form they are post-Christian (*c.* fourth century A.D.) and contain no specific references to Orphic doctrines. All that they indicate is that a movement called Orphic survived in the Graeco-Roman age in an atmosphere of mysticism which comprehended everything in the realm of *teletae* (initiatory rites).[39]

Although the influence of a so-called Orphic theogony on philosophy has been greatly exaggerated, mystical cult-societies associated with the mythical figure of Orpheus and of the followers of the historical Pythagoras certainly did exist in the early period and differed radically in type from the rationalistic Ionian school. For the Milesians φιλοσοφία meant intellectual "curiosity" while for Pythagoreanism and Orphism it represented a way of life in which union with, or likeness to, God was to be sought through knowledge directed towards the purification of the individual soul with the aid of ascetic rules, ritual prohibitions and contemplation of the divine order manifest in the universe and its processes. Thus, knowledge was regarded as an essential element in the quest of salvation through sanctification in a world in which good and evil were in fundamental opposition. Therefore, neither the Orphics nor the Pythagoreans shared the detached curiosity of the Ionians since they were primarily concerned with the problem of right living and the purification of the soul rather than with the pursuit of knowledge for its own sake. But they exercised an important function in the transition from sacred to secular learning through their emphasis on philosophy as a way of life with a transcendental goal in which traditional lore had its place side by side with scientific speculations.

While neither of them was a sacerdotal movement, both enjoined a way of living with a prescribed ritual of initiation and *katharsis* dependent upon a dualistic conception of body and soul. Therefore, they belong to the tradition in which priestly learning took its rise, with their roots laid in the Dionysiac, Apollinism, Hyperboreianism, and probably the Eleusinian cultus.[40] Moreover, as the late Dr Cornford has recently urged, Ionian philosophy was itself closely related to the mythical and poetical cosmological tradition that lay behind it,[41] in spite of its attempt to introduce a rational inquiry into the impersonal functions of the universe as a natural order. In its search for universal factors of a non-personal character in a cosmos hitherto regarded as under the control of intervening gods, it lacked, however, any stabilizing influence or institution comparable to that of the priesthood in the earlier tradition. Detached from the social structure or the recognition of an ultimate reality it led to a distrust of reason and a fundamental scepticism until, under the influence of Plato, the function of philosophy was made more or less analogous to that exercised by sacred learning in the priestly régimes. It then became the means by which the mind trained under its guidance comes to self-consciousness of the rational principles which direct man towards the Good, correlating and organizing all the various groups of interests in orderly relationships for the public weal, and the improvement of behaviour.[42] Behind all existence lay an eternal pattern—the sum total of all the Forms—as the Supreme Reality and the model of what ought to be. But as the idea of the Good and the doctrine of God developed independently in the mind of Plato, the conception of providential beneficence was never completely reconciled with the existence of evil, or the world of Ideas related to that of sense experience, except through a quest of philosophic knowledge open only to the few, and then dependent upon the process of reincarnation.[43]

Aristotle, approaching the problem empirically, substituted a dualism of Form and Matter, of Actuality and Potentiality, for a world of sense experience distinguished from a world of intellect. He, however, only arrived at a universal Unmoved Mover as the eternal immutable Cause of the universe, so transcendent and "wholly other" as to stand completely outside mundane affairs and human interests.[44] Indeed, being pure Actuality—"thinking of thinking"—He was unaware of the world with all its imperfections and never left the eternal repose in which His blessedness consisted. In the Deity of the Stagirite will, intellect and purpose had no place. Consequently, for the practical purposes of religion and its function in society, Aristotelian theism was of little avail until in the Middle Ages it was reinterpreted in terms of Scholastic theology, very much as the Platonic "Good Soul", to become a genuinely theistic conception of Deity, had to be restated in Neoplatonic and Christian Platonic terms by Plotinus, Origen, Clement of Alexandria and St Augustine of Hippo.

Plato and Aristotle, in fact, represent the culmination of metaphysical speculation in Greek thought. After the break-up of the Greek States in the new political and social structure of the cosmopolitan Macedonian Empire, Stoicism provided a comprehensive philosophy which was able to accommodate its teaching and outlook to other disciplines, including dialectic rhetoric, physical science, logic and ethics, grounded ultimately on a pantheistic monism in which Providence was conceived as the dynamic principle in the universe. As a rational being it was the duty of man to discover the laws and operations of nature, and to adjust himself to them: in short, "to live according to nature."[45]

A skilful blending of traditional polytheism and philosophical speculation enabled the Stoic philosopher to play a role in the Graeco-Roman world not very different from that of the priest as the spiritual guide of his time and the guardian of learning.[46] He was sought for advice on problems of right conduct, to prognosticate events, for divination and to minister to the sick and dying. The Stoic contribution to knowledge was, in fact, considerable as was its influence on Roman thought. In the Republic it was adopted by many of the most intelligent men of the day, and under the Empire it made a still wider appeal, although it failed to meet the more fundamental religious needs of the human spirit. Indeed this "final utterance of the speculative genius of Greece", although it absorbed and conserved the learning of the oriental and occidental metaphysical systems it synthesized, and deeply influenced subsequent mysticism and theology and the Platonic tradition of the West, was scientifically and theologically retrogressive. In trying to integrate the religions of antiquity in an all-embracing mystical philosophy it retained the allegiance of few except a small eclectic intelligentsia in a declining civilization that had run its course.

THE PATRISTIC CONTRIBUTION TO LEARNING

Christianity, its most serious rival, had the advantage of being uncompromisingly monotheistic and, therefore, of standing apart from the struggle between a philosophic monism and popular polytheism. Its faith claimed to be a new revelation foreshadowed in the sacred literature of Israel and fulfilled in a historic Figure not altogether unfamiliar in the conception of the Man-god in the myth and ritual of the Graeco-Roman world, but freed from its earlier legendary character and content. The Christian tradition, moreover, proved to be capable of re-statement in terms of current philosophic thought—Stoic, Peripatetic and Platonic—in which many of its Apologists had themselves been trained, notwithstanding strenuous opposition from the more obscurantist section of the Early Fathers (e.g. Tertullian). But if a philosophic basis was to be given to the Faith, the Church had to formulate its own creed and firmly establish its ecclesiastical organization centred in the priesthood as the guardian of its formularies. Only so could it be held to-gether as a catholic body in a disintegrating society.

In the process of the fusion of sacred and secular learning St Augustine (354–430) occupied a unique position as the connecting link between Greek and medieval thought. Drawing his inspiration mainly from Plato through the medium of Neoplatonism, supplemented by such knowledge of Stoicism, Epicureanism and Scepticism as he had gleaned from Cicero and contemporary writers, the search for knowledge of the Supreme Good was for him an indispensable stage in the acquisition of that perfect happiness which comes with the possession of God. This, he maintained, must be the aim of the true philosopher. But, anticipating Descartes and our con-temporary existentialists, he emphasized the certainty of self-knowledge and the part played by the will as against that of the intellect in the interpretation of reality. In him, however, the philosopher and the ecclesiastic were always in opposition, so that the two strains in his thought were never harmoniously blended. Moreover, the need of the hour was a firmly estab-lished authority, and this the Church alone could supply.

Therefore, he threw into the scales all the weight of his learning and prestige on the side of an infallible faith based on an absolute ecclesiastical authority. For him the spiritual order—the *City of God*—was a dynamic force manifesting itself in human society rather than a static metaphysical principle. Outwardly through the priesthood and the sacraments, and inwardly in the soul by the operation of the spiritual will, the Divine Spirit carried on His work of redemption and sanctification, controlling the course of history towards a goal beyond time through the interaction of the two cities, Babylon and Jerusalem, the earthly and the heavenly communities, founded respectively upon self-love and love of God.[47]

Although St Augustine was not a systematic thinker, his interpretation of the relations and function of Church and State constituted the most elaborate philosophy of history that had ever been attempted and virtually laid the theoretical foundations on which medieval civilization was built. The age was ripe for the originality which could contribute a deeper insight into a reality of the spiritual life and divine purpose and activity in a tumultuous world, such as he supplied as a philosopher, a psychologist and a theologian. Under his influence Western Christianity became a dynamic social and moral power rooted in the supremacy of the Spirituality and its hierarchy though he marks the end of the Patristic period at the fall of the Empire.

LEARNING IN THE DARK AGES

During the Dark Ages into which Europe then passed no really original thinker appeared until the ninth century, unless Dionysius the Areopagite be so regarded in his efforts to synthesise orthodox Christianity with Neoplatonism, and Boethius whose logical commentaries of Aristotle broke new ground in a static age. What learning there was was concentrated upon the collection of factual knowledge, and only in the monasteries did the ancient culture survive. Thus, in Ireland and Northern Britain scholars like Bede (673–735) in the Religious Houses devoted themselves to sacred study and the liberal arts. The principal aim, however, was to hand on the learning of the Fathers rather than to make any new contribution, and to expound the scriptures by the aid of an allegorical method which often assumed fantastic proportions, as has not been uncommon in later ages. They codified and classified the material inherited from the Patristic period without making any attempt to develop it or restate it in terms of progressive exposition. They were content to acquire an equipment sufficient for copying manuscripts, the recitation of the Divine Office, and the offering of the Sacrifice of the Mass—i.e. reading, writing, calligraphy, music, painting, a knowledge of the calendar and Latin, together with rhetoric, dialectic and arithmetic.

Notwithstanding their limitations, it was the Celtic and Saxon monks—Boniface, Willibrord, and Alcuin—who set about the revival of education and laid the foundations of Carolingian learning and culture. In England Theodore (602–690) and his abbot, according to Bede, were "well read in sacred and secular literature", and from them flowed "rivers of knowledge to water the hearts of their hearers" whom they gathered round them in the school at Canterbury to be instructed in the wisdom in which they themselves had been trained at Tarsus, Athens and in North Africa. Both Bede and Alcuin were genuine scholars though remaining men of their age, combining simple piety and faith, often indistinguishable from credulity, with considerable erudition. While uncritical in the use of his authorities, Bede selected his material with great skill and carefully distinguished between the transitory and ephemeral and the things of permanent value and significance. When the devout lived in the realm of the marvellous and saw divine interventions in all the occurrences of everyday life and its events, it is not surprising that miracles are recorded on almost every page of the *Ecclesiastical History*. But, true to the priestly tradition, Bede was the guardian of knowledge, having preserved for all subsequent generations the local history of his time, literature, prosody, hymnology, astronomy and the *computus,* chronology, medicine, rhetoric, hagiology, exegetical works of profound interest and importance for students of medieval letters and learning, and accounts of current theological controversies (e.g. the Council of Whitby). Indeed, he made England the first nation in Western Europe to have such a record in the vernacular. If Alcuin (735–804) lacked Bede's power of co-ordinating information, he transmitted the learning of his predecessors and gave to English scholarship a range of influence stretching from York to Tours, Fulda and Rheims.

THE MEDIEVAL SYNTHESIS

It was, however, not until the time of John Scotus Erigena (810–880), probably a native of Ireland where scholarship in some measure had survived during the long night of intellectual stagnation, that a new creative period in thought opened. Although Erigena's philosophy was not understood by his contemporaries, he was the most original thinker since Boethius, and he exercised a great influence on the development of Western thought in the Middle Ages and its aftermath. From Latin writers and the works of St Augustine he revived the transcendentalism of Neoplatonism with its graded hierarchy of existence, and raised the question of the reality of universals which eventually divided medieval thinkers into two opposed camps. He attempted to harmonize his Greek sources of knowledge with Christian doctrine and the interpretation of the scriptures. Claiming the autonomy of reason in theology he laid the foundations of medieval rationalism.

Between the ninth and eleventh centuries the growth of rationalism became a predominant feature in Western Christendom. As against the mysticism of St Bernard and the extreme Realism of Anselm, for whom faith was prior to reason and preceded knowledge, Abelard adopted a conceptualist position midway between extreme Realism and Nominalism. "A doctrine", he declared, "is not to be believed because God has said it, but we are convinced by reason it is so." If in his own day this attitude was regarded as heretical, and in consequence his influence on contemporary thought was slight, it was very considerable on the Scholastic movement in the thirteenth

Q

century, largely through Peter Lombard. Indeed, the fame of Abelard had made Paris one of the most important intellectual centres in France, and opened the way for the development of the *universitas* as a corporation of Masters under a Chancellor.

The rise of the universities in the latter half of the twelfth century gave a fresh impetus to the widespread interest in learning and had a far-reaching influence on the remarkable achievements of the following century. It only required the stimulus of the Aristotelian revival, fostered by the Crusades and the Moorish invasion of Europe, to bring these intellectual activities to fruition in the Scholastic movement, under the influence of such thinkers as St Bonaventure, Alexander of Hales, Robert Grosseteste, Roger Bacon, Albert Magnus and St Thomas Aquinas. The *studium* at Paris having grown up round the cathedral of Notre Dame and the collegiate church of St Geneviève in the Latin quarter of the city, it was essentially a clerical foundation concerned mainly with the interpretation of theology and philosophy, against that at Bologna which was originally a lay association devoted especially to the study of Roman and canon law, medicine and the arts. This, however, did not prevent Bologna being a bulwark of the Papacy exercising a powerful influence through its canonists on the ecclesiastical and social structure of medieval Europe. In fact it occupied a key position since it was responsible for the training of the administrators in both Church and State.

As the universities developed grammar schools were established in increasing numbers to teach the subjects of the Trivium (Latin grammar and syntax, rhetoric and dialectic) as a preparation for the wider curriculum of the Quadrivium (arithmetic, geometry, music, astronomy) which their pupils would be required to study at the university before graduating in theology, law or medicine. Thus, secular and sacred learning were brought into conjunction from an early age among the literate section of the community and consolidated by being placed in a religious framework of a common faith, worship and discipline, as in the ancient priesthoods. In the thirteenth century this process reached its greatest achievement in the remarkable synthesis of Greek, Roman, Jewish and Arabic culture and learning for which St Thomas Aquinas (1225–1274) was mainly responsible as the master mind of the Scholastic movement.

Building on the foundations laid by his predecessors, St Thomas with his unique powers of synthesis constructed a hierarchical system by means of the Aristotelian concepts of form and matter in which body and soul, matter and spirit, natural and revealed religion, secular and sacred learning, reason and theology, the spirituality and the temporality, were integrated as integral elements in a single structure resting ultimately on God as the ground and summit of all existence and unified under the stabilizing influence of the Church as the divinely ordained grace-bearing body. The truths of revelation being supra-rational they could be accepted only on the basis of a faith in a supreme spiritual authority, and so long as the mysteries of the Faith were not brought within the sphere of the natural reason, all other aspects of knowledge were regarded as legitimate fields of philosophic and scientific inquiry.

THE DISINTEGRATION OF SACRED LEARNING

Thus, the tension between sacred and secular learning was relieved. But the Thomist attempt to combine in one massive synthesis all available knowledge as the handmaid of theology on the basis of a fundamental dualism of revelation and reason, opened the way for a rationalism that was destined to end in a widespread scepticism when two centuries later, under the influence of the Renaissance, thought moved from the ecclesiastical to the secular sphere, and Aristotle was either interpreted naturalistically or discarded altogether. Already Bonaventure had rejected the Aristotelianism of Aquinas, and Roger Bacon had insisted, against the moderate Realism of the Angelic Doctor, that "an individual possesses more reality than all the universals taken together". William of Ockham carried the Nominalist position further by asserting that individual things are the only realities, thereby undermining the philosophic basis of the supremacy of universals on which the medieval solidarity, including the Papacy, was built. The part now became greater than the whole.

Thus, the stage was being set for a new act in the drama of civilization. The old order was clearly in process of disintegration. Scholasticism had run its course. The scientific interest that had been aroused through contact with Islamic learning and the works of Aristotle led more and more to concentration on factual knowledge in particular fields of inquiry in place of all-embracing philosophic and theological systems, syntheses and generalizations. Increasing emancipation from the ecclesiastical monopoly of learning, the growth of Humanism under the influence of the Renaissance, the break in the priestly tradition and the emphasis on individualism and private judgment fostered by the Reformation, opened the way for a new approach to scholarship in a secularized society in which the Church and its hierarchy were no longer able to fulfil the time-honoured function of the priesthood in the guardianship of learning and of the sacred tradition of culture.

In the centuries that have intervened since the break-up of medieval civilization the gains and losses have been considerable. On the credit side a new world order has been called into being in which human ingenuity has built up a vast superstructure on the basis of the scientific method, applied to every aspect of material culture, with results which have proved to be highly beneficial to mankind. On the debit side, however, stands the absence of ultimate concepts and standards, or of any unifying transcendental principle essential for the stability of an integrated system of values, such as the priestly tradition supplied. Devoid of a universal unity the universe, history and the life of the individual cease to have any fundamental purpose and meaning, and the social structure becomes faced with disintegration.

This outcome of the divorce of sacred and secular learning in the modern period has given rise to a new attempt to meet the situation by the creation of a totalitarian State in which the former priestly tradition is replaced by a secular hierarchy through whom the individual can communicate with the supreme authority (i.e. the State)—the particular with the universal—and so discern the reality of the unified whole. Learning under these conditions is concentrated in the first instance on scientific knowledge applied to industrial techniques as the means by which man gains control over nature and his own well-being. But no "deviationism" in the pursuit of learning in any domain is to be tolerated, and, therefore, freedom of thought and inquiry is as rigidly circumscribed as ever it has been in any priesthood, ancient or medieval. This can hardly be the final solution of the problem. Yet the fact remains that if mankind is to survive, the social structure must be integrated and stabilized on a spiritual basis, and in this achievement sacred and secular learning require to be brought into an effective relationship, maintained by a guardianship at once learned, liberal and transcendental, to serve the purposes of a unifying force.

CHAPTER VIII

Priesthood and Jurisdiction

THE exercise of priestly functions invariably has carried with it juridical authority. As the official representatives of the supernatural powers on whom the community depends for its physical and spiritual sustenance and the right ordering of its social relationships, the religious leaders, be they tribal elders, medicine men, seers, diviners, prophets, priests or divine kings, usually have been concerned *ex officio* with the administration of justice and the maintenance of law and order, alike in the temporal and the spiritual spheres. Thus, for instance, in primitive society when an accusation is made of the practice of witchcraft, black magic, the infringement of the law of incest, or some other offence against the common weal, the adjudicators normally are the priests or their equivalents.

TRIAL BY ORDEAL

If the method adopted to test the suspected person is that of trial by ordeal their presence frequently is required as being the most competent to conduct the procedure in view of their specialized knowledge and mediatorial status in a situation which pre-supposes transcendental intervention. Since the appeal is to the supernatural order, of which the priest is the duly commissioned agent, this mode of arriving at a decision falls within his jurisdiction even though he may merely preside, or receive the oath which is usually an essential preliminary to the order. But inasmuch as the operation may be actually magical, having within it its own inherent conditional curse, it need not necessarily demand sacerdotal intervention.[1] Nevertheless, trial by ordeal at first was carried out by the priests in conjunction with the civil power, and in Europe it survived in the Dark Ages under the combined sanction of the State and the Church, until in course of time it was discountenanced by the clergy. Although it made an advance towards practical justice, and often may have been successful in the detection of a conscience-stricken criminal when divine judgment was unquestioned, it was too crude in its methods, and liable to serious abuse and official trickery, to be more than a passing phase in judicial procedure, notwithstanding its persistence until the thirteenth century in England.

SUPERNATURAL SANCTIONS IN TRIBAL JURISDICTION

The trial by ordeal, however, was only one method by which jurisdiction based on supernatural sanctions has been exercised. In primitive states of culture tribal government was wholly, or to a very considerable extent, under the control of a hierarchy of sacred men who by virtue of their status in society, their esoteric knowledge and transcendental powers enforced discipline and explicit obedience to the established order. Law and order, social and spiritual stability and consolidation have been maintained by the recognition of an unconditional sacred standard of obligation to which each and every tribesman is bound. Therefore, each new generation has been subjected at adolescence to the rigorous discipline of initiation by the guardians of the traditional lore, its rites and customs, and the tribal organization, grounded in the remote past and made secure in the present by unquestioning obedience to the established régime.

The sacrosanct character of the things done, the teaching given, and the entire experience under immensely awe-inspiring conditions, has been such that it could not fail to have a lasting impression on the minds and convictions of the novices as imperatives and values demanding unquestioned acceptance. In this way the power and influence of the sacred rulers and their absolute jurisdiction became assured. Thus, Dr Howitt records that a young man in the Yuin tribe of New South Wales admitted his scepticism concerning what he was told in his childhood about the powers of the medicine-men until he actually saw them producing their magic crystals from their insides during his initiation.[2] By actions of this kind, tumultuous dances, long and elaborate mysterious rites, taxing to the utmost limit their physical and mental powers of endurance, a proper respect for authority, vested in the senior members of the tribe and the professional sacred leaders in their several departments, is inculcated, and religious and social stability is secured by placing on an unassailable foundation the traditional behaviour and belief. Once authority and jurisdiction have been definitely asserted and firmly established, a measure of freedom usually is allowed to the initiated section of the community provided that it does not conflict with the administration of tribal affairs by the official leaders.

ROYAL JURISDICTION IN AKAN

With the introduction of herding and agriculture the ultimate source of authority and jurisdiction became centred in the sovereign power of a single ruler, very frequently regarded as the embodiment of the beneficent forces of nature by virtue of his or her divine origin and significance. How this was accomplished, as we have seen, can only be conjectured,[3] but when society was regulated on a theocratic basis the divine ruler became the fountain-head of the government. Thus, among the Akan peoples of the Gold Coast the *Ohemmaa,* or queen-mother, was regarded as the owner of the sacred State, and it was she who appointed the king (*Omanhene*) after consultation with the council of the royal clan (*abusua*) and the elder counsellors (*mpanyimfo*), consisting of the paramount chiefs. As the daughter of the Moon, the female aspect of Nyame, the Supreme Creator of the universe, she occupied a unique position in the State, and although civil jurisdiction was exercised by the king she was his legal advisor in matters concerning female litigation and other disputes in which women were involved. Such cases could be transferred from the king's court to her own court, and although her powers have been considerably modified under British rule, she still plays a major part in administration in her own domain. She presided over the initiation of girls at puberty (*beragoro*), held a watching brief over the laws protecting the marriage and property rights of women, and those connected with divorce, rape, seduction, betrothal and dowries. As patron of agriculture she was thought to be able to control the weather, and, therefore, the conduct of the rain-making ceremonies fell within her jurisdiction.[4]

Having once been chosen by the queen-mother and installed, the king, however, was the sacred ruler of the State, exercising his jurisdiction in his royal capacity as the son of the Sun-god.[5] His sacredness then was such that lest he be defiled by contact with his subjects, his administrative functions were performed by deputies (*okyeame*) under a chief "spokesman" (*akyeam-chene*) who alone held converse with him. As the priest *par excellence* the king represented the hierarchy (*okomfo*) in the state council, and was responsible for the correct performance of the ritual on which the well-being of the community depended. Throughout his life four officers were constantly in attendance, whose duty it was to minister to all his needs, and to surround his bed after his demise. When in his priestly capacity as the mediator between his ancestors and the people he officiated at the *Adae* ceremonies, held every 43 days to propitiate the royal ancestors, he was accompanied by the chief of his household (*gyasehene*) as well as by the chief spokesman (*akyeamehene*), and some of the most important members of the council of elders.[6] At the conclusion of the rites the king received the homage of the chiefs. Apart from ceremonial functions of this kind his principal duties were in connexion with military affairs, though in theory he was the actual ruler of the State.

THE JURISDICTION OF THE KING AND HIS COUNSELLORS IN ANCIENT EGYPT

It would seem, therefore, that statecraft on the Gold Coast has borne a striking resemblance to that in the Nile valley where, as we have seen, the divine kingship was the dynamic institution in a complex hierarchical society.[7] The queen as the "god's wife" never, however, occupied the position in Egypt of the "queen-mother" in the matrilineal Akan tradition, notwithstanding the power wielded by the sacred princesses in Thebes. The only serious rivals to the divine occupant of the throne were the local priesthoods, and their jurisdiction was kept in check by the Pharaoh as the living Horus claiming the relationship of sonship with all the gods and goddesses in the pantheon. Although during weak reigns the high-priesthoods might become hereditary offices,[8] their appointment was vested in the monarchy[9] and their functions were primarily in connexion with the administration of the temples over which they presided,[10] assisted by a governing body composed of ministers of State who were also priests.[11] This jurisdiction included the control of the very large staff engaged in the administration of the wealth and estates of the temples and the care of the buildings,[12] until in the Roman period the temples were taken over by the local Senates. In addition to these administrative and cultic priests, in the New Kingdom six prophets and three priests acted as judges with a layman serving as a scribe,[13] together with other important offices involving civil and military administration held by the higher members of the priesthoods, who thereby ceased to exercise sacerdotal functions. But behind all jurisdiction was the absolute authority of the kingship vested in the reigning Pharaoh who, as we have seen,[14] was the upholder of "justice" (*maat*) controlling every aspect of human life, social organization and cosmic process.

THE CODE OF HAMMURABI

In Mesopotamia where gods, kings, priests and subjects were all interdependent upon each other, and each city seems to have had its own code of laws, it was not until about 1750 B.C. that the State was unified as an empire under Hammurabi.[15] The emperor then claimed to reign as "king of righteousness" by divine permission in order that "justice might appear in the land".[16] When subsequently he was confirmed in the throne by Marduk, who as the god of the new capital, Babylon, was raised to the supreme position in the pantheon, Hammurabi promulgated his great Code and gave it divine authority. Since earlier codes have now been brought to light—those of Urukagina (*c.* 2700 B.C.) and of Gudea (*c.* 2450 B.C.)—it is not improbable that before the time of Hammurabi other City-states were dominated by priestly organizations under priest-kings responsible for the administration of justice embodied in collections of judgments of great antiquity, issued originally by Sumerian kings and their counsellors and recorded from time to time by their successors for the express purpose of establishing a higher degree of justice. It was, in fact, in Mesopotamia that a succession of rulers and their priests and officials took the lead in the form of legal abuses, until, at the beginning of the second millennium B.C., the sixth monarch of the First Dynasty of Babylon, Hammurabi, was able to issue a Code that became the basis of all subsequent legislation, whether Semitic or Sumerian.

The temple being the most important factor in the Babylonian City-state, in theory the god owned all the land and to him a rent or tribute had to be paid by everyone who held a portion of the sacred territory. The inhabitants who had built the temple provided and maintained its priesthood, the priests having the right to enjoy the revenues of the temple and to exercise jurisdiction in the terrain. The king was a benevolent despot, and the prosperity of the land depended mainly upon his administrative ability. He was responsible for the wellbeing of his kingdom, and, therefore, he was the source of justice. Civic affairs were in the hands of the hereditary viceroys installed in the local palaces but they were subject to the royal approval. This centralization of authority in its fountainhead, which constituted the legislative basis of the Code, gave expression to the claim of Hammurabi to be "a father of his people"[17] and "the son of Babylon".[18]

In the exercise of his quasi-divine jurisdiction he kept in the background as far as was possible, and when he bought land as a private individual he tended more and more to employ his stewards to carry out the transactions on his behalf. Nevertheless, he directed the collection of temple revenues and superintended their shepherds and herdsmen. He constructed canals and controlled dredging and similar operations connected with their use and maintenance. He gave instructions concerning the enforcement of the law against bribery and money-lenders, upheld the just claims of debtors and supervised the regulation of food supplies, transport, public works, and the care of the royal flocks and herds. In the case of a breach of contract, the matter was decided in a court consisting of one or more judges together with the elders of the city acting as assessors, after they had carefully inspected the deed which usually was enclosed in a clay cover to prevent its being tampered with. Although oaths were taken in the temple or at its gate and referred to the judgment of the god, the judges were not necessarily priests. Their decisions were final so far as the court was concerned, but appeal to a higher court, and ulti-mately to the king, was allowed. Therefore, the jurisdiction of judges was local and limited to their own domain. Plaintiffs pleaded their own cases, there being no professional advocates available.

While the Code had its limitations and its legislation was based on the division of the community into feudal land-owners giving direct service to the crown and their retinue, commoners and slaves, each being assigned rights and duties appropriate to their status, it represents the high-water mark of legal practice in the civilizations of the Ancient East at the time of its promulgation. Its influence on the regulation of conduct in the adjacent countries was considerable, and not least in Israel where the Book of the Covenant in Exodus xxi-xxiii is now recognized to have been part of a much longer Hebrew analogue to the Code of Hammurabi, and to similar codes among the Babylonians, Assyrians, Hittites and Hur-rians between 2000 and 1100 B.C.[19]

HEBREW LEGISLATION

All these codes go back in their basic formulation to the Sumerian jurisprudence of the third millennium B.C., and are regarded as being ultimately of divine bestowal. Therefore, they fall within the province of the priests as the duly appointed agents of the gods and the custodians of sacred law. Being the only educated group they were the judges in civil and criminal cases as well as the arbiters on all theological and ecclesiastical matters and the keepers of the ancient traditions. A legal decision, in fact, was in the nature of an oracle, indicative of the will of the god, and so, as we have seen, the Hebrew *kohen* (priest), like the Arabic *kahin,* was a seer or diviner. His pronouncements declared the will of Yahweh, and the Hebrew word for law, *tôrah,* was the equivalent of the Babylonian *tertu,* the term for "omen". Hence the dogma concerning the divine origin of the Pentateuch as the code revealed on the Holy Mount to Moses, who wrote it down and taught it to the congregation of Israel as a divine oracle, without any clear distinction between ecclesiastical, civil and criminal procedures. How much of this heterogeneous legislation actually emanates from Moses cannot be determined, but the distinctive character of many of the laws (e.g. those on slavery, "holiness" and *lex talionis*) suggests that they were the product of independent legislative schools in Israel, like the Priestly Code drawn up by the priests in the time of Ezra (*c.* 444 B.C.), which was the result of a process of careful collecting and sorting of tradition by a skilled body of sacerdotal canonists and legislators. If they borrowed from Mesopotamian sources they also developed their own tradition behind which it would seem was the shadowy figure of a supreme legislator who was also a law-giver standing in a peculiarly intimate relation with the God of Israel and the cultus.[20] Some of this legislation at least may go back to the beginning of organized Hebrew monotheism, and it may have been codified at an early period in the cultic schools.

Inherent in the theocratic government of the "Chosen Nation", living as it claimed under a special dispensation of Divine providence, was the sovereign rule of Yahweh exercised through his earthly agents and instruments. Therefore their jurisdiction, like that of the divine king elsewhere, was vested in the peculiar relationship established between Israel and its god. The Law was the sacred and treasured possession of the Holy Nation and its dictates were absolute in their demands for explicit obedience. When the conception of Yahweh was moralized under prophetic influence his righteousness required right conduct in his people in accordance with the ethical standards and moral judgments of a perfectly holy god, who was at once the lord of creation, governor of the universe and ruler and judge of mankind and of human conduct. When the bond between the tribes and their god was that of a covenant-unity comparable to the social nexus that united desert folk on a family basis in a kindred group and blood brotherhood, the good life was centred in the mutual obligations which each owed to the other members of the clan, strengthened by their collective relationship with Yahweh, under whose jurisdiction they lived and prospered. Their first duty was to the theocracy and its god-given laws and institutions as administered by its duly appointed agents—the priests, seers, and prophets.

So long as the religious and civic observances, and the prescribed ethic, were interpreted in terms of non-moral sacredness as an irreducible datum, *sui generis,* the holy denoted that which was set apart from the secular, consecrated to the service of religion. It was in this sense that Israel was regarded as a sacred congregation, or the Nazarite was "separated" from the rest of the community;[21] while Yahweh himself was a holy god because he was the personification of the numinous, transcending the natural and commonplace and controlling the universe and its processes.[22] With the fuller moralization of the conception of sacredness he became the Holy One of Israel, and righteous Ruler of the world, absolute in goodness and truth.[23] Divine righteousness, however, retained a forensic quality meaning conformity to the proper norm or standard, as that of correct weights,[24] true speech,[25] or right paths.[26] Therefore, as a category of value it characterized the conduct required of every member of the Holy Nation, standing in a covenant relationship with the Holy One of Israel. Right and wrong were defined not by reason, reflection, custom or common consent, but by the revealed will of God made known through the cultus, the sacred oracle and the voice of prophecy.

The Hebrew ethic had a legal character inasmuch as the

Tôrah was regarded as a divine injunction resting on the righteousness of Yahweh disclosed to the Patriarchs and Moses. These regulations took the form of categorical commands, prohibitions, hortatory utterances, legal prescriptions, and in the later literature, wise sayings, pious aspirations, prophetic denunciations and Rabbinic interpretations and applications recorded in the *Mishnah*. Thus, the Deuteronomic and Levitical Codes were drawn up for the purpose of maintaining the religious and social structure of Israel free from the contaminations of the Canaanite cultus or of that of the surrounding nations. The function of the priesthood was the exercise of its divinely ordained jurisdiction over the laws, institutions and rites through which the sovereignty of Yahweh was made operative in the theocracy, and the holy people were kept in their covenant relation with him and distinct from their neighbours.

In the post-exilic community the priestly legislation centred round the sacrificial worship at the Temple[27] since upon it depended the preservation and restoration of that holiness essential for the realization of the vocation of the people of the holy God. This gave the priesthood its unique position and made its rule absolute. To keep the commandments of the Law was the first duty, whether it be that of worship, of burying the dead, or doing justly, loving mercy and walking humbly with God. To enforce this was the business of the priests. But the complex Priestly Code is a composite document compiled from more than one earlier collection of priestly *tôrôth* (e.g. the Holiness Code of Lev. xvii–xxvi) belonging originally to different priesthoods associated with the more important sanctuaries where they exercised their respective jurisdictions.

RABBINIC JURISPRUDENCE

According to the Rabbinic tradition, God gave to Moses on the Holy Mount not only the Tôrah but also the Prophets, the Hagiographical books, the Mishnah and the Talmuds,[28] together with commandments and their interpretations and all the rules deduced from them.[29] From Moses the divine Tôrah was held to have been communicated through Joshua and the Judges to the Prophets and the men of the Great Synagogue in an unbroken tradition.[30] Furthermore, since the priests were the official interpreters of the Law as the living voice of God to His people—the divine benefaction *par excellence* to the world—the oral Law was invested with the same divine authority as the written Law.

After the Exile the compilation and editing of the sacred literature were undertaken by the sacerdotal schools, and the five books attributed to Moses were collectively designated the Tôrah, or "Teaching", and assigned supreme authority. To provide for regular instruction in this complex mass of material adequately trained exponents were required, and with the rise of the synagogues those who sought to know the will of Yahweh betook themselves thither where scribes as the official teachers gave instruction in the written Law. At first usually they were priests who were set apart to "seek (i.e. study) the Law of the Lord, and to do it, and to teach in Israel rules and duties".[31] But freed from sacerdotal functions in connexion with the cultus, they had wider interests and generally were cultivated men of leisure and culture,[32] until the Maccabaean revolt against Hellenism had a narrowing effect upon them. Then the office lost its priestly character and content, and attention was concentrated upon the adjustment and adaptation of the existing conditions and prevailing practices to the dictates of the Tôrah. In short, they "fenced the Law" by the aid of oral tradition and so became virtually adjudicators.

The rule to be followed (i.e. the *Halakha*) as the guide to conduct, although not contained in Scripture, was regarded as the Word of God because it was as an authoritative interpretation of the Tôrah to meet the needs of practical morality and customary law. It included the temple ritual, the synagogue procedure, civil transactions such as buying and selling, betrothal, marriage and divorce, dietary prescriptions and the administration of criminal law. While this Halakhistic exegesis constituted an obligatory jurisdiction which had the force of law, like the Talmud it was a *corpus juris ecclesiastici* rather than a code. The purity rules referred chiefly to the priests in their official capacity rather than to the laity, but in the words of the Talmud, "the crown of the Tôrah surpassed that of the priesthoods and of royalty." And it was the duty of the scribes to preserve intact the *Halakha*, to maintain its teaching, uphold its juridical authority and enforce its discipline. Since they sat in Moses' seat all that they commanded had to be obeyed,[33] and however self-righteous, ostentatious, unscrupulous and stereotyped some of them may have been, well-instructed scribes were revered[34] and their injunctions were eagerly followed. Generally speaking the Jews found joy and satisfaction in the fulfilment of the Law, and they were not oppressed by the demands it made upon them. On the contrary, they praised God daily for having sanctified them by His commandments, and rejoiced in the words of His teaching, for they were their life and "the strength of their days".

In any legalistic system casuistry is bound to arise when the law is applied to individual cases and particular conditions. It was so, as we have seen, in the medieval Church, and became a prominent feature in Rabbinic Judaism in the interpretation of the traditional rules, primarily in respect of ritual observance, after the fall of Jerusalem in A.D. 70. It then became necessary to safeguard Jewish faith and practice in a Gentile environment under the guidance and jurisdiction of experts who could give authoritative and precise directions in the form of judicial decisions. In the schools which were established at Jamnia, Ludd, Sapphoris and Tiberias this consolidation of the nation as a religious entity was achieved, and from their deliberations the Mishnah took definite shape, and was handed on from generation to generation through the Sanhedrin.

The dispute between the followers of the rigorist Shammai and the more accommodating Hillel in their respective schools, which figure prominently in Rabbinical literature as Beth Shammai and Beth Hillel, continued to divide allegiances for a considerable time, and exercised a powerful influence on Jewish legalism in the Tannaite period. The scribes became rabbis and continued their debates within the framework of the Mishnah

R

for the next three centuries. When these discussions at length became systematized as Gemara (i.e. additions to or commentaries on the Mishnah), laws were formulated in the light of the conclusions, and in due course the Talmud emerged as the combination of the Mishnah and the Gemara in the form of a dialectic exposition. With this immense literary equipment at hand the scope for casuistical judgments was almost limitless and bewildering until Maimonides (1135–1204) intervened and became a "guide for the perplexed". Great as was his influence on medieval Judaism, however, "spicing" the Law by ingenious juridic disputation survived and reached fantastic lengths, especially between 1460 and 1540. Nevertheless, it was under Rabbinic jurisdiction based on Talmudic jurisprudence as a supplement to the Pentateuch that the national life of Judaism was consolidated and its traditional faith maintained when the unifying centre of the temple and the priesthood was destroyed and the sacrificial system abrogated.

APOSTOLIC JURISDICTION

When the Christian Nazoraean community released itself from Judaism in which it arose as a sect and became an "ecclesia",[35] it exercised apostolic jurisdiction over its adherents by virtue of the authority it claimed to have received from Christ Himself. The equation of Jesus with the Messiah was interpreted in terms of a divine sovereignty here and now— "the time is fulfilled, and the kingdom (i.e. the reign of God) is at hand".[36] Therefore, if the Messianic reign in fact had begun, the Church as "the Israel of God"[37] was a divine sovereignty, a "realized eschatology", brought into being to actualize the redemptive process for all time, though its completion was yet to be fulfilled in the future.[38] At first it would seem to have been regarded as an interim movement awaiting the Parousia which was, it was thought, likely to occur at any moment.[39] When this eschatology was abandoned in favour of a missionary enterprise extending throughout the Graeco-Roman world, an ecclesiastical administration and discipline were required to strengthen the organization of the rapidly growing community.

When the Jerusalem Church ceased to be an effective force and new centres began to arise throughout the Empire, often faced with heresies and persecution, the development of a stable form of government and a properly constituted authority became a matter of urgency. Moreover, as the apostles passed away the maintenance of apostolic jurisdiction had to be determined.

In the original Christian community at Jerusalem they were the recognized leaders, deriving their authority and status from the commission they were accredited with having received from Christ himself.[40] According to the Gospel tradition and that of the Acts of the Apostles, they were witnesses of the resurrection and the nucleus of the kingdom bequeathed to them.[41] The reference to their occupying twelve thrones corresponding to the twelve tribes of Israel[42] connected them with the Hebrew patriarchs as the "princes" of the New Israel. In this capacity they exercised authority by virtue of their apostolate as the "essential ministry",[43] whether or not this status and function carried with it an exclusive right of appointment of their successors. They were in a class by themselves, and if the selection of Matthias to take the place of Judas be a historical fact,[44] particular significance would appear to have been attached to the maintenance of the original nucleus, exactly as it had been constituted by Jesus before the Crucifixion. In any case, the tradition of "The Twelve" is very deeply laid in apostolic Christianity.

In addition to this inner circle within the general body of disciples, three of whom in the persons of Peter, James and John are represented as having occupied privileged positions of priority, mention is made of "seventy elders" commissioned during the Galilean ministry.[45] The number would seem to have been suggested by the tradition that Moses appointed seventy to share his responsibilities,[46] on the same principle that the Twelve were equated with the Patriarchs. But this symbolism would be appropriate only if in fact, whatever their actual number may have been, a lesser ministry had been constituted to assist in the work of evangelization and exorcism, comparable in some respects to that which subsequently became a separate class of subordinate officials eventually known as διάκονοις and πρεσβυτέροις.

The "Seven" mentioned in Acts vi. 1–6, however, appear to have been concerned chiefly with the administration of relief, although in the case of Stephen and Philip they were also preachers of the new Gospel. St Paul in his letter to the Philippians referred to "bishops" and "deacons" as two types of officials,[47] and considerably later the author of the Pastoral Epistles represented the bishops as "overseers", and the deacons as an inferior order.[48] The presbyters, as the name suggests, probably bore some relation to the members of the Jewish Sanhedrin, and to the officials who had the care and supervision of local synagogues.[49] The ministry was centred apparently in local congregations so that when a Christian community was established in a district presbyters were appointed to organize and govern it,[50] and minister to the spiritual and temporal needs of its members.[51] But no clear distinction existed between the officers described as "presbyters" and "bishops" respectively in the apostolic period.[52] Nevertheless, despite a fluidity of phraseology, local presbyterates had their leaders (ἡγουμένος), corresponding in some measure to the "ruler of the synagogue" (ἀρχισυνάγωγος) in Judaism,[53] and in some churches the "episcopos" may have presided.[54]

In this connexion the position of James, the brother of the Lord, is of particular interest and significance. He first appears in the Acts of the Apostles as the established leader of the Jerusalem Church[55] without any introduction, presumably because he was such a well known and prominent figure in the movement that St Luke in drawing up his narrative did not consider it to be necessary to supply any biographical details about him. He is mentioned by St Paul among the witnesses of the Resurrection,[56] and is represented as presiding over the Council of Jerusalem without question with the "elders" as assessors and himself pronouncing judgment on the issue under discussion.[57] Although not one of the Twelve, he was the ruler of the mother church, and there is reason to think that he was highly respected in Jewish as well as in Christian circles.[58] Indeed, but for his early martyrdom and the appearance of the even more outstanding personality in Saul of Tarsus, the Church, like Islam, might have been governed by an hereditary caliphate in the family of the Founder of the Faith.

The advent of St Paul, who claimed to have received a special commission as an apostle by divine intervention,[59] introduced a new and powerful element in the movement destined to change the subsequent course of its history, since under his influence the Jewish sect was destined to become the Catholic Church. Moreover, the Judaeo-Christian nucleus centred at Jerusalem under the jurisdiction of James, the Lord's brother, as a result of the fall of the capital in A.D. 70, was reduced to a position of complete insignificance. Whatever fundamental antagonism, if any, there may have been between it and the Pauline section of the community,[60] the future clearly lay with the Gentile Church, and in the wider perspective of an international institution the apostolic jurisdiction necessarily acquired a less localized and Judaistic or Hellenistic constitution. It is true that the synagogue tradition remained the basic pattern of the organization and its worship,[61] but as the pagan converts preponderated it was adapted to the needs and conditions of the Graeco-Roman environment in which it functioned.

As the apostolate was extended after the Resurrection to include such prominent leaders in the Christian community as the Lord's brother and St Paul, with Silas and Barnabas, Silvanus, Timothy and John Mark among others, closely associated with them, so when churches were established outside Palestine in Asia Minor, Macedonia, and the Levant, they were placed under delegated apostolic jurisdiction.[62] This involved a transmission of authority which apparently normally was bestowed through prayer and the laying on of hands by one who had been duly commissioned by the apostolic company.[63] The direct call to the apostolate presupposed in the case of St Paul and James, the Lord's brother, like the casting of lots at the appointment of Matthias, does not appear to have created a precedent in the Early Church.

Authority was delegated even though attempts to explain the status and function of the Twelve and their associates in terms of "plenipotentiaries" comparable to the Jewish *shaliachate*[64] have not proved to be very convincing in view of the absence of evidence that such an institution existed in Judaism in the first century A.D. Nevertheless, whether or not synagogue officials were emissaries (*shaliach*) acting on behalf of a superior authority (e.g. the high-priest or the Sanhedrin), in the Christian Church commissioned individuals were "sent" to exercise a specific ministry as the duly appointed agents of Christ and the Church in a particular place or region. Thus, Titus went to Crete and Timothy to Asia Minor, where later John is said to have exercised apostolic functions.

The beginnings of monepiscopacy may be detected possibly in the position occupied by James in the Mother church at Jerusalem, where the organization was based on that of the synagogue with presbyters as a normal part of the constitution, over whom he presided with "deacons" appointed as an emergency measure to act as almoners. At Antioch a different situation obtained, ministerial authority being exercised by prophets and teachers who based their claims on direct outpourings of the Holy Spirit.[65] Among them was Barnabas, who had been sent thither as a delegate from the Twelve, and he was soon joined by Paul. It was during their residence in the Gentile city that they were directed by a prophetic revelation to embark upon a wider missionary enterprise in the Empire. Dissensions, however, arose between the new Pauline churches and Jerusalem, and from the Corinthian and Galatian letters some question about the authority of their founder (St Paul) seems to have been raised. For a time St Peter was conciliatory, but eventually both he and Barnabas broke with Paul at Antioch.[66]

THE PETRINE SUPREMACY

The position of St Peter in the Apostolic Church is by no means easy to determine. As far as the testimony of the Acts is concerned he would appear to have been the most outstanding figure[67] until he was eclipsed by St Paul and his companions, with whom his relations became strained after the Antiochene controversy. After his escape from prison by angelic aid, he is said to have repaired to the house of John Mark and to have given directions for his deliverance to be communicated to James and the brethren[68] before going to "another place". At the Council of Jerusalem, although he did not preside, his evidence appears to have been thought to have decided the issue in favour of St Paul.[69] In the Epistle to the Galatians and in the first Corinthian letter, under the name of Cephas, the "Rock-man", repeated reference is made to his point of view, while in the Synoptic Gospels he is certainly represented as the leader among the original Twelve, and with the two sons of Zebedee to have made a bid for supremacy.[70] Moreover, the question of primacy seems to have been perennial,[71] and it is possible that the declaration of Jesus that the chief places had been reserved for them for whom they had been prepared[72] had reference to the position actually occupied in the apostolic Church first by Peter and then by James, the Lord's brother.

In the Matthaean narrative the Petrine supremacy is firmly established. In the list of the Apostles St Peter is placed first,[73] and his pre-eminence is given a special significance in the *logion* describing the commission which is alleged to have been bestowed upon him by Christ at Caesarea Philippi.[74] Having made his confession of faith in the Messiahship of his Master, Jesus in reply said to him "Blessed art thou, Simon Bar-Jonah: for flesh and blood hath not revealed it unto thee but my Father which is in heaven. And I also say unto thee that thou art Peter, and upon this rock I will build my Church; and the keys of Hades shall not prevail against it. I will give unto thee the keys of the kingdom of heaven: whatsoever thou shalt bind on earth shall be bound in heaven; and whatsoever thou shalt loose on earth shall be loosed in heaven." However these remarkable words be interpreted, it is impossible to escape from the fact that they are intended to confer upon Peter an absolutely unique status in the Church, and, as J. Weiss points out, this extraordinary exaltation of Simon Bar-Jonah at the expense of the rest of the Twelve is only conceivable in a community in which Peter was "the Apostle".[75]

If, as Weiss[76] and Streeter[77] maintain, the Matthaean narrative was compiled in Antioch in Syria not earlier than A.D. 80, it is possible that St Peter's connexions with the city[78] may have given rise to a Petrine tradition which, as Streeter has ingeniously argued, was subsequently fostered by Judaistic Christian refugees from Jerusalem after the martyrdom of the Lord's brother as a mediating influence between the Judaistic and Pauline factions.[79] This explanation, though by no means unreasonable, is merely a conjecture, but wherever the Matthaean tradition arose and whatever may have been the underlying causes, it is clear that the narrative was given its present form in the interests of a Petrine party. Thus, in the earlier Marcan account of the incident at Caesarea Philippi, which is generally regarded by New Testament scholars to have emanated from Rome between A.D. 60 and 70, and to have been dependent upon evidence supplied by St Peter,[80] there is no mention of a special commission having been given to St Peter as a result of his confession, "Thou art the Christ".[81] The same applies in the case of the Lucan record of the incident.[82] From these omissions it may be inferred that the Petrine supremacy was part of a floating tradition current in the centre in which the Matthaean narrative was compiled, not known or accepted elsewhere.

If St Mark's Gospel was in fact written in Rome, the absence of the text in its Matthaean form seems to indicate that the alleged pre-eminence of St Peter by Dominical decree was not in vogue in the capital of the Empire when the earliest Synoptic record was drawn up. This is the more remarkable inasmuch as the author appears to have been in very intimate contact with the apostle. To suggest that the *logion* was omitted from considerations of modesty on the part of St Peter[83] is a rather desperate expedient contrary to all that we know of the character of this forthright disciple. Similarly, St Luke, who claims to have been careful to trace the course of all things accurately from the first, and to have relied for his information upon "eye witnesses" and "ministers of the Word",[84] surely would have added the Matthaean remarkable *logion* to his account of the gathering at Caesarea Philippi if he had been acquainted with the theory, particularly in view of his Antiochene connexions,[85] unless, of course, it be supposed that he deliberately suppressed it in the Pauline interest. It would seem, therefore, that the Matthaean tradition concerning the Petrine supremacy was independent of, and probably subsequent to, the Marcan and Lucan sources, including the hypothetical document Q where it also does not occur.

Granting that the tradition associating the second Gospel with Rome is correct, the omission of the commission in the Marcan narrative suggests that it was not known in the capital between A.D. 60 and 70 in spite of the Patristic contention that the apostle was with St Mark at Rome and dictated the Gospel to the evangelist.[86] The only scriptural evidence for St Peter's connexions with the city is the cryptic reference to "Babylon" as the equivalent of Rome in the epistle that bears his name.[87] But the authorship of this letter is very uncertain and if it was in any sense a Petrine document it must have been written by an amanuensis, such as St Paul's companion Silvanus.[88] Why "Babylon" should have been substituted for "Rome" when Christians were exhorted to honour the emperor[89] is not very obvious. Nevertheless, the belief that Peter and Mark were together in the capital was current before A.D. 110, and as Streeter argues, if the epistle is not authentic, and as Professor Merrill contends "Babylon" means the Mesopotamian city,[90] the belief that Peter came to Rome must have been well established before the letter was written.[91]

The first Epistle of Clement (*c.* A.D. 96) records the martyrdom of St Peter and St Paul in the capitol, and a few years later Ignatius described them as "monitors" of Roman Christians,[92] but Eusebius in the latter part of the same century was the first writer definitely to assert that the two apostles lived in Italy,[93] and Irenaeus regarded them as the founders and organizers of the church in Rome.[94] Henceforth the tradition became firmly established in the Patristic writings. Tertullian

(1602–40), for example, referred their martyrdom to the Neronian persecution, and following the spurious *Clementine Homilies,* made Clement instead of Linus the successor of St Peter in the Roman See.[95] It was he who first alluded to the Petrine dominical commission in relation to its primacy, though it is very doubtful whether he regarded the power of the keys as conferring upon it jurisdiction over all other local churches. Tertullian being a Montanist his concern was to vindicate the exclusive right of this sect to remit sins rather than to establish the universal episcopate of the Petrine succession.[96] Indeed, he disallowed the appeal of Callixtus to the Matthaean *logion* in support of the apostle's jurisdiction as bishop of Rome.[97]

Similarly, while Irenaeus supported the foundation of the church in the capital of the Empire by "the two most famous Apostles Peter and Paul", when Pope Victor I in A.D. 190 took steps to excommunicate the proconsular province of Asia because it refused to fall into line with the Roman ruling concerning the date of Easter, he (Irenaeus) opposed the action of Victor and the excommunication was withdrawn.[98] It is unfortunate that our information concerning this much-discussed incident comes from the somewhat confused account of the issues at stake and their personnel given by Eusebius, who is never a trustworthy source in matters of this kind, and who on this occasion doubtless was influenced by the Paschal controversy current in his own day. Nevertheless, apart from the details of the dispute, the conflict would not have arisen unless at the end of the second century the Bishop of Rome had been in a position to speak and act authoritatively in respect of ecclesiastical procedure, at any rate within his own domain. This does not appear to have been questioned. What is much less certain is how far his action really was directed beyond the confines of his province. In Rome his predecessor, Soter, seems to have made some attempt to suppress the divergent Asian custom of keeping Easter on the fourteenth day of Nisan irrespective of the day of the week on which the date fell. Victor, however, on his accession took strong measures to enforce the

Latin practice of always observing the festival on a Sunday.[99]
It is possible, therefore, if it was this injunction, originally confined to Rome, that was communicated to other churches, that
the wider issue arose when the request for assent was refused by
the Asian provinces because of its reactions on the Roman
situation.

THE PAPAL SUPREMACY

Be this as it may, although the papal primacy of jurisdiction
did not become an established fact until after the Christianiza-
tion of the Empire in the fourth century, deference paid to the
occupant of the See centred in the capital prepared the way for
this consummation. Thus, Cyprian (*c.* 200–258), bishop of
Carthage, endeavoured to induce Pope Stephen I to excommunicate Marcion, bishop of Arles, because he had followed
Novatian in refusing to rebaptize those who had lapsed during
the Decian persecution.[100] In making this request Cyprian
seemed to acknowledge the Roman supremacy in matters of
discipline, though what the sequel of the suggestion was we are
not informed. That nothing was done is likely since Cyprian
subsequently despaired of Roman intervention in disciplinary
measures after Stephen had refused to regard a Spanish lapsed
bishop as *ipso facto* deposed,[101] and maintained that juridical
authority had been conferred on all the Apostles as well as on
St Peter. Therefore, the episcopate as a whole was the true
centre of unity and ecclesiastical jurisdiction since the apostolic
authority first entrusted to St Peter was extended to the other
eleven and transmitted by them to all Catholic bishops. Each
bishop, he thought, represented the particular church over
which he ruled, and possessed an undivided authority, but
limited in practice by the same jurisdiction exercised by his
neighbours, *episcopatus unus est cujus a singulis in solidum pars
tenetur.*[102]

As a practical proposition such a scheme based on a
collective sharing in a common Petrine inheritance would be
beset by formidable difficulties as was demonstrated by the
Novation controversy and the Donatist schism. In an age of

intermittent persecution coupled with rapid expansion the Church required a unifying dynamic comparable to that of the divine kingship in ancient society. This it was destined to find in the Bishop of Rome, who, as Harnack says, even in the eyes of Eastern Christians, had "something special attaching to him, which no other bishop had, a halo which gave him a quite peculiar authority".[103] But in the pre-Nicene period "it is as unreasonable to expect to find a bishop of Rome exercising a jurisdiction, universal or otherwise, as to exclaim at its absence",[104] since prior to the changed relations between Church and State when in the fourth century Christianity became the religion of the imperial court, it was virtually impossible to organize an ecclesiastical rule on an oecumenical basis. Therefore, however the Papacy may be regarded, whether it be as a divinely ordained universal jurisdiction centred in the Holy See as the mother of Christendom, deriving its absolute authority in matters of faith and morals from the alleged Petrine supremacy, or as the result of historical causes largely dependent on the prestige and significance of the imperial capital, the attainment of the goal was necessarily delayed until in the fulness of time the Christian Empire came into being. Once this was accomplished the supremacy of the See of Rome was assured, at any rate in the West.

Located in the capital of the Empire and claiming to have in its possession the mortal remains of the two Princes of the Apostles, in an age when such relics were thought to bestow great sanctity and favour upon those who housed them, the Church of Rome occupied a unique position in Christendom. This prestige was considerably increased after the Faith became the official religion, notwithstanding the fact that Constantine took up his residence in the ancient town of Byzantium on the European side of the Bosphorus and made it the seat of the Mediterranean Empire. But if the founding of Constantinople eventually led to the separation of East and West imperially and ecclesiastically, the venerable city of Rome, with its age-long tradition as mistress of the world, retained its ancient prestige and splendour. Even the Goths and Vandals felt compelled to reverence its magnificent buildings and leave them unimpaired, largely as a result of the statesmanship of the occupant of the Holy See. This left a lasting impression on the invaders, the Romans and the rest of the West.

Moreover, in the organization and administration of the Church at large it was Rome that took the lead, and rapidly gained precedence over its rivals, including Carthage, Alexandria, Antioch and Constantinople. When the great patriarchal metropolitan sees were created with jurisdiction over all other metropolitans included in their district, Rome retained priority. After the translation of the seat of the Empire to Constantinople its bishop was given patriarchal status as the Emperor's chaplain, but, nevertheless, he was second to the Roman Pontiff, whose primacy among the Latin churches became unquestioned. It was to the Bishop of Rome that disputes between local provinces and prelates were referred for judgment. The Council of Sardicia in 343 enjoined that a deposed bishop might appeal to Rome for a verdict against the local synod, and the Pope could then arrange for a retrial of the case by the bishops of the neighbouring province.[105] During the pontificate of Damasus I (366–384) attempts were made to extend the papal jurisdiction to the Balkan provinces and to prevent the subjection of the supreme ecclesiastical judge to the civil jurisdiction.[106] The somewhat ambiguous assent given to the latter demand doubtless enhanced the prestige of the Papacy even though it only ratified existing practice.

Subsequently, probably at the Council of Rome, the Petrine supremacy of the Holy See was affirmed in terms of the Dominical commission in Mt. xvi. and its foundation by SS Peter and Paul,[107] with the prerogatives these distinctions conferred upon it in the exercise of oecumenical jurisdiction. To this primacy Ambrose and Jerome lent their powerful aid.[108] As the Petrine rock on which Christ founded His Church, it was only in this "Ark of Safety" that security could be found, and those outside it awaited destruction when the floods came. So it appeared to Jerome,[109] while Innocent I (401–417) maintained that all the Churches in the West had been evangelized by St Peter and his successors. Therefore, they owed their allegiance to the Holy See. It only remained for Leo the Great (440–461) to unify ecclesiastical control through legatine metropolitans to complete the universal jurisdiction of Rome. The ancient capital, however, was declining politically and the Western Empire was threatened with dissolution. Realizing the implications of the menacing situation he set to work to establish the Church on the foundations of the crumbling secular authority before the collapse came. Boldly he proclaimed himself the successor of St Peter, the viceregent on earth of Christ, and if the claim was rejected by the Eastern churches, in the Latin West at the break-up of the Graeco-Roman world his spiritual authority was conceded by the decadent monarchy and became a rallying force and consolidating centre in an age of disruption.[110]

As Professor Toynbee has pointed out, the Roman Empire had provided Christianity with a universal State as an aid to the spread of the Faith round the shores of the Mediterranean, and when the civic life of Caesar's civilization had run its course and destroyed itself by its own inherent defects, it had served its purpose by bringing into being a spiritual organization that could endure the collapse of its secular matrix.[111] Now, whatever may have been the defects of the Papacy, and however obscure and insecure the foundations on which it rested historically and theologically, as an established institution it served a vital purpose in providing a transcendental authoritative leadership just when and where such a dynamic was most needed. Where Caesar was worshipped with divine honours Christianity had flung down its challenge in the name of a King whose kingdom transcended the world in which it was operative, and when the splendour of the imperial empire had vanished and crumbled into dust, His Church remained because it had been built upon a rock. The equation of this unshakable foundation with the Prince of the Apostles and his successors in the Roman See gave the papal jurisdiction an absolute authority which commanded respect in the civil as well as in the ecclesiastical sphere.

ECCLESIASTICAL JURISDICTION

Thus, when Christianity received imperial recognition by Constantine, although the Emperor continued to be the *Pontifex Maximus* of the Roman State until the title was abandoned by Gratian in 375 and transferred to the Pope as the *Pastor Pastorum* of the Christian hierarchy in the West, the Church was accorded juridical power, or *Forum*. As its rule extended and developed into a universal jurisdiction the papal prerogative was correspondingly enlarged until at length it passed outside the domain of spiritual causes in respect of the priestly and pastoral office of the Church and became an "external forum" governing social and public conduct.

In a complex society the "spiritual" and the "temporal" disciplines are so interwoven that the one cannot be completely separated from the other. Therefore, when the Papacy established its unique position in the empire, and eventually became the supreme spiritual authority in the West, legislation both ecclesiastical and civil fell increasingly within its domain, and was exercised either through conciliar decrees or by means of bulls . and briefs, general constitutions and encyclicals addressed to the episcopate as a whole or to the bishops of a province. All these authoritative utterances were binding on the faithful by virtue of the divine endowment which the Church claimed to have received in the capacity of a "perfect society" with judicial and executive power, and to dispense through the Apostolic See. And granting the papal claims, in purely spiritual matters concerning faith and morals, the sacraments and worship, it had every right to exercise its jurisdiction and be obeyed. But in a mixed society where is the line to be drawn between civil and common law and the respective jurisdictions of Church and State?

When the Church became the ally of the State during the reigns of Gratian and Theodosius (381–395) it was raised above the common law by virtue of the privileges granted to the clergy and the *custodes* of churches and oratories in exemption from taxation and civil jurisdiction. The right of sanctuary, whereby criminals and debtors placed themselves outside the law by seeking refuge in churches and other sacred places, became liable to grave abuse, as did the other ecclesiastical privileges, despite the efforts of Theodosius and his successors to define and restrict the limits of episcopal administration of justice. Although religious, doctrinal and disciplinary questions were left within the ecclesiastical jurisdiction, the State deprived heretics of the freedom of worship and assembly, and eventually of civil rights.[112] This gave the Church protection by the secular power against false doctrine as well as safeguarding her other privileges. Moreover, St Ambrose laid down the principle of ecclesiastical autonomy by declaring that "the palaces concern the Emperor, the churches concern the bishop".[113]

This union between Church and State, sealed in the time of Theodosius, was, however, a delicate adjustment, and as the investiture contest and the controversy between Henry II and Becket in England in the twelfth century demonstrated, it might readily lead to a serious conflict between the two authorities based on two opposed conceptions of the nature of Christian society. Both were agreed about its hierarchical structure but each adopted a different attitude towards the right ordering of Christendom. On the one side there was the view that the kingship represents the fundamental institution in the consolidation of a theocratic community. Against this was set the integrating influence of firmly established priesthoods as the most effective stabilizing force.

Now, as it has been our purpose in this volume to show, both these contentions are very deeply laid in the functioning of the sacerdotal type of society. The medieval struggle was in fact but a particular instance of a recurrent phenomenon in a setting which brings into high relief the dual nature of the hierarchy, at once monarchical and sacerdotal, combined together in an uneasy alliance for a common end—namely, the cohesion of the theocratic structure—but with conflicting jurisdictions and different interpretations of the observance of law and order. The time had not arrived when the very foundations of the priestly society were to be undermined. That a hierarchical basis centred in the Papacy was essential for the transformation of the kingdoms of the world into the kingdoms of the Lord and of His Christ was not in dispute. The question at issue was whether or not the form of the hierarchy should be sacerdotal, monarchic or monastic,[114] and how the respective jurisdictions should be adjusted.

In the Early Church bishops had been appointed with the concurrence of the clergy and influential laity of the diocese and the suffrages and acclamation of the people.[115] The Second Council of Arles decreed that "When a bishop is to be elected, three candidates ought, without any intrigue or ambition, to be nominated by the bishops of the province, and the clergy and people of the town should choose between them." In fact, however, the Merovingian kings not infrequently exercised their royal prerogative and appointed whom they would to vacant sees without election of any kind, until under the feudal system the episcopate automatically came under the sovereign rule of the monarch at its apex and his lay-lords who appointed to benefices in their own right, thereby trenching upon the bishop's control of his clergy. The Byzantine and Carolingian conception of the kingship as a divine ordinance carrying with it the predominance of the secular power, serves the purposes of a graded and segmented social order, as it did of the ascetic monastic ideal of withdrawal from the world. It was, however, a condition open to grave abuse when clergy and laity alike became more secular and ineffective, and the king increasingly absorbed in the organization and control of his kingdom. It was, therefore, not a state of affairs that could with impunity be allowed to endure. If the Church and its hierarchy were to fulfil their proper functions administrative freedom was essential and this demanded a drastic reform in the relations between the spiritual and secular jurisdictions.

It was to this task that Hildebrand (1025–1085) devoted all his energy and skill under the influence in the first instance of the reforming movement that had already begun at Cluny, and with which apparently he had become acquainted in his youth at the monastery of St Mary on the Aventine at Rome.

s

In many directions the general disorder in the Church and society was stimulating a return to more stringent discipline and to the anti-secularism of former ages. On his election to the Holy See in 1073 as Gregory VII, Hildebrand set to work to establish the absolute supremacy of the Papacy and its universal jurisdiction freed from all secular control. This involved bringing the Emperor, secular lords and nobles under the spiritual sovereignty of the Vicar of Christ as the consolidating centre of the social structure—the *potentior principalitas* and, therefore, the fountain of all jurisdiction.

For some time papal power, canon law and a sense of unity had been gaining ground in the Western Church. Thus, since the ninth century metropolitans had been required to receive the pallium from the Holy See before entering upon and exercising their functions, thereby acknowledging that they derived their administrative prerogatives from the *plentitudo pontificalis officii* conceded to them, and not as heretofore merely as an honorific emblem. The oath of obedience taken before its reception left them in no doubt about their position of subjection in respect of metropolitan and even of diocesan jurisdiction. So throughout the hierarchy the Bishop of Rome stood at the apex, firmly established by Decretals of as doubtful validity as they were of undoubted efficacy for the purposes for which they were produced as legal fictions in the consolidation of temporal power and universal dominion. From the Pope jurisdiction was delegated to the metropolitan and the diocesan episcopate, and thence to the archdeacons, chancellors, commissaries and rural deans, together with the network of officials, clerical and lay, ranging from vicars general, penitentiaries and *clerici familiares* to notaries apostolic, seneschals and stewards.

Over and above this diocesan administration unified in the supreme Pontiff was the legatine organization through which he exercised his ordinary primary jurisdiction (as distinct from the delegated jurisdiction entrusted to the episcopate) in an entire nation or particular country, without necessarily obtaining the sanction and approval of its sovereign and his government. Since in theory the legates take the place and exercise the jurisdiction of the Pope himself, the development and the extension of this method of administration met with strenuous opposition when the mission which they were sent to fulfil was directed against the policy of the secular authority, as, for example, in England during the controversy between Paschal II and Henry II in 1099–1118. When a cardinal was appointed to the office of *legati a latere,* as a member of the papal senate he was entitled to be treated with full papal honours, and his mission was regarded as of the highest importance and significance since he stood nearest to the Pope at the very heart of this complex organization, dispensed its authority, and gave coherence and uniformity to the exercise of its power in both the spiritual and temporal spheres.

However fatal to the spiritual authority of the Papacy may have been its temporal claims and administrative autonomy, so long as the organization was able to exercise its functions and maintain its universal jurisdiction, it constituted a remarkable achievement in social, political and religious cohesion, brought into being and sustained by the doctrine of the *plenitudo potestatis* of the supreme head of a priestly State acting in the capacity of the *Pastor Pastorum* of Western Christendom.

In claiming not only to have complete jurisdiction in faith, morals and ecclesiastical discipline, but also to be sovereigns over sovereigns, the popes held sway over kings and emperors as well as over ecclesiastics, excommunicating the one as freely as the other. The local hierarchy, jealous of its rights, was not unmindful of inroads on its jurisdiction and prerogatives but on the whole it preferred submission to its own order, even though it might be vested in a single autocracy, to accepting the yoke of its own princes. Struggles there might be with the Roman Curia, and complaints about the interminable delays in the exercise of its functions and the extortions of its charges, but, nevertheless, the elaborate system centralized at Rome worked efficiently considering the enormous demands made upon it from all directions, political, imperial, legal, theological, ethical, administrative, pastoral, ecclesiastical and liturgical.

By means of this intricate network of relations a common social, judicial, political and religious structure was sustained which gave expression to medieval civilization, and the medieval mind that conditioned it, under the guidance of the hierarchy of a united Church coincident with the whole of European society in the West. The tradition so deeply laid in the theocracies and their priesthoods in the Ancient East lived on, renewed, reinvigorated and re-enforced by religious sanctions no less whole-heartedly accepted by the great majority, and feared if not believed by an anti-clerical minority. Under such conditions as these Church and State became so closely associated that they were virtually identical, as were the sacred and the secular in primitive society, since, as Dante argued in *De Monarchia,* the Pope as the Head of the Spirituality and the Emperor as the Ruler of the Temporality were equally ordained by God to exercise their functions in their respective spheres for the welfare of mankind. If this duality of control did not endure, as the Church usurped more and more the civil jurisdiction and dominated emperors and kings as well as ecclesiastics under its all-embracing centralized rule, the unification of the body politic, interpreted in terms of the Augustinian "City of God", was rendered more complete as an integrated whole and determined the life and character of medieval civilization.

CHAPTER IX

The Nature and Function of Priesthood

THIS examination of the nature and function of priesthood at various stages of cultural and religious development has revealed that under primitive conditions the office and its status in society are much more fluid and less clearly defined than in the highly organized hierarchies of the advanced civilizations, notably in the Ancient Middle East. Nevertheless, although the officiants exercise a great variety of functions—e.g. those of healer, exorcist, rain-maker, bard or spirit-medium—they have this in common that they belong to a sacred order like priests, set apart from the "laity" by some form of consecration. Indeed, since medicine-men are always liable to lose their powers and so to be degraded from their office, it is important that they should keep themselves as free as possible from disturbing, defiling and desacralizing influences and occupations which may hinder or destroy their supernatural endowments. On the other hand, those who are successful in the pursuit of their craft, and are careful to develop their vocation, not infrequently rise to positions of considerable importance in the councils and administration of the tribe, not very different from those held by prominent members of organized priesthoods in higher states of culture, especially when they act as intermediaries between the community and the supernatural powers and forces under their control.

THE SPECIALIZATION OF TECHNIQUES

Although at this stage in the emergence of priesthood there is no clear-cut status or mode of operation, some measure of specialization occurs, since technical knowledge and vocational training are required in tribal lore, ritual, magic and shamanistic procedures; particularly in the case of those whose potency demands special psychic dispositions, training and the various traits and qualifications for the performance of ecstatic rites. Even when the office is hereditary, as not infrequently it is, before it is assumed the candidates have to be tested by a process of initiation in order that their competency may be assured and their necessary supernatural gifts bestowed by solemn installation. Although occasionally a spontaneous display of "possession" may suffice for the exercise of prophetic or oracular functions in a more or less private capacity, a prolonged preparation leading up to a formal and official consecration invariably is demanded of those who aspire to become professional practitioners in the tribal cult, with or without hereditary qualifications associated with certain ruling or sacerdotal families.

When the cultus is centred in a particular group or family it is usually under the direction of a council of elders, unless the exercise of sacred functions is vested in the head of the clan, or of the household. Thus, the chief, or the paterfamilias, may become the cult leader, though individuals with outstanding supernatural powers and proficiency in ritual techniques in such matters as rain-making and the control of the weather, and medicine-men who for various reasons have gained an established reputation and prestige often extending outside their own domains, may occupy a position of great importance and influence in society, rivalling or exceeding that of a local chief or sacred man. Moreover, with the development of specialized techniques, especially in settled agricultural communities, offices tend to become increasingly departmentalized, so that sacred functions are distributed among an hierarchy of diviners, exorcists, oracle-seers, physicians, augurs and astrologers, each class of practitioners working according to its own prescribed tradition, and invested with a measure of judicial authority appropriate to its assumed supernatural endowments. In this way the foundations are laid of the specialized techniques which merge within and around the office of priesthood—e.g. those of judge, physician, astronomer, archivist, scribe and scholar—as well as of the more specifically sacerdotal functions of sacrifice, expiation, absolution and mediation, for the purpose of maintaining and restoring a state of equilibrium between man and the sacred order.

CULT-LEADERSHIP

As societies become more complex differentiation of function increases. Rain-making, for example, frequently is assigned to a particular individual or group specializing in weather control, and experts in the healing art may attain not only a distinguished position in their own tribe but acquire a wider reputation in the surrounding district. Garden magic, again, offers opportunities for a successful career in Melanesia, as we have seen, just as in Babylonia astrology was practised with remarkable skill until it became a quasi-astronomy and mathematics.

As nothing is more awe-inspiring to the primitive mind than sacredness, anyone who can show evidence of being in possession of superhuman potency to a high degree, and of standing in a particularly close relationship with its source, is duly venerated and hedged round with tabus. He may rise to the chief place of leadership in the community in the capacity of chief or king, or he may be an independent power beside that of chieftainship or the throne, often competing with it as a rival authority; or, as in the case of the seer, as its opponent. Generally, however, in primitive society the temporal and the spiritual spheres not being differentiated, there is a tendency for leadership in the sacred, social and political organization to converge as a unifying force in the stabilization of the community.

HIERARCHIC ORGANIZATION

In the more advanced agricultural cultures segmented hierarchies have become a prominent and influential feature in the social structure. In these conditions an increasingly specialized sacerdotal organization is developed and the interactions between the various groups are more firmly established until the equilibrium is disturbed by internal rivalries and external influences.[1]

THE EGYPTIAN ROYAL PRIESTHOODS

Nowhere is this more clearly demonstrated than in the elaborate Egyptian hierarchic organization, which has been reviewed in some detail in the course of this inquiry. From the time when a centralized government was instituted in the middle of the fourth millenium B.C. all religious and political functions, as we have seen, were concentrated in the throne, and it was within this framework of theocratic monarchy that the hierarchical civilization was created and maintained in the Nile valley. The high-priests normally were appointed by the Pharaoh, and when the office was hereditary, or filled by recourse to oracular guidance, royal ratification was still required because the king remained the divinely ordained mediator between heaven and earth.

In the Imperial age, however, the wealth that poured into the new capital at Thebes from foreign conquests at the height of its splendour gave such enormous power and influence to the priesthood of Amon-Re that a clash with the monarchy was almost inevitable. The merging of all the priesthoods into a single sacerdotal organization under the sovereign rule of the high-priest of Amon produced a heretical movement in which Aton became a rival of Amon.[2] This opened the way for Amenhotep IV (Ikhnaton) on his accession in 1375 to break with the Amonite priesthood in Thebes, transfer the seat of government to Amarna (Akhetaton), and to institute the monotheistic worship of Aton as the sole sovereign lord of the universe dwelling in light invisible behind the solar disc.

That a sickly youth in his teens was able to inaugurate a new state religion in the face of the strenuous opposition of the mighty Theban priesthood at the height of its power, shows how unique was the position and power of the monarchy in the Nile valley, with all its divine prerogatives. The reform failed because it proved to be incapable of fulfilling its proper function, either in the consolidation and maintenance of the Empire before the rising tide of Hittite and Aramaean forces in Syria and Palestine, or in supplying the religious needs in a popular cultus. Therefore, at the death of Ikhnaton in 1358,

after ephemeral efforts to carry on Atomism, the Theban hierarchical rule was restored.

As a result of this abortive movement, although the divine
and sacerdotal functions of the ruling Pharaoh were emphasized
as the "herdsman" of his people and the "shepherd" of the two-
lands, temporal power passed more and more into the hands of
the high-priest of Amon-Re and his hierarchy. Thus, by the
time of Rameses III (*c.* 1198 B.C.) more than a tenth of the
entire country was owned by the Theban priesthoods who
henceforth dominated Upper Egypt. As the Heliopolitan hierarchy had been largely responsible for the creation of the
theocratic monarchy, so its Theban successor, by bringing the
throne under the control of its rigid hierarchical culture,
secured for itself the key position in the exercise of the functions
which in theory it derived by delegation from the kingship.

The enormous wealth acquired by these highly organized
priesthoods created an unhealthy situation which ultimately
destroyed the stability of the civilization it had done so much
to produce and consolidate. And this is a recurrent feature in
the history of priesthood at all times and in all states of culture.
As the records of Rameses III reveal, some fifteen per cent of
the available land of the country belonged to the temples, and
this was exempt from taxation, together with vast quantities of
cattle and of raw materials of various kinds. The priesthoods,
therefore, became an economic menace and placed the Pharaoh
in an impossible position, until at length the high-priest gained
absolute supremacy by himself occupying the throne. By this
expedient some stability was given to Egypt in the period of its
decline, until in the sixth century B.C. cultural leadership
passed to Greece with a very different tradition behind it.

THE MESOPOTAMIAN PRIESTHOODS

In Mesopotamia, on the other hand, the localization of the
kingship in the rulers of a city-state prevented absolute
sovereignty being vested in a single divine embodiment of the
entire pantheon having the sacerdotal prerogatives of the
Egyptian Pharaohs. As we have seen, the higher ranks of the

priesthoods were grouped round, and brought into intimate association with, particular rulers, and influential members of the Sumerian and Babylonian hierarchy often exercised the functions of the monarchy. Indeed, at the Annual Festival in Babylon the sovereign actually delivered up his regalia to the high-priest and was re-instated in his office by him, acting on behalf of Marduk. Such an act of humiliation would have been as unthinkable in Egypt as the Babylonian custom of providing substitutes for the king as a protective device.[3]

The royal office in Mesopotamia, in fact, was a curious combination of servitude and personal administrative power based on the duty of the king to interpret the will of the gods as the representative of the people under divine sanction. It was essentially a social rather than a cosmic institution, and as such its functions were divinatory and executive within the sphere of its jurisdiction. It was never the divinely appointed centre of the hierarchical organization, the social structure and the cosmic order. While rulers endeavoured to discover and interpret the will and purposes of the gods by portents, omens and dreams, the priesthoods, being the learned section of the community, were the teachers and guides of the people in their several capacities as diviners, exorcists, astrologers, physicians, scribes, and judges. In the temple-schools they fostered the study of astronomy, medicine and jurisprudence in association with the underlying magico-religious beliefs and disciplines. Since the gods were the ultimate source of all learning and law and the priests were their servants and agents, inasmuch as they (the priests) had a monopoly of all knowledge, human and divine, and virtually held in their hands the life and death of the people whose destinies they controlled for good or ill, their power was enormous. Moreover, it was through their vast and all-embracing hierarchic organization that the relation between religion and culture was maintained.

THE HEBREW HIERARCHY

In Israel, again, the priesthoods being originally the interpreters of the divine oracle at the local sanctuaries in which they exercised their functions as the guardians of the cultus,[4] gained increasing influence as the theocratic structure of Hebrew society developed. Since the consolidating centre came to be that of the covenant with Yahweh, which was assigned to the Mosaic period in the desert prior to the establishment of the monarchy, the priests as the personal attendants and ministers of the Holy One of Israel occupied a unique status in the community. The kingship appears to have arisen under pressure of Philistine and Ammonite oppression[5] mainly for reasons of security, and although Saul and David were regarded as the "Lord's anointed", neither they nor their successors were venerated as divine incarnations like the Pharaohs, or as servants of the gods as in the case of the Mesopotamian rulers. When a covenant was made between Yahweh and the house of David[6] the monarchy acquired a more specific priestly status and function, David having placed himself at the head of the Jebusite hierarchy. Indeed, from the time of Saul onwards, as we have seen, kings offered sacrifice, wore the ephod and prophesied as the "messengers" (*melek*) of Yahweh.[7]

If, however, the sovereign alone was the anointed of Yahweh, as the cultus developed at the larger sanctuaries, and eventually in the reigns of Hezekiah and Josiah was centralized at Jerusalem,[8] the activities and influence of the hierarchy became widely extended and independent of the monarchy. Thus, the fall of the dynasty in the northern kingdom in 721 B.C. had little effect on the Bethelite priesthoods.[9] In the south although the Jerusalem hierarchy at the royal temple on Mount Zion worked in close conjunction with the monarchy and officiated at a cultus in which the life of the king seems to have been bound up with the well-being of the nation, as elsewhere in the Fertile crescent,[10] it had its own independent organization and hypothetical line of descent. Thus were laid the foundations of the hierarchical theocracy of the post-exilic period which eventually emerged after the fall of the monarchy in 586.

With the return of the exiles and the re-establishment of the temple and its worship, the high-priest combined the royal cultic prerogatives formerly exercised by the kingship with those of the priesthoods.[11] Thus, when Zerubbabel became governor of Jerusalem in 520 B.C., as a descendant of David he was hailed as Yahweh's deputy and occupied a position in the cultus comparable to that assigned to "the prince" by Ezekiel.[12] He was, however, to rule in conjunction with the high-priest, who was to be the guardian of the temple and its worship.[13] With the failure of his mission the high-priest alone remained as the consolidating centre of the nation, and around him as the alleged descendant of Eleazar, Aaron's eldest son, the complex hierarchic organization developed with its distinction between the Zadokite priests and their servants the Levites.[14] Being at once the spiritual head of the post-exilic congregation of Israel and the substitute for the sovereign ruler in the monarchy, he stood at the apex of the sacerdotal theocracy and became the originating cause of the interaction between the members of the community and their hierarchy.

To restore the equilibrium after the disturbance of the Exile an intensive ritual system was required. This was provided by the sacrificial worship established at the temple rebuilt by Haggai and re-enforced by the powerful divine sanctions elaborated in the Priestly Code to preserve the correct relation between Israel and its God, on which the existence of the nation was thought to depend. The whole community made a concerted effort to maintain the temple cultus and to effect an "atonement" it agreed to the levy of the third of a shekel as a poll-tax for its support and that of the hierarchy.[15] This reached its climax in the annual public expiation on the tenth day of the seventh month when, as we have seen, the high-priest made a solemn atonement for himself and the priesthood and for the entire community.[16]

Therefore, the chief function of the hierarchy and its leader in post-exilic Judaism was to promote interactions between the priesthood and the congregation of Israel, and to preserve the equilibrium by the maintenance of an intensive ritual technique centred at Jerusalem. Like the Brahmins in Vedic India, the priests were the masters of the sacrificial ritual on which the stability of the struggling nation so largely depended, and the temple became the focal point in the consolidation of the theocracy because only there could the sacerdotal rites be duly performed. Even the Passover, which was originally a family feast observed by households in nomadic fashion,[17] became a temple institution,[18] though by the beginning of our era, after the sacrifice of the lambs by the priests in the sanctuary for the conveyance of the blood to the altar, the flesh was consumed in private houses[19] to preserve the earlier domestic character of the observance.

The destruction of the temple in A.D. 70 introduced a new situation with far-reaching consequences for the whole social and religious structure of Judaism. The hierarchy and its cultus inevitably ceased to exercise their former functions, though in theory they were abrogated rather than terminated. That the national cohesion survived this drastic disturbance in the most vital elements of its constitution and interactions, is a remarkable testimony to the consolidating force exercised by the conception of the Covenant, which transcended all other relationships and enabled the observance of the Tôrah, the Sabbath and the rite of circumcision to take the place of the temple and its hierarchy as the stabilizing centre in the re-organization of Judaism after the "second exile". The three annual festivals, the Passover with the Feast of Unleavened Bread at the vernal full moon, the Feast of Weeks in mid-summer, and the Feast of Ingathering (Sukkôth) at the vintage, together with the Day of Atonement as a "holy consecration", have also played their part in the cohesion of dispersed Jewry, though the observances have been shorn of their sacerdotal ministrations.

THE BRAHMANIC CASTE ORGANIZATION

Although nowhere has a priestly caste been more rigidly established than in Vedic India the Brahmanic tradition never functioned as a temple priesthood. The Brahmin was essentially a household priest, and, as we have seen, the sacrifice he controlled was a cosmic ritual to sustain the gods and maintain the structure of the universe rather than that of a human community and its divine relationships.[20] Yet notwithstanding the absence of a temple cultus and hierarchy, the priestly function was confined to a special class in the caste system with its roots deeply laid in Hindu social organization.

The origins of the very specialized form of segmentation which has characterized Indian society are a matter of conjecture,[21] but however it may have arisen and assumed its particular gradations, generally on a hereditary, occupational and endogamous basis, it has welded together a diversity of populations and cultures into a composite whole in a static social hierarchy of *varnas* supposed to have sprung from the body of the Creator as fixed states of life. Therefore, according to the Institutes of Manu, the four main castes—the Brahmanic priesthood; the Kshatriyas or warriors; the Vaisyas or merchants; and the Sudras or agriculturists and herders—must remain from birth to death distinct from each other in their respective groups without any interaction between their members. This rigid segregation, however, has been superimposed on a much more fluid organization when even the sacerdotal office was not hereditary and a Kshatriya could become a Brahmin and vice versa. Provided he took his first wife from his own caste, a Brahmin (who was allowed to have four wives) might select the rest from any of the three divisions.

Although the system became stereotyped by the Code of Manu and the doctrine of metempsychosis, it is not primarily a socio-political institution, as has been commonly supposed by Western interpreters. In the early texts of the Rig-veda and the Brahmanas, where it first appears in developed form, the divisions imply an organic structure functioning through the balance and co-operation of all its members, with the Brahmins as the head of the body of the Creator, the warriors as the arms, the farmers and merchants as the trunk and the servants as the feet. In this organic structure all the parts are equally necessary constituents in the organism as a multiplicity in unity. The function of the State is to preserve the social order, or Dharma (the law of nature and the universal order), as it is formulated and maintained by the Brahmins, whose duty it is to sustain the cosmic unity, while it is that of the second caste (the Kshatriyas) to guard and serve the Dharma. Since the State only exists in order that its members may exercise their respective functions aright, therefore the political is a secondary category. It is caste that forms the unity of the organic society, the unique position occupied in the organization by the Brahmanic priesthood being the result of the control the Brahmins alone exercise over the cosmic laws (*Rta*) as the masters of the sacrifice.

While they do not belong to a sacerdotal corporation attached to a sanctuary, as in the Ancient Middle East, their influence as "the lords of creation" (i.e. the sustainers of the universe and its processes) has not been less than that of divine kings and their royal priesthoods responsible for the consolidation and well-being of society and the maintenance of the seasonal sequence. Indeed, they occupied the highest place in the segmentation of Hindu society, whereas kings and chiefs belonged to the second, or Kshatriyas, caste, and in the Brahmanas great priests of the Rig-veda, such as Visramitra and the Prithivi Vainya, are occasionally represented as of royal origin. Since the Brahmins alone were permitted to engage in the occupations of the other castes, under certain circumstances they might assist in battle the princes they served as "chaplains", and the practice of medicine seems to have fallen within their sphere.[22] Some engaged in agriculture, the keeping of cattle, or in trade,[23] but for the most part their activities were concentrated upon their priestly vocation centred in the sacrificial cultus, the performance of domestic rites, especially in connexion with marriage and death, together with the repetition and teaching of the Veda (*Adhyayana* and *Adhyapana*).

Some of the more important ceremonies required a Brahmin who by descent and personal practice belonged exclusively to the priestly caste, or was a man of learning (*pandita*). Thus, in the Brahmanas the Brahmin *par excellence* who had charge of the entire rite, and was in possession of special knowledge, is introduced in the history of the ritual by the Vasistha family. But this was an innovation when the ritual had acquired great complexity in which magic and religion were intermingled freely, and Brahmins claimed privileges which made them superior to the royal jurisdiction, exempt from censure even by the king and sacrosanct in their person.

It was against this extreme expression of the Brahmanic caste organization that in about 600 B.C. the Upanishadic movement assigned to the sacrificial priest a new function based on a theory of the universe quite distinct from that which underlay the ritual order of the Brahmanas.[24] Thus, the horse sacrifice is interpreted in the *Brhadaranyaka Upanishad* as a meditative act in which the contemplative offers up the universe in place of the horse and by a supreme act of renunciation attains the ultimate identity of the individual self (*atman*) with the cosmic divine Reality (*Brahman*)—*tat tvam asi,* "That thou art."[25] Whether or not, as has been suggested, this divergence was due to a struggle for supremacy between the Brahmins and the Kshatriyas, the priests and the princes, it constitutes a definite break in the Brahmanic tradition and its organization. Moreover, it opened the way for the more radical refutation of the hereditary claims of Brahmin superiority by Mahavira and Gautama, the founders of Jainism and Buddhism respectively, both of whom probably were Kshatriyas.

Rejecting the Vedas and the caste system and embracing the doctrine of complete renunciation as the alternative to that of sacrifice or metaphysical Upanishadic mysticism, these two sages abandoned any permanent transcendental reality which alone can guarantee the hierarchic conception of society and of sacerdotal organization. Therefore, in the wheel of the Law (Dharma) which the Buddha set in motion neither caste segmentation nor the sacrificial offering found a place in the Eightfold Path leading to the passionless peace of Nirvana. The function of the priesthood was sublimated in a process of self-salvation, having for its purpose the deliverance of suffering humanity from the weary round of birth and rebirth. Since Desire (*Tanha*), the cause of the burden of *Dukka,* could only be removed by individual effort and the elimination of false views about the self (*anatta*), priestly intervention was of no avail. In the absence of any conception of Deity there could be no question of mediation between man and the eternal world through human agency, though in the substitution of a monastic order for a priestly caste the institutional tradition has survived, more especially in Mahayana, the Northern school of Buddhism, and in Tantric magic.

The spiritual assistance of the deified Buddha and the grace-bestowing *bodhisattvas* have acquired some of the characteristics of sacerdotalism. The monks perform prophylactic rites and incarnational recitations of the sacred texts at births, marriages and in sickness to keep at bay evil influences. In the temple shrines erected to the honour of the Buddha an image of the Blessed One seated on his lotus, bedecked with flowers, has become the central object of worship with prostrations during the recitation of verses of the ancient texts in Pali, as in the similar exercises in Islamic mosques. If the more sophisticated bonzes regard this type of invocation as a subjective mental discipline since the Buddha is unconscious, in popular devotion it is indistinguishable from prayer and spell. The recitation of the Sutras is believed to transmit merit acquired by the Buddha, or by holy men and women, inherent in the texts repeated, or in a sacred formula, such as *Namu O-mi-to* or *Amida-Butzu*. But as the presence of a priest is not required it is not a sacerdotal cultus. Buddhism, in fact, has never been able to produce an ecclesiastical organization, or a hierarchic segmentation, because it has interpreted unity in terms of Becoming instead of in those of Being, and replaced the Atman by its negation, *Anatta*, the unreality of the self.

In Hinduism, on the other hand, the transcendental principle which determines the activity of the four castes into which society is divided is Unity, or the Absolute (Brahman). The function of the first caste, the Brahmin, is to apprehend and formulate the nature of this Unity and to maintain in a multiple form the constituents of the organic society as a hierarchy. In justification of this hierarchic constitution Sir Radhakrishnan contends that "hierarchy is not a coercion but

T

a law of nature. The four classes represent four stages of development in our manhood. ... The highest of all is the Brahmin, who brings a spiritual rule into life."[26] It is his business "to lay down the science of values, draw out the blueprints for social reconstruction, and persuade the world to accept the high ends of life; it is the business of the Kshatriya to devise the means for gaining the ends ... to rule as the guardians and servants of the law."[27] The true Brahmin is said to be "one who has sensed the deepest self and acts out of that consciousness", and having sought and found knowledge communicates it to others and so makes it prevail in the world. Practical administration is not the task of the Brahmins. They are called to give moral guidance; to reveal but not to enforce.[28]

This is an idealized conception of the Brahmanic vocation which can hardly claim to be in accord with the checkered history of the institution. Nevertheless, it is true that "a class of disinterested seekers of truth supported by society, influencing it, and placed above the corrupting tendency of power, is the very life of social stability and growth."[29] The caste system in India, despite its anomalies, unquestionably has been a potent element in unification on a transcendental basis in the organic theory of Hindu society, having as its ultimate end the elimination of the illusion of individuality and relationship in a state of perfect unity in the Absolute. But so long as the divine is identified with the all-comprehensive primal source and inmost essence of the universe, or with absolute self-existent Pure Being in and beyond the self of man, an intervening Deity standing over and against His creation is excluded. Consequently, when the Vedic gods were resolved in an ultimate principle immanent in nature, or, as in the case of Prajapati, represented as a personification of the creative process, the priestly offering as the all-sustaining rite gave the Brahmins their unique position in the cosmic order and social structure, transcending that of the gods. When the ritual organization was superseded by the Upanishadic, Vedantic and Mimamsa sublimations, the hierarchic tradition survived in a new setting.

Notwithstanding the rise of theistic devotional movements the quest for absorption in the Absolute has remained the final goal and true end of all existence. Thus, Radhakrishnan affirms that "the worshippers of the Absolute are the highest in rank; second to them are the worshippers of the personal God; then come the worshippers of incarnations like Rama, Kṛṣna, Buddha; below them are those who worship ancestors, deities and sages; and lowest of all are the worshippers of the petty forces and spirits."[30] In this segmentation the Brahmins occupy the chief place in the hierarchic organization. Their role, however, is not that of an agent or servant, or the embodiment of a god with whom personal relations are possible, as in the case of the temple priesthoods in the Ancient Middle East, though in Vishnuism and Sivaism they approximate to it in the cultus of these theistic developments. As the masters of the sacrifice that sustains the universe their function has been to control the transcendental principle in which the gods have had no part, and their status has remained that of a sacerdotal élite in a closely integrated hierarchic society.

THE THEISTIC CONCEPTION OF DEITY

In the West, on the other hand, the emphasis in the priestly tradition has been on "representation" and "mediation" for the specific purpose of establishing and maintaining a vital relationship between man and a living God Who is the ultimate ground of the universe and the source and sustainer of all existence. Standing between the two extremes of a wholly transcendent extramundane unconditioned Being and an equally completely intramundane immanental principle, essence or substance in which God and the world are merged in a monistic or pantheistic unity, theism represents the Creator as the sovereign ruler of all things and yet at work in the universe which He has created, ordering the course of events in accordance with His will and purpose. As the most real Being, the ground and unity of all that is other than Himself, He is distinct from the phenomenal order. As the intelligent self-conscious will and the highest good, He is the living unity of existence and value in vital relationship with His creation.

An Absolute, monistically or pantheistically conceived, involves the absence of external relations, leaving the All either as a non-interfering deistic Creator completely dissociated from the universe, or as the sole Reality of which nature and man are partial manifestations and emanations, lacking permanence and individuality, or even independent existence when the phenomenal order is regarded as illusory. While such a conception of divinity finds expression in a mystical experience of impersonal unity with the Absolute, the distinctions of rational consciousness are absorbed in a divine essence beyond good and evil. As on this hypothesis everything proceeds from the One, so everything leads to the Source of all reality, but only by way of emancipation, absorption and identity, precluding a personal relationship with a living active God Whose sovereign will has called the created universe into being in its entirety, transcending the cosmic process and its ritual control.

DIVINE INTERVENTION AND PRIESTHOOD

From rudimentary inklings of Providence to the highest conceptions of personal theism divine intervention, guidance and disclosure in time and space have been conceded in divers ways and manners. The gods, ancestral spirits, or culture-heroes responsible for the creation and moulding of the world, have been thought to exercise transcendental control over natural events and human destinies, communicating their will and power to man through divine kings, priests, seers and prophets. This belief has found expression in transitional rites at critical junctures associated with birth, adolescence, marriage, death, illness, and the sequence of the seasons, when the equilibrium in the life of an individual and his family, or in that of the group as a whole, has to be restored and renewed. In a precarious environment crises, disturbances and rhythmic variations of this kind are of perennial and periodic recurrence, and call forth, as we have seen, a complex ritual organization ranging from domestic ceremonies, agricultural calendrical rites and the practice of divination to ecstatic experiences and astrological techniques, until at length Deity is thought to unveil Himself as a Person to persons through divinely controlled cosmic events, the vicissitudes of history, and human agencies, prophetic and priestly.

It is in this context that sacerdotal intervention normally has functioned throughout its long and varied history. Priesthoods are the duly accredited and spiritually endowed official instruments and representatives of God or the gods under whom they serve and on whose behalf they exercise their office in its several capacities. They are set apart for the specific purpose of establishing, maintaining and restoring intercourse and adjustment between the sacred and the secular spheres, theistically interpreted in terms of a personal Deity at once transcendent and immanent. As this very delicate equilibrium is always liable to be disturbed, either inadvertently or through human frailty, perverseness and inability to refuse the evil and choose the good, the function of the priesthood consists in restoring the balance, as and when required, and in strengthening the bond by the prescribed techniques and ministrations. As occasion demands the priest has to mediate, expiate and absolve; reveal, conserve and guard sacred learning and knowledge; administer and maintain the hierarchic organization in relation to the social structure; and above all to stand between heaven and earth at the altar as the master of sacrifice.

THE MEDIATORIAL FUNCTION OF PRIESTHOOD

The ritual functions of priesthood, it is true, have sometimes been secondary to those of declaring divine oracles and prophetic utterances, but, nevertheless, mediatorial intervention always has been the fundamental element in the priestly office and vocation. In the more rudimentary and primitive aspects of this process, as the instrument of divine power its official activities are largely concerned with the control of the weather and the seasons, with the fertility of the crops, and, in fact, with everything upon which man depends for his well-being, sustenance and survival, here and hereafter, and for the consolidation of human society. Like the Pharaoh in his mediating position, the priest is, in short, the stabilizing influence in the social structure and in the personal adjustment of the individual in his relations with his physical, social and ethical environment, and the supernatural order as its ultimate ground.

At higher levels of culture and of religious organization and spiritual experience, when the relationship between God and man acquires a theistic significance, mediation involves a more spiritual bond which finds expression in a covenant organization transcending the community interactions. In some measure this holds true of its prototype in the primitive age-grade and secret society, and in the mystery cults, while in Israel it assumed the form of a theocratic nation with its prophets and hierarchy fulfilling their respective mediatorial functions as revealers of the divine will in prophetic utterance, and as reconcilers through sacerdotal intervention, enabling sinful man to approach a holy God and have communion with Him as members of a society of which He is the head.

In Christianity the Founder becomes "the mediator of a new covenant",[31] and in this capacity he is represented as having established a new relationship between God and man by himself taking human nature into union with his divine nature in order to become the reconciler of the redeemed humanity as its saviour, head and high-priest.[32] His function as mediator is considered to be inherent in, and to proceed from, his divine nature and office. Therefore, unlike that of other priesthoods, it is not a delegated mediatorship. By virtue of his Godhead hypostatically united with his manhood, as priest and victim he is able in his own right and by his own redemptive power to reconcile man with God. This is accomplished through the remission of sins ascribed to his redeeming sacrifice on behalf of the human race, of which he is the divinely appointed head.[33] But what has been wrought by a special divine intervention in time and space, at a particular moment in history, has to be made actual and efficacious throughout the ages. That was the situation which faced the Church at its inception, once this interpretation of the office and function of its Founder was adopted.

Therefore, the carrying on of the work of mediation became the *raison d'être* of the Christian priesthood and the primary purpose of its hierarchic organization. To this end its principal function always has been that of perpetuating the sacrificial act of redemption by the offering of its *anamnesis* on earth in union with its heavenly presentation by the eternal high-priest. Next to the Eucharistic oblation as the centre of Christian worship, it has become the duty of the priest, standing between God and redeemed humanity, to absolve the penitent and so to effect the work of reconciliation as the duly commissioned agent of Christ, the redeemer and mediator. Moreover, in this capacity the priest acts as judge since he is required to estimate the spiritual condition of the penitent and to pass judgment accordingly. This presupposes his having received the necessary jurisdiction to fulfil the office, be it either "ordinary" or "delegated" jurisdiction.

The nature and function of priesthood, in fact, only becomes intelligible on a basis of spiritual authority in a graded hierarchic institution in which divine power or grace is mediated from its ultimate source through a sequence of instrumental agents set apart for their respective purposes, and judicially regulated in their several offices. In its Catholic mode of operation, in addition to the sacrifice of the Mass and the sacrament of Penance, sacerdotal ministrations include the administration of Baptism, the giving of Holy Communion and of Extreme Unction, the solemnization of marriage, the instruction of the faithful, and the pastoral care of the souls entrusted to the parochus. At a higher level the episcopate is invested with supreme authority to rule a diocese as its chief pastor and to perform those functions (e.g. Ordination and Confirmation and jurisdiction) which are reserved to the highest of the sacred orders.

THE DELEGATION OF PRIESTLY POWER
AND AUTHORITY

Behind this hierarchic organization lies the conception of mediation and delegation rooted and grounded in the Christian doctrines of the Incarnation and the Atonement interpreted in terms of the sacerdotal tradition operative in and through the Church as a grace-bearing institution (i.e. "the Body of Christ"). Within this divinely constituted society, as it is understood to be, there resides the fullness of divine power and authority dispensed by its duly commissioned officers, who are set apart from the rest of the congregation of the faithful for this purpose as the agents of Christ the high-priest. Thus, at his ordination a priest is held to receive spiritual power to enable him to exercise his functions, conferred by the imposition of "apostolic hands", together with the laying on of the hands of the representatives of the priesthood (i.e. the second order in the hierarchy).[34] For the fulfilment of the sacramental and administrative offices peculiar to the episcopate a further consecration is demanded, after election to the status of a diocesan bishop has been confirmed by the cathedral chapter, or, in the case of a suffragan, by the diocesan under whose jurisdiction he is called to serve.

In the Roman jurisdiction the manner of electing bishops has varied from direct papal appointment (sometimes, as in England, on the recommendation of the canons under the presidency of the metropolitan) to nomination by Catholic sovereigns, as in former times in France, Spain, Portugal, Austria, Bavaria and the smaller kingdoms (e.g. Naples, Sicily and Sardinia). But since the Holy See is regarded as the fountain-head of all ecclesiastical power and authority, in the last resort the government of the Church is vested in the Pope alone as the Vicar of Christ on earth. Therefore, he stands in the same position as the Pharaoh in Ancient Egypt who delegated his functions and jurisdiction to his priesthoods in their varying orders and degrees.

In both cases, as has been shown, this centralization of the mediatorial office in a single head by divine appointment and sanction has given great stability to the social and ecclesiastical structure of society. But inevitably it has involved a complex process of delegation which has opened the way for the establishment of rival hierarchies and reforming movements calculated to have a disintegrating effect on the former solidarity. The internal decay and widespread rivalries which characterized the final phases of the New Kingdom in Egypt, and in the later Middle Ages in Western Europe, are a melancholy story of disintegration with short interludes of partial recovery.

Nevertheless, the function of the priesthood has been that of a stabilizing force within the sphere of its influence, be it in a tribe, a nation, a civilization, a theocracy, or a divinely constituted Church established for the purpose of transmitting divine life and power through its hierarchy. This has been most efficacious when the royal and priestly functions and prerogatives have been merged in a unified system covering the entire range of social, cultural, economic and religious activities in a graded order of delegated power and authority, each segment being responsible for some particular office. When, as in China, these restrictions have been rigidly preserved, the development of a Brahmanic caste with its independent status and privileges has been prevented. In Israel the basic theocratic covenant had much the same effect, while in Christianity the derivation of supernatural grace and authority solely from Christ through a stratified apostolic ministry and a local diocesan and parochial system, mitigated the development of a rigidly exclusive priestly caste in isolation from the rest of the community. The mendicant Friars (e.g. the Dominicans and Franciscans) also played an important part in breaking down the barriers between the clergy and the masses and in bringing the influence of the Church to bear upon secular life.

Although in the Roman jurisdiction the impact of the Reformation had the effect of increasing centralization which found expression in post-Tridentine ultramontanism with the Pope as the absolute sovereign ruler of a spiritual monarchy, it opened the way for a non-papal sacerdotal structure to be established in England in conjunction with the royal supremacy. The movement at first being political, the king virtually replaced the Holy See as the supreme head of the new hierarchy, so that the monarchical organization remained little changed in its structure. The episcopate, the apostolic succession, the catholic creeds and the sacramental system were retained in spite of mildly Protestant Articles and other concessions in faith and practice to the Puritan opposition. Here, again, the retention of the hierarchic institutional principle has held together a composite and comprehensive ecclesiastical structure embracing a great variety of traditions, religious and secular, organized in the first instance on a nationalistic and Erastian basis, but, as subsequent events have shown, capable of preserving the identity of the Anglican Communion as an institution in the course of its diffusion throughout the English-speaking world.

THE FUNCTION OF PRIESTHOOD IN SOCIETY

Thus, the function of priesthood in its many and varied modes of expression, spheres of influence, cultural settings and ecclesiastical disciplines, has always been that of consolidating and stabilizing the social and religious structures in which it becomes established, and in the creation of which it has so often played an important part. Notwithstanding the despotism of sacerdotal government and the static conservatism of the organized priesthoods, in addition to their more specific religious offices at the altar and in the sanctuary, they have fulfilled a significant cultural role as the guardians of sacred tradition and learning, the producers and preservers of archives and documentary records, the promotors of education, of literary and linguistic activities, and of technical knowledge and skill as the intellectual guides of the cultures they have created, fostered and stabilized.

Thus, a hierarchic society invariably has produced a unified and integrated community because the priestly tradition has been a cohesive force enabling its members to live together in an orderly system of social and religious relations consolidated on a transcendental basis. Moreover, it has afforded a means of personal adjustment with the higher powers on which they feel themselves to be dependent for their well-being in the temporal order and for their ultimate destiny in the eternal world. In short, in a precarious, unpredictable and hazardous environment the institution of priesthood has enabled struggling humanity to advance on life's pilgrimage with hope and confidence and with a sense of security by supplying a power to help and to heal, to renew and to reassure, to cohere and to conserve.

NOTES

CHAPTER I

1. E. Smith, *J.R.A.I.*, vol. lxxxii, part 1, 1952, p. 34

2. S. Ella, *Report of Fourth Meeting of the Australasian Association for the Advancement of Science*, 1892, pp. 622 ff., 638; Hans Schinz, *Deutsch-Südwest-Afrika*, Oldenburg, 1891, p. 314.

3. D. Kidd, *Savage Childhood*, 1906, pp. 45 ff.; S. Johnson, *The History of the Yoruba*, 1921, p. 80; E. C. Parsons, *Pueblo Indian Religion*, Chicago, 1939, vol. ii, p. 1055.

4. Malinowski, *Argonauts of the Western Pacific*, 1922, pp. 392 ff., *Coral Islands and their Magic*, vol. i, 1935, pp. 218 f., 435 ff.; A. R. Brown, *The Andaman Islanders*, 1933, pp. 176 ff.

5. Evans-Pritchard, *Witchcraft, Oracles and Magic among the Azande*, Oxford, 1937, pp. 258 ff.

6. Spencer and Gillen, *Native Tribes of Central Australia*, 1938, pp. 119 ff.

7. *Op. cit.*, pp. 526 ff.

8. Spencer and Gillen, *Northern Tribes of Central Australia*, 1904, pp. 484 ff.

9. *Native Tribes of Central Australia*, pp. 522 ff.; *Northern Tribes of Central Australia*, 1904, pp. 480 ff.

10. *Native Tribes of Central Australia*, p. 526.

11. Spencer and Gillen, *Across Australia*, vol. ii, 1912, pp. 481 ff.

12. Howitt, *Native Tribes of South-east Australia*, 1904, p. 404.

13. *Op. cit.*, pp. 406 ff.

14. Cf. Howitt, *op. cit.*, pp. 389 ff.

15. R. Firth, *Human Types*, 1952, pp. 166 ff.; *The Work of the Gods in Tikopia*, 1940, pp. 23 ff.

16. Spencer and Gillen, *Native Tribes of Central Australia*, pp. 170 ff.; *The Arunta*, vol. i, pp. 81 ff., 148 ff.

17. *Native Tribes of Central Australia*, p. 174.

18. *Op. cit.*, p. 204.

19. Cf. Malinowski, *Festkrift tillagnad Edvard Westermarck*, Helsingfors, 1912, pp. 81 ff.

20. Malinowski in *Science, Religion and Reality*, 1926, pp. 41 ff.

21. Batchelor, *The Ainus and their Folklore*, 1910, pp. 471 ff.; J. R. Swanton, 26th *R.B.A.E.*, Washington, 1908, pp. 455 f.; W. Jochelson, *Memoirs of the American Museum of Natural History*, vol. x, 1905–8, pp. 88 ff.

22. J. Layard, *Stone Men of Malekula*, 1942, pp. 642 f.

23. A. B. Deacon, *Malekula, A Vanishing People in the New Hebrides*, 1934, p. 665.

24. Malinowski, *Coral Islands and their Magic*, 1935, vol. i, pp. 62 ff.
25. A. S. Thomson, *The Story of New Zealand*, vol. i, 1859, p. 114; D. Kidd, *The Essential Kaffir*, 1925, p. 114; H. Callaway, *The Religious Systems of the Amazulu*, 1870, p. 419; H. H. Johnston, *The Uganda Protectorate*, vol. ii, 1904, p. 779.
26. A. R. Brown, *The Andaman Islanders*, Cambridge, 1933.
27. Howitt, *Native Tribes of South-east Australia*, p. 314; Spencer and Gillen, *Native Tribes of Central Australia*, pp. 9, 15 f.
28. J. N. B. Hewitt, "Chiefs", *Handbook of American Indians*, part 1, pp. 263 f.
29. J. G. Frazer, *Early History of Kingship*, 1905, p. 127.
30. J. G. Frazer, *The Golden Bough*, part 1 (Magic Art), p. 234. For the latest criticisms of the Frazerian theory of the kingship, see Evans-Pritchard, *The Divine Kingship of the Shilluk*, Cambridge, 1948.
31. Boule, *Annales de Paléontologie*, vol. vi, 1911, pp. 110–72; Boule, *Les Hommes Fossiles*, Paris, 1922, pp. 268 ff.; E. Verneau, *Les Grottes de Grimaldi*, vol. ii, Monaco, 1905, pp. 298 ff.
32. Luquet, *The Art and Religion of Fossil Man*, Oxford, 1830, pp. 96 ff.; M. C. Burkitt, *Our Forerunners*, 1924, pp. 208 f.; Mainage, *Les Religions de la Préhistoire*, Paris, 1921, p. 314.
33. B. Laufer, *American Anthropologist*, new series, vol. xix, 1917, pp. 361 ff.; M. A. Czaplicka, *Aboriginal Siberia*, Oxford, 1914, pp. 169 ff.
34. Czaplicka, *Aboriginal Siberia*, Oxford, 1914, p. 178.
35. V. M. Mikhaïlowski, *J.R.A.I.*, vol. xxiv, 1895, pp. 85 ff.; W. Jochelson, "The Koryat", *Jesup North Pacific Expedition*, New York, 1905–8, p. 47.
36. Mikhaïlowski, *J.R.A.I.*, vol. xxiv, 1895, p. 86.
37. W. Radloff, "Aus Sibirien", *Lose Blätter aus dem Tagebuche eines reisenden Linguisten*, vol. ii, Leipzig, 1884, pp. 16 ff.
38. *Op. cit.*, p. 87.
39. G. Tschubinow, *Beiträge zum psychologischen Verständnis des sibirischen Zauberers*, Diss. Halle, 1914, pp. 34 ff., 48, 51, 55 ff.
40. Czaplicka, *op. cit.*, pp. 243 ff.
41. C. G. and B. Z. Seligman, *The Veddas*, Cambridge, 1911, pp. 133 ff.
42. J. Warneck, *Die Religion der Batak*, Göttingen, 1909, pp. 8 ff.
43. *Op. cit.*, pp. 89 ff.
44. G. A. Wilken, *Verspreide Geschriften*, vol. iii, The Hague, 1912, pp. 376.
45. B. Hagen, *Tijdschrift voor Indische Taal-Land-en-Volkenkunde*, vol. xxviii, 1882, p. 538.
46. W. W. Skeat, *Malay Magic*, 1920, pp. 440 ff.
47. W. Mariner, *An Account of the Natives of the Tonga Islands in the Southern Pacific*, vol. i, 1817, pp. 106 ff.
48. Codrington, *The Melanesians*, Oxford, 1890, pp. 209 ff.
49. *Op. cit.*, pp. 154, 224 ff.
50. T. G. Frazer, *Belief in Immortality and the Worship of the Dead*, vol. i, 1913, p. 322.

51. Cf. Skeat and Blagden, *Pagan Races of the Malay Peninsula*, vol. ii, 1906, p. 226; Mikhaïlowski, *J.R.A.I.*, vol. xxiv, 1895, p. 134.

CHAPTER II

1. Zimmern, *Beiträge zur Kenntnis der Babylonischen Religion*, Leipzig, 1901, no. 11: 1, 2, p. 87. Nos. 1–20: 11, 122, 126. No. 24: 1, 23; G. Contenau, *La divination chez les Assyriens et les Babyloniens*, Paris, 1940, pp. 171 ff., 235 f.

2. C. J. M. Weir, *A Lexicon of Accadian Prayers*, 1934, p. 52.

3. P. Dhorme, *La religion assyro-babylonienne*, Paris, 1910, p. 298.

4. Guillaume, *Prophecy and Divination*, 1938, p. 40 f.

5. A. Haldar, *Associations of Cult Prophets among the Ancient Semites*, Uppsala, 1945, p. 14; G. Reisner, *Sumerisch-babylonische Hymnen*, Berlin, 1896, no. 4: 11, 53 ff.

6. Zimmern, *op. cit.*, p. 86; Dhorme, *op. cit.*, p. 197; Haldar, *op. cit.*, p. 18.

7. F. Wetzel, *Zeitschrift für Assyriologie und verwandte Gebiete*, vol. xxx, 1915, p. 16 ff., 101 ff.

8. C. Bezold, *Babylonisch-assyrisches Glossar*, Heidelberg, 1926, p. 167; Langdon, *Journal of the Royal Asiatic Society*, 1932, p. 392; B. Landsberger, *Göttingische gelehrte Anzeigen*, 1915, p. 366; The Kouyunjik Collection of Cuneiform Tablets, B. Mus. 4310, col. i, 11, 13–15, col. ii, 11, 16–18.

9. E. Ebeling, *Keilschrifttexte aus Assur religiösen Inhalts*, no. 11, Rev. i, 9.

10. Cf. Malinowski, *Magic, Science and Religion*, ed. R. Redfield, 1948, p. 249; cf. C. K. Ogden and I. A. Richards, *The Meaning of Meaning*, 1936, p. 315; G. N. Mead, *The Philosophy of the Act*, Chicago, 1938, pp. 518 ff., 547.

11. *Rig-veda*, i, 14, 163, 179; ii, 2, 10; vi, 5, 7, 19; viii, 3, 9.

12. *Satapatha Brahmana*, vi–x.   13. *Aitareya Brahmana*, vii, 18.

14. Acts ii, 4, x, 46, xix, 6; 1 Cor. xii, 10, 30.

15. Acts ii, 17.

16. Eph. v, 18 f.   17. R. A. Knox, *Enthusiasm*, Oxford, 1950.

18. Aeschylus, *Eumenides*, I ff.; Pausanias, II, xxxiii, 2; Strabo, VIII, C.

19. *Od.* viii, 79–81; *Iliad* 404 f.

20. Farnell, *Cult of the Greek States*, Oxford, 1909, vol. iv, p. 188, vol. v, pp. 88 ff.; J. Harrison, *Prolegomena to the Study of Greek Religion*, Cambridge, 1922, pp. 363 ff., 560; R. Rhode, *Psyche*, 1925, p. 256; Bouché-Leclerc, *Histoire de la Divination*, vol. i, p. 353, vol. ii, p. 51, Paris 1878–82.

21. Plutarch, *de defect. Orac.*, 43; Farnell, *Cult of the Greek States*, vol. iv, pp. 181 ff.

22. Pliny, *Nat. Hist.*, II, 208; Livy, I, lvi, 10; Cicero, *de Div.*, I, xxxvi, 79; Strabo, *Geography*, ix, 419; *Pausanias*, X, v, 7, 12.

23. Stützle, in *Programm des Kön. Gymnasiums zu Ellwangen*, 1886–7, 1890–1, p. 14.

24. F. Courby, *Fouilles de Delphés,* vol. ii, 1915–7, pp. 59 ff.; A. P. Oppe, *Journal of Hellenic Studies,* vol. xxiv, 1904, pp. 214 ff.
25. Cf. Virgil, *Aen.,* VI, 46 ff.
26. Cf. K. Latte, *Harvard Theological Review,* vol. xxxiii, 1940, pp. 9 ff.
27. A. B. Cook, *Zeus,* vol. ii, Cambridge, 1925, pp. 233 ff.; E. R. Dodds, *Euripides' Bacchae,* Oxford, 1944, p. 103.
28. Herod, iv, 13.
29. W. K. C. Guthrie, *The Greeks and their Gods,* 1950, pp. 78 ff.
30. Plato, *Laws,* i, 1A, vi, 759C; *Rep.,* iv, 427B.
31. Farnell, *Cult of the Greek States,* vol. iv, p. 198.
32. Guthrie, *Orpheus and Greek Religion,* 1935, pp. 41, 43 f.
33. Pausanias, x, 6, 24.   34. Dem. Macart., 1072.
35. Pindar, *Frag.* i, 35, Bergk, 127, Bowra; Plato, *Laws,* 70C; *Phaedo,* 70C.
36. *Cratylus,* 400C; *Phaedo,* 64, 66 f.; *Phaedrus,* 247 ff.
37. Demosthenes, xlvii, 68; Plato, *Laws,* xi, 916C.
38. H. W. Parke, *A History of the Delphic Oracle,* Oxford, 1939, pp. 47 ff.
39. Plato, *Apol.,* 19A.   40. Dill, *Syll.,* 697E.
41. Plato, *Laws,* 759C, D, 865B, 988A.
42. Plutarch, *Demosthenes,* 20; Cicero, *de Div.,* ii, 57, 118.
43. Diodorus Siculus, XVI, xxvi, 6.
44. Cicero, *de Div.,* I, xxxvii, 81, D.S. XXII, *frag.* ix, 5.
45. Pausanias, X, xxii, 12–xxiv; Justin, XXIV, vii, 1 ff.
46. Diodorus Siculus, XXII, ix, 4; Strabo, IV, C, 188; Livy, XXXVIII, 2, 9, 48; Hymn to Apollo, 23f.
47. Dio Sic., XXXV, xiii, Suidesms. v, ἀτταλος.
48. Livy, xxix, 10–14; Ovid, *Fasti,* IV, 247 ff.
49. Tacitus, *Annals,* III, 63.
50. Tacitus, *Hist.* IV, lxxxiii; Plutarch, *Mor.* 984A; Clem. of Alexandria, *Protrep.,* 42P.
51. *Bulletin de Correspondance hellénique,* vol. vi, p. 451.
52. *Op. cit.,* vol. xx, p. 719.   53. *Op. cit.,* p. 728.
54. *Op. cit.,* p. 730; Julian, *Contra Galilaeus,* 198C.
55. Julian, *Contra Galilaeus,* p. 198C; Pauly-Wissowa, *Real-Encyclopädie,* "Delphoi", 2583.
56. Cf. Origen, *Contra Celsum,* book vii, chaps. iii–iv; Justin Martyr, *Apologia,* xviii.
57. Heraclitus, *Frag.* xii, ad. Bywater.
58. Virgil, *Aeneid,* vi, 42, *Ecologue,* iv; Ovid, *Fasti,* iv, 158, 257.
59. Warde Fowler, *Religious Experience of the Roman People,* 1911, pp. 257 f.
60. Livy, xxix, 10–14; Ovid, *Fasti,* iv, 257 ff.
61. Warde Fowler, *Religious Experience of the Roman People,* 1911, p. 259.
62. Livy, xxii, 27.   63. Cf. book III, 97–294, 491 ff.
64. Cf. books I, II, VIII, 217–501 (beginning with an acrostic on the Christian symbol *ΙΧΘΥΣ*).

65. Cf. books XI–XIV.

66. Cf. C. Alexandre, *Oracula Sibyllina,* Paris, 1841–56, abridged ed. 1896, E.T.; M. S. Terry, *The Sibylline Oracles,* New York, 1890.

67. Hermas, Vis., ii, 4; Justin Martyr, *Quaest. et resp. ad Orthoxos,* 74; *Apol.,* i, 20, 59; Origen, *Contra Celsus,* vii, 56; Clem. of Alex., *Strom.,* vi, 5.

68. Origen, *op. cit.*; Lucian, *Sibyllines,* i, 140–6, 326–31.

69. Tertullian, *Adv. Nationes,* chap. xii; Arnobius, *Adversus Gentes,* i, 62; Lactantius, i, 15 ff., 42, 245 ff.

70. Eusebius, *Orat. Constantine,* xviii, p. 574 f.

71. *De Civ. Dei,* xviii, 23.

72. Harnack, *Texte und Untersuchungen zur Geschichte der altchristlichen Literatur* viii, 108.

73. Tertullian, *Apol.,* 23; Origen, *Contra Celsum,* vii, 4; Apost. Constit., viii, 26.

74. Eusebius, *Hist. Eccles.,* VI, xliii.

75. R. Campbell-Thompson, *Devils and Evil Spirits of Babylonia,* 1904–5.

76. *Op. cit.,* vol. i, tablet IV, col. v, 23 ff., tab. V, i, 54 ff.

77. *Op. cit.,* vol. i, pp. 16 ff., vol. ii, pp. 152 ff.; *Semitic Magic,* 1908, pp. 7 ff.

78. *Western Asiatic Inscriptions,* II, 51B, line i ff.; Utukku series, tablet III, I, 204.

79. Tablet N, col. iii, line 37 ff.

80. Langdon, *Expository Times,* vol. xxiv, 1912, pp. 11 ff.

81. Surpu series, tablet vii.   82. Tablet "T", line 30 ff.

83. Zimmern, *Beiträge zur Kenntnis der Babylonischen Religion,* vol. ii, Leipzig, 1901, p. 33.

84. *Pap. Turin,* 131, 1–8; *Metternich Stele,* 3–8.

85. *Op. cit.,* 136, 8–9; *Pap. Leyden,* 347, 4, 11 f.

86. *Pap. Turin,* 131, 7; *Pap. Leyden,* 348, 3, 4.

87. Cf. Chabas, *Bibl. Egyptol.,* xii, 127–335; Budge, *Egyptian Magic,* 1899, pp. 224 ff.

88. *Pap. med. Berlin,* 8, 10; *Pap. med. London,* 8, 12; Petersburg, 1116B, recto 9; *Ebers Pap.,* 99, 2.

89. *Pap. mag. Harris,* 6, 10.   90. *Pap. med. Berlin,* 3027 (I, 9–II, 6).

91. Mark v, 1–20.

92. Cf. Warde Fowler, *The Religious Experience of the Roman People,* 1911, p. 260; Livy, x, 47 (*Epitome*); Ovid, *Metam.,* xv, 622 ff.

93. Aesculapius frequently appeared in the form of a serpent and it was in this guise that he was manifest to those who slept in the sanctuary at Epidaurus. In his temples live serpents were kept for the healing of the sick. G. Dittenberger, *Sylloge Inscriptionum Graecorum,* II, pp. 662 f.; Pausanias, ii, 3, 118; iii, 237; Livy, xi (*Epit.*); Pliny, *Nat. Hist.* xxix, 72; Aristophanes, *Plutus,* 733.

94. *Aen.* vii, 81 ff., cf. Ovid, *Fasti,* iv, 649 ff.

95. R. Heinzey, *Vergil's epische Technik,* Leipzig, 1908, p. 174, n. 2.

96. Cf. M. Besnier, *L'Ile Tibérine dans l'antiquité*, Paris, 1902, pp. 223 ff.; Plaulus, *Curculio*, 266; Flavian, *Corpus Inscrip. Latinarum*, vi, 8, 14.

97. *Frag.* 27.

98. Ovid, *Fasti*, ii, 267–446; Plutarch, *Caesar*, 61.

99. Warde-Fowler, *The Religious Experience of the Roman People*, 1911, p. 96; Frazer, *Golden Bough*, part 9, pp. 231 ff.

100. Cicero, *de Har. Resp.*, 9, 18; *de Div.*, i, 16, 28.

101. Horace, *Odes*, iii, 27, 1 ff.

102. Horace, *op. cit.*; Cicero, *de Div.*, i, 16, 28.

103. Wissowa, *Religion und Kultur der Römer*, Munich, 1912, pp. 523 ff.; Warde Fowler, *The Religious Experience of the Roman People*, 1911, pp. 301 f.

104. Dio. Cass. xlii, 51.   105. Livy, i, 18.   106. Festus, 378, cf. 45.

107. Cicero, *de Div.*, i, 47, 105; Dio Cassius, xxxvii, 24; Tacitus, *Ann.*, xii, 23.

108. Bouché-Leclerc, *Hist. de la divination dans l'antiquité*, vol. iv, Paris, 1882, pp. 205 ff.

109. Varro, *de ling. Lat.*, v, 33.   110. Wissowa, *Rel. und Kultus*, p. 470.

111. Livy, xxxi, 5; *Corpus Inscript. Lat.*, vi, 32328, 1, 78; Servisu, *Aen.*, iv, 56.

112. C. Thulin, *Religionsgeschichtliche Versuche und Verarbeiten*, Giessen, 1906, iii.

113. C. Bezold, *op. cit.*, ii, 1905, pp. 246 ff.

114. Jastrow, *Zeitschrift für Assyriologie*, xx, 1907, pp. 118 ff.; *Die Religion Babyloniens and Assyriens*, Giessen, 1912, ii, 213 ff.; Contenau, *La divination chez les Assyriens et les Babyloniens*, pp. 235 ff.

115. Lam. ii, 11; Prov. vii, 23.   116. vi, 4–16.

117. For a consideration of the scientific aspects of astrology, see chap. VII, pp. 212 f.

118. ii, 600 ff.   119. Cf. chap. VII, p. 215.   120. vi, 577 ff.

121. Manilius, iv, 14 f.

122. *de Agri. Cult.*, 5.

123. Valerius Maximus, i, 3, 3.

124. Matt. ii, 6, 12 f., 19, 22.

125. Acts i, 26.

126. 1 Sam. xiv, 41; x, 20 f.; Joshua vii, 16–18; Prov. xvi, 33; Deut. xxxiii, 8–11.

127. Gen. xx, 3; xxvi, 24 f.; xxviii, 10–22; 1 Kings iii, 4–15.

128. Col. ii, 8–10; Gal. iv, 8–11; *Shab.*, 146A, 536.

129. Wisdom, xiii, 1 f.

130. viii, 9; xiii, 6; xvi, 16; xix, 19.

131. Irenaeus, *Hoer.*, I, xiii, xxiii, 4; Didache, c. 2; Hermas, *Mand.*, xi, 4.

132. de Doctr., c. ii, 24.

133. *Decr.* p. ii, caus. xxvi, qu. v, 12.

134. Cf. chap. VII, pp. 216 ff for a further consideration of these developments.

CHAPTER III

1. Num. xxii–xxiv.   2. Num. xxiii, 9 f.   3. Num. xxiii, 18–23.
4. Num. xxiv, 3 f.   5. Gen. xii, 6 f.   6. Gen. xxviii, 10–22.
7. Gen. xxviii, 16.   8. Exod. iii, 2–5.   9. Deut. xxxiii, 16.
10. Num. xii, 6 f.   11. Exod. xxv, 22, xxxiii, 7; Num. vii, 89.
12. Num. xi, 25 f., xii, 5.   13. Exod. xxxiii, 9 f.; Num. xi, 16.
14. Exod. xix, 3 ff.
15. Deut. xviii, 15, xxxiv, 10; Hos. xii, 13; Ps. xcix, 6; Exod. iii, 10 ff.
16. Exod. iv, 2 ff., 16 f., vii, 1.   17. Deut. xii, 2 ff.
18. 2 Kings xxiii, 5 ff.   19. Jer. vii, 18, xliv, 15–25.
20. Ezek. viii, 14.   21. Judges ix, 37.   22. Gen. xii, 8, xxxv, 4.
23. Joshua xxiv, 26; Deut. xi, 30.   24. 2 Sam. v, 24.
25. Joshua vii, 16 f.; 1 Sam. iv, 5, 8, x, 20 f.; Prov. xvi, 33.
26. Exod. xxviii ff.; Lev. 1 ff.; Deut. xxxiii, 8–11.
27. 2 Sam. viii, 18.   28. 1 Kings iv, 5.   29. Judges xvii, 5.
30. 1 Sam. vii, 1.   31. Exod. xxxiii, 11.   32. Gen. xlix, 5–7.
33. J. T. Meek, *Hebrew Origins,* 1950, pp. 121 ff.; Waterman, *Journal of the American Oriental Society,* vol. lvii, 1937, pp. 375 f.; *Amer. Journal of Semitic Languages and Literatures,* vol. lv, 1938, pp. 25, vol. lvi, 1939, pp. 113 ff.; Gray, *Sacrifice in the Old Testament,* Oxford, 1925, pp. 181 ff., 244 f.
34. Deut. xxxiii, 8–10.   35. Num. xii, xvi; Deut. xxxiii, 8–11.
36. Cf. Lods, *Israel, from its Beginning to the Middle of the Eighth Century,* 1932, p. 442.
37. Num. xvi–xviii, cf. xii.   38. Num. xviii, 2–7; Lev. viii.
39. Num. xxv, 13 (P); 1 Chron. xxiv, 3.
40. Gray, *Sacrifice in the Old Testament,* p. 209.
41. Mowinckel, *Ezra den Skriftlaerde,* Kristiania, 1916, p. 109, n. 2; Bentzen, *Studier over det zadokidiske Praesteskabs Historie,* Kobenhavn, 1931, pp. 10 ff.
42. Kennett, *Journal of Theological Studies,* vol. vi, 1905, pp. 161–86.
43. 1 Kings xii, 28; Exod. xxxii, 1–6, 22–25.
44. Judges xvii–xviii; 1 Sam. xix, 13 ff., xxi, 9 f.
45. Judges, xviii.   46. Ezek. xliv, 10 ff.   47. 2 Kings xi, 4 ff.
48. 2 Chron. xxiv, 2 ff.   49. 1 Chron. xv, 13.
50. Cf. Exod. xx, 24 f., 1 Kings xix, 10, xviii, 30.
51. Joshua xviii, 7; Deut. xxxiii, 8 ff.
52. 1 Sam. ix, 9.   53. 1 Sam. i, 24 f., ii, 18, iii, 1.
54. 1 Sam. ix, 12 f., xi, 15, xiii, 7 ff.
55. 1 Sam. i, 20.   56. 1 Sam. xiii, 9 ff.   57. 1 Sam. xiv, 35.
58. 2 Sam. vi, 14.   59. 1 Kings ix, 25.   60. 1 Kings, xii, 33.
61. 2 Kings, xvi, 12 f.   62. Cf. chap. IV, pp. 139 f.
63. Hos. iii, 3–5, x, 9, xiii, 9–11.
64. 1 Sam. viii, 7, x, 17–19. Cf. xii, xv.
65. Hos. x, 9.   66. Judges iii, 7–11.   67. 1 Sam. x, 1.

68. 1 Sam. x, 1–13.   69. 1 Sam. xvi, 13 f.
70. 1 Sam. x, 5 ff.; 1 Kings xviii, 20 ff., xxii, 11 f.
71. Cf. chap. II, p. 37.
72. Meek, *Hebrew Origins,* New York and London, 1950, pp. 148 ff.
73. Op. cit., pp. 172 f.
74. Jepson, *Nabi,* Munich, 1934, pp. 144 ff.
75. 1 Kings xviii, 19 f.   76. 1 Kings xviii, 4.
77. 1 Kings xxii, 6 ff.
78. Guillaume, *Prophecy and Divination,* 1938, p. 145, n. 2.
79. 1 Kings xx, 13 ff.   80. 2 Kings xiii, 15 ff.
81. 2 Kings ix, 11; Hos. ix, 7; Jer. xxix, 26; 2 Sam. xviii, 40.
82. 2 Kings ii, 23.
83. Exod. iv, 14 ff.; Deut. xviii, 18; Jer. xv, 19, xxiii, 31; Isa. 1, 20; Ezek. xii,
    21–28.
84. Isa. lv, 10 f.   85. Hag. i, 13.
86. Gen. xvi, 7–14; Judges vi, 11–24, xiii, 3 ff.
87. Johnson, *The One and the Many in the Israelite Conception of God,* Cardiff,
    1943, p. 37.
88. Gen. i, 20.   89. Exod. xxii, 3–8.
90. Job x, 10 f.; Ps. cxxxix, 13–16; 2 Macc. vii, 22; Prov. xxx, 19.
91. Ps. civ, 29; Gen. ii, 7; 1 Kings xvii, 12.
92. Exod. xv, 8; Hos. xiii, 15; Job ix, 9.
93. 1 Sam. x, 6, 10.   94. 1 Sam. iii, 1 ff.
95. Isa. xxxvii, 36; from 2 Kings xix, 35; Hos. xii, 4.
96. Hag. i, 13.   97. Mal. ii, 7.   98. Mal. iii, 1.
99. H. G. May, *Amer. Journal of Semitic Languages and Literatures,* vol. clviii,
    1931, pp. 32 ff., 81 ff.; A. Haldar, *Associations of Cult Prophets,* Uppsala,
    1945, p. 129; cf. chap. IV, pp. 119, 126.
100. xxiii, 16 ff.
101. Amos v, 15, ix, 7; Isa. v, 16 f., xl, 6, 8, xlv, 5, 6, 18, 20, xlvi, 9, xl, 21 f.,
     26, xlii, 5, li, 9 f.; Hag. i, 10 f., ii, 17 ff.
102. Exod. iii, 2, xix, 16; Lev. x, 2; Num. xi, 1–3, xiv, 35; Deut. iv, 12; 1
     Kings xviii, 24, 38; Job xxxvii, 10 f.; Ps. x, 17, xviii, 7, cxlvii, 16 f.;
     Jer. i, 13.
103. Ps. cxlv, 9.   104. Isa. xlvi, 13.   105. Isa. lvi, 1; Amos v, 4.
106. Isa. i, 16 f.
107. Hos. vi, 5; Jer. xii, 2, xxxi, 31 ff.; Mic. v, 8.
108. xxxi, 31–34.
109. J. Skinner, *Prophecy and Religion,* Cambridge, 1922, pp. 320 ff.
110. iii, 6 ff.   111. xxxi, 31.   112. xi, 4, cf. vii, 23, xxiv, 7.
113. xviii, 13 ff.   114. Ezek. xviii, 4 ff.   115. Joshua vii, 24 ff.
116. Ezek. xviii, 4 f.   117. Amos vii, 10–17; Mic. iii, 5.
118. Amos vii, 14; Zech. xiii, 5; J. Morgenstern, *Hebrew Union College Annual,*
     vol. xi, 1936, pp. 256 ff.

119. Isa. vi, 1 ff.; cf. Pederson, *Israel, Its Life and Culture*, vol. ii, 1926, p. 168 f.
120. Jer. i, 1; Ezek. i, 3, xxxvii.   121. Isa. xx, 2 f.
122. Jer. xxvii, 3 ff.   123. Amos v, 25.   124. Hos. ix, 10.
125. Amos iv, 4.
126. Jer. vii, 22 f.; cf. Amos v, 21.
127. Welch, *Prophet and Priest in Old Israel*, Oxford, 1953, p. 24.
128. *Op. cit.*, pp. 76 ff.   129. Jer. xxiii, 26 ff.
130. Isa. xvii, 12 ff.   131. Isa. xiv.
132. Mowinckel, *Psalmenstudien*, vol. iii, Kristiana, 1924, p. 17; cf. Johnson, *The Cultic Prophet in Ancient Israel*, 1944, pp. 59 f.
133. Cf. T. Nöldeke, *Corpus Inscriptionum Semiticarum*, 2, nos. 611, 1358, 1748.
134. *C.I.S.*, 2, nos. 1358, 1748. Eutang, 249, 348, 350.
135. *Neue Beiträge zur semitischen Sprachwissenschaft*, Strassburg, 1910, p. 36, n. 6.
136. Gray, *Sacrifice in the Old Testament*, Oxford, 1925, p. 184.
137. Robertson Smith, *The Prophets of Israel*, 1895, p. 390.
138. Ibn al-Kalbi, *Kitab al-'asnam*, p. 54.
139. *Op. cit.*, p. 28 f.
140. *Op. cit.*, p. 29; cf. Abu l'Farag, *Kitab al-agani*, Cairo, 1285, 8, pp. 11, 16 ff., 67.
141. Wellhausen, *Reste arabischen Heidentums*, Berlin, 1897, p. 9.
142. H. S. Nyberg, *Bemerkungen zum Buch der Gotzenbilder Ibn al Kalbi*. Skrifter utg av. Svenska institutet i Rom. Serie 2, 1939, p. 360.
143. Qur'an, Sura xcvi, 1–5.   144. Sura liii, 2–18.
145. Sells, *Faith of Islam*, Madras, 1907, p. 509.
146. Ibn Klaldun, *Prolégomènes*, Paris, 1862, i, p. 195.
147. Sura lxxxv, 21, xliii, 3.   148. xl, 15, xlii, 52.
149. xxii, 51, xxiii, 99, x, i, 36, xvi, 100.
150. Cf. M. Cheragh Ali, *Critical Exposition of Jihad*, Bombay, 1885, p. lxix.
151. Cf. M. Smith, *Studies in Early Mysticism in the Near and Middle East*, 1931, pp. 103 ff.
152. *Mishkatu'l-Masabih*, book 1, chap. vi, 2.
153. Cf. Guillaume, op. cit., pp. 326 ff.; G. F. Moore, *Judaism*, vol. i, Cambridge, 1927, pp. 411 ff.

CHAPTER IV

1. *Report of the Wellcome Tropical Research Laboratories*, 1911, pp. 216 ff.
2. Frazer, *The Golden Bough*, part 4, pp. 9 ff.
3. Cf. Seligman, *Pagan Tribes of the Nilotic Sudan*, 1932, pp. 90 ff., *Egypt and Negro Africa*, 1934, pp. 28 ff.; Meek, *The Northern Tribes of Nigeria*, vol. i, 1925, pp. 255 ff., vol. ii, pp. 58 ff.; *A Sudanese Kingdom*, 1931, pp. 164 ff.
4. W. Hofmayr, *Die Shilluk, Geschichte, Religion und Leben eines Niloten*

Stammes, 1925, pp. 152 f.; M. E. C. Pumphrey, *Sudan Notes and Records,* 1941, pp. 19 f.

5. O. S. Oyler, *Sudan Notes and Records,* 1920, pp. 296 ff.

6. Evans-Pritchard, *The Divine Kingship of the Shilluk of the Nilotic Sudan,* Cambridge, 1948, pp. 18 f.

7. Evans-Pritchard maintains that the tradition was a fiction arising from the dual personality of the king as both himself and Nyikang, an individual and an institution. He agrees that Shilluk kings generally met a violent death, but through leading a rebellion, *op. cit.,* pp. 21, 34 f.

8. P. Munro, *Sudan Notes and Records,* 1918, pp. 147 ff.; Howell and Thomson, *op. cit.,* 1946, pp. 41 ff.

9. Cf. Driston, *L'Egypte,* Paris, 1938, p. 597.

10. Frankfort, *Kingship and the Gods,* Chicago, 1948, pp. 24 ff.

11. M. S. Holmberg, *The God Ptah,* 1914; cf. B. M. Stela, No. 498.

12. Frankfort, *The Birth of Civilization in the Near East,* 1951, p. 54; *Kingship and the Gods,* pp. 150 ff.; cf. Quaritch Wales, *The Mountain of God,* 1953, pp. 8, 16.

13. Breasted, *Religion and Thought in Ancient Egypt,* 1914, p. 15.

14. Although the Osiris myth is not recorded *in extenso* in the Egyptian texts, the allusions to it agree with the account in Plutarch's narrative in *Isis et Osiris,* 12–20; cf. Breasted, *op. cit.,* pp. 24 ff.; Frazer, *The Golden Bough,* part 4, vol. ii, pp. 3 ff.

15. Budge, *Tutankhàmen, Amenism, Atonism and Egyptian Monotheism,* 1923, p. 79.

16. M. A. Murray, *J.R.A.I.* vol. xlv, 1915, pp. 308 ff.

17. Erman, *Handbook of Egyptian Religion,* 1907, pp. 57 ff., 72 ff.; Breasted, *Ancient Records of Egypt,* vol. ii, Chicago, 1905–7, pp. 187 ff., 190; Sethe, *Urkunden der Aegypt. Altertums,* Leipzig, 1908, iv, pp. 26, 29, 219.

18. Breasted, *Ancient Records of Egypt,* vol. iv, p. 943; Brugsch, *Dictionnaire géographique de l'ancienne Egypte,* 1877–80, p. 1361.

19. Cf. Cumont, *Les Religions Orientales dans la Paganisme Romain,* Paris, 1909, pp. 140 f.

20. Frankfort, *Ancient Egyptian Religion,* Columbia University Press, 1948, pp. 54 ff.

21. C. J. Bleeker, *De beteekenis van de Egyptische godin Maat,* Leiden, 1929, p. 33.

22. Breasted, *Ancient Records,* vol. ii, p. 299; *The Dawn of Conscience,* p. 148.

23. Frankfort, *Ancient Egyptian Religion,* p. 54.

24. Breasted, *Religion and Thought in Ancient Egypt,* p. 56; Frankfort, *Kingship and the Gods,* pp. 61 ff.

25. Breasted, *Ancient Records,* vol. iv, p. 870; vol. ii, p. 222.

26. Erman, *Life in Ancient Egypt,* 1894, p. 57; Blackman, *Luxor and its Temples,* 1923, p. 167.

27. Breasted, *op. cit.,* vol. ii, p. 99; D. R. MacIver, *Buhen,* Philadelphia, 1911 (13s.), p. 34; Blackman, *Proceedings of Society of Biblical Archaeology,* vol. xl, 1918, p. 90.

28. Sethe, *Urkunden des Aegypt. Altertums,* IV, p. 262, note b.
29. Blackman, *Journal of the Manchester Egyptian and Oriental Society,* 1918–19, pp. 30 ff.; *Recueil de Travaux,* vol. xxxix, pp. 44 ff.; *Encyclp. of Rel. and Ethics,* vol. xii, pp. 778 ff.; Moret, *Le rituel du culte divin journalier en Egypte,* 1902, p. 5 f.
30. Budge, *History of Egypt,* 1902, pp. 17 ff., 44 ff.; Moret, "Du caractère rel. de la royauté Pharaonique," in *Ann. du Musée Guimet,* 1902, p. 310.
31. Naville, *Deir El-Bahari,* vol. ii, 1895, p. 10.
32. Brugsch-Bey, *Egypt under the Pharaohs,* vol. i, p. 519.
33. Naville, *Old Egyptian Faith,* p. 267.
34. Erman, *Life in Ancient Egypt,* pp. 63 ff.
35. Cf. Foucart, *E.R.E.,* vol. v, p. 855.
36. Brugsch, *Zeitschrift für aegyp. Sprache und Altertumskunde,* XIX, 1881, pp. 77–111; Loret, *Recueil de travaux relatifs à la Philologie et à l'archéol. Egypt. et Assyriennes,* vol. iii, 1882, pp. 43 ff., vol. iv, 1883, pp. 21 ff., vol. v, 1884, pp. 85 ff.
37. *Journal Egypt. Archaeol.,* vol. ii, 1915, p. 123.
38. Budge, *Osiris and the Egyptian Resurrection,* vol. ii, 1911, pp. 131 ff.
39. Brugsch, *Religion und Mythologie der alten Aegypter,* Leipzig, 1885–8, p. 621.
40. *Op. cit.,* pp. 90 ff., 96 f., 98.
41. R. V. Lanzone, *Dizionario di Mitologia Egizia,* pp. 743 ff., pl. cclxxvi; Hornblower, *Man,* XXXVII, 1937, p. 157.
42. Budge, *Osiris and the Egyptian Resurrection,* vol. i, p. 51.
43. Brugsch, *Thesaurus,* 1891, p. 1190; Blackman, *Myth and Ritual,* Oxford, 1933, pp. 22 f., fig. 4.
44. M. A. Murray, *The Osireion at Abydos,* 1904, pp. 27 ff.
45. *Untersuchungen,* III, pp. 136 f.
46. *Journal of Egyptian Archaeology,* vol. ii, 1915, p. 124.
47. Sethe, *Urkunden des Aegypt. Altertums,* IV, p. 134.
48. Cf. Hornblower, *Man,* XXXVII, Nov. 1937, p. 173.
49. Moret, *Du caractère rel. de la royauté Pharaonique,* pp. 256 ff.
50. *Op. cit.*
51. Breasted, *Religion and Thought in Ancient Egypt,* p. 39; M. Murray, *Ancient Egypt,* II, 1926, pp. 33 ff.
52. Seligman, *Egypt and Negro Africa,* 1934, p. 2.
53. Cf.
54. Frankfort, *Kingship and the Gods,* p. 86.
55. Moret, *Du caractère rel. de la royauté Pharaonique,* p. 105, fig, 21.
56. Breasted, *Religion and Thought in Ancient Egypt,* p. 39; Seligman, *Egypt and Negro Africa,* p. 2; Frazer, *Golden Bough,* part 6, pp. 153 ff.; Petrie, *Researches in Sinai,* 1906, pp. 186 ff.; S. B. Mercer, *Religion of Ancient Egypt* 1945, pp. 122, 362 f.
57. *J.E.A.,* vol. xxviii, 1942, p. 71; Gardiner, *op. cit.,* p. 123; Frankfort, *Kingship and the Gods,* p. 79.

58. Moret, *Du caractère rel. de la royauté Pharaonique*, p. 256.

59. Jacobsen, *The Intellectual Adventure of Ancient Man*, pp. 126 ff.

60. Frankfort, *op. cit.*, pp. 221 ff.

61. Jacobsen, *Journal of Near Eastern Studies*, vol. ii, Chicago, 1943, p. 166, n. 44.

62. *Op. cit.*, pp. 159 ff.

63. F. Thureau-Dangin, *Sumerische und Akkadische Königsinschriften*, Leipzig, 1907, pp. 156 ff.; Gadd, *Ideas of Divine Rule in the Ancient East*, Oxford, 1948, p. 38; Jacobsen, *Journal of American Oriental Society*, vol. lix, 1939, pp. 486 f.

64. Frankfort, *op. cit.*, p. 228.

65. M. Wetzel, "Tammuz-liturgien und Verwandtes," *Analecta Orientalis* X, 1935, p. 17.

66. Jacobsen, *The Sumerian King List*, Chicago, 1939, p. 58.

67. Frankfort, *Op. cit.*, p. 297.

68. *Op. cit.*, and Zimmern, *Berichte über die Verhandlungen der Kgl. Sächsischen Gesellschaft der Wissenschaften, Phil-hist. Klasse*, Band 68, 1916.

69. Chiera, *Sumerian Religious Texts*, no. 1, col. v, 11, 18 ff. (Thorkild Jacobsen); Langdon, *Journal of the Royal Asiatic Society*, 1926. pp. 15 ff.; Lambert and Tourney, *Revue Biblique*, 1948, pp. 408 ff.; *Revue d'Assyriologie*, 1949, pp. 128 f.

70. Langdon, *Tammuz and Ishtar*, Oxford, 1914, pp. 6 ff.

71. Cf. T. Jacobsen, *The Intellectual Adventure of Ancient Man*, Chicago, 1946, pp. 126 ff.; Frankfort, *Ancient Egyptian Religion*, Chicago, 1948, pp. 54 ff.

72. W. W. Baudissin, *Adonis und Esmun*, Leipzig, 1911, pp. 27, 56, 94 ff., 480 ff.

73. Ezek. viii, 14.

74. Langdon, *Semitic Mythology*, 1931, pp. 342 ff.; *Tammuz and Ishtar*, 1914, pp. 11, 14 ff.; Ebeling, *Tod und Leben nach den Vorstellungen der Babylonier*, Leipzig, 1931; Wetzel, *Analecta Orientalis*, X, 1935, pp. vi f.; A. Moortgat, *Tammuz*, Berlin, 1949, pp. 81 ff.

75. Zimmern, *Der alte Orient*, 1926, p. 18.

76. Delitzach, *Mitteilungen der Deutschen Orient Gesellschaft*, no. 33, p. 34, no. 38, p. 19.

77. Pallis, *The Babylonian Akitu Festival*, 1926, p. 198.

78. S.Smith, *J.R.A.S.*, 1928, pp. 849 ff.; Pallis, *The Babylonian Akitu Festival*, 1926, p. 109; Tallquist, *Sumerischakkadische Namen der Totenwelt*, Helsingfors, 1934, p. 26, n. 4, Frankfort, *op. cit.*, p. 331.

79. C. H. Gordon, *Ugaritic Handbook*, Rome, 1947; T. H. Gaster, *Thespis*, New York, 1950, pp. 57 f.; R. de Langhe, *Les textes de Ras Shamra-Ugarit*, Paris, 1945.

80. *Syria*, XIII, 1932, pp. 113–63.

81. *Syria*, XV, 1935, pp. 29–45; XVII, 1936, pp. 150–73; *La déesse 'Anat*, Paris, 1938, pp. 91–102.

82. *Syria*, XII, 1931, pp. 193 ff.; *Eranos-Jahrbuch*, 1939, pp. 21 ff.
83. Cf. Hooke, *Origins of Early Semitic Ritual*, Oxford, 1935, p. 32; W. C. Graham-May, *Culture and Conscience*, Chicago, 1936, pp. 122 ff.; Engnell, *Studies in Divine Kingship*, Uppsala, 1945, pp. 97 ff.; F. F. Hvidberg, *Gradd og. Latter i det Garnle Testamente*, Kavanharm, 1938, pp. 37 ff.; Gaster, *Thespis*, New York, 1950, pp. 56, 59, 232.
84. Albright, *Journal of the Palestine Oriental Society*, vol. xiv, 1934, pp. 135 n., 186; Dussaud, *Revue de l'histoire des religions*, vol. cviii, 1933, pp. 10 f.
85. Virolleaud, *Syria*, XVII, 1936, pp. 202 ff.; Ginsberg, *Orientalia*, VIII, 1939, pp. 317 ff.
86. *J.R.A.S.*, 1938, pp. 37 ff.
87. Virolleaud, *Bibliothèque archéologique et historique*, XXI, 1936, pp. 126 ff.; cf. Isa. vii, 14.
88. Cf. K. Marti, *Jahwe und seine Auffassung in der ältesten Zeit*, Gotha, 1908, pp. 322 f.; Zimmern and Winckler, *Die Keilinschriften und das A.T.*, Berlin, 1902, pp. 66, 262. Rowley, *From Joseph to Joshua*, 1950.
89. Gen. iv, 26.   90. Exod. iii, 16.   91. Exod. iii, 13–15, vi, 2–3.
92. II Kings xvii, 25–33; I Sam. xxvi, 19; Jer. xvi, 33; Ruth i, 15, ii, 12.
93. Cf. chap. III, pp. 73, 76 f.
94. Chap. III, pp. 78 f.   95. I Sam. x, 6, xvi, 13 ff.
96. I Sam. viii, 4 ff.; Hos. x, 9, xiii, 10.
97. I Kings xii, 12, 16.
98. 2 Sam. vii, 12 ff.
99. Ps. cx; Gen. xiv; Heb. vii, 13.
100. I Sam. x, 1–13; cf. i, 24 f., ii, 18, ix, 12 f., xi, 15, xiii, 7 ff.; 2 Kings x. 11; Isa. iii, 2; Jer. i, 14 ff., v, 18.
101. Cf. chap. III, p. 73; W. C. Graham and H. C. May, *Culture and Conscience*, Chicago, 1936, pp. 170 ff.
102. Mal. ii, 1–7.   103. Ps. lxxxix, 26 f.   104. Test. Judah xxiv, 1,
105. Test. Levi. viii, 14, xviii, 2–14.
106. I Macc. xiv, 35.
107. Hab. iii, 13; Ps. xxviii, 8, cv, 15; Isa. xliv, 23; Dan. vii, 13; Enoch xlvi, 2 ff.
108. *The Re-discovery of the Old Testament*, 1946, p. 197; cf. *The Servant of the Lord*, 1952, pp. 61 ff.
109. Isa. 1, 6, liii, 5, 7 ff.
110. Rowley, *op. cit.*; Strack-Billerbeck, *Kommentar zum Neuen Testament aus Talmud und Midrasch*, vol. ii, 1924, p. 274; Lagrange, *Le Judaisme avant Jésus Christ*, 1931, p. 385.
111. Jeremias, *Deutsche Theologie*, vol. ii, 1929, pp. 106 ff.; W. D. Davies, *Paul and Rabbinic Judaism*, 1948, pp. 276 ff.; W. Manson, *Jesus the Messiah*, 1943, pp. 110 ff., 171 ff.
112. *The Ebed Yahweh Songs and the Suffering Messiah in Deutero-Isaiah*, 1948, pp. 11 f., 42.

113. Cf. Snaith, *Studies in Old Testament Prophecy*, ed. by H. H. Rowley, 1950, p. 191.

114. Mark viii, 31–33; Matt. xvi, 21–23.

115. *Journal of Biblical Literature*, vol. xli, 1922, p. 143 (Bacon); vol. xlvi, 1927, pp. 1 ff. (Case); vol. lx, 1941, pp. 151 ff. (Parker); T. W. Manson, *The Teaching of Jesus*, Cambridge, 1935, pp. 227 f.

116. W. Manson, *Jesus the Messiah*, 1943, p. 99.

117. Rev. v, 6 ff., xii, 7 ff., xiii, 8, xix, 1–9.

CHAPTER V

1. W. R. Smith, *The Religion of the Semites*, 3rd ed., 1927, pp. 269 ff., 405.

2. E. O. James, *The Origins of Sacrifice*, 1933, pp. 256 ff.

3. *Primitive Culture*, vol. ii, 5th ed., 1913, pp. 375 ff.

4. *Religion in Essence and Manifestation*, 1938, p. 351.

5. *Essai historique sur le sacrifice*, Paris, 1920, p. 22.

6. *Religion of the Semites*, 1927, pp. 245 f., 405 ff.

7. Cf. Hubert and Mauss, *L'Année Sociologique*, 1898, II, pp. 41, 133.

8. M. Mauss, *L'Année Sociologique*, 1925, N.S. I, pp. 50 ff.; Money-Kyrle, *The Meaning of Sacrifice*, 1930, pp. 248.

9. Sahagun, *Histoire générale des choses de la Nouvelle Espagne*, Paris, 1880, pp. 52 ff., 61, 96 ff.

10. *Manu*, vii, 3–7, ix, 303–311, v, 96.

11. *Rig-veda*, i, 46, 164.   12. *Manu*, ix, 1, 13, 85, 100.

13. *Rig-veda*, I, lxv; *Sacred Books of the East*, vol. xlvi, 54, 220.

14. *Satapatha Brahmana*, V, 1, 1, 2, 111, 2, 2, 4.

15. *Op. cit.*, VI, 5, 1 ff., cf. I, 9, 2, 29.

16. *Op. cit.*, VI, 1, 1, 7.

17. In the Brahmanas Agni is made to affirm, "in me they shall sacrifice for all of you and thus I give you a share in me." Similar words are applied to Soma and Indra., *op. cit.*, I, 6, 3, 20–22.

18. *Op. cit.*, VI, 1, 1, 8.

19. *Op. cit.*, X, 6, 4, 1.   20. Cf. chap. IX, p. 288.

21. *Satapatha Brahmana*, I, 1, 4 ff., II, 5, 1, 7.

22. Chap. IX, p. 288.

23. *Svetasvatara Upanishad*, ii, 6, 7; *Maitri Upanishad*, I, i; *Bhadaranyaka Upanishad*, IV, iv, 22; *Chandogyan Upanishad* II, xxiii, 1; *Kena*, 33.

24. 1 Kings xviii, 1–8.   25. 2 Kings xxii, 8.   26. 2 Kings xxiii.

27. Exod. xxiv, 4–8 (E); Lev. xvii, 11.

28. Ps. i, 5.   29. Gen. xxxi, 54; Exod. xxiv, 11.

30. Lev. ii, 13; Num. xviii, 19; 2 Chron. xiii, 5.

31. Lev. xvii, 11 f.   32. Exod. xiii, 13, 15, xx, 22–xxiii, 35.

33. Joshua vi, 26; 1 Kings xvi, 34; R. A. S. Macalister, *The Excavations of Gezer*, vol. ii, 1912, pp. 426 ff.

34. 2 Kings xxiii, 10.   35. 2 Kings iii, 27.   36. Judges xi, 30 ff.
37. Gen. xxii, 1–14.   38. Exod. xxii, 29; Gen. xxii, 2.
39. Exod. xii, 2 (P), 12 f. (J), xxii, 29, 30 (E).
40. Exod. xii, 12 f., xvi, 1–8.
41. Frazer, *The Golden Bough,* part 4, p. 176.
42. Robertson Smith, *Religion of the Semites,* p. 345.
43. Firmicus Maternus, *De err. prof. rel.* VI, p. 16 (Zeiler).
44. Robertson Smith, *op. cit.,* p. 338.   45. Exod. xii, 22 f.
46. Curtiss, *Primitive Semitic Religion To-day,* Chicago, 1902, pp. 226 ff.
47. Exod. xii, 27, xi, 4.   48. Exod. xii, 13, 23, 27, xi, 4.
49. *Sacrifice in the Old Testament,* Oxford, 1925, pp. 364.
50. Exod. xiii, 15 ff.
51. Exod. xiii, 15 ff.; xxiv, 18; Lev. xxiii, 10; Deut, xvi, 9.
52. Lev. xxiii, 5; Deut. xvi, 6; Exod. xii, 6.
53. Nielson, *Handbuch der altarbischen Altertum skunde,* 1927, i, 213.
54. Exod. xxiii, 15 ff., xiii, 4, xxiv, 18; Lev. xxiii, 10 ff.; Deut. xvi, 2 f.
55. Lev. xxiii, 17.
56. Thackeray, *The Septuagint and Jewish Worship,* 1921, pp. 40 ff.; Oesterley, *Myth and Ritual,* pp. 115 ff.
57. Cf. Exod. xii, 26, xiii, 14.   58. *Pesahim,* 10.
59. Lev. xvii, 11.   60. Ezek. xlv, 18, 30.
61. Lev. viii, 14 f., xvii, 11; Deut. xii, 23.
62. Lev. xiv, 4 ff.; Zech. v, 5, 11.
63. Isa. lv. 6, 7, xliv, 22; Ps. xlv, 1, 6, 8–14, li, 16 f., lxix, 30 f.
64. Mic. vii, 18 f.
65. *Yoma,* viii, 9.   66. *Yoma,* viii, 8, cf. Lev. xvi, 30.
67. *Shabbat shabbaton,* Lev. xxiii, 32.
68. *Yoma,* viii, 1.
69. Abot de R. Nathan, 4, 5; Bacher, *Tannaiten,* 1, 39.
70. Isa. xliii, 1–4, xlix, 1–6, 1, 4–9, lii, 12–liii.
71. Isa. liii, 10 ff.   72. Isa. liii, 10, cf. 5, 8.
73. Num. xix, xx.   74. Num. xx, 27, 29; *Jer. Yoma* 38 b.
75. Isa. xlix, 5 ff.   76. Rom. v, 8.
77. Heb. v, 5 ff., vii, 24, viii, 1, ix, 25 f.
78. Heb. v, 6 ff.   79. Heb. x, 4.
80. Heb. ix,, 24.   81. Heb. x, 1.
82. Chryst. *Ep. ad Heb. hom.* xiv, i, 2; Ambrose, *In Psal,* xxxviii, 25; *de Officiis,* book 1, xlviii, 238; *Dial.,* iv, 58.
83. Paschasius, *De corp. et Sang, Dni,* 8, 12.
84. Cf. R. Leivestad, *Christ the Conqueror,* 1954, pp. 179 ff.
85. Heb. ii, 17, iii, 1, iv, 14, v, 1 ff., vii, 1 ff.; 1 Pet. ii, 5; Rev. i, 6, v, 10.
86. 1 Pet. ii, 5; Rom. xii, 1; Jas. 1, 27; Heb. xiii, 15 f.
87. Mark xiv, 22 ff.; Matt. xxvi, 26 ff.; Luke, xxii, 19 f., cf. 1 Cor. xi, 23 ff.
88. J. Jeremias, *Die Abendmahlsworte Jesu,* 1949, pp. 8–13.

89. Mark xiv, 12 ff.; John xviii, 28, xix, 14.

90. It is not improbable that the stories of a miraculous feeding of a great multitude were connected with ritual gatherings of this nature, and so were put in a sacramental setting by the Fourth Evangelist. John vi, 2 ff.

91. S. Mendelsohn, *Jewish Encyclop.*, vol. vi, 123 f.; Dugmore, *J.T.S.*, vol. xlvii, pp. 108 f.

92. Oesterley, *Jewish Background of the Christian Liturgy*, 1925, pp. 167 ff.; Elbogen, *Der Jüdische Gottesdienst in seine geschictliche Entwicklung*, Frankfort, 1934; Leitzmann, *Messe und Herrenmahl*, Bonn, 1926, p. 202; Circlot, *The Early Eucharist*, 1939, pp. 1 ff.; K. Völker, *Mysterium und Agape*, Gotha, 1927, pp. 3 ff.

93. Luke xxii, 15 f.

94. *Messe und Herrenmahl*, Bonn, 1926, p. 221.

95. Cf. Acts ii, 42, 46, xx, 7, 11, xxvii, 35.

96. G. Dix, *The Shape of the Liturgy*, 1945, p. 69.

97. H. A. A. Kennedy, *St Paul and the Mystery Religions*, 1913. A. D. Nock, in *Essays on the Trinity and the Incarnation*, 1928, pp. 51 ff.

98. 1 Cor. x, xi.

99. Justin Martyr, *Ap.* 65–67; *Dial. c. Tryph.*, 41; Tertullian, *Apol.*, 39.

100. I. Clement, 44; Hippolytus, *Apos. Trad.*, iii, 4, ix, 11; Ignatius, *Smyrn.*, 8.

101. *Apost. Constit.*, viii; *Test. of our Lord*, i, 34; *Older Didasc.*, ii, 57; cf. Maclean, *Ancient Church Orders*, Cambridge, 1910, pp. 46 ff.; Bright, *Canons of First Four General Councils*, 1892, pp. 59 ff.

102. Ignatius, *Magn.*, vi, i; *Smyrn*, viii, 1–2; I. Clem., *op. cit.*, Didache, xv; *Apost Const.* xxiv, p. 43 f.

103. Can. 18.

104. G. Dix, *The Apostolic Ministry*, ed. K. E. Kirk, 1946, pp. 246 ff.

105. Justin Martyr, *Apol.*, i, 65, 67; Cyprian, *Ep.*, v, 2; Ignatius, *Smyrn.*, viii, 1.

106. Irenaeus, *Ep. ad Victor.* Eusebius, *Eccl. Hist.*, V, xxiv, 14; Dix, *op. cit.*, p. 221.

107. Hippolytus, *Treatise of the Apostolic Constitutions*, ed. Dix, 1937, p. lxxx.

108. *Didascalia Apostolorum*, XXVI, 4–8, ed. R. E. Connolly, 1929, p. 80 f.

109. Cf. chap. VIII, pp. 267 f.

110. Cf. C. Jenkins, *Journal of Theological Studies*, 1922, pp. 1–30.

111. Despite the ambiguities in the phrasing of the rubric and the different interpretations placed upon the injunction, it left open the way for the widespread restoration of the Eucharistic vestments which are now a common feature in Anglican churches and cathedrals.

112. In fact only in England south of the border and west of Wales is the Anglican Communion an Established Church.

CHAPTER VI

1. Cf. chap. II, pp. 49 f.   2. Cf. chap. V, pp. 146, 162.

3. 1 Sam. v, 19 f.; 2 Sam. vi, 6 f.; Isa. vi, 3; Lev. x; Num. iv, 15, 20.

4. The Hebrew root *kpr,* from the second stem of which the technical terms connected with atonement are derived, seems to mean both to "cover" (after the Arabic) and to "wipe clean" (after the Syriac); cf. W. R. Smith, *The Old Testament in the Jewish Church,* 1895, p. 381.

5. Lev. xvii, 11 f., cf. *Yoma,* 3, 5.   6. Prov. x, 12.

7. Prov. xxi, 3, xv, 8; 1 Sam. xv, 22.

8. Ecclus. vii, 29–31, xlv, 14 f., 1, cf. chap. IX, p. 285.

9. Ecclus. xxxiv, 25 f., xxxv, 1–12.   10. Ecclus. xxxv, 1, 3.

11. *Yoma,* 8. 9., cf. Matt., v, 23 f.   12. Matt. xviii, 15 ff.

13. *Tanhuma,* 30, Matt. vi, 14 f. cf. v, 12, xviii, 21 f.

14. Num. v, 6 f., xiv, 40; Lev. v, 5; Ps. xxxii, cvi, 6; 2 Sam. xii; 1 Kings viii, 47; Prov. xxviii, 13.

15. Cf. chap. V, pp. 161 f.

16. *Yoma,* 3, 8; 4, 2; 6, 2; *Sifra Ahare Perek, 4, on Lev. xvi,* 21.

17. 2 Sam. xii, 13; 1 Kings viii, 47; Dan. ix, 5.

18. *Yoma,* 87b; *Ber.,* 17a; Singer, *Prayer Book,* p. 263.

19. *Shulhan 'Anuk. Tur. Or. Hay.,* 607.

20. *Yoma,* 87b.   21. Singer, *Prayer Book,* p. 259.

22. *Sanh.,* vi, 2.   23. Ps. cxlv, 8 f.

24. Maimonides, *Commem. on M. Sanhedrin,* 10, 2; *Hilkor Terhubah,* 3, 6 ff.

25. Cf. R. Simeon ben Yohai, *Sifre Deut.,* p. 252 on Deut. 23, 8.

26. *Yoma,* 23a; *Baba batra,* 9a; *Taanith,* 16a.

27. *Jer. Rosh ha-Shanah,* 59c; *Pesikta Rabbati,* ed. Friedmann, f. 169a.

28. 2 Cor. v, 18–2; Rom., 10 f., xi, 15; Col. i, 20 f.

29. Gal. ii, 20; Rom. v, 20 f., vi, 5, xi, 15; Col. iii, 1.

30. Gal. ii, 20; Rom. vi, 3 ff.

31. Rom. vi, 1–11; 1 Cor. xii, 13.   32. Rom. vi, 11.

33. 2 Cor. v, 18 f., 20.   34. Matt. xvi, 13–20, xviii, 18.

35. Acts x, 47; Ep. Clementis ad Jacob, 2, 6; Migne, *Pat. Graec.* ii, 26, 41.

36. John xx, 19–23.   37. Gen. ii, 7.

38. Cf. 1 Cor. xv, 45.

39. John xiii, 20, xvii, 18, cf. xiv, 18, 27, xv, 11.

40. Justin, *Tryph.,* 106.

41. Origen, *de princip.,* 1, iii, 2; *Comm. in Jn.,* 388; Cyprian, *de unit.,* 4; *Ep.* lxxiii, 6; Luke iii, 3; Acts ii, 38, xix, 4; Matt. xxviii, 19.

42. Matt. iii, 6; Mark i, 5.

43. Tertullian, *De Baptismo,* 7, 8, 20. For the most recent discussion of the relation of Baptism to Confirmation in the Early Church see G. W. H. Lampe, *The Seal of the Spirit,* 1951.

44. Mark, iii, 28–30; Matt. xii, 31 f.

45. 1 John v, 16.   46. 1 Cor. v, 3–5.   47. *Maud.* iv, 3.

48. *Sim.* ix, 19.   49. Strom. II, 13.   50. *Op. cit.,* II, 23.

51. *De Orat,* 28.   52. *Refutatio omnium haeresium,* IX, 7.

53. *De Poen.,* v.   54. *De Poen.,* iv, v.

55. *De Pud.,* i, ii, iii, v.   56. *De Pud.,* xxii.

57. Sermo, cli, n. 3.

58. *Homil. in Ps. xxxvii,* n. 6, in Migne, *Patres Graeci,* XII, 1386; *In Lev.* ii, 4, in *Patres Graeci,* xii, 418.

59. *Ep. Can.,* ii, 34.   60. *Ep.,* 168, 2.

61. St Innocent, *Ep.,* 25, ad Decentium.

62. Council of Trent, sess. xxi, de reform., ch. 9, sess. xxv.

63. Aquinas, *Summa Theol.,* III, q. 84–90, suppl. q. 1–28, Sent. IV, dist. xvii, xviii, xix.

64. A. Lehmkuhl, *Theologia Moralis,* 8th ed., Friburg, 1896, ¶ 418.

65. *Op. cit.,* 392; Alphonso de Liguori, *Theologia Moralis,* Ratisbonae, 1846, vi, n. 560, 561; J. P. Gury, *Compendium Theologia Moralis,* Ratisbonae, 1874, 576.

66. Lehmkuhl, *op. cit.,* 410.

67. *Op. cit.,* 455; Gury, *op. cit.,* ii, 647; *Council Lateran,* IV, *c.* 21; *English Canons of 1604,* can. 113.

68. A. Liguori, *Theologia Moralis,* VI, n. 634. The Anglican Canons of 1604 make an exception in the case of crimes against the laws of the realm involving danger to the life of the confessor. But cf. Pusey, *Entire Absolution of the Penitent,* II, 1846; p. 14; T. T. Carter, *The Doctrine of Confession,* 1885, chap. XVI.

69. Trent, sess. XIV, 4.   70. Cf. Canon, 26.

71. Herbert Thorndike, *Just Weights and Measures,* 1662, p. 120.

72. J. Wickham Legg, *English Church Life,* 1914, pp. 258 f.

73. *Memoirs of William Wordsworth,* ed. by C. Wordsworth Maxon, 1851, I, p. 8.

74. Legg, *op. cit.,* p. 278.

75. In the subsequent revisions in 1552 and 1662 this last sentence was omitted, but otherwise the same form of service remained unaltered except for the insertion of the parenthesis, "if he humbly and heartily desire it," inserted in the rubric in 1662 after the words "the priest shall absolve him".

76. Cf. Mabillon, *Museum Italicum,* II, Paris, 1689, 70–76. H. A. Wilson, *Order of Communion,* 1548 (Henry Bradshaw Society), p. xv.

77. *Whitgift,* vol. i, p. 489.   78. *Eccles. Polity,* IV, 4.

79. *Op. cit.,* VI, 16.

80. Church and Paget, *Hooker,* Oxford, 1888, I, p. 85.

81. *Diary of John Evelyn,* 1655, March 31, Bray, Wheatley, Bickers, II, 1879, p. 76.

82. *The Remains of Dennis Granville,* 1865 (Surtees Society), XLVII, pp. 49 f.

83. *Life of John Sharp,* vol. i, 1825, p. 301.

84. *Tom Jones,* book 5, chap. VIII.

85. 8th ed., London, 1681, Sign. D.

86. Cf. Thorndike, *Of the Laws of the Church,* book 3, chap. XI, 20, 21; in J. H. Parker, *Works,* vol. iv, part 1, Oxford, 1852, pp. 258 f.; Ken, *A*

Manual of Prayers for Use of Scholars of Winchester Colledge, 1675, p. 27; Wetenhall, *Enter into thy Closet,* 1672, p. 444; E. Churton, *The Minor Theological Works of John Pearson,* vol. ii, Oxford, 1844, p. 237; W. Wake, *An Exposition of the Doctrine of the Church of England,* London, 1686, p. 42; W. Beveridge, *Works,* ed. by Bettesworth and Innys, vol. i, 1729, p. 7; I. Barrow, *Theological Works,* ed. by A. Napier, vol. vii, Cambridge, 1859, p. 365.

87. *Questions and Answers Concerning the two religions,* London 1723, p. 37, Bodleian Library, Pamphlet, 374.
88. *Sermons on several Subjects,* vol. vi, London 1771, p. 357.
89. *Elements of Christian Theology,* vol. ii, London, 1799, p. 424.
90. Newman in a letter, dated August 13th, 1844, refers to a friend of Henry Wilberforce (one Fortescue), a member of a non-juring family, who had been in the habit of making his confession from a child. But the context suggests that he regarded the case as exceptional, cf. *Letters and Correspondence,* vol. ii, ed. by Mozley, 1891, p. 435.
91. Cf. H. P. Liddon, *Life of Dr Pusey,* vol. iv, 1898, pp. 266 ff.
92. Matt. v, 48.
93. St Alphonso di Liguori, *Theologia Moralis,* vi, 631, v, n. 461; Lehmkuhl, *Theologia Moralis,* 418, 426; K. E. Kirk, *Some Principles of Moral Theology,* 1920, pp. 213 ff.
94. Gury, *Compendium Theologia Moralis,* 599, 605; Kirk, *op. cit.*
95. The principle of "reserved cases" should be extended to cover those requiring more expert direction.
96. *Modern Man in Search of a Soul,* 1933, p. 260.

CHAPTER VII

1. *Patterns of Culture,* 1935, p. 60. 2. *Op. cit.,* pp. 71, 96.
3. H. J. Spinden, *Ancient Civilization of Middle and Central America,* New York, 1928, pp. 228 ff.
4. *Op. cit.,* pp. 35, 99, 130 ff.; T. A. Joyce, *Mexican Archaeology,* 1914, pp. 368 ff.; G. C. Valliant, *The Aztecs of Mexico,* 1941, pp. 93 f.
5. B. de Sahagun, *A History of Ancient Mexico,* E. T. by F. R. Bandelier, Nashville, 1932, pp. 196 ff.
6. Cf. chap. II, pp. 61 f.
7. Cf. R. C. Campbell-Thompson, *The Reports of the Magicians and Astrologers of Nineveh and Babylon,* 1900.
8. The Avesta, Yasna, XXX; Vendidah, I ff.; Yasht, X, 97, XLIII, 77; Yasna, LX, 8, X, 15; Bandahisu, I, 1–28.
9. Cicero, *De div.* i, 38 (82).
10. Enoch lxxv, 3, lxxx, 6; 4 Esdras vi, 3; Matt. xxiv, 29; 2 Kings xvii, 16; Cant. vi, 10.
11. 2 Kings xxi, 3 ff., xxiii, 5 ff., 11 ff.; Deut. xviii, 10; Isa, xlvii, 13 f.

12. Gen. i, 14.

13. Isa. xlvii, 13.

14. *Shab.*, 67b, 156a; *Pes.*, 1136.

15. *Shab.*, 146a, 536.

16. Targum, *Ec.*, vii, 15, ix, 1 f.

17. *Suk.*, 29a; *Sanh.*, 65b, *Pes.*, 120.

18. *Yad. Ab. Cochab.* xi, 8.

19. Cf. chap. III, p. 97.

20. Abu'l-Qasim 'Isa ibn Alf, in Ibn Qayyim al-Jauziyyah, *Miftāh dār as-sa 'ādah*, ii, Cairo, 1905–7, pp. 156–196; Al-Fārābi, *Philosophische Abhandlungen*, tr. Dieterici, Leyden, 1892, pp. 170 ff.

21. A. F. Mchren, *Muséon*, III, Louvain, 1884, pp. 383 ff.; L. Goldziher, *Abhandlungen d. Berliner Akad. d. Wissenschaften*, 1915, pp. 20 ff.; Al-Ghazali, *Ihya'utum ad-din*, Cairo, 1885, i, p. 27 f.

22. *Miftāh dār as-sa 'ādah*, ii, pp. 132 ff.

23. Cf. J. E. Harrison, *Themis*, Cambridge, 1912, pp. 328 ff.; Malinowski, *Myth in Primitive Psychology*, 1926, pp. 21 f.; Hooke, *Myth and Ritual*, Oxford, 1933, pp. 1 ff.; *The Labyrinth*, 1935, p. ix f.

24. *Science, Religion and Reality*, 1926, p. 30 f.

25. L. Bruhl, *Les Fonctions dans les Sociétés Inférieures*, Paris, 1915; *La Mentalité primitive*, Paris, 1921.

26. Cf. C. Dawson, *Religion and Culture*, 1948, pp. 137 f.

27. *Rig-veda*, 1–36, I, 9, II, 1, 9.

28. *Rig-veda*, ii, 1, 2, iv, 9, 3, vii, 7, 5, 33, 11, x, 71, 11.

29. Cf. Sethe, *Die altägyptischen Pyramidentexte*, Leipzig, 1908–10.

30. Breasted, *Religion and Thought in Ancient Egypt*, 1914, p. 93.

31. Chap. IV, p. 133.

32. C. H. Gordon, *Ugaritic Handbook*, Rome, 1947; R. de Laughe, *Les Textes de Ras Shamra-Ugarit et leurs rapports avec le milieu de l'ancien Testamente*, 1945, i, ii.

33. Foreword to *Thespis* by T. H. Gaster, 1950, p. vii.

34. Hos. iv. 1–10; Mic. iii, 11; Zeph. iii, 4; Jer. ii, 8; Ezek. xxii, 26; Mal. ii. 8 ff.

35. Exod. xviii, 16, 19, xxxiii, 7–11.

36. Mal. ii, 6 f.; Jer. ii, 13.

37. Cf. Holscher, *Kanonisch und Apokryph.*, 1905, pp. 36 ff.

38. Guthrie, *Orpheus and Greek Religion*, 1935, pp. 45 ff.

39. J. M. Linford, *The Arts of Orpheus*, Berkeley, 1941; Nilsson, *Harvard Theological Review*, vol. xxviii, 1935, pp. 185 ff.; O. Kern, *Orphicorum Fragmenta*, Berlin, 1922, pp. 80 ff.

40. Guthrie, *Orpheus and Greek Religion*, 1935, pp. 153 f.

41. *Principium Sapientiae*, Cambridge, 1952, pp. 159 ff.

42. *Rep.* VI, 505, 508D; *Phaedrus*, 247C.

43. *Timaeus*, 30 A–C; *Laws*, 896E, 898D.

44. *Met.*, XII, ix, 1074b.

45. Cleanthes, *Hymn to Zeus*, in Stob. *Ecl.* I, i, 12.

46. Cicero, *De Natura Deorum*, ii, 23, 60.

47. *De Civitate Dei*.

CHAPTER VIII

1. Westermarck, *Origin and Development of Moral Ideas,* vol. i, 1906, p. 505 vol. ii, p. 687.
2. *Native Tribes of South-east Australia,* 1904, p. 533.
3. Chap. I, pp. 25 f.
4. E. L. R. Meyerowitz, *The Sacred State of the Akan,* 1951, pp. 27, 37 ff., 48; J. Gros, *Voyages, aventures et Captivité de Bonnet chez les Ashantis,* Paris, 1884, p. 218.
5. Rattray, *Ashanti Law and Constitution,* Oxford, 1929, pp. 81 ff.
6. Rattray, *The Ashanti,* Oxford, 1923, pp. 92 ff, 116 f.
7. Chap. IV, pp. 107 ff, 126 ff.
8. Breasted, *A History of Egypt,* 1906, p. 126; *Ancient Records of Egypt,* vol iv, Chicago, 1907, pp. 787 ff.
9. *Ancient Records,* vol. i, pp. 622 f., 778 ff., vol. iii, p. 565; Brugsch, *Thesaurus, Inscriptionum Aegypticarum,* Leipzig, 1883–91, pp. 908 f., 942.
10. Sethe, *Urkunden des Aegypt. Altertums,* Leipzig, 1903, ii, pp. 126, 153.
11. Erman, *Life in Ancient Egypt,* 1894, pp. 291 ff.
12. *Op. cit.,* pp. 104., 294.
13. *Ancient Records,* vol. iii, pp. 64 f.
14. Chap. IV, p. 116.   15. Cf. chap. IV, p. 127.
16. *Code of Hammurabi,* col. xxiv, 11 ff.
17. Col. xxv, 21 f.   18. Col. v, 4.
19. W. F. Albright, *From the Stone Age to Christianity,* Baltimore, 1946, p. 204.
20. Cf. chap. III, p. 71.   21. Num. vi, 8.
22. 1 Sam. vi, 20; Isa. ii, 6–21.   23. Isa. i, 4, vi, 10, vi; Amos, iv, 2.
24. Deut. xxv, 15.   25. Ps. lii, 3.   26. Ps. xxiii, 3.
27. Lev. i–vii.   28. *Berakoth,* 5a.   29. *Sofra,* 112c.
30. *Abot.,* i, 1.   31. Ezra vii, 10.   32. Eccles. xxxviii, 33–xxxix, 11.
33. Matt. xxiii, 2 f.   34. Matt. xiii, 52.   35. Gal. i, 2, 15.
36. Mark i, 15.   37. Gal. vi, 16.
38. C. H. Dodd, *The Parables of the Kingdom,* 1935, p. 34 ff.; *History and the Gospel,* 1938, p. 181.
39. 1 Thess. iv, 15 ff.; 1 Cor. xv, 51 f.; James v, 8; 1 Pet. iv, 17; cf. Mark viii, 38–ix, 1.
40. Matt. xxviii, 18; John xx, 21; Acts i, 21–26.
41. Mark iii, 14; Luke iv, 13 ff., 20, iv, 13 ff.
42. Luke xxii, 30.
43. Cf. K. E. Kirk, *The Apostolic Ministry,* 1946, pp. 8–10, 12, 15, 531.
44. Acts i, 23.   45. Luke x, 1–24.   46. Num. xi, 4–25.
47. Phil. i, 1.
48. 1 Tim. iii, 1–13. For the date and authorship of these epistles, cf. P. N. Harrison, *The Problem of the Pastoral Epistles,* Oxford, 1921.
49. Acts xi, 30, xv, 2, xvi, 4, xxi, 18.

50. Acts xiv, 23.   51. James v, 14.
52. Acts xx, 17 f.; Titus 1, 5–7; J. B. Lightfoot, *Philippians*, 1903, pp. 96 ff.
53. 1 Thess. v, 12; Heb. xiii, 17.
54. Rom. xii, 8; Epistle of Clement, c. 1; Hermas, *Visions*, III, ix, 7.
55. Acts xii, 17, xv, 13 ff.; Gal. ii, 9.
56. 1 Cor. xv, 7.   57. Acts xv, 13–21.
58. Cf. Hegessipus, in Eusebius, *Eccl. Hist.* II, xxiii, 1–19.
59. 1 Cor. xv, 8; Gal. i, 12.
60. Cf. Brandon, *The Fall of Jerusalem and the Christian Church*, 1951.
61. E. C. Ratcliff, in *The Study of Theology*, 1939, pp. 410 f.
62. 2 Cor. viii, 23; 1 Thess. iii, 2.
63. Cf. 1 Tim. iv, 14; 2 Tim. 1, 6; Acts vi, 6; xiv, 23.
64. *The Apostolic Ministry*, pp. 228 ff.
65. Acts xiii, 1.   66. Gal. ii, 11–13.
67. Acts i, 15; ii, 14, 37; iii, 23, 104; viii, 14–25.
68. Acts xii, 17.   69. Acts xv, 7 ff.
70. Mark, x, 35, 45; Matt. xx, 20–28.
71. Mark ix, 33–37; Matt. xviii, 1–3; Luke ix, 46–48.
72. Mark x, 40.   73. Matt. x, 2.   74. Matt. xvi, 17–19.
75. *Das Urchristentum*, Göttingen, 1914, p. 585.
76. *Op. cit.*   77. *The Four Gospels*, 1924, pp. 504, 515.
78. Gal. ii, 11 f.
79. Streeter, *The Four Gospels*, 1924, pp. 515 f.
80. Cf. Rawlinson, *St Mark*, 1925, pp. xv f.; Streeter, *op. cit.*; Moffat, *Introduction to the Literature of the New Testament*, 1933, p. 213; Eusebius, *Hist. Eccles.*, III, 39, 15. For a recent critique of the priority of St Mark, cf. B. C. Butler, *The Originality of St Matthew*, Cambridge, 1951.
81. Mark, viii, 29.
82. Luke ix, 20.
83. Butler, *The Originality of St Matthew*, pp. 168.
84. Luke i, 1–3.
85. Acts xi, 10 ff., xiii, 1 ff., xv, 1 ff.; Eusebius, *Hist. Eccles.*, III iv, 6.,
86. Eusebius, *op. cit.*, iii, 39, 15, v, 8.
87. *Op. cit.*, II, xv; 1 Pet. v, 13.
88. v, 12, cf. Selwyn, *The First Epistle of St Peter*, 1946, pp. 9 ff.
89. ii, 17.
90. Merrill, *Essays in Early Church History*, 1924, pp. 311 ff.
91. Streeter, *The Four Gospels*, 1936, pp. 489 ff.
92. *Ad Romanos*, iv, 3.   93. *Hist. Eccles.*, II, 25, 5–7.
94. *Adv. Haer*, III, iii, 2 f.   95. *De Praescriptione*, xxxii, xxxvi, 3·
96. *De pudicitia*, xxi, 1 f., 9.   97. *Op. cit.*, i, 13, 21.
98. Eusebius, *Hist. Eccles.*, v, xxxiii f.
99. Cf. Zernov, *Church Quarterly Review*, vol. cxvi, 1933, pp. 28 ff.; Jalland, *The Church and the Papacy*, 1944, pp. 120 ff.

100. Cyprian, *Ep.* lxviii.   101. *Ep.* lxvii.
102. *De unitate,* 4, 5.
103. *Dogmengeschichte,* 4th ed., vol. ii, p. 103.
104. Jalland, *The Church and the Papacy,* p. 182.
105. *Conc. Sard.,* can. 3, tome I, 1930, pp. 455 ff.
106. Migne, *Patr. Lat.,* 13, 575.
107. *Decretum Gelasianum,* ed. E. Dobschutz, 1912, 3, 1, p. 29.
108. Migne, *Patr. Lat.,* 14, 1134; 16, 861; 22, 1091; Ambrose, *De Fide,* 4, 56; *Ep.* 11, 4; Jerome, *Ep. ad Damasum,* 15, 1; 16, 2.
109. *Ep.* 15, 1.   110. Migne, *Patr. Lat.,* 54, 146, 213, 622, 879.
111. Cf. *Civilization on Trial,* Oxford, 1948, pp. 236 f.
112. *Cod.* Theodosius, XVI, i, 3, xvi, 16, 20 f.; XVI, v, 29.
113. *Epist.* XX, 8, 19; XXI, 17; *Contra Auxentium,* III, XXIV, XXXI.
114. Cf. G. Tillenbach, *Church, State and Christian Society,* E.T., by R. F. Bennett, Oxford, 1940, pp. 55 ff.
115. Cf. Cyprian, *Ep.* xxxii, xxxviii, Athanasius, *Apol.,* c., *Arian,* 6.

CHAPTER IX

1. Cf. E. D. Chapple and C. S. Coon, *Principles of Anthropology,* 1947, pp. 283 ff., 408 f.
2. Cf. *Zeitschrift für aegyptische Sprache und Altertums-kunde,* 59, pp. 109 ff.
3. Cf. Labat, *Le caractère religieux de la royauté assyro-babylonienne,* Paris, 1939, pp. 352 ff.
4. Cf. chap. III, p. 73.   5. 1 Sam. viii, 19 ff.   6. 2 Sam. vii, 12 ff.
7. 1 Sam. 1, 24, ii, 18, ix, 12 f. x, 1–13, xi, 15, xiii, 7 ff.; cf. chap. IV, p. 83.
8. 2 Kings xviii, 1–8, xxii, 2 ff.   9. 2 Kings xxiii, 15, 19.
10. 2 Kings xi, 2, xii, 16, xxii, 3 f.; 2 Chron. xxii.
11. Ezra iii, 10; Neh. xii, 45 f., cf. 1 Chron. xxiv–xxv; 2 Chron. vii, 6, xxxv, 15.
12. 2 Sam. vii, 12 ff.; Ps. ii, 7, lxxxix, 28 f., cf. Mic. v, 2; Zech. vi, 9 ff., xii, 8; Hag. ii, 23.
13. Zech. iii, 4 f., vi, 9 ff.; Ezra iii, 1–6; Hag. i–ii.
14. Cf. J. Morgenstern, *American Journal of Semitic Languages and Literature,* vol. lv, 1938, nos. 1, 2, 4.
15. Neh. x, 33.   16. Lev. xvi, cf. chap. V, p. 162.
17. Exod. xii, 46 f.; Hos. xii, 10.
18. Ezra vi, 19 ff.; 2 Chron. xxx; Jubilees xlix, 16.
19. *Pes.* V, viii, 13.   20. Cf. chap. V, p. 151.
21. J. H. Hutton, *Caste in India,* 1951, pp. 133, ff.; pp. 182, ff.
22. *Rig-veda* IX, cxii.   23. Cf. *Manu,* X, 80–82, 101, 102; IX, 319.
24. Cf. P. Deussen, *Philosophy of the Upanishads,* Edinburgh, 1906, pp. 61 f., 396.
25. *Brhad. Upan.,* 1, i, ii; *Chhandogya Upan.,* VI, viii, 7.

26. *Eastern Religious and Western Thought,* Oxford, 1939, p. 366.

27. *Op. cit.,* pp. 359, 362.   28. *Op. cit.,* p. 357.

29. *Op. cit.,* p. 358.   30. *The Hindu View of Life,* 1927, p. 22.

31. Gal. iii, 19 f.; Heb. viii, 6, ix, 15, xii, 24.

32. 1 Tim. ii, 3–6; Col. 1, 13–20; Eph. v, 30.

33. Heb. ii, 11–15, iii, 1; Eph. v, 30.

34. Cf. 1 Tim. iv, 14; 2 Tim. i, 6.

BIBLIOGRAPHY

CHAPTER I

Batchelor, J., *The Ainus and their Folklore*, 1910.

Brown, A. R., *The Andaman Islanders*, Cambridge, 1933.

Codrington, R. H., *The Melanesians, their Anthropology and Folklore*, Oxford, 1891.

Chapple, E. D. and Coon, C. S., *Principles of Anthropology*, 1947.

Czaplicka, M. A. *Aboriginal Siberia*, Oxford, 1914.

Evans-Pritchard, E. E., *The Divine Kingship of the Shilluk of the Nilotic Sudan*, Cambridge, 1948. *Witchcraft, oracles and magic among the Agande*, Oxford, 1937. *The Nuer*, Oxford, 1940.

Frazer, J. G., *Early History of Kingship*, 1905; *Belief in Immortality and the Worship of the Dead*, 1913; *The Golden Bough*, Pt. I (The Magic Art), 1914.

Howitt, A. W., *Native Tribes of South-east Australia*, 1904.

Kidd, D., *The Essential Kaffir*, 1925.

Landtman, G., *The Origin of Priesthood*, Ekenaes, 1905.

Layard, J., *Stone Men of Malekula*, 1942.

Luquet, G. H. *The Art and Religion of Fossil Man*, Oxford, 1930.

Mainage, Th., *Les Religions de la Préhistoire*, Paris, 1921.

Malinowski, B., *Coral Islands and their Magic*, 1935; *Argonauts of the Western Pacific*, 1922.

Marett, R. R., *Sacraments of Simple Folk*, Oxford, 1933.

Mikhaïlowski, V. M., *Journal of the Royal Anthropological Institute*, vol. xxiv, 1895.

Oesterreich, T. K., *Possession*, 1930.

Parker, K. L., *Australian Legendary Tales*, 1896.

Rivers, W. R. H., *Medicine, Magic and Religion*, 1909.

Seligman, C. G. and B. Z., *The Veddas*, Cambridge, 1911; *Pagan Tribes of the Nilotic Sudan*, 1932.

Skeat, W. W., *Malay Magic*, 1920; and Blagen, C. O., *Pagan Races of the Malay Peninsula*, 1906.

Spencer, W. B. and Gillen, F. J., *The Native Tribes of Central Australia*, 1899; *Northern Tribes of Central Australia*, 1904; *Across Australia*, 1912; *The Arunta*, 1927.

CHAPTER II

Bouché-Leclerc, A., *Histoire de la Divination dans l'antiquité*, Paris, 1878–82.

Budge, E. A. W., *Egyptian Magic*, 1899.

Campbell-Thompson, R., *Devils and Evil Spirits of Babylonia*, 1904–5; *Reports of the Physicians and Astrologers of Nineveh and Babylon*, 1901.

Cook, A. B., *Zeus*, vol. ii, Cambridge, 1925.

Coste-Messalière, P. de la, *Delphes*, Paris, 1943.

Dhorme, P., *La religion assyro-babylonienne*, Paris, 1910.

Eisler, R., *The Royal Art of Astrology*, 1947.

Farnell, L. R., *The Cult of the Greek States*, Oxford, 1909, vols. iv, v.

Fowler, W. Warde, *Religious Experience of the Roman People*, 1911.

Guillaume, A., *Prophecy and Divination*, 1938.

Guthrie, W. K. C., *The Greeks and their Gods*, 1950; *Orpheus and Greek Religion*, 1935.

Haldar, P., *Associations of Cult Prophets among the Ancient Semites*, Uppsala, 1945.

Harrison, J. E., *Prolegomena to the Study of Greek Religion*, Cambridge, 1922.

Halliday, W. R., *Greek Divination*, 1913.

Jastrow, M., *The Religion of the Babylonians and Assyrians*, 1912.

Jean, C. F., *La Religion Sumérienne*, Paris, 1931.

Parke, H. W., *A History of the Delphic Oracle*, Oxford, 1939.

Rhode, R., *Psyche*, 1925.

Poulsen, F., *Delphi*, E. T. by G. C. Richards, 1920.

Terry, M. S., *The Sibylline Oracles*, New York, 1890.

Wissowa, G., *Religion und Kultur der Römer*. Munich, 1912.

Zimmern, H., *Beiträge zur Kenntnis der Babylonischen Religion*, Leipzig, 1901.

CHAPTER III

Bentzen, Aa., *Studier over det zadokidiske Praesteskabs Historie*, Kobenhavn, 1931.

Cheragh, Ali M., *Critical Exposition of Jihab*, Bombay, 1885.

Gray, G. B., *Sacrifice in the Old Testament*, Oxford, 1925.

Guillaume, A., *Prophecy and Divination*, 1938.

Haldar, A., *Associations of Cult Prophets among the Ancient Semites*, Uppsala, 1945.

Hooke, S. H., *Prophets and Priests*, 1938.

Ibn al-Kalbi, *Kitab al-a'snam*, ed. Ahmed Zeki Pacha, Cairo, 1924.

Ibn Kladun, *Prolégomènes*, Paris, 1862.

Jepsen, A., *Nabi, Soziologische Studien zur alttestamentlichen Literatur und Religionsgeschichte*, München, 1934.

Johnson, A. R., *The Cultic Prophet in Ancient Israel*, Cardiff, 1944; *The One and the Many in the Israelite Conception of God*, Cardiff, 1943.

Lods, A., *Israel, from the Beginning to the Middle of the Eighth Century*, 1932.

Meek, J. T., *Hebrew Origins*, New York and London, 1936.

Mowinckel, S., *Ezra den Skriftlaerde*, Kristiania, 1915. *Psalmenstudien*, vols. i–vi, Kristiania, 1921–24.

Nöldeke, T., *Neue Beiträge zur semitischen Sprachwissenschaft*, Strassburg, 1910.

Nyberg, H. S., *Studien zum Hoseabuche*, Uppsala, 1935; *Bemerkungen zum "Buch der Gotzenbilder" Ibn al-Kalbi* (Skrifter utg. av. Svenska institutet; Rom. Ser. 2. 1939).

Pedersen, J., *Israel, Its Life and Culture*, vols. i–iv, London and Copenhagen, 1926–40.

Sells, E., *Faith of Islam*, Madras, 1909.

Skinner, J., *Prophecy and Religion*, Cambridge, 1922.

Smith, M., *Studies in Early Mysticism in the Near and Middle East*, 1931.

Smith W. R., *The Prophets of Israel*, 1895.

Welch, A. C., *Prophet and Priest in Old Israel*, Oxford, 1953.

CHAPTER IV

Baudissin, W. W., *Adonis und Esmun*, Leipzig, 1911.

Blackman, A. M., *Luxor and its Temples*, 1923; "Priest" in *Encyclopaedia of Religion and Ethics (E.R.E.)*, vol. x; "Worship" in *E.R.E.*, vol. xii; in *Myth and Ritual*, Oxford, 1933 (ed. S. H. Hooke).

Breasted, J. H., *Development of Religion and Thought in Ancient Egypt*, 1912; *Ancient Records of Egypt*, Chicago, 1905–07; *The Dawn of Conscience*, 1935.

Budge, E. A. W., *Hieratic Papyri*, 1911; *History of Egypt*, 1902; *Osiris and the Egyptian Resurrection*, 1911.

Chiera, E., *Sumerian Religious Texts*, Upland Pa., 1924.

Deimel, A., *Enuma Elish und Hexaëmeron*, Rome, 1934.

Dhorme, P. E., *Les religions de Babylonie et d'Assyrie*, Paris, 1910.

Engnell, I., *Studies in Divine Kingship in the Ancient Near East*, Uppsala, 1945.

Erman, A., *Aegypten und aegyptisches Leben im Altertum*. Tübingen, 1885; *Handbook of Egyptian Religion*, E. T., 1907; *Life in Ancient Egypt*, 1894.

Evans-Pritchard, E. E., *The Divine Kingship of the Shilluk of the Nilotic Sudan*, Cambridge, 1948.

Foucart, G., "King" (Egyptian) in *E.R.E.*, vol. vii, pp. 711–15.

Frankfort, H., *Kingship and the Gods*, Chicago, 1948; *Ancient Egyptian Religion*, Columbia Univ. Press, 1948; *The Intellectual Adventure of Ancient Man*, Chicago, 1946; *The Problem of Similarity in Ancient Near Eastern Religions*, Oxford, 1951.

Gaster, T. H., *Thespis*, New York, 1950.

Heidel, A., *The Babylonian Genesis*, Chicago, 1942.

Hocart, A. M., *Kingship*, Oxford, 1927.

Holmberg, M. S., *The God Ptah*, 1914.

Hooke, S. H., *Origins of Early Semitic Ritual*, Oxford, 1935; *Myth and Ritual*, Oxford, 1933.

Jacobsen, Th., *The Intellectual Adventure of Ancient Man*, Chicago, 1946.

Jastrow, M., *Religion of Babylonia and Assyria*, Boston, 1898.

Kramer, S. N., *Sumerian Mythology*, Philadelphia, 1944.

Labat, R., *Le Poème babylonien de la création*, Paris, 1935.

Langdon, S., *Tammuz and Ishtar*, Oxford, 1914; *The Babylonian Epic of Creation*, Oxford, 1923; *Semitic Mythology*, 1931.

Langhe, R. de, *Les Textes de Ras Shamra-Ugarit*, Paris, 1945.

Moortgat, A., *Tammuz*, Berlin, 1949.

Moret, A., *Mystères Egyptiens*, Paris, 1913; *Du caractère religieux de la royauté pharaonique*, Paris, 1902.

Murray, M. A., *The Osireion at Abydos*, 1904.

Naville, E., *The Temple of Deir el Bahari*, 1898–1908.

Pallis, S. A., *The Babylonian Akitu festival*, Kobenhavn, 1926.

Peters, P. J., *The Psalms as Liturgies*, New York, 1922.

Petrie, W. M. F., *Researches in Sinai*, 1906.

Rowley, H. H., *The Servant of the Lord*, 1952.

Schmidt, Hans, *Die Thronfahrt Jahwes am Fest der Jahreswende*, Tübingen, 1927.

Seligman, C. G., *Egypt and Negro Africa*, 1934; C. G. and B. Z., *Pagan Tribes of the Nilotic Sudan*, 1932.

Sethe, K., *Urkunden des Aegypten Altertums*, IV, Leipzig, 1908.

Tallqvist, K. L., *Sumerisch-akkadusche Namen der Totenwelt*, Helsingfors, 1934.

Wainwright, G. A., *The Sky-religion in Egypt*, Cambridge, 1938.

Wales, H. G. Quarith, *The Mountain of God*, 1953.

Woolley, L., *Ur of the Chaldees*, 1929.

Zimmern, H., *Zum babylonischen Neujahrfest*, Leipzig, 1918.

CHAPTER V

Barth, A., *The Religions of India,* E. T. by J. Wood, 1889.

Bloomfield, M., *The Religion of the Veda,* New York, 1908.

Caland, W., and Henry, V., *L'agnistoma: description complète de la forme normale du sacrifice de Soma dans le culte vedique,* 2 vols., Paris, 1906.

Curtiss, S. I., *Primitive Semitic Religion To-day,* Chicago, 1902.

Dix, G., *The Shape of the Liturgy,* 1945.

Duschesne, L., *Origins of Christian Worship,* 1919.

Dussaud, R., *Les Origines canaanéennes du sacrifice israelite,* Paris, 1921.

Evans Pritchard, E. E., "The Meaning of Sacrifice among the Nuer," *J.R.A.I.,* 1954.

Gayford, C. S. *Priesthood.* 1951.

Gray, G. B., *Sacrifice in the Old Testament,* Oxford, 1925.

Griswold, H. D., *The Religion of the Rigveda,* Oxford, 1923.

Hillebrandt, A., *Ritual Litteratur,* Strassburg, 1897.

Hochmann, J., *Jerusalem Temple Festivities,* 1908 (for sources).

Holloway, H., *The Norwegian Rite,* 1934.

Hopkins, E. W., *The Religions of India,* Boston, 1895.

Hubert, H., and Mauss, M., *Mélanges d'Histôire des Religions,* Paris, 1909.

James, E. O., *Origins of Sacrifice,* 1933.

Leeuw, G. van der, *Religion in Essence and manifestation,* E.T., 1938.

Leitzmann, H., *Messe und Herrenmahl,* Bonn, 1926.

Loisy, A., *Essai historique sur le sacrifice,* Paris, 1920; *Les mystères païens et le mystère Chrétien,* Paris, 1914.

Macalister, R. A. S., *The Excavations of Gezer,* 1912.

Monier-Williams, M., *Brahmanism and Hinduism,* 4th ed., 1891.

Oesterley, W. O. E., *The Jewish Background of the Christian Liturgy,* Oxford, 1925; in *Myth and Ritual,* Oxford, 1933; *Sacrifice in Ancient Israel,* 1937; and Box, G. H., *The Religion and Worship of the Synagogue,* 1911.

Satapatha Brahmana, Sacred Books of the East, J. Eggeling, xii, xxvi, xli, xliii, xliv.

Schürer, E., *Geschichte des Jüdischen Volkes im Zeitalter Jesu Christi,* Leipzig, 1886.

Smith, W. R., *Lectures on the Religion of the Semites,* 3rd ed., S. A. Cook, 1927.

Stone, D., *A History of the Doctrine of the Eucharist,* 2 vols., 1909.

Thackeray, H. St John, *The Septuagint and Jewish Worship,* 1921.

Tylor, E. B., *Primitive Culture,* 2 vols., 5th ed., 1913.

Yalverton, E. E., *The Swedish Rite,* 1929 (Henry Bradshaw Society).

CHAPTER VI

Aquinas, St Thomas, *Summa Theologica,* III.

Batiffol, P., "Les Origines de la pénitence" in *Etudes d'histoire et de théologie positive,* vol. i, Paris, 1902.

Bückler, A., *Studies in Sin and Atonement,* Oxford, 1928.

Burney, C. F., *The Old Testament Conception of Atonement fulfilled by Christ,* Oxford, 1921.

Carter, T. T., *The Doctrine of Confession,* 1885.

Casey, P. H., *Notes on a History of Auricular Confession,* Philadelphia, 1898 (cf. H. C. Lea).

Chardon, M. C., *Histoire du sacrement de pénitence,* Paris, 1745; and in Migne, *Cursus Theol.* Paris, 1840–45, xx.

Drury, T. W., *Confession and Absolution,* 1904.

Frank, F., *Die Bussdiscipline der Kirche,* Mainz, 1868.

Gury, J. P., *Compendium Theologia Moralis,* Ratisbonae, 1874.

Harrington, H., *Sacrament of Penance,* 1928.

Kirk, K. E., *Some Principles of Moral Theology,* 1920; *Conscience and its Problems,* 1927.

Legg, J. Wickham, *English Church Life from the Restoration to the Tractarian Movement,* 1914.

Lea, H. C., *History of Auricular Confession,* 1899 (cf. P. H. Casey).

Lehmkuhl, A., *Theologia Moralis,* Friburg, 1896 (8th ed.).

Liguori, St Alphonso de, *Theologia Moralis,* Ratisbonae, 1846.

Montefiore, C. G., *Rabbinic Literature and Gospel Teaching,* 1930.

Morin, J., *Commentarius hist. de disciplina Poenitentiae,* Paris, 1651.

Mozley, J. K., *The Doctrine of the Atonement,* 1918.

Mortimer, R. C., *The Elements of Moral Theology,* 1947.

Oesterley, W. O. E., *The Jewish Doctrine of Mediation,* 1910.

Prummer, M., *Manuale Theologiae Moralis,* 3 vols.

Pusey, E. B., *Entire Absolution of the Penitent,* Oxford, 1846.

Rashdall, H., *The Idea of Atonement in Christian Theology,* 1920; *Theory of of Good and Evil,* 1917.

Slater, T., *Manual of Moral Theology,* 2 vols., New York, 1908.

Thorndike, H., *Just Weights and Measures,* 1662.

Watkins, O. D., *A History of Penance,* 2 vols., 1920.

CHAPTER VII

Benedict, R., *Patterns of Culture,* 1935.

Bezold, C., *Ninive und Babylon,* Leipzig, 1909.

Bieber, M., *The History of the Greek and Roman Theatre,* 1939.

Breasted, J. H., *Religion and Thought in Ancient Egypt,* 1912.

Budge, E. A. W., *Literature of the Egyptians,* 1914; and King, L. W., *Annals of the Kings of Assyria,* 1902.

Burney, C. F., "Stars" in *Encyclopaedia Biblica,* vol. iv, 1903.

Canney, M. A., "Sun, Moon and Stars" (Hebrew) in *Encyclopaedia of Religion and Ethics,* vol. xii, 1921.

Campbell-Thomson, E. K., *The Reports of the Magicians and Astrologers of Nineveh and Babylon,* 1900.

Cumont, F., *Astrology and Religion among the Greeks and Romans,* 1912.

Darmesteter, J., and Mills, L. H., "Avesta" in *Sacred Books of the East,* iv, xxiii, xxxi; *Le Zend-Avesta,* 3 vols., Paris, 1892–93.

Dawson, C., *Religion and Culture,* 1948; *Mediaeval Religion,* 1934.

Eisler, R., *The Royal Art of Astrology,* 1947.

Erman, A., *The Literature of the Ancient Egyptians,* E. T. by A. M. Blackman, 1927.

Farnell, L. R., *The Cult of the Greek States,* Oxford, 1907 (vol. iii).

Gaster, T. H., *Thespis,* New York, 1950.

Gordon, C. H., *Ugaritic Handbook,* Rome, 1947.

Gregory, R., *Religion in Science and Civilization,* 1940.

Harrison, J. E., *Themis,* Cambridge, 1912.

Hooke, S. H., *Myth and Ritual,* Oxford, 1933; *The Origins of Early Semitic Ritual,* Oxford, 1938; *The Religion of Babylonia and Assyria,* 1952.

Joyce, T. A., *Mexican Archaeology,* 1914.

Keith, A. B., *Religion and Philosophy of the Vedas,* 2 vols., 1925.

Kugler, F. X., *Sternkunde und Sterndienst in Babel,* 1907.

Laughe, R. de, *Lex Textes de Ras Shamra-Ugarit et leurs rapports avec le milieu de l'ancient Testamente,* 1945.

Lockyer, N., *Dawn of Astronomy,* 1894.

Lobeck, C. A., *Aglaophamus,* 1928.

Macdonell, A. A., *History of Sanskrit Literature,* 1900.

Max-Müller, F., *History of Sanskrit Literature,* 1859.

Nallino, C. A., "Sun, Moon and Stars," (Muhammadan) in *E.R.E.,* vol. xii, 1921.

Pearse, A. J., *Textbook of Astrology,* 2 vols, 1879–89.

Sahagun, B. de, *A History of Ancient Mexico,* E.T. by F. R. Bandelier, Nashville, 1932.

Schiaparelli, G., *Astronomy in the Old Testament*, Oxford, 1905.

Sethe, K., *Die altaegyptischen Pyramidentexte*, Leipzig, 1908–10.

Spinden, H. J., *Ancient Civilization of Middle and Central Mexico*, New York, 1928.

Valliant, G. C., *The Aztecs of Mexico*, 1941.

CHAPTER VIII

Albright, W. F., *From the Stone Age to Christianity*, Baltimore, 1946.

Blunt, J. H., and Phillimore, W. G. F., *The Book of Church Law*, 1899.

Brandon, S. G. F., *The Fall of Jerusalem and the Christian Church*, 1951.

Breasted, J. H., *A History of Egypt*, 1906; *Ancient Records of Egypt*, Chicago, 1907.

Brooke, Z. N., *The Canon Law of the Church of England*, 1947.

Brugsch, H. C., *Thesaurus Inscriptionum Aegypticarum*, Leipzig, 1883–91.

Butler, B. C., *The Originality of St Matthew*, Cambridge, 1951.

Cook, S. A., *The Laws of Moses and the Code of Hammurabi*, 1903.

Danby, H., *The Misnah, Translated from the Hebrew*, 1933.

Daube, D., *Studies in Biblical Law*, 1947.

Dodd, C. H., *The Parables of the Kingdom*, 1935; *History and the Gospel*, 1938.

Erman, A., *Life in Ancient Egypt*, 1894.

Fournier, P., and Bras, G. le, *Histoire des collections canoniques en occident*, 2 vols., Paris, 1931.

Galante, A., *Fontes Juris Canonici*, 1906.

Harper, R. F., *The Code of Hammurabi*, 1904.

Holdsworth, W. S., *History of English Law*, 1903.

Jalland, T. G., *The Church and the Papacy*, 1944.

Johns, C. H. W., *The Laws of Babylonia and the Laws of the Hebrew Peoples*, 1914.

Kent, C. F., *Israel's Laws and Legal Precedents*, 1907.

Kirk, K. E., Editor of *The Apostolic Ministry*, 1946.

Maitland, F. W., *Canon Law in the Church of England*, 1928.

Maimonides, M., *Mishneh Torah*, Latin translation by W. Surenhusius, Amsterdam, 1698–73.

Malinowski, B., *Crime and Custom in Savage Society*, 1926.

Meyerowitz, E. L. R., *The Sacred State of the Akan*, 1951.

Palanque, J. R., Bardy, G. and others, *The Church in the Christian Roman Empire*, 2 vols., 1952.

Rattray, R. S., *Ashanti Law and Constitution*, Oxford, 1929; *The Ashanti*, Oxford, 1923.

Sethe, K., *Urkunden des Aegypten Altertums*, II, Leipzig, 1903.

Strack, H. L., *Introduction to the Talmud and Midrash*, 1931.

Streeter, B. S., *The Four Gospels*, 1924.

Tillenbach, G., *Church, State and Christian Society*, E.T. by R. F. Bennett, Oxford, 1940.

Weiss, J., *Das Urchristentum*, Göttingen, 1914.

Westermarck, E., *Origin and Development of Moral Ideas*, 2 vols., 1906.

Whitney, J. P., *Hildebrandine Essays*, Cambridge, 1932.

INDEX

333